Creating the Creole Island

MEGAN VAUGHAN

Creating the Creole Island

Slavery in Eighteenth-Century Mauritius

DUKE UNIVERSITY PRESS ❧ *Durham & London 2005*

© 2005 DUKE UNIVERSITY PRESS. All rights reserved.
Printed in the United States of America on acid-free paper ∞
Designed by Rebecca M. Giménez. Typeset in Adobe Minion by
Keystone Typesetting, Inc. Library of Congress Cataloging-in-
Publication Data appear on the last printed page of this book.

Contents

Acknowledgments

In researching and writing this book over a number of years I have incurred more debts of gratitude than I can acknowledge here. Producing a book may feel like a peculiarly solitary activity, but this is never the whole story.

My thanks go to the archivists and librarians of the Archives Nationales in Paris, the Archives d'Outre-Mer in Aix-en-Provence, the National Archives of Mauritius, and the Congrégation de la Mission, Paris.

Philip Baker, Robin Briggs, Natalie Zemon Davis, Stephen Ellis, Colin Lucas, and Jane Shaw gave me invaluable advice on different aspects of the book. My colleagues and friends Ruth Harris, Robert Young and Lois Mc Nay, provided me with intellectual stimulation and encouragement in Oxford. Laurence Brockliss read and commented on a draft of the book, for which I am extremely grateful. I owe particular thanks to Pavi Ramhota of the Mahatma Gandhi Institute in Mauritius, who shared his rich knowledge with me and facilitated my introduction into Creole communities. Gerard Noyau first made me aware, as a teenager, of the existence of this Indian Ocean island and its Creole community. My debts to the work of the following historians of Mauritius will be obvious: Richard Allen, Marina Carter, Raymond d'Unienville, Marcelle Lagesse, Huguette Ly-Tio-Fane Pineo, and the late Auguste Toussaint. Ned Alpers (in whose footsteps I seem to follow) has been characteristically generous with his vast knowledge of Indian Ocean and African history. I would like to give my particular thanks to Vijaya Teelock of the University of Mauritius, who has worked tirelessly and courageously to ensure that the history of slavery on Mauritius is not a history of silence. Thanks also to Ken Wissoker, Christine Dahlin, and Justin Faerber of Duke University Press.

In the process of writing I have been inspired by recent work on historical consciousness and slavery by two anthropologists: Michael Lambek and Stephan Palmié. Unfortunately I have not been able to emulate them here—perhaps next time.

My research was made possible through the generosity of the University of Oxford, Nuffield College, Oxford, and, in particular, by the award of a British Academy Research Grant and a Research Readership.

*I*n 1787 the French slave ship *Licorne* cruised the ports of the Mozambican coast in search of slaves—slaves for the colony of St. Domingue in the Antilles. The ship's captain, Brugevin, who was experienced in the business, found this particular commission a frustrating one (Debien n.d.). He had been here, on this coast before, but this time everywhere he went, from the island of Ibo, to Cape Delgado, he found other ships, with commissions for the French Mascarene islands of Île Bourbon and Île de France. Filling the hold with the requisite five hundred slaves was not an easy task—competition had forced prices up and supply could not, apparently, keep pace with demand. When, eventually, he set sail on the long voyage to St. Domingue via the Cape, with his hold full, he faced a revolt by Makua slaves on board. The revolt was crushed; its leader threw himself overboard. Disease and death were not so easily defeated, however, as Brugevin made clear. Mortality among slaves from this part of Africa was, he contended, higher than among those from the West Coast. The central cause of death was everywhere the same—a form of dysentery, which the French called *chéringose*, and which, when it became, in his words, "putrid," was almost always fatal. Those suffering from it died an agonizing death. Opening up the bodies for cursory postmortems revealed that they were internally gangrenous, rotting from within.

Like all whose livelihoods rested on the business of slavery, Brugevin was centrally concerned with mortality. Death stalked the slave and vexed the slave trader and the slave owner. Most slave ships' logs from this period read as the bald and brutal statistics of morbidity and mortality. Brugevin's account is different. No doubt this is because it is addressed to a well-known member of the antislavery lobby in Paris.[1] He fleshes out the statistics, goes into the details of the course of diseases suffered by the slaves and the manner of their deaths. And beyond that, he speculates on the psychology of slavery.

It was both a convention and an organizing principle of the slave system that different ethnic groups of slaves possessed different qualities. These ethnic designations (the French called them "castes," or sometimes "nations") were, of course, crude—constructions of the market as much as they were signifiers of any real cultural differences or origins—but they took on a real life of their own. Brugevin, in his "observations on the different 'castes' of slaves traded at the coast," and the following section of his report, entitled "the prejudices of 'nations,' " described the different dispositions of ethnic groups. Disposition bore directly on the material question of mortality for, in Brugevin's view, some groups (the Makonde, for example), though physically robust, lacked "courage" in the face of illness, grew dispirited, and died. The worst, in this respect, were the Yao. Often slave traders themselves, perhaps they knew too much, had seen too much to have hope when they themselves were herded on board a slave ship. Even the slightest illness sent them into despair—too weak to take either the medicine or the food offered to them, they died in large numbers. This tendency was, of course, reflected in the price they fetched. Brugevin expanded on his theory. The real cause of mortality, or so it seemed to him, was not so much the dysentery (deadly as this was), but deadly fear: "What is most detrimental to the preservation of the lives of these 'castes' [the Yao in particular] is the prejudice, inculcated in them since childhood, that the whites come to their shores to abduct them, to take them to their own land in order to eat them and to drink their blood" (105). This "misconception," so Brugevin went on, was actively propagated among Africans of the interior, by the slave traders who promised their captives that if they caused no problems en route, then they would be protected from this fate on arrival at the coast; if, on the other hand, they attempted to escape, they would be "sold to the white men, who would eat them, preserve their flesh as salted meat, drink their blood." Cowed into docility, the slaves would reach the coast only to find that their worst fears were to be realized. Finding themselves sold to white men, they are "seized by terror" and never recover from the shock: "Despair overtakes them, illness follows, and an infinite number are lost in this way."

In an attempt to right this misconception that slavery involved the consumption of black by white, Brugevin employed, as sailors, a number of slaves from Île de France. These latter, he explained, should be dressed and fed well, and above all, should never be seen to be beaten (nor eaten, one assumes). Their example would serve "pour encourager les autres." Slavery—don't despair (above all, don't die, please), it's not so bad really.

But it was bad, and it got worse. On board the packed slave ships epidemics of the dreaded "chéringose" were common. Ships' surgeons were alert to the first signs of this disease and had a strict routine for dealing with it, one from which, according to Brugevin, they were very reluctant to deviate—for "one cannot depart from the rules of medicine." First, sufferers were placed on a diet (rice and a tisane) so limited (so Brugevin noted) as to constitute a starvation regime. In addition to the medicines administered orally, which were viewed with great superstition by the slaves, who feared they were poison,[2] the surgeons ordered repeated enemas. It was this latter form of treatment which produced horror, terror, and repugnance among the sick slaves: "They are not familiar with this form of treatment, which they view as humiliating, so much so that those who are well show the greatest repugnance at having to eat from the same dish as those who have undergone it." All of this, Brugevin noted, affected them greatly and weakened them.

One can see why. If, as is implied here, these East and Central African captives viewed the business of export slavery as one which was essentially cannibalistic, if their worst fear was that their flesh was to be consumed by white men, then the surgeon's regime of starvation, enema, and evacuation may well have seemed like preparation for butchery.

Horrifying as a direct testimony of the slave trade, and powerful in its metaphorical possibilities, Brugevin's account at once repels and compels. Historians of slavery debate the kind of retelling I have engaged in here. Should we feel a responsibility to continue to bear witness, to remind, to tell the horror story again, or should we rather be wary of indulging in a kind of pornography of violence, stimulating the senses of the spectator, reproducing the righteousness of the antislavery campaigners, their magic lantern shows in darkened rooms where the light falls on images of the most debased of humankind, again and again and again; the intake of breath, the rattling of the collection box, the relief and release of philanthropy.

This question hovers over this study of the world of slavery, as it hovers over so many others. I have chosen to begin with this glimpse of horror, in part because in the rest of this book I do not dwell on horror, or address the terror of the slave trade in a systematic way. Horror and terror become, implicitly if not explicitly in my account, a kind of trauma —an absence, a hole, a forgetting which is at the same time always and everywhere present in the world I describe. Brugevin's account, like all accounts, cannot be read in any simple way, but my own view is that it moves us some distance at least beyond mere horrified spectatorship to a point where we look, only briefly, and only tangentially of course, with the slaves into the abyss. Many, as Brugevin indicates, did not survive that moment—death was produced by disease and starvation but hastened by the horror that theirs would be no ordinary death.

In the rest of this book I describe the world of those who survived that moment to live and to contribute to the creation of a complex world of *créolité* on a small island in the Indian Ocean—Île de France, now Mauritius. This was the place from which Brugevin drew his slave sailors— reminding us, in passing, that a slave destination can become a place of origin within a lifetime. What follows is an account of destinations and new creations, but it is not a celebratory story.

Creating the Creole Island

D oubtless there was a time when the island of Mauritius was uninhabited, but those who landed on it either by design or misfortune from the late sixteenth century found a place full of traces, real or fantastical, of others who had trodden there before. There were traces of those who had come and gone, and of those who had come and died, but the most haunting of all were the traces left by those who might still be there: the real terror faced by the marooned was not that they were alone, but that they might not be alone after all. This small island always had internal islands of habitation within it: an interior which was simultaneously exterior, repudiated. But most exclusion is an illusion, as we shall see.

Mauritius, as it is now known, and as it was known to the Dutch in the seventeenth century, lies in the middle of the Indian Ocean. This is a simple and obvious point, but it is an important one. This is not an island from which one can see another island, let alone a mainland of any description. It does not sit in the shadow of any large continent. The French island of La Réunion lies some 164 kilometers to the west; further west (over 800 kilometers away) is the larger island of Madagascar, and beyond that the east coast of Africa. To the east lies the small island of Rodrigues, a dependency of Mauritius. Originally the remains of a volcanic shield in the ocean, Mauritius is an island subject to frequent buffeting from hurricanes that, even in these days of reinforced concrete, have the capacity to undo the landscape. One can feel a little stranded, seasick, despite the fact that the island is now linked, instantly, by millions of threads of communication, to all parts of the world. At its center is a hub of international industrial and financial activity; around the edges a skirt of beaches from the vantage point of which thousands of mostly European tourists lie, facing outward to sea: westward to Africa, eastward toward Australasia, north to the Indian subcontinent.[1]

Throughout its history of human habitation Mauritius has been a profoundly cosmopolitan place (reminding us that globalization has a long history) and a profoundly parochial one. This was an island without natives, and its unique fauna and flora attest to its long historical isolation. Though Indian and Arab seafarers may have periodically landed on it over the centuries, the island did not play any notable role in the rich pre-modern history of the Indian Ocean, unlike neighboring Madagascar with its ancient human settlement from diverse sources.[2] More recent attempts to "inscribe Mauritius into a larger Islamic map" are, as Shawkat Toorawa argues (Toorawa 2000), "wishful thinking," and one of the many instances of Mauritian historical ethnic imagining. The island's lasting inscription on the world map would come only with the Portuguese exploration of the southwest Indian Ocean at the beginning of the sixteenth century, when Diego Fernandez Pereira and his sailors landed on the island—from now on it would feature on European charts and sketches (Grove 1995, 130).

Without natives, the island's beginnings were necessarily the product of no one thing or people but of many, more or less foreign, more or less "naturalized." It has always been a creole island. *Creole* is a notably slippery term, and its meaning in relation to Mauritius shifts historically, as we shall see. But here, by "creole," I simply mean that the island, without natives, has always been the product of multiple influences, multiple sources, which to differing degrees merge, take root, and "naturalize" on this new soil. Without natives there is no recourse to nativism,[3] but this appears to make a concern with origins more rather than less evident. Much vaunted as an island of racial and communal harmony, a "rainbow" nation reflecting its many colors in the ocean, Mauritius earns this reputation only partially, for Mauritian society is in fact deeply anxious and divided, containing many different islands of exile and exclusion, and one "off-shore" one, the even smaller island of Rodrigues.[4]

Concern with origins is also a concern with authenticity. Though everyone on the island speaks a French *créole* language specific to the island, and although every Mauritian shares in the history of creolization, only one group is designated as the "Creoles."[5] This is both a racial category (those who allegedly look most "African" in their features are members of it, though their descent is likely to be very mixed) and a residual category, and therefore one that signifies lack. The Creoles in contemporary Mauritian terms are those who are *not:* they are neither Hindus nor Muslims nor Tamils nor Chinese nor "whites" of either the Franco or Anglo variety. The Creole community is the residue of these racial/ethnic/cultural categories, a residue that purportedly lacks a distinct culture and suffers from what is known as "la malaise créole," a "disease" not only of poverty, but of social marginality and abjection. In Mauritius, *culture* has a very specific meaning closely tied to a narrative of origins. For while every other ethnic and religious group on Mauritius traces its origins, somewhat obsessively and with a great deal of imaginative invention, to an "elsewhere" in India, China, or Europe, Creoles have little in the way of remembered origins. Their origins in West or East or Central Africa, in Madagascar, and in India, China, and Europe have been forgotten. They have no "authentic" culture, since authenticity can come only from origins elsewhere, as if nothing which the island had produced itself, through its own complex history, could be real.[6]

Because there was originally no one there, or so they say, there are no independent witnesses to early accounts of occupation. The instability of these accounts (to say that fact and fiction are intertwined is to simplify greatly), the remoteness of the island from reliable metropolitan scrutiny, the possibilities (and in the case of the slave population, the imperative) of reinvention of self, all produce uncertainty. Which accounts are "real" and which the product of a feverish Robinson Crusoe imagination?[7] It is symptomatic of this anxiety over origins and authenticity, that modern Mauritius has created its own native in the form of the dodo, a native which suffered the fate of so many others—extinction—and which can therefore induce a sense of loss and mourning. We used to have something of our own, this seems to say, but then we lost it. Worse, it was eaten to extinction, consumed by the Dutch.[8] The dodo represents authenticity and so is used as a kind of test of reliability of early accounts: was *X* really there, and was he a reliable witness, is answered by reference to the supposed accuracy of any description of the dodo within that account. Dodology, as it is called, is a many-faceted science, but there is nothing stable about this native, against which all else is judged.[9] Recently scientists in Britain have suggested that the dodo has been seriously misrepresented: they have even gone so far as to deconstruct the model of the bird which has sat in the University Museum in Oxford since the last century.

In their view the dodo was not as fat as we have been led to believe, and they base this view on a piece of evidence that represents the ultimate in late-twentieth-century ideas of authenticity—genetic material from a real dodo's head ("New Light" 1999).

"Under the Blue Sky": Pirates, Maroons, and Dutch Ambitions

In late September 1598 the exhausted and sick crew of five Dutch ships commanded by Rear Admiral Wybrandt van Warwick set foot, gratefully, on an island they knew to be known to the Portuguese, and which had appeared on nautical charts since the beginning of the sixteenth century.[10] They found an island that abounded with fresh water and fresh foodstuffs: coconuts, fish, parrots, doves, and tortoises whose "shells were so large that six men could sit together on a single one." And, of course, the dodos—*Walg-vogels* (disgusting birds) to the Dutch, who found all but their stomachs hard to swallow. They knew, or at least they believed, the island to be uninhabited, because of the behavior of the birds that, fearlessly, fell directly into the arms of their captors, trusting and willing victims. Uninhabited it may have been, but traces, even inscriptions of earlier traffic remained. They found on the island "three hundred pounds of wax" on which were inscriptions. In some accounts these are Greek, in others Arabic. Recognizing that they were onto a good thing, this first Dutch party set about leaving something more than a trace in the shifting sand, more than a few letters in wax. Not only did their vice admiral fix a wooden cross to a tree and engrave it with the words *Christianos Reformados*, but also, in an unmistakably colonizing gesture, he began the process of attempting to mark out and domesticate this island wilderness by sowing seeds and leaving behind hens, which he hoped would "naturalize." The wilderness, the native environment into which the Dutch abandoned their hens, was, however, already a creolized environment. The Portuguese sailors had already left rats, monkeys, and goats. Most of the "wild" mammals of Mauritius were, in fact, foreign imports, some of which had gone native with alarming speed (Grove 1995, 130). Goats and pigs went "maroon" in the woods; rats, thousands and thousands of them, were to be the scourge of future human colonists.

On 8 January 1599, the Dutch sailors set sail again, leaving the island once more deserted. But not for long. Just as nature abhors a vacuum, so it seems that human society cannot, for long, imagine without extreme unease an uninhabited space. In an oft-repeated, archetypical story said to have influenced Defoe, it is related that when the next party of Dutch sailors landed in 1601 they found a lone Frenchman on the island.[11] The veracity of this incident is perhaps less relevant than the nature of its telling. The Frenchman, we are told, had been traumatized into dumbness and was living without fire. It took some time for the Dutch to coax any words out of him, but when he finally spoke he said that he had been alone on the island for eighteen to twenty months, without fire or clothing, living on dates and raw tortoise flesh; his four English companions (they were all mutineers) had apparently abandoned him after a week and set sail in a junk for England (de Rauville, 1889). In one retelling of this story the Frenchman is rescued into civilization and sanity by a boy, a dog, and a "good" pirate. As this particular retelling makes clear, it is very unlikely that the Frenchman (if he existed) was ever completely alone.[12] The Dutch were not the only ones to come and go—this part of the Indian Ocean swarmed with a very multicultural collection of pirates, and more or less permanent piratic communities existed on the "grande île" of neighboring Madagascar. The lone Frenchman, this version suggests, was far from alone, spending his time avoiding encounters with hostile others. The fear of being stranded alone was nothing compared to the fear of being stranded with alien others. This is a theme that recurs in Mauritian history.

Between 1599 and 1638 there was no formal Dutch settlement on Mauritius. The island was not, however, forgotten. Van Warwick had returned to the Netherlands in 1600, and his expedition was lauded as a huge commercial success. An engraving of 1601 illustrated the activities of his men during their short stay on the island, engraving, perhaps, the image of Mauritius on a number of influential minds: the tortoises "so large that a grown man could stand on one and take a ride. They catch and eat crabs as large as feet"; the dodos; the palm trees "with leaves so large that a man can shelter from the rain with one leaf without getting wet" (quoted in Moree 1998, 54–55). So widely distributed was this engraving and so great the interest in maritime exploration at this time that, according to Moree, everybody in Western Europe with an interest in overseas trade and exploration knew of this wonderful place, this fruitful and salubrious land, blessed with ebony, dodos and tortoises (1998).

In the following years pirates came and went, as did Dutch seafarers,[13]

FIGURE 1. Plate depicting the denizens of Mauritius, from *The Dodo and Its Kindred*, by Hugh Edwin Strickland, 1848. Bodleian Library, University of Oxford, 18.9 h. 77. Plt. opp. p. 9

and who knows who else. Despite the undoubted strangeness of the native wildlife—the tortoises "monstrously large," the bats with heads like foxes, and the dodos with their pinions—the Dutch seamen had already begun to treat the place with some familiarity. They left messages for each other in bottles in prescribed places, so that the island became a kind of poste restante in the middle of the Indian Ocean. The earlier colonizing gestures had meanwhile produced an orchard of orange trees and a few cotton bushes, as well as the rats. Finally, in 1638, spurred on by rumors of impending English occupation, the first permanent Dutch settlement came into being. This stab at colonization was to last some twenty years.

Dutch explorations and ambitions in the western Indian Ocean at this time need, of course, to be set in context (see Ross 2000; Chan Low 2000). The Dutch Republic had come into being only in 1581, a federation of states originating from the revolt against Phillip of Spain in 1566. The following century has often been described as a "Golden Age" for the Dutch, a period of economic prosperity and cultural flowering (Schama 1987; Boxer 1977). Though they were barely born as a nation, the Dutch had far-reaching commercial ambitions, evidenced by the phenomenal growth in the shipping industry in the period between 1585 and 1650 and the establishment, in 1602, of the Dutch East Indies Company (the VOC).

In the course of the seventeenth century the Dutch, through the Company, would establish bases in Mauritius, Japan, the Cape, India, and Ceylon.

The slow process by which Batavia became "Dutch" has been described by Jean Gelman Taylor (1993). Though the Company aimed to have a total monopoly of trade in the Indonesian archipelago, which would be backed up by naval power, the reality of seventeenth-century European trade expansion was that it involved constant negotiation with existing powers and cultures. The Dutch used both Malay and Portuguese to communicate with the peoples they encountered—outside the narrow confines of the Company offices "neither culture nor language were Dutch" (Taylor 1993, 18; Ross 2000, 9). Indeed, though the Dutch tended to monopolize senior Company posts, many of the other Company employees were not Dutch. In 1622 over half the 143-strong Batavia garrison consisted of foreigners—Germans foremost among them, but also Scots, French, English, Danes, Flemings, and Walloons (Taylor 1993, 6). Furthermore, voc policy was to recruit unmarried men, who would then be encouraged to engage in unions (both informal and legally sanctioned) with Asian women, both slaves and free (Taylor 1993; Stoler 1991; Blussé 1986). The result was that in the seventeenth century Batavia developed its own complex Eurasian culture, in which locally born women were central actors.

By the middle of the seventeenth century, however, Dutch maritime power, operating out of the secure base of Batavia, was winning out in Southeast Asia, and their position was strengthened when, in 1652, they occupied the Cape of Good Hope. The point of all this activity east of the Cape of Good Hope was, of course, trade—the linking of the ports of Asia to those of Europe, and beyond to the Americas. With the movement of goods went the movement of people. The voc employed over a million men in the course of its existence, but also presided over a huge volume of involuntary human migration—a massive trade in slaves in and around the Indian Ocean (Ross 2000, 9–10).

The voc wanted to maintain its dominance in the Indian Ocean and feared that the English or French might take possession of the island, which led to the first Dutch colonization of Mauritius in 1638. Mauritius would never be more than a minor outpost of the voc and its Batavian Asian headquarters, and its garrison was never large enough to have any real deterrent effect (Ross 2000, 12). Nonetheless, in the period before the

Dutch occupation of the Cape in 1652, its possession probably performed an important psychological role in the mind games of great power rivalry in the Indian Ocean. And, perhaps more importantly, the Dutch found that, in occupying Mauritius, they had at their disposal a highly valuable source of ebony, a commodity in great demand in the seventeenth century (Grove 1995, 132; Sleigh 2000, 52).

Under their first commander, Cornelius Gooyer, the Dutch set up base at the southeast harbor, building a fort, an austere square fortification with bastions—a design also used in Ceylon and later in the Cape (Moree 1998, 25, includes a sketch). This early garrison comprised only twenty-five men and was armed with four bronze cannons, 150 cannon balls, and 600 pounds of gunpowder. By 1639 the garrison had grown to include fifty men, most from Dutch towns, but some of German origin. They included in their number a preacher, an administrator, a cook, and a blacksmith. But though they may have claimed the island, they were not in sole occupation of it, for on the northwestern side of the island a party of Frenchmen off a ship from Dieppe was busy cutting the ebony (Moree 1998, 27). The Dutch were also there for the ebony, and in some ways their colony is best thought of as a large logging camp. As such it made an irreversible mark on the island's ecology. The heavy demand for ebony and other tropical hardwoods was one of the central motivations for Dutch occupation of Mauritius, and they wasted no time in exploiting the island's forests. As Richard Grove has argued, Mauritius was seen by the Dutch less as a settlement and far more as a source of raw timber (Grove 1995, 132). However, even a logging camp requires some degree of social organization and this, as successive commanders discovered, was no easy matter.

The second Dutch commander, Adrien van der Stel, arrived with his pregnant wife, Marie Lievens, in November 1639. Marie gave birth on the island to a son, Simon, who would later become governor of the Cape.[14] Marie is the first woman mentioned in the archives of the island, and Simon's is the first birth. As human resources for colonization van der Stel had a garrison of eighty "unruly" men. Seventy of them had arrived from Batavia on the flute *Capelle* in 1639, and most of these were sick. Van der Stel complained to Batavia of the unruliness of the soldiers, sailors, and convicts who comprised his colony. In response the governor general in Batavia suggested that he replace them with slaves. The voc thought of slave labor as constituting a capital outlay they would prefer to avoid, if at all possible, but the problems with nonslave labor supply and control were, in this case, apparently insurmountable. If there was any assumption that slave labor would be more pliable, this was soon to be proven wrong.

For his slaves van der Stel went to the obvious source—Madagascar. It was from here that the French would also draw their first slaves when they took possession of the neighboring island of Bourbon in 1642 (Payet 1990), and Malagasies would continue to comprise a significant proportion of the slaves, both on the Mascarene islands and at the Cape, until the abolition of slavery (Shell 1994, chap. 2). But if Mauritius was little more than a logging camp in this period, the same cannot be said of Madagascar. With its complex layering of Indonesian and African cultural elements, and extensive external contacts, the "grande île" in the seventeenth century was hardly virgin territory.[15] The Dutch, like the Portuguese before them, the Omanis, the English and the French, were obliged to deal with sophisticated chiefs and kings possessed of considerable power and autonomy. In 1641, van der Stel set off for the Bay of Antongil in the northeast of the island with orders to establish contact with the Malagasy kings and armed with the usual trade goods—combs, linen, iron pans, and mirrors. He persuaded, or coerced, a treaty out of the local king, left behind a couple of men and a fort (which was to survive only a few months), and returned to Mauritius with 105 slaves, both men and women. Within weeks half of them had disappeared into the forests, some subsequently to escape on French ships anchored on the northwest coast.

The embarrassment of riches the Dutch had initially perceived as characterizing the island, depicted in their engravings (the ebony, the abundant water, the rich tortoise meat, the fruits), had already worn thin. Visitors began to describe the island as a place from which everyone, not least the Malagasy slaves, desired to escape. Everyone was in some sense marooned here, including the Dutch convicts from Batavia, who made up a significant proportion of the nonslave population. From the beginning the implied omnipotence of colonization was challenged from both within and without the small Dutch community. The fort in the southeast looked out to sea, on guard against external enemies. Meanwhile, inland, behind Dutch backs, maroon slaves, alone or in groups, colonized the interior, with its still dense forest.

Nevertheless, van der Stel's successors continued to pursue the dual policy of extracting ebony and extending Dutch trading relations with Madagascar. The Dutch in this period, argues Richard Grove, were rather more aware of the importance of conservation and land management than were any of their European rivals, but in Mauritius, where the threat of a French or English invasion was always present, the voc made a conscious decision to cut as much ebony as quickly as possible (Grove 1995, 132). Gradually the ebony frontier moved inland, creating problems of transportation, which of course implied further demands for labor. In December 1645 a large consignment was shipped to Batavia. It had taken three months of felling and six months of transportation to the coast (Moree 1998, 36).

With the Dutch voc's occupation of the Cape in 1652, and the falling price of ebony on the world market, the limited role of Mauritius in Dutch colonial ambitions was reduced still further. In 1655 the small community of Company employees, "burgers," and slaves was still largely concentrated in the southeast settlement, leaving plenty of scope for both foreigners and pirates to come and go on other shores. Convicts sometimes escaped this way, on foreign ships, as in 1647 when the English vessel *Greyhound* left after a six-month stay on the island. Escaped slaves, sometimes joining force with escaped convicts, proved elusive, reputedly living in caves in which they kept their stores of smoked beef, culled from the gone-native cows that shared the forest pastures with them. Arguably, becoming a maroon was a rational survival strategy for both slave and technically free inhabitants of the island. Hunger was a constant condition of the Dutch settlement. The Dutch fought a losing battle against the rats, which regularly destroyed food crops and left them at the mercy of irregular supplies from Batavia. In 1652, Commander Reiner Por found himself obliged to send the population out into the woods to forage for whatever food they could find, while awaiting the arrival of a cargo of rice from Batavia. Not surprisingly, and despite several attempts to destroy the maroon community in the 1650s, this alternative settlement, mostly of Malagasy origin, was reproducing itself. This was more than could be said of the Dutch.

We do not know the size of the maroon community left behind when Van Riebeck issued the order to abandon the island in 1658, but when the Dutch returned in 1664 they must have known, even if they preferred not to acknowledge it, that this time the island could not be uninhabited, and that they were not colonizing on a blank slate. Indeed, in the intervening period there had been two Dutch visits to the island. The first, extremely well publicized in several written accounts, was the shipwreck of the *Arnhem* in 1662. Shipwrecks, floods, and inundations featured prominently in the Dutch imagination in this period (Schama 1987, 28–34). Tellingly, not all the *Arnhem* survivors chose to be rescued. Seven individuals were left behind, six of whom were later picked up by an English yacht. The seventh had, apparently, been murdered by a group of five African slaves, themselves escapees from a ship owned by the highly successful Dutch privateer Hubert Hugo, who had come to rescue the survivors. Hugo appears again later in this story. When the Dutch ship *Landsmeer* arrived on the island in 1663 to look for more survivors, its crew does not appear to have encountered these Africans but did report traces of human habitation, in a description that continues the enduring theme of shifting, elusive, and ghostly habitation: "Here and there had found some signs, such as an axe, a chopping-knife, ironwork, an old baftas shirt, shards of porcelain saucers, fresh tobacco etc., from which one could conclude that people had been there shortly before" (quoted in Moree 1998, 46).

The second Dutch colonization (from 1664–1710) was a more determined one, but it was shaky nevertheless. Despite its lure as a source of ebony and of amber, and its useful strategic position, the island was more of a burden than an asset to the voc, and successive governors engaged in daily battle with a perverse natural environment (rats, cyclones, and mysterious plagues), with the unruliness of their small community (wives poisoned husbands with apparent regularity, convicts escaped their chains), and with the persistent shadowy threat from the communities of the forest. The propensity of slaves to escape made a mockery of the master/slave relationship. If the ultimate authority of master over slave could not be seen to hold up, what hope for that of husband over wife, parent over child? Even the "domestic" animals of Mauritius were unruly. It seemed to many a particularly godless place.

The material conditions of this second colonizing period have recently been described by Daniel Sleigh (2000). The new lodge at what is now Vieux Grand Port was a long narrow wooden building with few military pretensions. Later on a number of stone built and thatch-roofed houses would be built within the compound, but there is no evidence of the Dutch colonial architecture characteristic of other Dutch settlements of the period. A sense of impermanence must have pervaded the settlement, not helped by periodic hurricanes and fires, which razed the lodge to the ground on several occasions. But the voc did have uses for the island, the supply of timber being the most constant. Ebony, cut and sawn into planks, was exported to the Cape, where major construction was taking place, and rare finds of ambergris (over which the Company had a monopoly) kept greater expectations alive.

The occasional colonial visionary did arrive on this unpromising stage. One of the earliest commanders of this second colonizing period was George Wreede, a German explorer and linguist who had been in South Africa, where he had compiled a Latin-Dutch-Hottentot vocabulary (Moree 1998, 77). Later came Isaac Lamotius, a botanist of some eminence (Moree 1998, 84–85; Grove 1995, 138–139). Between the two, and most colorfully, was Hubert Hugo, commander from 1673–1677. Hugo had been born near Rotterdam and worked as an assistant clerk for the voc in Batavia and Surat. He had then pursued a successful career as a privateer, working on his own behalf and for French sponsors, specializing in preying on ships of pilgrims in the Arabian seas, ransacking them on their way to Mecca. It was he who had called at Mauritius to rescue some of the survivors of the *Arnhem*. On his return to Amsterdam he presented the voc with an ambitious scenario that had Mauritius at the center of a largely East African trade in amber, slaves, and ivory. He may have regretted ever having been given the chance to realize these ambitions, for arriving as the new commander of the island he found things in a sorry state. He made some progress, rebuilding the lodge in stone, remaking the garden, establishing a mill, a distillery, and a tannery, and constructing a ten-mile road. His relationship with the company was to sour, however, and his term of office ended in acrimony (Moree 1998, 82).

Hugo's journal, summarized by the late-nineteenth-century Mauritian historian, Albert Pitot, presents us with another fact/fiction/fantastical cameo, mirroring the earlier story of the abandoned Frenchman. We should not doubt that the existence of communities of maroon slaves in the interior of the island evoked real terror on the part of those who lived in the Dutch encampment, but the maroon, like the pirate, was simultaneously a figure of terror and of romance. Of course, Hugo himself had been a "pirate" before becoming a company commander, a fact that serves to remind us that the boundaries between inside and outside the established order were far from rigid.

The story Hugo told goes like this (Pitot 1905, 170–171). A detachment of men who had been sent west of the lodge returned with a black man, completely naked, with long tangled hair and a beard that covered his face. The Dutch cut his hair and beard and gave him clothes. Then they had him put in chains. It was the effect of this last act that so struck Hugo, for at the first sight of his "rescuers" he claimed that the man had seemed pleased, appreciative, but once in chains he appeared overwhelmed by a terrible sadness and refused the food offered to him. He was questioned (how, and in what language we are not told—an omission from the story that, perhaps, increases our suspicion that the whole event is Hugo's fantasy), and on questioning he explained that he could not come to terms with seeing himself in chains once more. This response apparently evoked something powerful in Hugo. Here was an escaped slave who, it seemed, shared a respect and desire for freedom with his captor, a fact that put him in the frame of humanity. Impressed, Hugo struck a deal with him. He would release him from his chains if he promised not to escape. He agreed to this readily, and once released began to tell Hugo his story. He had lived, he said, with four other maroons in a hut in the forest, but two of his companions had died and a third had disappeared. Hugo proposed that, if he would show them the way to this forest encampment and promise not to escape, he would not only guarantee his safety (not, we should note, his freedom) but would also give him a woman. The man agreed "readily," we are told, to this very male deal and continued to tell his story. He had been around fifteen years old, he said, when he had been abducted and taken into the forest. Many a time he had wished he could return to the lodge, and more than once he had even approached it, but each time he had been frightened off by the sight of guns and swords. But now, he said, he had had enough of his roving existence, and as long as he knew that his life was not in danger, it did not matter to him if he were beaten from morning to night. Four days later he led the soldiers to his former hideout in the forest and to his former companion. They found a large hut surrounded by a palisade, four additional shacks, a stable for the cows, and a well-tended garden of tobacco. In one corner of the garden were the tombs of his two dead companions. Having fulfilled his side of the bargain the man, now named Simon by his captors, received his recompense—a woman—and went on, according to Hugo, to be a loyal and hardworking slave in the service of the Dutch. But an additional part of Hugo's story is that Simon became a storyteller at the lodge, regaling them with accounts of his amazing adventures in the forest.

If this entry in Hugo's journal is one of fantasy rather than fact, it is a revealing fantasy nonetheless. Simon was an example of the good maroon, a figure who recurs in various forms throughout the history of slavery on the island. In the post-abolition romance of slavery,[16] Simon made the transition from forest to lodge. In Hugo's account, he was a domesticated maroon, who could tell *stories* of the real lives of maroons in the forest. The real terror of maroons the lodge residents undoubtedly experienced was transformed by Simon into a bedtime horror story—still horrifying, but a story. Hugo's account also alludes to a process of recognition between the two men, in positions of master and slave, an issue I explore further in later chapters. Hugo is impressed by Simon's deep abhorrence of the physical chains of captivity and his desire for freedom. This sentiment earns Simon recognition, and so Hugo arranges a deal with him, a bargain. But Hugo's deal does not go as far as granting Simon his freedom in return for intelligence on the whereabouts of maroons: instead, Simon will get a woman (for he is also a man) and will be guaranteed his safety—by which is meant a certain assurance that he will not be murdered.

The Dutch in Hugo's time had reason to be wary of their slaves, for in this second period of colonization, as in the first, they escaped with apparent ease. The frustration of the "masters" is palpable in contemporary accounts. In their attempts to prevent escape the Dutch resorted to shackling their slaves (and, indeed, their convicts), which in turn rendered their labor tantalizingly inaccessible.[17] Mastery of the island, as this account by an English visitor indicates, was continually contested by communities of individuals like Simon:

> Divers of their slaves, disliking both work and food and *wages* fled into the mountains and though thereby they little bettered their condition, yet many of them are thereby freed from servitude. Some of these miserable people were again *attacked* and are now voyagers toward Batavia, yet upwards of thirty men, women and children are so hid and *fenced* in the mountains that they cannot be recovered, notwithstanding the commander's utmost industry for their apprehension, so that in all probability they may become the populace and masters of this rugged island.[18]

Despite being fenced in and fenced out, the maroon slaves, as we have seen, were hardly strangers to the Dutch. Both real and fantastical, they acted as a repository of Dutch fears, for it is so much easier to be fearful of something or someone outside and definable than it is to be anxious about a more amorphous everything.[19] Onto the maroons, real and fantastical, the Dutch hysterically projected the violence within their own small community, and there was no shortage of that.

There were conflicts at all levels within this community, between administrators and *vrijburgers* (free burgers), between vrijburgers and convicts and administrators and convicts, between everyone else and slaves and between slaves. Much of this violence (at least according to the accounts of it that have come down to us) took a sexually transgressive nature. In 1694, for example, Commander Deodati despatched a number of suspected criminals to the Cape. Among them was Hestor Pietersz, charged with attempting to poison her husband, Roelof Cartense. But Roelof Cartense was also sent over at his own request, for after his allegation against his wife she had been detained at the house of another vrijburger. Cartense had been caught there in the act of "impregnating" the wife he accused of attempting to poison him. Deodati was horrified by this trangression: "What such a man deserves, who stretches forth his hands in such a manner to those who are in the hands of the law, we recommend to your wise judgement" (Liebbrandt 1896, 49). He also reported on the case of a slave who had been charged with the rape of a "half-caste" girl of four or five years old. But it had turned out that the girl was unmolested and that she had accused the slave falsely, at the instigation of her father: "We therefore believe the charge to be calumnious and false. The slave has, however, been put in irons temporarily, to prevent him from running away through fear." Finally, there was the slave owned by Pieter Jansz, found guilty of committing sodomy with a dog, having been "caught in the act." Such an act, it seems, was beyond the application of the law: "As we did not wish to send such a person over with the ship, we quietly did away with him."

Analyzing the census of 1706, Barnwell gives a more detailed account of "colonists and convicts" on the island. There was a total of about three hundred freemen and company servants at this point. The colonists were scattered across the island. At Flacq, for example, there were twelve households listed, including that of Hans Balthasar Pigt, who twenty years earlier had been kept in irons for six months on the orders of Commander Lamotius. It was alleged that Lamotius was implicated in the rape of Pigt's wife, Mary May, by a slave. That slave belonged to another colonist, Jan

Hendrik Tauke, and he had escaped from prison. According to Barnwell, Tauke blamed Mary May for the loss of his slave. Tauke's wife, Katherina Kel, had been married previously and was thought to have killed her first husband by poisoning him, assisted by two other women (Barnwell 1948, 99).

The Company was relying on its vrijburgers to make the settlement viable, yet they had very few rights, and their attempts to move beyond self-sufficiency were not helped by vacillating Company policy. They never owned the freehold title to their land, and when (despite the chronic problem of control over slave labor) they managed to produce a surplus (of tobacco or sugar, for example), the voc did not always buy it (Sleigh 2000, 55). Tellingly, many vrijburgers chose to settle in present day Black River and Port Louis, on the opposite side of the island from the Company's base in the southeast. Here they were close to the harbors frequented by foreign ships, with whom they could more easily and profitably trade. In 1702 and 1704, for example, the vrijburgers in the northwest benefited from the two-month-long visits of the pirate John Bowen, with his crew of two hundred (Sleigh 2000, 55).

A taste of disgust permeated dispatches from this island frontier. For some it was all too much. Feeling himself abandoned on such a godless island, Commander Momber wrote that he was desperate to "reach a place where he might practice his reasonable religion with tranquillity of mind" (Barnwell 1948, 92). There was a phrase often used in correspondence through which the Dutch administrators expressed this feeling of abandonment—we are "under the blue sky," they wrote, or "sitting under the blue heaven." There was no roof over their heads. In 1695 Commander Deodati used this phrase to justify his improvisation of a legal process, the trial of suspected maroon slaves. In theory, all criminal cases were to be referred to the Cape, but Deodati explained that there had been a serious arson attack on the lodge and that justice could not, in this case, wait. Four slaves had been apprehended and had "confessed" (Barnwell 1948, 59)

Confession, whether coerced or not (and one must assume a background at least of coercion), was a central act of the drama which was the maroon trial. Maroon confessions expressed and articulated the fears of the nonmaroons, the Company officials, the vrijburgers, the servants, and slaves who all, besieged in the headquarters, or in their small scattered homesteads around the island, felt themselves to be captives of the maroons. But confessions, even when coerced, may also have expressed the fears and ambiguous hopes of the escaped slaves—for slaves had fantasies, too. The public confession of the maroon trial aimed at the elaboration of a shared fantasy and underscored the interdependence of master and slave. Maroons, it seems from these "confessions," were more threatening when they were simply "out there" somewhere, roaming aimlessly. Maroons were preferred with clear-cut designs, the design to become masters themselves.

In the arson case the four arrested slaves "confessed readily," saying that they had "determined to do it months ago . . . so to make themselves masters of the island." Deodati then improvised a legal process. The law was invoked, a higher, if distant authority brought to bear. Four men from the garrison were selected to constitute a Council that drew up and inscribed the "confessions" of the suspects and reexamined them on the basis of what was now a text. Duly convicted, their punishment was clearly intended as a display of judicial terror. The three male slaves were fixed to a cross, their flesh torn from their bodies "in six different places where it is thickest"; the female slave was strangled and scorched with palmetto leaves. All four were finally given the "stroke of mercy" at sunset, their bodies left exposed "under the blue sky," on a gibbet, as an example to others. As Deodati wrote to the Cape, he was aware that "all this is contrary to the orders given to us, but as we were sitting under the blue heaven, without any arms, and did not know whether any more slaves were implicated, and we had no prisons for the criminals" (Liebbrandt 1896, 49).

Repressive power and the spectacle of public punishment were, as this incident makes clear, central to this skeletal and shaky regime. Yet Deodati's improvisation of a legal process, his extraction of "confessions," and inscription of those "confessions" indicates, that even "under the blue sky" repressive power needed to be supplemented with something else. It was important that the apprehended slaves "confessed," and the stories of their dreadful deeds were heard from their own mouths.

A few years later, in 1706, the maroon theme was elaborated on through the arrest and trial of "Piet of Bali," a freeborn escaped prisoner who found himself at the head of a small and motley group of maroons whose aim, so it was said, was "to set fire to all the dwellings, murder the people and escape from Mauritius." Here, it appears, was a real conspiracy. Piet's gang was a cosmopolitan one, reflecting the social composition of the island, its creole beginnings. There were eleven of them altogether, including Piet of Bali, Jacob of Madagascar, Antonie of Batavia, Antonie of Malabar, Louis of Bengale, Jan the Kaffir of Goa, Ventura of Mozambique, Abas of Padang, Domingo of Patti, and Posjen of Madagascar.[20] The beginnings of the group appear to have been modest and domestic. As the trial progressed, so, it seems, their ambitions retrospectively grew. Sixteen months previously (or so the "confessions" went), Jacob, who was a slave, had been sent by his master to look for cattle, and fearful of returning without having found them, absconded. Some months later Antonie of Batavia had been sent out by his master to fish and had run away into the forest. A few months on, the two were joined by Antoine of Malabar. He was just too old and too ill to work for his master—refuge in the forest was likely born of desperation. The three set up camp together, improvised their subsistence and a system of basic care, a family of sorts. The younger men went "to and fro" in search of food, while the older Antonie stayed on the spot and did the cooking. Piet of Bali claimed in the trial that on joining them in the forest, he expanded their maroon ambitions. In his "ready confession" he claimed that he had instructed them that "as soon as they met a christian man in the forest" they were to "attack him, cut off his nose and ears and then, for their pleasure, bind him to a tree" (Barnwell 1948, 92).

There is power in a confession. Emboldened perhaps by Piet of Bali's claims for them (and what had they to lose?), Jacob and Antonie of Batavia are credited with more. Jacob confessed that he had "often intended to set fire to his master's house and to kill his master," while Antonie declared that he had intended to kill his master's son and young male and female slaves (not, apparently, his master) and after that to eat their hearts.

Despite the confessions, the trials, the subjection of fantasy to the law, the Dutch remained captives on their own island, subject to internal and external eruptions and overrun by rats. Added to the maroon slaves were the escaped convicts like Piet of Bali, the pirates and the deserters from passing ships—in 1706 fourteen "Europeans" deserted onto the island, including an Englishman, a Muscovite, and a Portuguese.

Meanwhile, thanks to its trust in foreigners, the smallness of its wings and the weight of its body, the island's famous native was no more. The dodo was well and truly dead by the end of the seventeenth century. Abandoning the island, which the Dutch finally did in 1710, was, however, easier to command than to execute. No one knew for sure how many people were there, but the commander's estimate was three hundred (not, apparently, including slaves or maroons). Commander Momber was charged not only with rounding everyone up and ensuring that the island was once more uninhabited, but also with making certain that everyone, slaves included, was exported to either the Cape or Batavia decently clad, so as not to disgrace the Dutch nation. Over a period the boatloads left, until finally Momber himself sailed for Batavia.

French Beginnings: Plus Ça Change

On abandoning Mauritius the Dutch feared that it would fall to their archrivals, the English, but in fact it was the French who laid claim to it with a *prise de possession* in 1715 and, under the control of the Compagnie des Indes (French East Indies Company), began to settle it in 1721.

Compared to their European rivals, the French had been somewhat slow off the mark when it came to overseas expansion and the development of international commerce.[21] But French colonial ambitions had been furthered in the reign of Louis XIII by Cardinal Richelieu, who saw overseas commerce as a form of state aggrandizement. Mercantilist ideas dominated in the seventeenth century—the purpose of colonial trade was to provide France with items it could not produce and in return to buy manufactured goods from the metropole. The agent of French colonial and commercial ambitions would be the chartered companies facilitated by the system of the *exclusif*, through which trade, theoretically, re-mained in French hands and thus guarded against the exodus of capital from France. The companies, the nomination of whose directors was to be approved by the king himself, would exercise a monopoly over com-merce in the colonies in which they operated, and in return would fulfill an administrative (and political) role on behalf of the Crown.

The initial focus of French activity was, unsurprisingly, the Americas, where 1626 saw the founding of the Compagnie de St. Christophe, and the following year the Compagnie de la Nouvelle France. In 1635 the Compagnie des Îles d'Amerique took possession of the islands of the Antilles. For France, as for Britain, the production of sugar would come to dominate colonial policy, and with sugar came slavery. In 1642, Louis XIV authorized the use of slavery in the colonies and the trade in slaves from the West African coast.

Though all eyes were on the Americas, where important sites of

French settlement already existed (in Quebec and Louisiana, for example), nevertheless, it was also in 1642 that the first Compagnie des Indes Orientales was founded, with a monopoly over trade to and from Madagascar and "adjacent islands." Although the last of the great powers to arrive in the Indian Ocean, the French took a keen (and enduring) interest in Madagascar and began establishing outposts on its east coast, the most important of which was Fort Dauphin. Beyond Madagascar, of course, lay the anticipation of the great wealth that might be derived from trade with India, the islands of the East Indies, and China—a trade already being tapped by the Dutch and the English. Furthermore, though European commercial expansion in the Indian Ocean had its own dynamics, it also linked directly with the development of the sugar colonies of the Atlantic world. The link came in the goods (Indian textiles and cowrie shells in particular) that were essential items in the trade for slaves on the West African coast. The evolving "triangular trade" of the Atlantic, then, would depend, in part at least, on access to the products of the Indies.

French ambitions in the Indian Ocean were further advanced by Colbert in the 1660s. In 1664 a new Compagnie des Indes Orientales was founded, with Lorient as its designated port. The new company's fortunes would fluctuate in the 1670s and 1680s, but it was in this period that the French established an important foothold in India with the establishment of a *comptoir* at Pondichéry, on the Coromandel coast (Singaravelou 1993; Haudrère 1993). But the costs of war in Europe and a new fervor for protectionism in France (in 1709 the government banned the importation of Indian textiles) meant that the development of Pondichéry and of Indian Ocean commerce in general, would not take off until the foundation (driven by John Law) of yet another Compagnie des Indes in 1719. By this time, other events had led the French to take a greater interest in the islands which lay to the east of Madagascar—Bourbon and the island of Mauritius, now abandoned by the Dutch.

Since 1643, the French had been in possession of Île Bourbon, a sleepy agricultural backwater, settled in part by Franco-Malagasies expelled from Fort-Dauphin in Madagascar and by slaves of mainly Malagasy origin.[22] Nothing much happened on Île Bourbon for the rest of the century. In 1686 a visiting priest reported that the island's population consisted of around three hundred people (presumably not counting slaves). They included families of mixed French and Malagasy origin, and of those arising from marriages between French and Portuguese from India. There were also fifteen Indians, prisoners from San Thomé (Vaxelaire 1999, 1:84). But from around 1710 Île Bourbon began to assume a much greater significance for the French Company and the Crown because of its nascent coffee industry (Ly-Tio-Fane Pineo 1993, 29–37). Île Bourbon now looked like a valuable asset and it seemed dangerously exposed by the "emptiness" of the neighboring island the Dutch had abandoned, and of course by the great power games of the Indian Ocean. French nervousness increased when, in 1721, the captain of a French ship stopped off on Mauritius, now known to the French as Île de France. This account, like much of the early history of the island, is disputed and contentious,[23] but according to one version the captain found on the island a worrying number of inscriptions to the glory of Emperor Charles VI. His response was to declare a new French prise de possession at Île aux Tonneliers (on the northwest of the island, near present-day Port Louis) where he erected a thirty-foot cross, engraved on it a fleur-de-lis and the following inscription of his own: "Lilia fixa crucis capiti mirare sacratae ne stupeas; jubet hic Gallia stare crucem. Anno M DCCXXI."[24]

What the inhabitants of the island (pirates? maroons?) made of these repeated gestures and overlaid inscriptions, we cannot know,[25] but so nervous were the inhabitants of Bourbon about the possibility of a foreign neighbor that they took matters into their own hands. The Company had appointed a governor for the new Île de France, de Nyon, who had left France in June 1721. De Nyon was an engineer—a member of a profession that would play a crucial role in the eighteenth-century empire—and he had already been at work on the French *comptoir* of Pondichéry, constructing its fortifications (Frémont 1993, 72–73). His journey from France was reportedly nightmarish, even by the standards of the time, so that by December, a group of sixteen settlers (*habitants*) of Île Bourbon, under the direction of Le Toullec de Ronguet, had already taken matters into their own hands and left for Île de France. They landed on the northwest of the island ten days later and built themselves a few huts. Le Toullec de Ronguet then made a tour of the island, declaring that it appeared to a large extent uncultivable and perhaps uninhabitable due to the rocks scattered over the landscape: good for a *poste de garde*, he suggested. There was no mention of maroons in these early reports.

Though the French were well aware of the history of the earlier Dutch settlement, they often described the island as if it were a wilderness, newly discovered. De Nyon arrived on Easter Sunday, 5 April 1722. With him, on the ships *Atalante* and *Diane*, were seven further Company employees, four priests of the Lazarist order, six Swiss officers, eighty-four Swiss soldiers, two domestic servants, six married women, and four children.[26] This first group arrived, apparently, without slaves.

De Nyon's first task was to secure the island against any coup de main by a foreign power. For this he needed to find some colonists and some slaves to serve them, and so, having once again formally claimed the island (just in case), he set off again to Île Bourbon to find some recruits. What the Company envisaged was a settlement along the lines of that which had been established on Île Bourbon: a few families to start with, and their slaves, of course, who would set about growing the new and profitable crop of coffee. Expectations of coffee production on Île Bourbon were already phenomenally high, but the very value of the crop was thought to pose a security problem, encouraging the attention of foreign enemies. According to the governor of Île Bourbon, Desforges Boucher, the word had spread that "the Arabs who produced [coffee] would come to slit their throats and the Dutch who conducted a lucrative trade in the coffee of Moka and Java would come to ravage the island" (Ly-Tio-Fane Pineo 1993, 53). The initial purpose of colonizing Île de France, then, was to protect Île Bourbon from attack. The new colony would be productive *and* strategic: populating the island in itself acted as a deterrent to foreign powers, or so it was thought. Returning with his recruits, a few habitants from Île Bourbon and around thirty slaves, de Nyon decided to create the first French settlement on the ruins of that which had been left by the Dutch at what became known as Port Sud-Est.

There is no moment in the human history of Mauritius that is prior to creolization, or "pre-creole." The Dutch settlers and their slaves, as we have seen, were a varied and cosmopolitan group, a product of the far-flung colonial world in which they lived. Piet of Bali's small maroon group was drawn from Madagascar, Africa, South India, and Batavia, and many "Dutch" colonists were from Germany, Switzerland, and England. Likewise, some of the early French settlers and their slaves already had a long history of creolization behind them: those who were drawn from Île Bourbon, for example. Île Bourbon was largely peopled by small agriculturalists whom one might have labeled "peasants" were it not for the crucial fact that they owned slaves. The majority of their slaves would have come from Madagascar (Barendse 1995; Larson 2000; Gerbeau 1997;

Ho 1997; Filliot 1973) itself a complex mélange of cultures, and while some of the slave owners had come originally from France, others had reached the island by a more circuitous route. These were the exiles and descendants of exiles from the French settlement of Fort Dauphin on Madagascar, finally abandoned in 1674. European settlement on Madagascar had always been a negotiated affair, involving strategic alliances with powerful rulers, political brokerage, marriage ties, and the perpetuation of shared economic interests—including that of the slave trade. The resulting community of Fort Dauphin must have been a complex one, culturally and linguistically. This is hinted at by the account of a Lazarist priest on Île Bourbon in 1739 describing an elderly Fort Dauphin exile, Mme. Cadet, who had been born in Madagascar of a Malagasy mother and French father. According to the priest, whom she regaled with stories of life at Fort Dauphin and of the French "Messieurs" who had presided over the settlement, she spoke, in addition to her "poor" French, Malagasy, Portuguese, English, and "Malabar."[27] Within this one transported life were traces of earlier journeys and other places. More layers would be added to this history in Île de France.

De Nyon's instructions from the Company were instructions to create the physical, economic, and social skeleton of a colony;[28] they did not, and perhaps could not, take into account the multilayered and unruly reality of this distant frontier post. The island's strategic importance was uppermost—de Nyon was to build a fort capable of resisting attack, and within it a chapel and some stores. He was to create for the Company a plantation on which to grow essential food supplies, with an enclosure for animals. He was to distribute both land and slaves to the settlers to enable them to produce wheat, rice, spices, and, above all, coffee.[29] He was to attend to the preservation of precious hardwoods (Grove 1995, 173), to build roads, and finally, and importantly, to produce an accurate map which would indicate the cultivable parts of the island, the areas on which different crops might be grown, the location of different tree species and of rivers, ports, and anchorages.

Things went well for a short while. Building on the ruins of the Dutch settlement, de Nyon and his colleagues had encouraging success with their first attempts at cultivation. They (or more accurately, their slaves) produced in 1722 harvests of rice, wheat, maize, and tobacco. In December of that year a new cargo of slaves arrived from Madagascar—twenty-seven men, eighteen boys, twenty women and girls. By 1725, when de

Nyon took a census, there were 213 known people on the island: 20 officers of the Company, 100 troops, 28 workers, 5 servants, 13 women, 24 company slaves (*Noirs de la Compagnie*) and 10 privately owned slaves (*Noirs des particuliers*) (Baker and Corne 1982, 142). This was the only moment in the history of Île de France when free people outnumbered slaves; the situation would soon be reversed. But, as in the Dutch period, the census did not tell the whole story, for there may have been as many slaves outside de Nyon's tenuous control as there were under it. In a letter to the Company in 1724, he had complained of what he called the "sad" and "deplorable" situation on the island.[30] Work that had started on the port in the northwest of the island (later to become Port Louis) was hampered by lack of labor, and agricultural production was continually thwarted by an "incomprehensible multitude" of rats. Furthermore, he was engaged in what he termed a *guerre intestine* with a band of some fifty maroon slaves who continually attacked the northwest camp and port. Social disorder was indeed widespread. The Company had embarked in France 210 soldiers of the Compagnie Suisse, 20 women, 30 children, and a number of officers and workers for the island. Many had died on the voyage over—in fact, only 67 of the soldiers had survived, and half of these were considered unfit for duty. Those who had survived were hardly willing colonial servants. Duval de Hauville, who as de Nyon's deputy commanded the northwest port, complained of the seditious tendencies of officers and the continual threat of flight into the forests made by the ordinary soldiers. He had never, he wrote, been in a place so dominated by "mutinous, diabolical and pernicious spirits." Even Job, he went on, with all his patience, would have been severely tried ("bien embarrassé," quoted in Ly-Tio-Fane Pineo 1995, 67). He asked to be relieved of his duties, as did de Nyon soon afterward.

The dominant tropes of the early French correspondence, then, echoed those of the earlier Dutch administration: maroon slaves, rats, disloyalty, and intrigue. There is little doubt that the reality was harsh and the intrigue real enough in a system of government and employment based so heavily on personal reputations and personal relations. One could never be certain what one's enemies were up to far away in Paris, what lies were being manufactured at home. The line between political realism and paranoia was not always an easy one to maintain, especially when stranded, or so it must have seemed, in the middle of the Indian Ocean. French administrators did not employ the Dutch motif of being "alone under the blue sky," but they expressed similar sentiments. The brief years of de Nyon's administration contained many themes that would recur for decades to come. They were parochial, sometimes personal themes but simultaneously large, global economic and political ones. At their heart were big questions of the definition, purpose, and viability of a colonial enterprise and of the institution of slavery within it. De Nyon could not control his labor, either enslaved or technically free, and in any case there was never enough of it. He could not control a natural environment that, though rich in some ways, was hostile in others. The rats, products of earlier human intervention, really did plague the island, and periodic and terrifying cyclones destroyed in a matter of minutes work that had taken years to complete: life on the island reads like a description from Freud's account of phobic anxiety.[31] The priest Ducros described, graphically, the psychological effect of the plague of rats:

> This island might be called the kingdom of rats. They are seen coming down from the mountains in battalions, climbing the most rugged rocks, roaming over the level plains, assembling in the marshes. They lay all things waste, especially at night, I have seen them myself, at nightfall, swarm out of the earth as numerous as ants, and spread desolation everywhere. Nothing escapes their teeth. How may one sleep quietly amid this cursed breed? You wrap yourself up like a corpse, and try to grow accustomed to feeling them running, jumping and fighting upon you. (Quoted in Barnwell 1948, 143)

Only the rats, it seemed, were organized with the kind of military precision expected of a colonial army. Meanwhile the Company's plans for the island were confused and confusing, and the responsibility for securing the western Indian Ocean for the French monarchy daunting in the extreme. The officers did not trust one another; they were fearful of their workers, soldiers, servants, and above all the slaves upon whose labor the entire enterprise depended. Their fear could turn to paranoia, and their paranoia may well have fed the fantasies of those without power. Slaves and soldiers probably really did plot to murder officers in their beds.

Over the next few years the island staggered from one disaster to another (famines and cyclones among them), and things were made no easier by vacillation in the Company and the Crown's commercial and political priorities. Initially conceived of as the poorer sister to the coffee-producing Île Bourbon, the maritime advantages of Île de France's harbors (and particularly those of the northwest port) were slowly recognized. Gradually the respective status of the two islands would be reversed, with Île Bourbon becoming something of a backwater, and Île de France the crucial link in French colonial and commercial policy in the Indian Ocean. But these ambitions were slow to be realized and were never, in any case, without complications.

In 1726 Christophe Lenoir, appointed by Louis XV as Commander of all the French establishments in India and the Indian Ocean, visited Île de France after de Nyon's disgruntled departure. The administration of Île Bourbon and Île de France was, for a brief period, subordinated to Lenoir and the Conseil Supérieur established at Pondichéry, now experiencing a period of prosperity. Île de France was another matter. When he arrived in May he found a desperate situation. The island was virtually without food, its inhabitants all living in the direst poverty, and, unsurprisingly, in a state of revolt. The missionaries had left in disgust for Île Bourbon (Ly-Tio-Fane Pineo 1995, 97). But he had plans for the island, which he rehearsed in a long *mémoire* to Paris.[32] Lenoir observed that the island's natural resources had been mismanaged and suggested greater regulation. This was to be an enduring theme of Île de France history. But though Lenoir was undoubtedly correct to recognize that effective exploitation of resources in a fragile island environment depended on careful conservation, there was, as he acknowledged, a more intractable problem. This was the absolute shortage of people to effectively exploit the resources in the first place. By "people," of course, Lenoir meant the right kind of people, specifically colonists, habitants. As he wrote in his dispatch to Paris, there was no possibility that the island could fulfill its envisaged role with so few habitants at its disposal, and so peopling the island had to be a priority.

The earliest formal settlers, as we have seen, came from Île Bourbon, but their reports home had not been favorable and many had left. Certainly the idea of peopling Île de France from Île Bourbon looked implausible to Lenoir. His proposed solution to the "peopling" problem (which to an extent became policy) was to recruit from France the non-agricultural workers the island required (such as masons and carpenters), to encourage them to bring their wives and families, and to make them into permanent agricultural settlers, habitants, once their contracts were over. Yet Lenoir acknowledged that in practice it was hard to retain such people—many left as soon as their contracts were over, complaining of the harsh conditions on the island. At the very least, he suggested, they needed appeasing with the provision of hats and shoes. There were some employees of the Company, he noted, who had begun to carve out and cultivate small plots of land beyond the confines of the two main camps (the southeast and northwest ports), but they did so in constant fear of attack from maroon slaves. The existence of maroons thus rendered colonization outside the camps dangerous but also, as he noted, led to further demands on the already stretched labor resources of the island, since a constant supply of men was required for the maroon capturing and killing expeditions, chillingly named *chasse des marons*, maroon hunt.

Reading Lenoir's dispatch, and many like it, one is easily drawn into the logic that dominated the minds of these colonial administrators. They certainly had problems; creating a viable colony is clearly not easy. But their logic obscures what, when viewed from another place and time, is a glaring reality: a large part of their problem was created by the one institution that seemed to them to be utterly indispensable—slavery. Slavery was itself a law and order problem, which in turn created a demand for loyal labor. But both loyalty and labor were in short supply. This is not to argue that slavery itself was irrational or uneconomic, but that in these particular circumstances the physical repression used to contain the slaves not only made their labor unproductive but also tied up further labor. In particular, it appears that the apparently intractable problem of the island's food supply was at least in part the result of contradictions inherent in the slave system. The island needed agricultural producers, but agricultural producers were conceived of as playing social and political roles, as well as economic ones. The agriculturalists were to be the habitants, the colonists, the families who would ensure that this distant island loyally served the king. Slaves "naturally" could not perform these social and political roles, though they might fulfill the economic ones. Economic and social functions, though perceived in the eighteenth century as closely, if not inextricably, bound together, sometimes appeared to be at odds. The siege mentality of these early years meant that the labor of slaves could never be fully materialized—a milder version of the dilemma facing the Dutch when they shackled their slaves to prevent their escape. At the same time, slaves (and all other Company dependants—the whole population, in fact) needed to be fed. In fact, the inadequacy of their food supply was one factor impelling slaves to escape to the forests, where they could at least fend for themselves through hunting, fishing, and gathering. Once in the forests, their raids posed a further threat to habitants, and more labor had to be diverted to hunting them down. And so a vicious circle was perpetuated.

The project of "peopling" the island continued. Lenoir's observation that perhaps some white women would help was followed up. In a sometimes farcical, certainly tragic episode, women and girls were sent from France expressly for the purpose of providing their labor of biological and social reproduction. The first group to arrive in 1728 were *filles de la Compagnie* (Ly-Tio-Fane Pineo 1995, 101; Baker and Corne 1982, 160; Lagesse 1972, chap. 4). They were followed by a group of twelve *filles paysannes* from Brittany. These were girls from poor families (rural Brittany was in the midst of deep economic depression); the Company provided them each with a trousseau in anticipation of their marrying when they arrived on the island. The feminization project faltered, however, at this point. The presence of the girls was said to have caused "disorder" on board the ship that brought them to the island, and many had arrived in a "poor condition," afflicted with venereal diseases. Henceforth an effort was made to recruit girls from religious communities, in the hope that they might at least arrive in the colony uncorrupted. Despite doubts about their suitability as representative female subjects, many did at least fulfill their biological role, and the small group of habitants grew. But while Île de France had acquired more families, they were not necessarily ideal ones. When the new governor Nicolas de Maupin, arrived on the island in 1729, he was not impressed. The habitants, he wrote, are "louts."

Disaffection among the settler population, never absent, became ever more apparent under the administration of de Maupin, who was eventually the target of an assassination plot. The objects of disaffection were maladministration and the abuse of power, but there were two main issues over which this large theme was played out. One was the apparently ubiquitous question of sexual morality and "decency"; the other was the question of *la distribution des noirs*, or the allocation of the island's most precious resource, its slaves.

As in the Dutch period, sexual scandals were highly political, touching at the heart of issues of governance and abuse of power. One long-running case involved one M. de Bellecourt, an ensign at the northwest port who, in 1726, was accused of making a calumnious attack on the morals of a priest of the Lazarist order, Jean-Baptiste Borthon, but whose conviction and sentencing by the court in Île de France was overturned by an appeal to the Conseil Supérieur, now located in Île Bourbon.[33]

Complaints of arbitrary punishment were frequent against Nicolas de Maupin, who was often accused of being "despotic" and of taking the law into his own hands. In 1730, when a young girl, Elizabeth La Basserie, had taken refuge in a priest's house in order to avoid an unwanted marriage, he had, with the help of fusilliers, forcibly removed her.[34] In 1728 the Lazarists had complained that an employee of the Company had arbitrarily inflicted a punishment on the wife of a habitant that was "contrary to decency," since it was a punishment normally reserved for men. Mme. Coupet had been subjected to the *cheval du bois*.[35] The priests had further and more general complaints, which they directed to the Company in Paris. After eight years on the island, they had founded two parishes, which they described colorfully as "two small corners of prostitution, of debauchery, of desertions, duels and all sorts of crimes." They had been subjected, they said, to the most insulting and sacrilegious treatment; they had been accused of a wide range of crimes, including that of selling confessions. It was, they said, the officers who were responsible for the deplorable state of affairs on the island. The greatest crimes went unpunished, while at the same time innocent people were often falsely accused. This, they said, also applied to the treatment of slaves, and with dangerous consequences. An innocent slave had been hanged on the evidence of just one other slave, who hoped to save himself by implicating others. Incidents such as this, they argued, "irritated" the maroon slaves in the forests who previously had harmed no one, but who now went as far as murdering *les blancs*.[36] The Lazarist order on the islands was in fact itself deeply riven by scandals and dissensions, and so their testimony is hardly innocent, but they were not the only ones to express deep dissatisfaction.

There were many deep fault lines within this small colony, even leaving aside the more obvious ones between Company settlements and maroon camps, between slave and free. The small elite of Company officers was despised by other employees and by habitants; their rule was considered less than legitimate, and their corrupt practices were only too evident. The priests and administrators were often at loggerheads, as we have seen, as were administrators and military men. Accusatory and self-justificatory mémoires must have taken up a significant amount of space in ships' holds—they certainly take up a great deal of space in the colonial archive.

One early example of this—a 1730 mémoire against the administration of Maupin—also highlights the other enduring scandal of this period. This was the allocation, or misappropriation, of imported slaves. Slaves were the most sought-after commodity on Île de France, and the most fought over. Aware of the problem posed by the earliest maroon slaves, who were probably all Malagasies, the Company had from early on encouraged the island's administrators to diversify their sources. A favored, if distant, source was West Africa: ships from France stopped off at the Company's establishment on the island of Gorée and filled their holds with human beings there. The East African coast would become an important source later. The slave trade, as with all trade at the time, was a Company monopoly, and officers of the Company were frequently accused of exploiting their position to keep the best part of these precious cargoes for themselves. Indeed, distinguishing between Company trade and the private enterprise of individual administrators was and is difficult, but less favored inhabitants of Île de France tried to do just that. In a letter of 1729 the Company had urged Maupin not to favor employees of the Company when it came to the allocation of newly arrived slaves but to ensure that the habitants, the potential agricultural producers, received their share.[37] But Maupin was accused not only of favoring employees in the *distribution des noirs*, but of keeping many slaves for himself.[38] In 1731 one M. de Souilleuse wrote a very disgruntled mémoire to the Company.[39] He had been contracted by the Company in 1728 as a habitant, and had left France for Île de France with his wife and a worker. His assumption had been that he would be given slaves, but on his arrival on the island he was told that none was available, that they were all required by the Company. Eventually a ship, the *Méduse*, arrived from West Africa.[40] Du Souilleuse was allocated two slaves—a man and a woman—but this, he argued, was hardly sufficient to enable him to exploit his *habitation* in the rather remote area of Plaines Wilhems (a mountainous region in the center of the island) where, to add to his problems, he was also vulnerable to attack from maroons. When, in August, M. de Maupin arrived to take up his post as governor, du Souilleuse approached him, requesting slaves from the ship on which he had arrived, but he was rewarded with just one *négritte* (by which was usually meant a male teenager or older child). Others made the same charge. M. Teinturier de

Gennincourt produced a long mémoire (later found to be libelous) addressed directly to the king, copies of which he distributed as far afield as Paris and India. He had made, he wrote, the "long and dangerous" journey from France in the expectation of finding the prosperity the Company had promised him in Île de France. He was, he said, rewarded instead with poverty and near starvation. To de Gennincourt, the cause of this poverty was all too obvious: the misappropriation of slaves by officers of the Company, to the detriment of the ordinary habitant. The colony will never flourish, he wrote, or do honor to the French nation, until the habitants are provided with sufficient slaves to enable them to put their land to use.[41]

In 1730 the contradictions of slavery were, indeed, writ large on the island, for while de Gennincourt was complaining of the lack of slaves, another group of habitants was leaving Île de France, either for France or for Île Bourbon. Among these settlers' complaints about the island was that there were "too many blacks" there.[42]

Maupin may have been a bully, as was often alleged, but the conditions of his administration were not easy. Company policy toward the island vacillated in a way which, from a distance in particular, must have appeared quite whimsical. Such habitants as the governor had at his disposal had built their hopes on the potential profitability of coffee, but Maupin was soon instructed that coffee production on Île de France should cease and be left to Île Bourbon. A number of precious habitants were sufficiently annoyed and discouraged by this to leave, some taking their slaves with them. Underlying the confused policy was a serious financial crisis in the Company leading to more limited, less ambitious activity in the East Indies and Indian Ocean. In Paris, the directors of the Company puzzled over the difficulty they were having in making their Indian Ocean possessions (and particularly Île de France) into profitable concerns. The Indian Ocean possessions consumed relatively few French manufactured goods, but vast quantities of valuable silver were required to keep them afloat. This was not how things were supposed to work.[43] Among other problems, the credit the Company extended to each habitant on Île de France proved almost impossible to recover. The habitants of Île Bourbon, though continually accused of laziness, did at least produce coffee (120,000 pounds of it in 1728); the habitants of Île de France produced nothing. Île Bourbon was by now a known quantity; assessing the potential of Île de France remained extraordinarily difficult. From the time of the second Dutch occupation, right through to the end of the period of French rule, descriptions and assessments of the island had a marked tendency to be either romantically optimistic (an island of multiple rainbows and bountiful soil) or excessively pessimistic (an island of cyclones, rocks, and rats). One set of information fed back to the Company in the late 1720s proved decisive: the reports of ships' captains concerning the relative advantages and disadvantages of the ports at their disposal on the two islands.

Gradually it became apparent that in the northwest port on Île de France the Company had possession of a potentially exceptional harbor. Maupin was therefore instructed, firstly to develop the fortifications at that port and then, in 1731, to move his headquarters there. The Company's plan now focused on the northwest port as a potential port of call for its ships. The move to the northwest created further friction between Maupin and the already unhappy habitants, most of whom resided in or around the southeast port. If the northwest port was to be a port of call, then foodstuffs would have to be grown sufficient not only to feed the islanders, but also to supply the ships. But in 1731 this hardly seemed realistic. The island was hit by a cyclone; the habitants were disgruntled and complained, directly to the king, of the injustices of Company policy and the shortage of slaves at their disposal. As work on construction at what became known as Port North-West got underway, so agricultural production may have seemed even less attractive than before. For though there was a growing market for produce, it was much easier to make a living through direct involvement in the construction process. Yet the problems occasioned by the new Company policy toward the island were probably outweighed by the fact that new investment was being made. The construction of a new colony had now really begun.

Chapter Two

*A*mong the national mythologies of present-day Mauritius is that surrounding the role of Governor Mahé de Labourdonnais, the "founding father" and architect of the island colony. Tourists making a day trip from the beaches to the capital of Port Louis will find a statue of this imposing figure facing out to sea, the old administrative headquarters which he had helped to construct at his back. With Labourdonnais, we are led to believe, came order and development. He is credited with the erection of both a durable physical infrastructure and the colony's social infrastructure. He was an engineer, in both senses. He built an aqueduct, a large hospital, and a *salle de spectacle*, and he pressed home a vision of Île de France as a real colony, not simply a *rélache* or stopping-over point in the middle of the Indian Ocean. And he achieved these things despite the hesitancy, and sometimes the opposition, of the Company. In this story, vision and heroism are thrown into further relief by tragedy: the great war hero suffered the death, on the island, of his wife and child and was eventually defeated by the machinations of his enemies, which landed him in the Bastille and left him a broken man. Yet despite the clear mythologization of the founding patriarch (aided by Bernardin de Saint-Pierre's portrayal of him in his best-selling novel *Paul et Virginie*),[1] there is much truth in this account. Creating a colony really was the work of a visionary, whatever we might now think of its social cost and of the result. While Governor Maupin had ranted and raved and finally despaired of making anything of the island and its wretched inhabitants, Labourdonnais forged ahead with his ambition of creating Île de France as *the* entrepôt of the Indian Ocean, one he hoped would be the envy of France's political and economic rivals, the English and the Dutch. In this ambition he was immeasurably assisted by another dominant institution of the eighteenth-century world: war.

Warfare was the backdrop to everything that happened on Île de France in the eighteenth century, yet it appears curiously absent from many accounts. It is there, clearly, in the biographies of many of the island's administrators (Labourdonnais prominent among them), and it is there in the economics and demographic structure of the island. Port Louis, like most eighteenth-century ports, was socially complex, extremely fluid and very masculine,[2] but much more so during periods in which it served as a base for French conflicts with England over India, which would end in French defeat. During these periods (1744–1746, 1755–1762, 1778–1783, and 1794–1802) the port played host to large fleets of ships that required repairing and reprovisioning. The huge crews of these ships constituted multicultural and multiracial microsocieties, with their own naval patois, their own rules of conduct, their own hierarchies. Recent work on Atlantic history by Peter Linebaugh and Marcus Rediker (2000) explores the social and political consequences of a cosmopolitan, transatlantic maritime economy; the role of African American seamen in the Atlantic world has also been described by Jeffrey Bolster (1997). More directly relevant, however, is Janet Ewald's analysis (2000) of seafarers of African and Indian origin in the northwest Indian Ocean in the eighteenth century. Ewald argues that East African and Indian men played vital roles on European ships in the Indian Ocean from at least the sixteenth century, and that wars and growth in commerce increased demand for them in the eighteenth century. Maritime workers, she argues, were boundary crossers; they "traversed often vast and open seascapes, yet lived in the tightly bounded confines of ships, where life was, to varying degrees, hierarchical and regimented" (70). Many of the sailors who landed on Île de France were undoubtedly "black," some of them slaves and ex-slaves, their very existence immediately creating havoc with (but certainly not dissolving) the social and racial distinctions upon which the colonial project rested. Throughout the century, administrators struggled to exert some control over these crews (and those of merchant ships), struggled to feed them and tend to them in the overcrowded hospitals. Eighteenth-century seamen, both slave and free, were notoriously poorly fed and prone to sickness. It is unsurprising, then, that so many French medical innovations in the eighteenth century derived from naval experience (Brockliss and Jones 1997, chap. 11; Vaughan 2000).

Despite the problems war created for the island, in some sense war was its raison d'être. Île de France was never a jewel in the crown of French colonialism, never the source of riches represented by the sugar colonies of the Antilles.[3] Its value to the French lay in its geographical position. It was, they liked to think, the "key to India" and even when the French had decisively lost India after the Seven Years' War, it retained its position in French strategic thinking. In the life of the inhabitants of Île de France, then, and of its slave population, war, preparations for war, reparations of war, and the anxieties induced by war were in some sense ever present. Though the actual conflict took place somewhere else, in the "theater of war," its debris and its casualties continually washed up on the island's shores.

Independent of great power politics and treaties, the island was, in a sense, always at war. As many commentators noted, while patrols looked out to sea from its coastal fortifications, ever on guard against the possible approach of the enemy, in the center of the island the *guerre intestine* against maroon slaves continued to rumble on, throughout the century. As the island's forests were increasingly depleted (not least for the purpose of repairing war ships), so the possibilities for creating self-contained maroon communities also receded. The maroons of Île de France were forever on the move, often within earshot—the war against them was a guerrilla war, erupting here and there unpredictably. But their continual unseen presence, their night raids and kidnappings, created considerable anxiety, just as they had for the Dutch and the very first French settlers. Maroons were a reminder of the violence on which slavery was built. And so the island was constantly on alert against the enemy without and the enemy within.

∾

MAHÉ DE LABOURDONNAIS, born in St. Malo in 1699, was one of many "Malouins" to make his name in the French naval service (Crepin 1922; Ly-Tio-Fane Pineo 1993). He took his first voyage at the age of ten and entered the service of the Compagnie des Indes when he was twenty. Over the next ten years or so he was initiated into the arts of navigation, engineering, war, and, significantly, commerce. He took part in the French taking of Mahé in 1725 and stayed on in India, using the advantages of his position as a Company employee to engage in the lucrative commerce *d'Inde en Inde*—by which was meant the trade (which the Company had opened up to entrepreneurs) based in India but extending from Moka in the west to the Philippines in the east. "One goes to the Indies only to do business," he is reported as saying (Haudrère 1993, 59). By the time he was nominated to the post of governor of both Île de France and Île Bourbon in 1734, he had made a considerable fortune, and as Company employee, military man, and entrepreneur he would come to embody the contradictions inherent in colonial policy in this period.

Arriving on Île de France, La Bourdonnais was initially greeted by all the problems that had beset his predecessors. He had visited the islands before, and so these would not have come as any surprise to him. The inhabitants continued to complain of the lack of slaves, of their "poor quality," of the unfairness of their distribution. The Company controlled everything and had a monopoly on all trade. Reluctant habitants, many of whom were ex-soldiers and sailors who had been persuaded to take concessions, were heavily indebted to the Company and had no incentive to become more independent. Food shortages were constant and sometimes severe and there was not enough clothing for either habitants or their slaves. Rats continued to plague the island, while maroon slaves created a backdrop of terror. Finally, for a significant proportion of the (free) population, there was an overwhelming sense of injustice, of ill treatment, a sense of being stranded far away from France and subject to the overbearing, illegitimate power of unscrupulous and greedy administrators.

Labourdonnais's first task was to secure the island's defenses—particularly those of Port North-West (later Port Louis) with its valuable harbor. A start had already been made to this work under the governorship of Maupin, and the driving force behind it was Philibert Orry, the Company's new *contrôleur général des finances*. The island might look peculiarly unpromising from Maupin's close quarters, but from a distance things appeared very different. Orry had great expectations of the wealth that could be generated by commerce with the Indies, and for very practical reasons Île de France was essential to his plan. Winds and weather were critical. The passage from France to the Indies was long, arduous, and hazardous, and the rhythm of navigation between France and India and beyond was determined by that of the southwest monsoon, which dominated the Indian Ocean between the months of April and October and carried ships eastward. In order to take advantage of this, one had to leave the Company's port of Lorient in Brittany in the dead of winter and endure harsh sailing conditions en route to the coast of Africa, before stopping off either at the island of Gorée on the Senegambian coast or on the Cape Verde islands. This was followed by the long haul around the Cape (some three or four months after leaving France)—the point at which scurvy usually set in (Haudrère 1993, 48). Both on the way to India and beyond, and on the return journey (often in the cyclone season), Île de France could perform an invaluable role—a role enhanced, of course, in periods of war.

Throughout the century, as we shall see, disappointment with this colonial outpost would periodically surface and someone would suggest that perhaps it was not worth holding onto. But always this argument was rebutted with a few hard facts about weather and navigation. In 1752, for example, arguing against a very negative assessment of the island's worth, one mémoire writer insisted that the directors of the Company bear in mind two basic facts: first, that the passage to India was too long to be undertaken without a stopping-over point, and second, that the Company had no choice—Île de France was the only feasible site for this.[4] Securing the harbor was crucial, then, and to this end the Company had, in 1731, dispatched a highly qualified engineer to the island.[5] This was Charpentier-Cossigny, captain of infantry, Ingénieur Ordinaire du Roi, and recipient of the military order of St. Louis, an irascible and controversial character who was to be an important figure in the island's development (Crepin 1922; Toussaint 1936). Cossigny's assignment was to build batteries and to create a fort, similar to that which had been erected by de Nyon at Pondichéry (Frémont 1993, 73), with "strong walls," which might serve as a place of "retreat or defence" (Toussaint 1936, 16). Cossigny produced his plans in 1732 and got the go-ahead to begin work in 1734, but meanwhile the colony had slipped into near anarchy and he lacked both labor and materials to begin his work. Disgruntled and complaining, he returned to France.

Arriving in Port North-West in 1735 as the new governor general, Labourdonnais found some primitive defenses and the making of a harbor in the Trou Fanfaron. Cossigny had constructed the beginnings of an enclave for government buildings, with a store (begun in 1731 but uncompleted), a mill, and his own house. Around this were some sixty shacks, among which "nothing distinguished the house of the governor, the church, or the seat of the Conseil Provincial" (Crepin 1922, 57), a primitive hospital and huts to house soldiers. Impermanence was the main feature of Port North-West—many of the port's inhabitants lived in small, fragile structures, the one advantage of which was that they could be physically moved from location to location. The image is a powerful one: the early French colonists resembling a nomadic tribe, or perhaps a version of the island's famous giant tortoises, moving their houses on their backs.

Despite these inauspicious beginnings, the seeds were already being sown for the "urban bias" that would characterize eighteenth-century Île de France. The earliest habitants were already migrating from Port South-East to the new center of government, attracted by the opportunities offered by construction. As a result the number of habitations under cultivation on the island actually fell between 1731 and 1735 (Ly-Tio-Fane-Pineo 1993, 140).

And the site had a certain grandeur, surrounded as it was by impressive mountains. The French had built ports in similar sites elsewhere—in the islands of the Antilles, for example (Pérotin-Dumon 2000; Butel 2002, chap. 6) and in Canada (Johnston 2001)—and there was a kind of template for them. Nearer to hand, and within Labourdonnais's direct experience, was the now thriving settlement of Pondichéry on the Coromandel coast of India. Here Pierre Lenoir had presided over not only the building of a fort, but also the construction of a town, dominated by two large tree-lined streets. Lenoir had insisted that the houses be built with two stories. By 1735 there were some 100,000 inhabitants (Frémont 1993, 81).

Labourdonnais may have had Pondichéry in mind, then, when he advanced his plans for Port North-West, but the Company was insistent that this was to be a mere *escale* (stopover), not a town, and that therefore he should confine himself to the erection of batteries, goods stores, a hospital, and barracks. Labourdonnais replied that it was important to enable colonists to live an *agréable* existence. The Company retorted that he seemed not to have considered the consequences of such a policy: "If you unite all the habitants in the town, what will become of their habitations, where the presence of the master is so essential? Who will guard the habitations when the master is absent? The maroon slaves will have free reign" (quoted in Toussaint 1936, 28). And, they might have added, who will grow the food to feed these new urban dwellers? This was a problem

Labourdonnais himself soon had to face, but he was determined that Île de France should be much more than a relâche.

There were plenty of detractors who thought his ideas unrealistic and grandiose. In 1738, for example, when he argued that the island could become a valuable entrepôt for the Company, comparable to Batavia, one writer referred to this comparison as ridiculous, a "chimera."[6] But Labourdonnais appears to have been undeterred. As he explained in his long mémoire written to the Company in 1740 (Lougnon 1937), if Île de France were to perform the tasks expected of it, even as a relâche, it would need colonists who were more than transient, who were committed to the place. A lack of commitment to colonial life was, he argued, a peculiarly French problem, not one experienced by their rivals, the English. Why was this? His explanation was a touchingly patriotic one: life in France was so very agreeable, why would anyone wish to stay away for long? His solution was to create a "society" on the island, which would incorporate, crucially, both a solid "town" and a "country," and he set the tone himself by buying a large habitation, in the northern settlement of Pamplemousses, which he named Mon Plaisir (Grove 1995, 175).

Labourdonnais was surely right to link the projects of physical and social engineering—the early colonial history of the island demonstrates this clearly, and the key linkage is provided by labor. The governor's first tasks were to create a harbor and the facilities to build and repair ships, and to construct the basic elements of a headquarters that could receive and supply large numbers of men. And all of this needed, of course, to be protected, fortified, both on land and at sea. This was a huge task. Merely creating a usable harbor, for example, was a significant work of engineering, and in addition to this he would have to build a basin in which ships' repairs could take place. Building supplies (stone, wood, sand, lime, iron goods) had to be found or imported and transported and a range of skills was also needed, including those of pilots and sailors to man the small boats which supplied moored ships with water, wood, and other provisions.[7] And so it was very early on in his administration that Labourdonnais made a decision that was to have a lasting impact on the social structure of this nascent colony—he drew on his Indian experience and decided to import a number of skilled Indian sailors, known by the name of Lascars.[8] They were, he argued, cheaper and more readily available than their French equivalents, and equally skilled. They were also of free birth and many of them were practicing Muslims—a fact that enraged the island's priests.

Labourdonnais used the skilled Lascar seamen to construct the beginnings of an apprenticeship system for the work on the port, and he would do the same for other tasks on land. Slaves, both Company owned and, increasingly, rented from private owners, were apprenticed to skilled workmen (both French and Indian) in ateliers. From very early on, then, he was engineering a labor system that would allow him to put slaves to productive use—something that the Dutch and his earlier French predecessors had found hard to achieve.

This pattern of slave utilization was, of course, not at all unique to Île de France, but common in other parts of the world, particularly in colonies dominated by ports and by urban development.[9] Many slaves, as Gwendolyn Hall has noted in her study of colonial Louisiana (Hall 1992, 132) brought with them significant skills as metalworkers, sailors, and shipbuilders. Foremost among these in Île de France as in Louisiana were the Bambara slaves (sometimes also glossed as *Guinées* in the Île de France documentation),[10] who were greatly valued for their marine skills and regarded as a good substitute for the Indian Lascars—for even Lascars were sometimes in short supply, and, it was argued, had a tendency to go "soft" on land ("These Indians, good enough on board ship, become soft and effeminate on land").[11] Even before Labourdonnais's arrival, an alternative source of skilled maritime labor had been found among Bambara slaves from West Africa, whom the Company had employed at the post on the island of Gorée.[12] Another specialized occupational/ethnic group, they were highly valued, and constantly in demand, especially in the first part of the century when administrators repeatedly stressed their superiority. In the early part of the century West Africans dominated among Company-owned slaves. In 1738 there were 1,432 Company slaves (785 men and 647 women) with 242 children. Of these, 630 were so-called Guinées exported from the Company's base in Gorée, 440 were Malagasies, 145 were Mozambiques, which meant that they had been exported from the east coast of Africa, and 142 were of Indian origin.[13]

For work on the construction of the harbor, Labourdonnais apprenticed (as he reported in 1740) 158 slaves—as carpenters, caulkers, coopers, sailmakers, ropemakers, and sailors. For the construction of the buildings on land and fortifications he also apprenticed slaves as masons, ironworkers, carpenters, and so on. A detailed breakdown of Company workers in 1742 reveals a hierarchy of skilled workmen and slaves attached to them, both as apprentices and as more menial labor. The twelve blacksmiths, for example, worked with six apprentice slaves and sixteen further slaves whose job was to work the bellows and to beat out the metal.[14] The same document hints at an ethnic division of labor, enumerating separately skilled Indian workers and Indian slaves attached to them as masons, blacksmiths, and carpenters. Since building and repair work became such an enduring feature of the life of Port Louis, this form of organization of slave labor would persist.

The engineer Charpentier-Cossigny returned to the island in 1736, highly critical of the work of the "amateur" Labourdonnais. Later, in the 1750s, Cossigny would resume work on the port's fortifications, using an apprenticeship system very similar to that devised by Governor Labourdonnais. But as Cossigny's journal from this period demonstrates, the fact that some slaves were trained and even paid wages did not imply that the Company slave regime as a whole was a soft or easy one. For every skilled slave there were many others whose work consisted of the most harsh manual labor—transporting materials and hewing stone, for example. Short of their own slaves, the Company increasingly rented slaves from private owners, but the conditions under which they worked were, according to Cossigny, appalling. In September 1753, for example, he reported that some two hundred slaves had been rented from one owner, a number of whom were sent out to the fortifications on the Île des Tonneliers, at the entry to the port. But most of these soon took the risk of drowning and deserted—for good reason, wrote Cossigny, for they were starving. Stranded on banks of coral and therefore with no recourse to wild foods or to any trade in foodstuffs, they were fed a wholly inadequate diet consisting of cakes of manioc (a crop which Labourdonnais had introduced to the island for the express purpose of feeding the slave population). Enraged, Cossigny told the Governor that he would not attempt to put to work slaves who were dying of starvation.[15] Alongside this Cossigny noted his own attempts to differentiate, police, and motivate slaves who were apprenticed to various ateliers. Each atelier had its own uniform: decorated bonnets the slaves were obliged to wear on work days, which enabled Cossigny to identify "at a glance" those at work on lime, those making bricks, and those whose jobs took place inside the lodge building. He claimed that the slaves regarded the wearing of these bonnets, with their bright colors, as an enormous honor. This may or may not have been the case, but it does seem likely that slaves would have appreciated Cossigny's other innovation, the provision of sandals made from imported hide. He made a particular point of distributing these to the women slaves employed to remove the coral from the foundation of the battery on Île des Tonneliers.

Labourdonnais was a rational man and well aware of the value of keeping slaves alive—he had passed regulations supplementing the Code Noir,[16] which governed slavery over the entire French empire, specifying minimum food and clothing rations and empowering slaves to bring complaints to the Company. But clearly, like the Code Noir itself, Labourdonnais's own regulations were largely unenforceable. And it was not only the slaves who suffered. All over the Atlantic and Indian Ocean worlds nominally free workers labored alongside slaves under appalling conditions (Ewald 2000; Linebaugh and Rediker 2000), and Île de France was clearly no exception. Later in the century the naturalist and novelist Bernardin de St. Pierre would describe the plight of the Breton peasants employed as sailors on the Company's ships, and the feudal mentality that made their exploitation possible:

> The peasant in Lower Britanny is contented. He considers himself free, close to an element on which all the roads are open . . . If he is too hard pressed, he boards a ship. On the ship where he has taken refuge he finds the oak wood of his enclosures; the linen woven by his family, and the wheat in his fields, household gods who have abandoned him. Sometimes he recognizes the lord of his village in the officer on the ship. In their common misery he sees that the officer is but a man, more to be pitied than himself. At liberty concerning his reputation, he becomes master of it . . . (Bernardin de St. Pierre [1773] 2002, 66)

Other evidence, however, points to the experience of labor in the colonies as more radicalizing. Unsurprisingly, workers recruited from France regularly employed the idiom of slavery to describe their situation. In the personnel records of the eighteenth-century colonial administration,[17] among the long service records of senior administrators, judges, and military leaders, is a file on a carpenter, Jean Louis Pobequin. In late 1737 he wrote (or, more likely, dictated) a letter to his wife in France:

My dear and honored wife these lines are to assure you of my humble respect and, at the same time to testify to my state of health which is good, thanks to the Lord, and I pray to God that yours is too, as well as that of your relations and friends in general, and [to say] that I am mortified that you have not told me whether you received the four hundred *livres* which I sent you; you have not said whether you received it, yes or no. On the subject of the coffee which you asked for I gave the money to a man who has affronted me since he has given me neither the coffee nor the money. My dear wife I beg you to be a little more careful to write to me and tell me the news of the country—my mother is dead, but you did not tell me. If you want me to come you will have to ask [the authorities] since we are not allowed to make such a request and if we do they tie us to a cannon on a cheval de bois in the dungeons and we see nothing but this unjust treatment . . . and so I ask you to use your friends to get me out of this country and to ensure this I will not be sending you anything until my return to France . . . I ask you to embrace my father, my sister, your sister, and to abbreviate, all our relations and friends in general, on your side as well as mine, and to assure them of my humble respect and my compliments . . . from your humble and faithful husband who will love you for as long as the soul beats in his body, with every respect possible, your faithful husband.

A second letter survives. This is dated two months later, 23 February 1738. The opening lines are exactly the same, with their formulaic enquiries on the health of the family. "I do not know how I will get away from here," he goes on, "and this is why I ask you to pray for me and for all my friends here who are in the same difficulties as myself." After repeating the request to his wife to find some means of releasing him from Île de France, he ends, "Take good care of my little daughter and I will bring her a beautiful dress, and one for you too."

It is thanks to Pobequin's wife that these letters have reached the archive, for she did act on her husband's request and in June 1738 employed a scribe to address a letter to the Naval Commissioner in Port Louis:

Marie Francoise Sauvage, wife of Jean Louis Pobequin, ship's carpenter living in the town of Port Louis has the honor to beg you, humbly, to order the return of her husband whom M. de Labourdonnais,

Governor for the Company on Île de France, is keeping there despite the fact that he has completed the three years of his engagement which came to an end in the month of March 1737. The supplicant has received two letters, one dated 15th December 1737 and the second 23rd February 1738 in which he remarks that it is only a [higher] authority which can deliver him from the colony, that the Government has prohibited him, and others like him, from making any such request . . . and that those who are bold enough to make such a request are tied to a cannon and beaten with ropes, others are exposed to the cheval du bois and others are held in prison, and that every day he sees nothing but punishment, bad treatment, such that makes these wretches despair seeing themselves so inhumanely treated, and without any hope of changing their unhappy lot if a higher authority does not come to their help. This is why the supplicant, who has a large family and needs her husband to provide for them, asks for your protection to order his return to this country, having completed the contract for which he was engaged.

Among Company workers, then, as this one case illustrates, Labourdonnais may not have enjoyed the reputation now attributed to him. There is no doubt that Labourdonnais's plans transformed the physical appearance of Port Louis and increased its ability to perform the defensive and naval roles the Company and the Ministère de la Marine envisaged for it. Huguette Ly-Tio-Fane Pineo (1993) lists over twenty substantial structures built in Port Louis under Labourdonnais, including government buildings, a hospital, stores, batteries, and mills. But this had been achieved at enormous human cost. Seemingly all-powerful, the Company and its representatives were highly unpopular among "poor whites," who regarded them as something like feudal lords without the legitimacy conferred by history. Plots against them were regular occurrences. The harsh regime created another problem for Labourdonnais, which endured well beyond the period of his governorship: the difficulty of persuading individuals such as Pobequin to stay on the island at the end of their contracts, marry, settle down as rural habitants, and produce the food so badly needed to feed the urban population and the crews of ships. Labourdonnais pondered this problem in his mémoire to the Company of 1740. The island, he argued, needed colonists, like those who existed in large numbers on neighboring Île Bourbon.

Though over the years numbers of writers would undoubtedly exaggerate the contrast between the societies of Île de France and Île Bourbon for dramatic effect, nevertheless the divergence between them was real. Île Bourbon's economy was driven by coffee production—not, by and large, on large plantations, but on small concessions occupied by "white" families, each with a handful of slaves (Vaxelaire 1999, vol. 1). The economy of Île de France was centered on its port, and its society was increasingly dominated by an elite of Company officials and merchants (often one and the same). From early in the century, observers worried about the overpopulation of Île Bourbon and the damaging effects of the inheritance system,[18] which led to the *morcellement*[19] of concessions and the multiplication of "poor whites." On Île de France, by contrast, the same observers worried about rural depopulation, the underutilization of concessions, and the socially corrosive effects of wealth generated by war and commerce. Indeed, comparing the evolution of the colonial societies of Île Bourbon, Île de France and Pondichéry in this period is highly instructive and points to the conclusion also drawn by Johnston in his study of Île Royale (2001, xxix) that though the French might claim to have a single colonizing system emanating from Versailles, local conditions differed greatly.

Labourdonnais's plan was to ensure that Île de France became indispensable to the Crown. But he knew that if the island was to be both a linchpin of power politics in the Indian Ocean and the thriving entrepôt he hoped for, it was also essential not only that it feed itself but also that it was able to provision a large number of ships every year. Eighteenth-century war ships and cargo boats were vast floating communities of the hungry, thirsty, and sick, their crews requiring food, fresh water, and medical care.[20] But the island's supposedly agricultural habitants were a peculiarly unproductive lot, as the Company Directors repeatedly pointed out, and Labourdonnais was obliged to address the causes of this lack of productivity. He saw two central problems: the Company's monopolistic policies, which, he argued, produced perverse results, and the enduring problem of labor supply. The two issues were, in fact, closely connected through the question of the supply and allocation of slaves.

The Company's policy had been to grant land concessions to potential habitants and to extend them credit in the form of goods and, crucially, slaves. In return the habitant was obliged to pay a *redevance seigneuriale* (a seigneurial rent) to the Company. The Company here explicitly placed itself in the position of the feudal lord. But, as Labourdonnais quickly discovered, many habitants never reached the point of being able to repay anything. Some, he suspected, had no real intention of doing so, but had become nominal habitants with a view to securing as many Company benefits as possible. The result was an island prone to frequent near-famine and almost constant dearth; a population of habitants who, by convention, spent at least a part of the year away from their land and homes, hunting for subsistence in the forests; and an enormous food bill for the Company, which was obliged to import from India, Île Bourbon, Madagascar, and France. Labourdonnais ordered (through the Conseil Provincial) that there be no more credit extended in the form of food or utensils, and that though the Company would continue to buy any produce brought to it by a habitant (taxing it, as before, at a rate of 33 percent), habitants would also be free to sell food directly to the captains of ships.

Key to everything, of course, was the supply of slaves. Habitants would continue to be able to secure slaves on credit from the Company, but they would also be taxed on the basis of slave ownership. In recognition of the fact that slaves were what everyone most desired, Labourdonnais devised an incentive scheme. Ships' captains would be supplied with "tickets," an accounting system which allowed them to record how many fowl each habitant had supplied. When the time came for the Company to allocate newly arrived slaves, their distribution would be proportional to the number of tickets any given habitant had earned. Those who had been exceptionally productive would be given first choice. Slaves for chickens.

How effective these incentives were is not clear, since food production on the island was to remain a problem for decades to come. But Labourdonnais did address the related question of the supply of slaves in other ways. First, and most importantly, as an experienced slave-trader himself, he set out to extend the trade with Madagascar, and through his personal contacts with Portuguese royalty, to develop a new source of supply in Mozambique and its East African hinterland. Under his governorship, the number of slaves imported increased considerably, though their numbers were always insufficient. Philip Baker estimates that there were 2,429 new slave imports between 1736 and 1740, and that just under half of these were Malagasies (Baker 2002, handout). In his 1740 mémoire Labourdonnais detailed the island's increase in population, both slave and free. In 1735 he enumerated a total of 190 members of free families on the island (including children); by 1740 this number had risen to 379. Meanwhile, the number of slaves had risen from 648 to 2,612.[21] The sex imbalance within both the free and the enslaved population was marked. There were 613 adult women slaves to 1,263 men, and 70 free women to 112 men. The governor declared himself concerned by the lack of women who might make suitable wives for the workers he was hoping to persuade to stay on the island as habitants. He and his wife had taken it upon themselves to import a number of girls from France and to educate them as potential wives.

The supply of slaves raised for the governor another very large issue—that of the Company's monopoly over all trade. Private trade, Labourdonnais wrote, was absolutely essential: "I will tell you what this fraudulent commerce is, and then I will tell you why it is indispensable." Treading carefully on sensitive ground, he argued (using his own experience as an entrepreneur for evidence) that the profit motive of the private trader operated not against the interests of the Company, but in their favor. The fact that the Company labeled "illicit" anything that entered the islands through private trade contributed to privation and discontent, he argued. For example, in 1737 the Company had sent 1,500 plates to Île de France. Since this was clearly insufficient, Labourdonnais, the experienced trader, had independently procured more, but this had earned him a strong reprimand from Paris. "Whatever the losses and gains of this commerce," he wrote, "we will never be able to prevent it, other than at great expense." This was an issue that would continue to preoccupy administrators through most of the century. In 1742 he persuaded the Company to allow a degree of freedom of trade to the island's colonists—though this would later be rescinded, and in any case the majority of these colonists had insufficient funds to allow them to participate (Ly-Tio-Fane Pineo 1993, 248). This period of liberalization did, however, give a boost to the evolving small elite of entrepreneurs based on the island, including Labourdonnais himself, and other ex-officials and military men.[22] A distinctive pattern of development was already emerging, then, one in which agriculture took second place to commerce and in which wealth was concentrated in a very small number of hands. The other important characteristic of the island, and one about to be further emphasized, was its military (and more specifically, naval) character.

Labourdonnais's golden opportunity to prove, definitively, the value of Île de France to the French crown came with the declaration of war in

1744 and its extension into the Indian Ocean. This could not have come at a worse time for the island, which had experienced a cyclone in 1743 and a subsequent severe food shortage. The squadron Labourdonnais put together was ramshackle, ill equipped, and many of its largely inexperienced crew (3,342 men, including 720 slaves) were both hungry and sick. In military terms, however, the expedition to India was a success—the French had held the English to ransom in Madras—and he returned triumphantly to Île de France. But Labourdonnais's military strategy had also brought to a head the rivalry between himself and Jean-François Dupleix, governor of Pondichéry (Vincent 1993, 127–131). He was now accused of taking money from the English. In 1746 he was recalled to France and eventually imprisoned in the Bastille. He died a ruined man in 1753.

The new governor of Île de France was a son of a director of the Company, Pierre Félix Barthèlemy David, who had previously been the governor of the Company's post in Senegal.[23] Like Labourdonnais, he was a man of considerable personal fortune, and like Labourdonnais was frequently accused of advancing his own economic interests above those of the Company.[24] The first two years of his governorship (1746–1748) were almost entirely taken up with the continuing war in India and defending the island against English attack. Nineteenth-century writers would celebrate his apparent taste for romantic exploits, alleging that he had built a large mansion, Le Réduit, to accommodate his lovers (Pitot 1899, 56–59). Beyond that, he is credited with expending considerable efforts to advance agricultural production and to conserve the island's natural resources (by banning hunting, for example). But when there was another spate of report writing on the island in 1752–1753, the old themes recurred. Île de France had proved its worth in times of warfare, but against this had to be set the fact that maintaining it cost a huge amount of money. It was also clear that, unless it began producing its own food, it was extremely vulnerable to a blockade by the English navy.[25] Dupleix wrote to his successor, Lozier-Bouvet, in 1753 acknowledging the immense strategic importance of the island but also pointing out the problems of provisioning it. Lack of provisions, he argued, could lead to severe disciplinary problems as, for example, when soldiers had to be fed on nothing but bread and eau de vie.[26] Lozier-Bouvet would complain that Company agents in India and China paid little attention to the island's food needs and frequently tried to offload huge cargoes of porcelain instead.[27] The island was still regarded as having insufficient colonists of the "right sort." A majority of observers argued that *petits colons* (essentially peasants) were likely to be more efficient than large (and largely absentee) landholders and that more "girls" were needed to encourage workers to stay.[28] Two other themes dominated the correspondence of this brief period of peace (war would break out again in 1755): one was the question of the supply and control of slaves; the other the issue of freedom of trade.

Though the numbers of slaves on the island continued to increase steadily, there appeared never to be enough of them—no doubt in part because mortality rates were so high. Successive administrators reiterated the importance of having the "right kind" of slaves as well as the "right kind" of colonists. In 1753 the new governor, Lozier-Bouvet, was once more stressing the value of the (minority) group of West African slaves for their marine work,[29] a preference also expressed by the engineer Charpentier-Cossigny, at work again on the fortifications of Port Louis. The trade in slaves was not itself without hazard. David had attempted to extend the slave trade with the east coast of Africa begun by Labourdonnais, but this had been interrupted by the war. In 1753 M. Abbé de la Tour was urging the Company to open a base in Mombasa for this purpose.[30] East Africa would, eventually, supply a much greater proportion of the island's slaves, but for the time being Madagascar continued to be the main source. Slave revolts on board ship were frequent, and conditions in areas of supply like Madagascar could be hazardous. Here, as in Africa, the trade itself was helping to fuel internal conflict and the militarization of politics (Larson 2000). Lozier-Bouvet complained that on one trading expedition to the east coast of Madagascar, he had lost more sailors in combat than he had gained slaves.[31] Meanwhile the problem of marronnage continued to trouble the island's colonists and administrators, despite the gradual erosion of the forests in which maroon slaves usually lived. The colonist Baron Grant referred to this issue in a letter of June 1749: "The danger arising from hostilities of these runaways is increased by the perfect knowledge they possess of the plantations which they have deserted. Besides, their old comrades and mistresses will frequently give them information of the most convenient opportunities to descend on their pillaging parties, and second their designs, so that they may be said to keep us in a state of continual disquietude and hostility" (Grant 1801, 297). Like others, Grant thought Malagasy slaves most prone to escape, since they "seem to have an instinctive knowledge that the distance of that country is not in proportion to the length of the voyage," and frequently took to the sea in small boats. Neither was Port Louis immune from maroon attack; Charpentier-Cossigny complained of this in 1754.[32] It had been Labourdonnais's initiative to create a company of selected slaves who were armed and sent in pursuit of maroons, and this strategy was continued by his successors, with mixed success. Despite the anxious state of the island, there was relatively little debate about the merits and demerits of arming slaves, the general consensus being that the shortage of manpower made this absolutely necessary. Slaves were armed, then, both for pursuit of maroons, and for the purposes of defending the island against external enemies (Ly-Tio-Fane Pineo 1993, 172; Toussaint 1936).

Meanwhile the not unrelated issue of freedom of trade continued to be debated, here as in France and in the French Empire as a whole. According to Daniel Roche (1998, 150), between 1700 and 1789 some 1,800 works were published in France on this question, most of them by government officials and military men. Unsurprisingly, it dominated colonial correspondence and was a source of friction between colonists and the state throughout the colonial world. Yet, as Roche points out, this was not a simple question of "freedom" versus "protection." Traders and government officials often shared common interests, not least because the state itself was a very important consumer, offering credit and a unique market (145). These shared interests (and tensions) were clearly demonstrated in Île de France, where an elite of merchants both benefited from and resisted Company control. Merchants and officials were, as we have seen, often one and the same. As one mémoire author perceptively wrote in 1753, "the Company seems to be in contradiction with itself."[33]

The limited freedom of trade granted in 1741 had been reversed in 1746 and, in any case, had been regarded by many as a failure. Most of the island's colonists were simply too poor to be able to take advantage of the new opportunities for trade. The real problem, as one commentator wrote, was that of wealth creation within the islands. Mercantilist-oriented theories held that colonies should be not only producers, but also consumers: "The Company has forgotten [that] . . . the interest of the state in founding a colony is to increase consumption that might benefit the state."[34] Why then, he went on, did the Company appear to be so wedded to the maxim that the colonies should be inhabited by *petits habitants* and the poor. The interests of the Company lay, he argued, in ensuring that the colonists of Île de France not only produced goods for India and France, but also became wealthy enough to consume more themselves. The solution proposed by this commentator, among others, was a limited freedom of trade for colonists and a simultaneous ban on Company employees engaging in commerce. Freedom of trade for Île de France would, however, also have to be organized in such a way that it did not contradict the interests of the Indian colonies.

Among other impassioned pleas for greater freedom of trade was one of 1755 that, typically, linked economics with the social development of the colony and invoked the metaphor of slavery:

> A free man accustoms himself to the place in which he lives, defends his property fiercely, works with satisfaction in commerce or agriculture, raising his family, for whom he is always aiming to increase his fortune, which is good for the colony and the state, while the man who is restricted and without his freedom, dislikes all work and becomes useless. . . . he hardly works and lives only for the moment when he can leave this country where he lives in slavery, and frequently he dies there, from poverty.[35]

Not everyone favored greater freedom of trade. The island's Lazarist missionaries, for example, equated greater commercial freedom directly with moral laxity and *libertinage*.[36] There is no doubt that in this period discussions over freedom of trade were inherently moral discussions (Vaughan 1996), but, argued M. Abbé de la Tour, the position of the missionaries was deeply hypocritical. They are fond of preaching, he wrote, "with odious rhetoric on hundreds of occasions against *libertinage* and against the balls the Governor gives, but say nothing about usury. The reason is simple—they indulge in it themselves."[37] Certainly illegal trade (not least the illegal importation of slaves) was widespread, as one of the directors of the Company, Godeheu, remarked during his visit in 1754. Virtually no one, he wrote, appeared to be working for the good of the Company.[38]

Not for the first time, such discussions on the long-term development of the island would be interrupted by the outbreak of war. The Seven Years' War began in Europe in 1756 and once again India become a site of conflict between the French and the English—the latter now keen to drive the French out of India for good. On the eve of war, Île de France was better defended than it had been during the conflict of the 1740s: Charpentier-

Cossigny (still at odds with the islands' administrators) had completed many of the defenses around Port Louis. The town itself had also begun to more closely resemble the kind of settlement Labourdonnais had had in mind, but had never achieved. Symbolically important was the fact that in 1752 work had begun on a large church building. But greater physical permanence did not necessarily imply any greater social stability, and in any case, the island would soon be subject to a massive influx of soldiers and sailors. The crucial question of the island's food supply also continued to plague administrators, as the new governor, René Magon, would soon discover. In 1755 the island had, exceptionally, produced a large surplus of foodstuffs, so large in fact that the Company had refused to buy more than a fraction of it. The disgruntled colonists watched as the rest went to waste. In the following year, the very year in which war broke out, they planted very little and a famine ensued.[39] This episode seemed to indicate that the island's recurrent food shortages were, as advocates of trade liberalization might have argued, less due to structural constraints in the production process (the frequently invoked lack of slave labor, for example) and more to the inefficiencies and constraints imposed by the *exclusif*.

René Magon (later *intendant* of St. Domingue),[40] arrived sick with fever in December 1755. The journal he kept over the next few years details his desperate efforts to keep the island afloat in the context of war.[41] On arrival he found that he had only two months' food supply in store to feed Company slaves, many of whom were already sick; reviewing the troops revealed that most of them lacked clothes, shoes, and arms, and that all of them lacked discipline. One of his first tasks was to set the price of foodstuffs in such a way as he hoped might encourage production, and to distribute newly landed slaves with the same aim in mind. In March 1756, for example, he distributed slaves from Bengal to the colonists of the Flacq quarter—one of the most productive parts of the island. Slaves were arriving in small numbers from India, East Africa, and Madagascar, mostly on privately owned ships engaged by the Company, but Magon, like his predecessors, favored West African slaves for Company use, despite the high mortality and morbidity rates entailed by the long crossing. In June a Company ship arrived with a cargo of 288 *Guinées*. Fifty had died during the crossing and most of the others were suffering from scurvy.

Throughout 1756 and into 1757 Magon struggled with the provisioning of the island, in anticipation of the warships that would eventually arrive in July 1757. In the course of 1756 he sent boats to Île Bourbon, Madagascar, Bengal, the Cape, and Goa in a desperate search for food supplies. If in France at this time the view was widely held that it was the king's duty to provide for the subsistence of his subjects, this expectation was doubtless exaggerated on an island colony in the middle of the ocean, dominated by an authoritarian Company administration. Magon desperately needed to find food. In 1757 he toured the island in an attempt to discover the causes of low levels of food production. While in Flacq he found colonists making good use of their land concessions and of the slaves the Company had advanced to them; elsewhere it was more generally a story of land and slaves remaining underutilized. He reserved his most scathing comments for the inhabitants of Port South-East, an area that lay at a distance from government scrutiny and where the inhabitants were a law unto themselves. Magon remarked that they had become used to "leading the life of savages" and subsisting on the products of fishing and hunting. The land was uncultivated, covered in weeds, and everywhere infested with rats and insects. The colonists had large numbers of slaves but appeared to have no use for them—they were more of a burden than an asset. Not all the culprits were poor petits colons. M. Vigoreux, for example, was an immensely rich entrepreneur from whom the Company rented a large number of slaves. Yet his huge concession in Port South-East was both uncultivated *and* deforested (cutting and selling timber being an easy way to get rich quickly).

Magon also worried about mortality rates among slaves on the islands —even before the disastrous smallpox epidemic of 1757 struck. He took as one of his examples a large habitation belonging to the Company and a timber enterprise in the southeast. In five months, ten out of the total of eighty-five slaves employed had died. In addition, thousands of days had been lost through sickness. Magon calculated that slaves had to live for more than three years after their arrival if their cost was to be defrayed. Magon, like any rational slave owner, knew the importance of keeping slaves alive and healthy, but conditions on Île de France frequently worked against this policy, even when it was being actively pursued. Meanwhile, the defense of the island, along with its provisioning, was a priority. In January 1757 some 560 slaves were being trained to use cannon, and Magon was urging colonists to send him more slaves for this purpose. They should of course choose for this purpose "trustworthy subjects," but Magon thought there was little risk in arming slaves, so long as they were properly treated as a "separate class."

Six warships arrived in July 1757, the advance guard of the expedition to India commanded by Thomas Arthur Lally, one of a number of military men of Irish origin serving the French crown at this time. The squadron set off for India, returning in October for repairs. In December, sixteen more warships arrived in Port Louis; in January 1758, eleven more. And so it went on for the next two years. In July 1759 one squadron, commanded by the Comte d'Aché (himself now wounded), set sail again for India, having been in port for repairs and provisioning. Some repairs had taken place, but as for provisioning, d'Aché commented that his sailors were literally dying of hunger. Famine was widespread on the island now, and ironically the islanders now placed their own hopes for survival on the warships they were supposed to be provisioning. It was hoped that d'Aché's ships would return from the war in India with both food and money. In fact, they returned in November with neither (Toussaint 1936, 53).

In 1758 the island's Conseil Supérieur had, in fact, warned d'Aché of the dire situation on the island. They calculated that if one included an expected 6,000 men on the naval squadrons, then there would be nearly 12,000 people (including 2,654 Company slaves) on the island whose food supplies came directly from the Company's stores. In addition, of course, the food shortage implied that many more colonists and their slaves would be seeking food from the Company—making a grand total of 18,962 expected mouths to feed.[42]

Casualties of the war were also placing a huge strain on the island's medical resources. In 1760 the surgeon in charge of the hospital in Port Louis reported that there were "continually at the hospital 500 or 600 black and white men, and the number does not diminish—as much by the almost continual presence of the naval squadron as by the work which this necessitates in port." He had insufficient beds, no bedding, and a shortage of drugs.[43]

None of this work to support the French war effort prevented the latter from failing disastrously. Pondichéry fell in January 1761, many of its largest and finest buildings destroyed by the English. It would be restored to the French in 1763 under the Treaty of Paris, but the war had effectively put an end to French power in India.[44] How many men had died in what sometimes seemed like a suicidal enterprise is not known. How many slaves from Île de France and Île Bourbon were among these is also not known, though a reading of Admiralty records might reveal this.[45] It seems likely, however, that the number was high. Slaves were widely used not only on French naval vessels, but also on the ships and boats armed by local mercenaries (or "pirates") whose contribution to the war effort consisted of engaging English ships in conflict and confiscating their cargoes. In 1759, for example, one resident of Île de France armed, at his own expense, two vessels for this purpose. According to Auguste Toussaint (1936, 53), the crew totaled five hundred, of whom four hundred were slaves. The exact toll (both human and financial) of the war on Île de France is difficult, if not impossible, to gauge, though we do know that the island's timber resources had been further depleted by ship repairs.[46] Yet warfare also brought wealth, for some at least. Rich entrepreneurs and concession owners made money through the sale of wood and the supply of slaves, and periodically booty from an ambushed English vessel would flood into port. According to the island's priests and other moralizing observers, the war had also brought a further influx of "undesirables."

In a report (of 1764) colorfully titled "monopolies, hoarding, commerce, depredations, embezzlement and abuses," the author set out some of the ways in which well-placed individuals (protected by the governor, or so it was alleged) had made a fortune during the war years. Some had made a killing in the slave trade from Madagascar, by using Company ships. And some of these slaves had then been sold on to the Cape (where ships went in search of food) and Batavia—thereby infringing the French law that slaves could be sold only to owners who were of the Catholic faith. Wood resources had been rapaciously exploited, also infringing regulations. Timber cutting, the author alleged, had been carried on day and night, such that local inhabitants referred to it as *bois de lune* (wood of the moon). And in the middle of a war, the valuable labor of Company slaves had been diverted for the purpose of carrying these favored individuals in style, in their palanquins, to and from their rural habitations.[47]

With the end of the war and the signing of the Treaty of Paris, the French empire appeared in disarray—no more so than in the Indian Ocean. Yet this was far from the end of the story for the island of Île de France, as we shall see.

Chapter Three

ENLIGHTENMENT COLONIALISM

AND ITS LIMITS, 1767–1789

*T*here are two images the contemporary tourist to Mauritius will find hard to avoid. The first is that of the dodo, the second that of the two young eighteenth-century lovers Paul and Virginie. At the airport shop you will find both—stuffed soft toys in the shape of the dodo, bright green liqueur bearing the names of Paul and Virginie. But this is not a uniquely twenty-first-century phenomenon. Thanks to the enormous popularity of Bernardin de St. Pierre's novel *Paul et Virginie*, the landscape of Île de France became familiar territory to thousands of late-eighteenth-century and nineteenth-century European readers.[1] First published in 1788, this story of naive love in the tropics rapidly went into hundreds of editions, was translated into all the major European languages, and inspired an extraordinary number of engravings, lithographs, songs, poems, ballets, and operas, not to mention decorations on clothing, china, and other domestic items.[2] For thousands of European readers (and nonreaders), this small island in the Indian Ocean was the setting for a drama representing early Romantic sensibility at its most lachrymose.

Bernardin de St. Pierre was one of a string of French Enlightenment figures to visit the island between the 1760s and the Revolution. Others included the famous astronomer and geographer Abbé de la Caille, the explorer Philibert Commerson, and the botanist (who became intendant of the island) Pierre Poivre. Bernardin de St. Pierre was born in Le Havre in 1737 to a modest family with aristocratic pretensions. His practical education began when he was twelve and accompanied his uncle on a voyage to the Antillean island of Martinique. He trained as an engineer in the prestigious École des Ponts et Chaussées in Paris and, with the outbreak of the Seven Years' War, embarked on military service in Holland, Russia, Poland, and Germany. Episodes of his early adult years read as if life might be imitating art. Like a number of other Frenchmen, he entered the service of Empress Catherine II of Russia. He tried (and failed) to persuade her to adopt a number of his visionary schemes, including the creation of a republican community on Lake Aral and the forging of a new route to the Indies via Russia. In 1764 he was in Poland, where he fell in love with the influential Princess Marie Lubomirska, who worked for the French secret service. After a string of disappointing experiences in Germany and Prussia, Bernardin de St. Pierre found himself, in 1768, employed as a king's engineer on an expedition to Madagascar. After falling out with the rest of the party, he did not disembark there, but sailed on to the island of Île de France. Here he worked briefly as an engineer, but spent most of his time studying the island's natural history and its society, returning to France in 1770. The intendant at the time was the botanist and physiocrat Pierre Poivre, and questions of environment and conservation were high on the government's agenda.[3]

The island motif occupied an important place in the early Romantic environmental thinking of Jean-Jacques Rousseau, one of the major influences on Bernardin de St. Pierre. But the latter's account of his 1768 *Voyage à l'Isle de France* (published in 1773) described the island as falling far short of utopia. For one thing, the institution of slavery cast a dark shadow over the mountainous tropical landscape the author so admired. Though Bernardin de St. Pierre would later refuse membership in the French antislavery organization the Amis des Noirs (Lokke 1932, 149), his antislavery sentiments became well known and were indicated by his descriptions of the mistreatment of slaves both in the *Voyage* and later in *Paul et Virginie*. The preface to the *Voyage* contained the following words: "Besides, I hope that I can be useful to mankind if my feeble picture of the fate of the luckless blacks can save them from one single lash of a whip, and if Europeans, who cry out against tyranny in Europe and who write such pretty treatises on morality, cease being barbarous tyrants in the Indies" (Bernardin de St. Pierre 2002). And he would end the whole book: "For thee unhappy African, who, on the rocks of Mauritius, bewailest thy truly wretched lot, it is not for my feeble hand to alleviate thy griefs, or dry thy tears—but if I have induced thy tyrant master to look upon them with regret, and upon himself with remorse as the cause of them—I have nothing more to ask of India—I shall have made my fortune" (270).

It was not only the treatment of slaves that shocked this man of sensibility, but the whole ramshackle enterprise of French colonialism on the island. A premonition of this seems to have come to him even before his boat lowered anchor at Port Louis: "Approaching land, many of the people found are ill. I felt uneasy and sweated profusely" (Bernardin de St. Pierre 2002, 88). Despite the improvements of Labourdonnais and his successors, Port Louis was still far from a sophisticated colonial city. Bernardin de St. Pierre found it marked by an attitude of "insensibility" and "indifference." Many streets were unpaved and treeless, most of the houses were mere wooden cabins "that could be carted anywhere on wheels"; they had no glass in their windows and no curtains, and such furniture as they contained he described as "miserable." He may have been exaggerating a little here for effect—we know that wealthier inhabitants of Port Louis lived in much grander style than this—but the point he was making concerned the long-term nature of the island's development, based on a reckless exploitation of natural resources, war, and commerce.

Reviewing the history of French occupation, Bernardin de St. Pierre made a number of interesting observations on the formative influences on the "character and manners of the inhabitants." These observations would, in time, take on the flavor of caricature when, in one version or another, they were repeated by subsequent visitors. Yet there appears to have been some truth in what were becoming standard tropes of the island's history. First, he described briefly the earliest French settlers from the island of Bourbon. These, he wrote, were agriculturalists who brought with them "simplicity of manners, good faith, love of hospitality and even an indifference to riches" (Bernardin de St. Pierre 2002, 118). He then went on to describe the work of the "founder of the colony," Labourdonnais (later to appear as the benevolent governor/father figure in *Paul et Virginie*), who "brought over his workers, good, honest men, and some evil types sent over by their relatives, but he forced them to be useful." But it was the next wave of colonists that, according to Bernardin de St. Pierre, began to sow the seeds of subsequent problems. "All kinds of people arrived," he wrote.

His social analysis was not entirely consistent. Sometimes he seems to be bemoaning the exaggerated attention paid to rank and status on the island, at other times the apparent lack of regard for social order. But he was consistent in his condemnation of the main economic activity of the island and the source of individual wealth—commerce. First, there were the officers of the Company, to which "everything and everybody" was subject. They had lived, he wrote, "rather like nobles in Venice. To their aristocratical manners they added that finance's spirit which scared off the impetus to carry out agricultural work." Then there were the military men, some of high birth, who "could not even imagine that an officer could sink so low as to accept orders from a man who had once been a merchant office boy." And there were the merchants who "quickly became loathed by the different classes of men" by indulging in underhand business practices. These men "claimed to scorn the distinctions of rank, engaging each person who had crossed the equator as if they were all equal." Finally, there were the "seamen," whose "gossip, the continuous arrivals and departures, give the island the manners of an inn."

Things had been made worse, he wrote, as a result of the Seven Years' War, which "threw there, like a tide, bankrupt men, ruined libertines, thieves, and scoundrals of every sort." This new influx had further added to and complicated the extreme mutual distrust familiar in France and already existing within island society between the "departments of the marine, the pen and the sword." Now levels of suspicion and discord reached new heights: "Reputations were strained with an Asiatic ingenuity unknown to our islanders. There were no longer any chaste women, nor any honest men; all trust was extinguished, all honor sullied. By vilifying everybody, they had reduced everybody to their level" (Bernardin de St. Pierre 2002, 120).

For Bernardin de St. Pierre, as for a number of others who wrote about the island at this time, the root of the problem lay in the island's economic dependence and, crucially, the lack of development of its agriculture. He was critical of the policy that had made this *the* strategic base for the French navy in the Indian Ocean. Port Louis, he wrote, was an environment where "the worms will totally destroy a ship in three years." In his view, the vast quantities of money expended on maintaining the island would have been much more fruitfully invested in India, now definitively lost to the British. While admiring Labourdonnais's success in creating something of a colony out of nothing, Bernardin de St. Pierre was also critical of the governor's unrealistic ambition to make the island a "second Batavia": "With the opinions of a great genius, he had his human weakness: place him on a point and he will make it to the centre of everything" (Bernardin de St. Pierre 2002, 171). For while Batavia produced spices, Île de France produced nothing: "I do not know any corner of the earth that extends its needs so far. This colony obtains its dishes and plates from China, linens and clothes from India, its slaves and cattle from Madagascar, a part of its provisions from the Cape of Good Hope, and its money from Cadiz, and its administration from France" (171). Bernardin de St. Pierre's account was written in the wake of French defeat in India and the reassessment of colonial policy that followed. Let us, then, take a step back.

At the end of the war in 1763 the Company was in ruins and was placed provisionally under the control of the Comité du Roi. French power in India had been effectively destroyed, and French colonial ambitions more generally given a rude shock. But the French had no desire to give up on their imperial ambitions—quite the contrary, for as Jean Tarrade has argued, the period between the Treaty of Paris in 1763 and the outbreak of the Revolution was one of unprecedented colonial prosperity (Mayer et al. 1991, 199). It was, of course, the sugar islands that mattered most to the French, and St. Domingue in particular. The economic dominance of St. Domingue within the French empire was phenomenal, as we have already seen. But, for different reasons, the islands of the Indies also drew the attention of the Ministère de la Marine in the aftermath of the war.

From 1761 to 1766 the Ministère de la Marine was headed by the duc de Choiseul, who also held the portfolios of war and foreign affairs. He was succeeded in the Ministère de la Marine in 1766 by his cousin, the duc de Praslin. Despite a bitter and expensive defeat, the French had no intention of giving up the role of world power in the aftermath of the war, and a great deal of national face-saving took place. Choiseul reportedly boasted that he had tricked the British into allowing him to keep Martinique in place of Quebec (Lokke 1932), but nothing could prevent the loss of India from being deeply humiliating. A war of revenge seemed inevitable, and so Choiseul's first task was to reconstruct the navy. The war had revealed serious weaknesses here, for though the French had built some impressively efficient new vessels, ships alone could not win a war without (as we have seen) massive logistical support and, crucially, enough sailors to man them.[4]

There were some doubting voices to be heard in the 1760s, but not as many as there would be later in the century. Pierre Poivre, for example, had published his *Voyages d'un Philosophe* in 1768, and a contemporary reviewer had remarked, "When one reads what the author has written on Bourbon and the Île of France, when one compares their history to the history of our other colonies, including that of Guiana in our day, one remains convinced that God has not granted the French nation the talent and the spirit to form colonies" (Lokke 1932, 22). But such despondency was less evident than new ambitions, even if some of the latter had disastrous consequences. Guiana was one such disaster. Choiseul was of the view that white men were able and fit to cultivate tropical lands, and he conceived a plan for a white colony along the Kourou River in Guiana. Settlers were recruited, not only from France, but also from Switzerland, Germany, Belgium, and Malta. An estimated 10,000 lost their lives in this experiment. Madagascar was another favored site for disastrous experiments in colonization, many of them using Île de France as a launching pad.[5]

In the Indian Ocean, the more pressing issue for the duc de Choiseul and then for his successor, the duc de Praslin, was the future of the Company and of Île de France and Île Bourbon. The Company was in ruins, but this was in part a result of the use that had been made of its ships during the war. After long and acrimonious disputes among shareholders, eventually, in 1764, a royal decision was made. The Company was to be reinstituted as a purely commercial enterprise, its ties to the state cut. But before this happened, the king would buy back both the Breton port of Lorient and the Îles of France and Bourbon. This transfer was finally effected in 1767.

The decision to buy back the islands was not made without a great deal of deliberation and analysis of costs and benefits. The correspondence of the years 1763 to 1765 contains little else.[6] Most of the mémoires must have made depressing reading for the duc de Choiseul. The themes closely followed those that dominated the previous spate of postwar postmortems, in the early 1750s. Indeed, some argued that little had changed since the days of Labourdonnais, some thirty years earlier. The failure of the Company and of the Île de France colonists to make agriculture prosper was widely reported and bemoaned. This was an old theme given an added impetus in the 1760s, with the rise in France of the Physiocratic movement, which placed agriculture at the heart of a vision of economic planning and development. Physiocrats placed land at the center of their analysis of political economy and morality, purporting to show how the rural order was opposed to the urban and commercial sectors. Not everyone agreed with them, but this influential movement would soon have a powerful representative in the Indies in the form of Pierre Poivre.[7] Île de France was, in fact, a Physiocrat's nightmare, and the contrast with neighboring Île Bourbon only served to highlight this. Île Bourbon might not be rich, but it was at least viable, with a much greater percentage of its land under useful cultivation, and though it had a problem with "poor whites," these were at least *rural* "poor whites," not the urban flotsam and jetsam that characterized Port Louis. The theme of degeneration, as Jean-Michel Racault has also argued (1996), was a dominant one in descriptions of Île de France in this period, and a more general leitmotif in the anthropology of the tropics. Certainly a number of stereotypes dominated writing on the islands of the Indian Ocean, but there was a reality underlying some of these. The underdevelopment of agriculture on Île de France and the relative depopulation of the countryside were real enough. Of course, for a non-Physiocrat, this would not necessarily matter—if the island generated enough wealth from commercial transactions, why should it have to produce its own foodstuffs, or even its own trade goods? But the two wars had dramatically demonstrated the vulnerability of an island in the middle of the ocean that depended on imports for its subsistence.

Self-criticism was a marked feature of the mémoires of the early 1760s, and sometimes the verdict on French colonial enterprise in the Indies was harsh. A *Mémoire relatif à l'Île de France* written around 1763 was not untypical.[8] Île de France, wrote the author, was entirely dominated by Port Louis, a "camp" containing a thousand or so huts, half of which were occupied by "Malabars," half by whites, of whom the major part lived by selling goods they had illegally obtained from the Company stores. The place was heaving with "employees, litigants, supplicants, military men, sailors and merchants," all living in this "pretence of a capital." At first glance the concentration of people gave an impression of a "certain kind of affluence," but this masked a deeper poverty and underdevelopment. The author noted that moving from town into countryside was a shock to the visitor, because the latter was almost completely depopulated, its land mostly lying idle: "It is hard to understand how, after forty years, the administration has failed to bring it alive." This writer, along with many others, could not help but draw a contrast between the French failure to develop this island and the apparent success of the Dutch at the Cape. The Dutch, he wrote, had learned out of necessity in their homeland to make the best of their environment and had produced works "worthy of the Romans," but "none of these miracles have made any impression on us—despite the poverty and weakness we have lived in over the last forty years."

Despite this pessimistic assessment of French capabilities as a colonial power in the Indian Ocean, the conclusion of this commentator was far from defeatist. The example of England, and rivalry with the English, made colonies in the Indian Ocean not a luxury, but a necessity for France: "Success as marked as theirs shows clearly the false reasoning of those who argue in favor of procuring the merchandise of India second-hand, rather than enter into the cost of the men and the vessels necessary for this commerce; it proves that without an active navy and without overseas possessions, France would not for long be able to maintain any equilibrium with its neighbors whose wealth, strength and extent of domination increase day by day."

Other mémoires of these years raised again the old issue of whether "large" or "small" colonists were to be preferred on the islands. A glance at the Île de France countryside was enough to convince most that the latter would be preferable. Much of the island was given over to a few large concessions, most of them only marginally exploited. A few years later, in 1766, a census would confirm this: only about half of the island's cultivable land had been allocated as concessions, and less than a quarter of that allocated was under cultivation.[9] Many of the large landowners of Île de France, as visitors noted, resided in Port Louis, where they made a living as merchants or military men or administrators: their habitations (where their wives and children lived for most of the year) were country homes rather than economic enterprises. There were a few exceptions to this by the 1760s, but not many. Commerce, it is clear, was far more profitable than agricultural production, despite the ready market for foodstuffs in the colony. A precise assessment of the profitability of commerce in this period awaits research, but contemporaries estimated that one could make a return of 25 to 35 percent on trade with India, and up to

100 percent on goods imported from Europe. There may not have been many large consumers on Île de France, but those that there were did their best to keep up standards. Merchant ships found a market for Bordeaux wines, hats, and clothes from Paris, as well as fine textiles and carpets from India. As one mémoire writer reminded his readers in 1763, it was a *duty* of colonists to consume goods coming from their home country.[10]

Not only land was very unequally distributed; so were slaves. Another old theme—that of the *maldistribution des noirs*—also featured prominently in the assessments of the 1760s. As one mémoire noted in 1763, there were many colonists in areas such as Plaines Wilhems who had only two or three slaves in the household (the usual calculation being that eight was the minimum to make even the smallest concession viable). Meanwhile others had large numbers they were not putting to any good use. A more "just" distribution of slaves was essential, wrote this author, and more slaves should be given to those who were making an effort to cultivate the land (echoing Labourdonnais's arguments of the 1730s).

It is not entirely clear from these sources how, exactly, the minority of large slave owners were employing their slaves. Presumably they were not leaving them idle. It seems likely that many were being rented out to large enterprises such as the large Forges de Mon Désir owned by Rostaing and Hermans, and to owners of sawmills, as well as to the administration itself for ongoing infrastructural works. We know too that many slaves were sent out by their owners to earn a living as carpenters, for example,[11] or to run shops and canteens on their masters' and mistresses' behalf. While more could be done with wills and taxation documentation, the general absence of detailed habitation records for Île de France creates a real gap in our knowledge here.[12] More than one mémoire noted, however, that a great deal more effort could be made by Île de France slave owners to improve the working conditions and productivity of their slaves and to keep them alive. Slavery on Île de France, it seemed, was an institution that could benefit from further rationalization. As one writer pointed out, merely ensuring that there was a greater balance of the sexes among imported slaves would go some way to help. The economic argument was, as ever, also a moral one: greater demographic stability in the slave population would cut down on the cost of importation *and* reduce the problem of *libertinage*.[13]

Critical as these assessments were, their conclusions (though not always arrived at by the same route of argument) were similar: though Île de France and Île Bourbon were expensive possessions, the Crown simply could not afford to do without them. They were, as one writer put it, the French "boulevard of the nation in the Indies."[14] However, most were also agreed that, to avoid further expense and corruption, some measure of free trade would have to be granted to the islands' colonists—the Company's *exclusif* seemed not, after all, to have been the most efficient way of ensuring that the nation benefited from its colonies. From now on the islands would be directly administered by the Crown.

Administering Enlightenment Colonialism: Pierre Poivre

On 14 July 1767, Pierre Poivre arrived on Île de France to take up the post of intendant under the new royal administration. He had been to the island before, and he had advised the ducs de Choiseul and Praslin on its development, so we must assume that he had some idea of the challenge ahead of him. But it is hard to imagine a more difficult posting for this idealist Physiocrat. Poivre was a lifelong admirer of the agrarian civilization of China; Île de France was a long way from China, in more senses than one. In many ways Poivre's period as a colonial administrator encapsulates the possibilities and limitations of a late-eighteenth-century reformist exercise in "Enlightenment colonialism,"[15] which coincided with increasingly vocal criticisms of the institution on which colonialism in this period depended: slavery.

Pierre Poivre' s life, philosophy, and influence have been described in detail by Richard Grove in his account of the evolution of environmentalist thinking in the colonies, and of the particular role of Mauritius (1993, chap. 5). As Grove shows, Poivre was to become an immensely important figure in the late-eighteenth-century world of learning. His expertise in botany and natural history, his fascination with the comparative study of agricultural systems, and his analysis of the relationship between man and nature brought him renown and, crucially, considerable influence. My interest here, however, is less with Poivre's undoubted importance as scientist and philosopher, and more with juxtaposing these achievements with the realities of colonial administration in Île de France. Poivre was unusual in one very important respect—an unabashed idealist, he was given a senior position in colonial government and instructed to apply his ideas. If Poivre could be said to represent one significant brand of Enlightenment thinking, then, was there such a thing as Enlightenment colonialism?

Poivre was born in 1719 in Lyons, where his family made a living from merchandising haberdashery. In her account of his life, the Mauritian historian Madeleine Ly-Tio-Fane Pineo implies an early link with China here, for Lyons was an important center of the silk trade.[16] Chinese civilization made a huge and lasting impression on Poivre, who first traveled to China as a young trainee priest with the Jesuit Societé des Missions Etrangères. During his two years in Canton he immersed himself in the study of the Chinese language and culture, agriculture, horticulture, water management, and aesthetics, becoming a lifelong admirer of Eastern learning. In his later hugely wide-ranging comparative works, no civilization (including that of France) would ever get close to his estimation of that of China. From China, Poivre traveled to Vietnam and then began a voyage back to France, but his ship was captured by a British vessel (during which encounter he lost an arm), and he was deposited on Dutch Batavia. Here began his fascination with spice cultivation and trade, over which the Dutch had a hugely profitable monopoly. Poivre conceived it his patriotic duty to break this monopoly and he offered his services to the Compagnie des Indes for this purpose. There followed a decade of activity in the area of spice espionage and transplantation, during which Poivre made several visits to Île de France, where he hoped to be able to acclimatize East Indies spice trees. In 1757 he retired to his estate near Clermont-Ferrand to live the life of a gentleman farmer. But his expertise and vast comparative knowledge were known and in demand. He was elected to the Royal Society in Paris, became president of the Royal Agricultural Society of Lyons, delivered a series of important lectures in 1763, and became a leading light in the Physiocratic movement.

Defeat in India had apparently helped to fuel French interest in points further east, and Poivre was *the* French expert on the Far East. According to Grove, his 1763 lectures were read by the duc de Choiseul, now flirting with Physiocratic ideas, and in 1766 Poivre was persuaded to take up the post of commissaire général-ordonnateur (later intendant) on Île de France, newly brought under the direct control of the Crown. But before exploring Poivre's career as intendant, it is important to have some idea of what his Physiocratic ideals implied in terms of human society and its organization.

The Physiocrats saw landed property as the only true source of value, and this led them to a critique not only of commerce, but also of systems of landholding in France. This was a social and political critique as much as it was an economic and environmental one. In Physiocratic thinking, the natural and human orders were inseparable, and nowhere is this link more evident than in Poivre's own writings on comparative society and government. According to him, the success of Chinese agriculture was directly related to the nature of Chinese government and society. This is just one example of what he would write on this subject (from his *Voyages d'un philosophe*, first published in 1768):

> Remind yourselves of what I have said of the laws, the morals, the customs of the different nations of Africa and Asia, whose state of agriculture I have examined. Compare nation with nation, judge whether the unfortunate Malabar, without property and subject to the tyrannical government of the Moguls, or a people in slavery, their heads bent under the iron scepter of the despot of Siam, or the Malay nation, forever agitated and oppressed by the abuses of their laws, [judge] whether they, even when in possession of the best land in the world, enjoy an agricultural system as flourishing as that of the Chinese, a people governed as a family and subject only to the laws of reason. (1797, 192)

Poivre must have been well aware of the paradoxes and contradictions that would face him as a Physiocratic colonial administrator of Île de France. It was not just that the island survived on commerce and war, but also that its entire existence rested on the system of slavery, an institution which, when he encountered it elsewhere in the world, he was quick to condemn. Poivre would have things to say about this, as we shall see, but ultimately he could not escape it. The abolition of slavery was, of course, not on the agenda of the Ministère de la Marine when Poivre was appointed as Intendant, but the instructions issued to him, and to the governor-elect, Daniel Dumas, were certainly reformist and rationalizing in spirit.

All those lengthy mémoires appear to have had some impact, for the Crown was now in possession of a clearer analysis of the costs and benefits of Île de France. In a preamble to the instructions, the duc de Praslin noted that the island was important, both strategically and commercially, and that it therefore needed a solid base of both political and economic laws. Even after a long period of occupation it was, disappointingly, not in good shape, and an important contributory factor to this was the distrust of the colonists. It was the job of Poivre and Dumas, then, to gain their confidence, and to do so through the application of the law and of the "science" of colonialism: "It is for the administrators to hasten the progress of Justice, and by the gentleness of their government; they must never forget that the science of establishing a colony and of raising it up is the science of rendering the colonist and his work useful."[17]

In the particular circumstances of Île de France, the two men were told, the object of government was to arrive at a "fair balance" between commercial interests and those of the colonist (clearly it was assumed that these were distinct), and to reconcile both of these with the object of keeping on the island a military force that would be capable not only of defense, but also of attack on the enemy in India. They were to encourage "useful" cultivation (but to remember that sugar, cotton, and indigo were crops reserved for the Antilles) and attempt to secure its food supply. The minister suggested that the island might have an important role to play in the cultivation of spices, and might even become the "new Moluccas." He instructed them to take a full census, and Poivre, as intendant, was also asked to produce a detailed report on every aspect of the island, and to do so under the following headings, themselves indicative of the Minister's conceptual framework of colonial rule:

Religion
Justice
Military
Finance
Commerce
Population
Agriculture
Naval

Poivre was also asked to write comments on the qualities to be found among individuals on the island—their morals, talents, and capabilities, vices and virtues—for "in a nascent colony it is important to make some use of everyone, and there are very few people who cannot be employed usefully once one has identified their true destiny."

Poivre would soon get to work on surveying the island, but not before he had made an extraordinary address to the island's colonists, an address that indicated the extent of his ambitions for colonial reform and, in Grove's words, a "polemic on the need to make a new beginning after a period of company corruption and decline" (Grove 1995, 200). He began by outlining a number of important changes and innovations. A land tribunal would be instituted to survey and adjudicate on concessions; agriculture would be reformed and a system of forest conservation instituted; colonists would be able to engage in free trade in the Indian Ocean area; the island's inflationary paper money would be replaced by the real thing; more ships and troops would be supplied by the king. Above all, he said, "the King desires . . . that you should be happy" (Poivre 1797, 203). There followed a discourse on how this happiness could be achieved (through cultivation), and what social and political benefits it entailed: "Think that you are at one and the same time the defenders and nourishers of this colony in peacetime. But you are more: in wartime the homeland regards us as the defenders of our bases in India and the suppliers of our squadrons, as well as of the troops which are sent to defend your property and our natural commerce in Asia" (Poivre 1797, 204).

Poivre went on at length, with (as Grove also notes) a mixture of flattery and admonition. He repeatedly asserted that the colonists of Île de France *should* be happy—after all, they were living in an "earthly paradise" and they were free of the feudal dues that burdened their countrymen at home. There were problems, however, with the way the island had been developed. Too many people had seen Île de France as a place to could get rich quick, then leave. The colonists' morals had been corrupted by the obsession with commercial wealth and, above all, by luxury: "*Quoi le luxe!* . . . all the more scandalous on an island which is short of bread and which produces not one item of trade! Ah! Sirs . . . let us admit frankly that if this island is poor, one must attribute this, not to the climate, but to the corruption of morals" (Poivre 1797, 229).

But for Poivre there was another deeply troubling feature of the island's development. This was its reliance on slave labor. One can only try and imagine how the assembled colonists reacted to the philosopher's statements on the institution that dominated their lives. He began by announcing that since Île de France lay under a "temperate sky," was "founded on agriculture," and was the "boulevard of our possessions in Asia," it should be cultivated only by "free hands." But, he went on, unfortunately the Company had relied on slaves for the establishment of the colony: "Be that as it may, the harm has been done, but happily there is a remedy." The remedy was the law, for "we can prevent all the evils which follow from slavery by obeying the law."

It was the law, he said, which enabled the French to have slaves in their colonies, for slavery was an inhuman institution, against the laws of nature, and it was tolerated only because of the conditions laid down by the law. He then went on to list some of the clauses of the Code Noir: the obligation on masters to ensure that their slaves were instructed in the Catholic religion; the obligation to encourage marriages between slaves. Good masters, he went on, would produce good slaves who "will be attached to the Catholic faith, will belong to our nation and think of themselves as French; they will have a horror of other religions and a terror of falling under the power of a heretical nation" (Poivre 1797, 223).

I will return to the question of the law later, since it is central to the stories I recount below. Clearly Poivre viewed the application of the law as integral to his mission to civilize the "barbaric" institution of slavery and prevent the "corruption of morals" that institution entailed. As he made clear, ideally he would have preferred that the island be cultivated by "free hands," small-scale agriculturalists enjoying the fruits of this "earthly paradise," but, as he put it, the harm had been done, and slavery was an inescapable fact of life.

Also inescapable was Poivre's colleague, Daniel Dumas. Dumas, a soldier who had fought in Canada, was appointed governor at the same time as Poivre was made intendant, and the two men had fallen out even before they left French soil. They were clearly very different characters, and Dumas may have been suspicious of Poivre's ambitious reformist agenda. At any event, the hostility between the two men reached epic proportions and permeated relationships among the island's elite.[18] The documentation of this period demonstrates vividly the difficulty Poivre must have had in reconciling his ideals with the realities of Île de France and of an ancien régime administrative system dominated by patronage networks and personal rivalries. Alongside the ambitious, rationalist, reformist schemes set out by Poivre, there is also the correspondence that records, blow by blow, the often seemingly petty disputes between the two men at the top of this island's administration.[19] Writing to each other from their respective official residences in Port Louis, Poivre and Dumas accused each other of misappropriating and misusing government slaves ("stealing" the best and dressing them in their own liveries)—an old and familiar theme in the history of island politics, as we have seen. There were larger issues at stake, however. The men disagreed on the question of liberalization of trade, for example, on the island's currency and on land speculation. Others were forced to take sides; one leading Poivre supporter was sent into exile on the even smaller island of Rodrigues,[20] and officials in the Ministère de la Marine looked on helplessly before eventually recalling Dumas in 1768.

Even without the hostility of his fellow officer, Poivre would have found it hard to put his ideas into practice, simply because the island was once more in desperate straits during the period of transition between Company and Crown rule. In 1767 Dumas and Poivre were agreed on one thing: that the "colony lacks everything, the Company stores are empty." Ships arriving in the course of that year had brought "almost nothing," and the sailors from them consumed a large proportion of the island's stock of eau-de-vie.[21] In January 1768, Poivre distributed a meager shipment of Indian cloth among the colonists, remarking that "There are here a large number of slaves who have not received clothes for six years, and the greater number of the colonists have no shirts for themselves, their wives and their children." He also noted that though a cargo of Malagasy slaves had arrived, no one could afford to buy them.[22] Both men detailed in their journals the perpetual war with maroon slaves, waged on their behalf by the *noirs de détachement* first instituted by Labourdonnais and the continuing need for labor to work on the island's defenses. And the prospect of another war with an external enemy was always on the horizon. In 1771 the king, fearing a new war, dispatched 10,000 men to Île de France. The duc de Choiseul wrote to Poivre: "I know only too well that you are wanting for everything, but we are counting on you" (Toussaint 1936, 107).

It is difficult, if not impossible, to assess the effectiveness of the very many ordinances enacted in Poivre's period of office, covering everything from timber conservation to pigs and goats in the streets of Port Louis—not to mention attempts to halt the perceived ongoing "decline of morality." Richard Grove has written admiringly of Poivre's visionary (but practical) measures against soil erosion, though how far they were put into practice is hard to tell. As I have already implied, other documentation of the period leaves one with the impression that enforcing anything on Île de France was extremely difficult. Yet it would be wrong to completely dismiss the attempts of Poivre and some of his successors to promote what the duc de Choiseul had called the "science of colonialism."[23] And though the reformists had their detractors, they must have been encouraged by the string of eminent scientists and explorers who dropped by from the late 1760s to the eve of the Revolution, allowing the island's elite to think of itself as a tropical learned society. In Poivre's time, there was not only Bernardin de St. Pierre (whom he instructed in botany), but also the naturalist Philibert Commerson, member of the Bougainville expedition (Grove 1995, 216–224). Astronomers (Le Gentil, Abbé de la Caille) passed through on the occasion of the Passage of Venus. The Mauritian historian Auguste Toussaint wrote in the 1930s that this was a period when the presence in Port Louis of all these *savants* created a diversion from the "mercantile spirit which the colonists had developed under the Company." The officers of the new royal government were, he wrote, of "a different intellectual worth" (1936, 115). This may have been something of an exaggeration, but, as he points out, there were a number of government employees on the island in this period who came with impressive amounts of learning. Just one of a string of names mentioned by Toussaint is that of Jean-François Caillaud (or Cailleau), a storekeeper.[24] Cailleau had arrived on the island on the same ship as Poivre. He and his colleague Laurent Mason Abraham, another storekeeper, were passionate about mathematics and formed part of the circle of scientists Commerson created around himself in Port Louis. In 1784 Cailleau constructed a hot air balloon, 32 feet in diameter, which he used to conduct his scientific experiments.

Though mathematicians in hot-air balloons no doubt created something of a stir, probably more relevant to the applied "science of colonialism" were the island's botanists, pharmacists, and physicians. Closely allied to Poivre's science of botany was that of medicine. As intendant, Poivre was in charge of the island's hospitals, and this was another sphere in which he attempted to put his scientific knowledge to practical use. But the story of hospital administration in this period also reminds us that this was a period (like many others) when scientific knowledge was much in dispute. Such disputes were frequently personalized—and in the eighteenth century this meant they were political.

Though the island's hospitals had been enlarged and improved since the time of Labourdonnais, they were still, for the most part, overcrowded and dangerous places to be, particularly during periods of warfare.[25] Government-run hospitals on Île de France were essentially naval and military hospitals, and they were governed by the legislation covering these. One of Poivre's first concerns when he took up his post was to cut the costs of running the Port Louis hospital, notorious as a place from which valuable resources of food and medicine "leaked" into private hands. In 1754 (during one of Poivre's earlier visits to the island) Godeheu, a director of the Company and *commissaire du roi*, had written a scathing account of the place, which he described as resembling a storehouse rather than a hospital. It was, he wrote, never subject to inspection and was directed by one Mademoiselle Emmanuel, a "fille d'esprit," who spent most of her time entertaining soldiers. The surgeon-major was Sr. La Coustrade, a famed "homme de plaisir," reportedly very rich, whom Godeheu accused of neglecting the sick. It was said that many patients went days without food and drink.[26]

Poivre began by trying to impose some order on the hospital staff. Its *directrice* was now one Dame Martin Lajust. Unfortunately the archival records for the Bureau de l'Hôpital are in very poor condition,[27] but enough is decipherable for us to have some idea of Poivre's orders. These consisted in part in a reiteration of existing legislation (the king's ordinance governing port hospitals of 1689 and another concerning military hospitals of 1747) accompanied by some explicit instructions, both to the directrice and to the surgeon-major. Dame Martin Lajust was to make an inventory of the contents of the hospital; she was to provide regular accounts of expenditure on food and linen and hold her nursing staff accountable for any goods under their control. The apothecary, the surgeon-major, and the hospital's clerk were issued with similar instructions, holding them to routines and to routine accounting in particular. The emphasis was on domestic economy, but Poivre also had a larger ambition, which was to put his botanical knowledge into practice by encouraging the use of local plant sources in place of some of the imported medicines. This, in fact, was a project begun in the 1750s by another botanist, Jean-Baptiste Aublet,[28] with whom Poivre had fallen out.

Poivre would also fall out with another of his scientific colleagues, the surgeon-major Jean Barthélemy Dazille.[29] Dazille had been educated in France by the famous Anthoine Petit, and he had served as a naval surgeon in Canada and Cayenne. In 1766 he was appointed as surgeon-major to Île de France, where he became involved in a bitter dispute with Poivre over the hospital regime the latter had put into place.[30] Poivre had decided that patients suffering from venereal diseases (there were apparently many) faired better on a more restricted diet. Dazille clearly felt that this policy was based less on demonstrable medical evidence and more on Poivre's desire to save money. This was also an implicit critique of Poivre's scientific knowledge and his lack of any formal medical qualification. In a long mémoire of 1768 Dazille set about attempting to prove that supplementing a diet of sago with some wine and lemonade was beneficial to sufferers. Poivre accused Dazille of subverting the order and economy of the hospital, dispensing and diverting medicines, and circumventing the rules Poivre had put into place. Dazille returned to France to defend his reputation with the Ministry, citing fifteen years of uninterrupted service, three shipwrecks, and three "maladies pestilentielles" as proof of his loyalty. He went on to a distinguished career in medicine and published two influential works on tropical medicine.[31] In this episode, then, Poivre's attempts to apply the "science of colonialism" clashed with Dazille's own experiment in the application of medical science. Perhaps there was not room on the island for more than one advanced scientific thinker.

Poivre resigned his post as intendant in 1772. With the fall of the duc de Choiseul in 1770 he had lost his key ally in France. As Grove points out, however, this did not mark the end of Poivre's influence on administrative policy, particularly in relation to forest conservation. And there had been other developments during his period of office that bore the mark of the rationalist regime of which he was a representative. Information gathering was one—the census of 1767 was more complete than earlier population counts, though still partial and difficult to interpret (Kuczynski 1949, 708),[32] and surveys of the island's natural resources had multiplied. More of the streets of Port Louis were now paved, and more of the houses were stone-built (though a later visitor, Milbert, would remark that the inhabitants of the town were adept at painting an impression of stone walls onto their wooden houses). Île de France now had a printing press, one of the very earliest to exist in the southern hemisphere—though it should be noted that it still had no school for the children of colonists. Poivre had also presided over considerable improvements in the port's defenses and in its capacity to store foodstuffs in the event of the outbreak of a new war (Toussaint 1933, 69). The population had increased—in particular, the population of slaves. The exact figures are a matter of dispute, but the slave population probably rose from just over 15,000 in 1767 to over 20,000 at the time of Poivre's resignation. An odd achievement, perhaps, for a man who had loudly declaimed his anxieties and distaste for the institution. Whether Poivre had succeeded in subjecting slavery to the law, as he had claimed he would do, is also open to dispute, as we shall see.

War, Plunder, and the Slave Trade: Wealth Creation, 1767–1789

When Louis XVI came to the throne in 1776, Île de France was beginning to flourish under the limited freedom of trade conferred to its inhabitants (and other French nationals) in 1769. This new prosperity would continue up to the outbreak of the Revolution. The "flowering" of the island's colonial society, the *bon vieux temps* later Mauritian historians would look back upon nostalgically, occurred, then, in the very period when the colonial system and the system of slavery that underpinned it were coming under increasingly vocal criticism in France. And insofar as Bernardin de St. Pierre was an important voice in this tide of criticism, then it can be said that the example of Île de France played a role in this pre-Revolutionary movement for reform. The islanders themselves, however, were resolute in their defense of slavery, as we shall see.

Though agricultural production grew slowly in the last two decades of the ancien régime, this was still very far from being a plantation economy. The relative prosperity of the 1770s and 1780s came from familiar sources: commerce and the spin-offs of war, the slave trade, and speculation. It may be true, as Jean Mayer has argued (1991, 229) that the period of freedom of trade in the Indian Ocean did not meet expectations. Nevertheless, the 1769 decree allowing the colonists of Île de France and Île Bourbon to conduct private trade within the Indian Ocean region does appear to have been an important spur to economic growth. Philip Haudrère has recently provided evidence for this in his study of commerce between France and Asia in the last quarter of the eighteenth century (Haudrère 1996), arguing that Port Louis in particular became the focus for an increasing number of independent shipowners trading in Asian goods, particularly after direct trade to China and India was once again consigned to a monopoly (with the creation of yet another Compagnie des Indes in 1785). This trend was greatly enhanced in 1787 when Port Louis was declared a "free port," open to ships of all nations, and it reflected a larger shift in European trade away from the Antilles (where profits were falling) and toward the East (Haudrère 1996, 35–36; Butel 1996, 85). Unfortunately we do not have a full study of the island's commercial relations, nor of the (undoubtedly) critical role played by a small group of merchants, such as the famous Monneron dynasty, but we do know that the volume of shipping in and out of the island increased in this period (Haudrère 1996, 37–38). In his 1967 study Auguste Toussaint not only scoured the archives for statistics on the comings and goings of ships of all sizes but also provided useful examples of ships' logs (Toussaint 1967). Smaller ships made the crossing to and from Madagascar, which remained an important source of both foodstuffs and slaves in the latter part of the century. Larger ships—some of which were French, others owned by islanders or by foreigners—conducted the so-called country trade within the Indian Ocean. Most of this trade was with the Bay of Bengal and the East African coast (a new and important source of slaves), but also to a lesser extent with ports in Arabia, Dutch possessions in Indonesia, and the Cape. Large vessels also arrived from France—most now originating not from the Company's port of Lorient, but from Bordeaux and Marseilles. Among the long-distance arrivals, Toussaint counted representatives of twenty nations and "races": American (the largest number), Arab, Armenian, British, Dalmatian, Danish (the second largest number), Dutch, Flemish, German, Imperial (Austrian), Indian, Indochinese, Portuguese, Russian, Savoyard, Spanish, Swedish, Tunisian, and Tuscan (Toussaint 1967, 143–144).

The evidence gathered by Toussaint points to the fact that in this period a great deal of traffic appears to have been directed *at* Île de France, not simply passing by it on the way to and from the East. This raises the question of what, exactly, was being traded. First, the population of the island was increasing, from a total of 18,777 in 1767 to 40,439 in 1787 and 77,768 in 1807. Given that the island still failed to produce anything much in the way of commodities, there was now a good trade in supplying its needs and those of the naval garrisons periodically stationed there. The most important item in these cargoes in quantitative terms was alcohol: French wine (or, when this was not available, madeira and beer), eau-de-vie, and *arack*. A study of 1806 estimated the consumption of wine alone on Île de France at 15,000 bottles per day for a free population of around 12,000—which, as Toussaint put it, was a "fairly high coefficient of absorption" (Toussaint 1967, 116). Next in importance came all kinds of foodstuffs, both staple (rice, wheat) and luxury items from France. Third were textiles, both French and Indian in origin. Fourth were the goods required for the maintenance of ships: wood, copper, iron, rope, coir, sailcloth, and so on. Fifth, a bewildering array of "domestic" items destined for the island's elite households, ranging from feathers for ladies' hats, antisyphilitic balsam, wardrobes, cabinets, and carriages. Next were the Spanish piastres that remained standard currency in the East to the middle of the nineteenth century and were imported into the island by merchants conducting trade in the region. And finally, there were slaves.

Slaves. Toussaint was not happy with his figures for slave cargoes arriving on the island, which he provided in an appendix to his book. Subsequent studies, by Filliot in particular (1974), used a wider range of sources in an attempt to provide a more accurate picture of the volume of slaves imported into the islands in this period. Filliot estimated that some 80,000 slaves arrived on Île de France and Île Bourbon in the period 1769 to 1793. But recent important work by Richard Allen (2001) using colonial census material indicates that this is almost certainly an underestimate. Allen's work also confirms earlier studies that noted that there was a dramatic increase after 1770 in the numbers of slaves arriving on the islands from East Africa, particularly from the Mozambican coast. While slaves of Malagasy origin comprised around 70 percent of the trade in the period to 1769, slaves of East African origin formed 60 percent of the trade from 1770–1810. As Allen argues, this marked increase in East African imports can be attributed in part to the 1769 decree opening up the island's trade.[33]

But Île de France was significant not only as an importer of East African slaves, but also as a base for slave traders operating on the East African coast and exporting slaves to the Atlantic world. The increased buzz of commercial activity on the island in this period was almost certainly partly attributable to its strategic position in the trade in slaves, which linked the Indian Ocean and the Atlantic. This trade was more complex than the familiar Atlantic "triangle," and it awaits further research, but the basic parameters have been outlined by Robert Louis Stein (1979, chap. 9), and more recently by both Philippe Haudrère (1996) and Paul Butel (1996). Stein argued that the lifting of trade restrictions in 1769 was one element fueling the growth of the East African slave trade; the other was the growth in the West Indian demand for slaves, to which French merchants responded by extending their range of sources. But, as Stein shows, this was not a simple case of substituting East African slaves for West Africans. The trade was more complex than this, in part because Île de France was an important source of Indian textiles, which were themselves essential goods in the slave trade.[34] Stein sketches out a number of ways in which slave traders operated within the Indian Ocean. First, there were the ships that sailed from France to India to buy the textiles necessary for the purchase of slaves and then sailed on to the Mozambican coast (or sometimes back to West Africa), bought the slaves and transported them to the Antilles. He adds that, particularly after Port Louis was made a free port, ships frequently stopped there to buy Indian textiles, rather than sailing to India itself. Other merchants engaged in "multiple" trade. For example, a ship might leave France filled with trading merchandise, a portion of which was exchanged on the East African coast for slaves who were then sold on Île de France or Île Bourbon in exchange for Indian cloth. The same ship then returned to the Mozambican coast and exchanged the cloth for more slaves, who were then shipped to the Antilles.

As Stein points out, the colonists of Île de France and Île Bourbon had one advantage over their Antillean equivalents: they had ready access to the merchandise on which the trade with Africa depended. The trade with India, condemned by Voltaire and others as an example of the worst kind of corrupting "luxury" trade, was in fact a great deal more than this—it was an essential element in the trade in slaves.

Although we need a great deal more research on the slave trade in this period, what evidence we have points to Île de France as a linchpin in the growing East African trade. In addition, as new research by Richard Allen is indicating, the trade in slaves from India (about which, as Toussaint noted, little has been known) appears to have been far more significant in the latter part of the century than anyone had previously imagined (Allen 2001). While the colonists of Île de France had always depended on slave labor, and while many of them had long engaged in the illegal importation of slaves, it was in the last quarter of the century that their involvement in the slave trade (both local and long-distance) reached new heights. One way or another, directly or indirectly, the island's prosperity rested on the trade in human beings. This was hardly the island of Enlightenment dreams.

There *were* other sources of wealth. War was one, as was its associated activity of privateering. Wild speculation in colonial projects on behalf of the crown was another—but less reliable. When the War of American Independence broke out in 1775, Île de France was once more given the opportunity to demonstrate its indispensability to the French crown. The first French engagement with the English took place in Pondichéry, and once more Port Louis played host to thousands of sailors and soldiers now under the command of the famous Admiral Suffren. Once again a period of war placed an enormous strain on the island's resources, but for some there was money to be made. Chronically short of manpower, the French navy in the Indian Ocean was supplemented with mercenaries and with slaves supplied by wealthier inhabitants acting as *rentiers*.[35] One of these was Jacques Leroux de Kermoseven.[36] Born in Lorient, Leroux de Kermoseven had arrived in Île de France in 1756 as an employee of the Company. He had soon acquired significant amounts of property: a large habitation in Pamplemousses, another in Rivière de Rempart, and a large house in Port Louis. By 1777 he was the owner of seven hundred slaves and was a significant slave trader in his own right. He also frequently supplied slaves (whom he had trained as artisans and sailors) to the island's administration and to the French navy. In the 1780s, however, he suffered significant losses as a result of having extended credit to another entrepreneur, Pierre Paul d'Arifat,[37] who had himself lent large amounts of money to the colonial administration.

D'Arifat's career sums up much about the political economy of this period, in particular the interdependence between the colonial administration and individual entrepreneurs, and between war and profit. Born at Castres in France of noble parentage, he arrived on the island in 1767 to join his brother. Beginning with one small boat doing trade between Île de France and Île Bourbon, he rapidly built up something of a fleet engaged in both "legitimate" commerce and privateering. With the outbreak of the War of American Independence, d'Arifat began supplying and arming ships, repairing ships, and supplying *noirs de marine* to Admiral Suffren. All of this was achieved through taking out enormous loans; in 1782 the colonial administration, who apparently saw d'Arifat as indispensable, lent him over a million livres to pursue an ambitious trading project in China. This failed, with enormous repercussions on the island and beyond—both for the colonial administration, and for other individuals who had been involved with him (Mayer et al., 1991,

270). D'Arifat's combination of activities—trade, privateering, and supplying goods and manpower to the French navy—was not untypical of the time, though on a larger scale than most. Privateering would continue to be central to the island's economy for the rest of the century, and Île de France earned a reputation as the center of a *guerre de course* that produced the periodic influx of riches (Mayer et al. 1991, 296).

The 1770s and 1780s saw a continuation of the regulatory and "improving" measures Poivre's administration had began to put into place. There were more attempts to enumerate the population more accurately, to control the proliferation of bars and canteens in Port Louis, to prohibit building in wood, to prevent fires, and to regulate (and segregate) burials. Attempts were made to segregate the population of Port Louis by reiterating the regulation that made it illegal for whites to reside in the so-called *camp des noirs* (the "free black" location). But this, as we shall see, was largely unenforceable, particularly in times of war. Island society (or rather a small part of it) could now boast a printing press and a Freemasons' lodge (1778) and enjoyed a great many balls. But while the consolidation of an elite was undoubtedly taking place through marriage and business alliances, this was a process continually disturbed by the influx of newcomers, particularly at times of war. Île de France elite society appears to have been somewhat schizophrenic when it came to attitudes to conventional distinctions of rank—these were repeatedly and anxiously referred to, yet at other times Île de France colonists seem to have prided themselves on the relative fluidity of their society. In 1772, for example, the administration had issued an order establishing a seating protocol for church services and public ceremonies, but during the War of American Independence fighting often broke out on the streets between islanders and military men from France with titles who were attempting to "lord it" over their colonial cousins. Visitors like Bernardin de St. Pierre made much of the "simplicity" of local colonial society on the island, and this picture was often repeated and reinforced (for example, by the historian Albert Pitot), but as the chapters below show, this was a society deeply riven by divisions of rank and wealth.

The display of wealth was much evident in the period during and after the War of American Independence, fueled no doubt by the booty acquired from English ships. This was the period of the governorship of the vicomte de Souillac, a popular man described as a *grand seigneur* of the old sort and very fond of entertainment (Toussaint 1936, 117). He instituted a ball on the occasion of the celebration of St. Louis at which, according to one contemporary observer (Chevalier de Mautort, a military man) the island society showed itself off as the "star of the Indian Ocean": "India furnished the most beautiful cloth, China also brought its tribute, France provided the fashion, the trinkets and the right note . . . to the occasion" (quoted in Toussaint 1936, 117). Even more lavish, according to Pitot, was the ball held in 1787 when news reached the island that Souillac was to be replaced. Present at this occasion were the ambassadors of Tippu Saib, passing through from India on their way to France. Pitot, no doubt repeating a mythologized account of the occasion, wrote that the visitors were "so stupefied by the exhibition of luxury, the spirit, the animation of the young people, the exquisite grace and elegance of our creole women, the urbanity and courtesy of everyone, that they could not help themselves declaring out loud that they were charmed and ravished" (Pitot 1899, 129). If nothing else, this description gives us a sense of how nineteenth-century Mauritians (now, of course, under British colonial rule) liked to look back on this period of their history.

Souillac was replaced as governor by d'Entrecasteaux, who arrived bearing a letter from the king to the colonists bemoaning the continuing underdevelopment of agriculture and reminding them that their first responsibility was to maintain the island as a military entrepôt from which French forces could launch at attack on India (Pitot 1899, 131). D'Entrecasteaux, in his turn, was replaced by one of the many Irishmen serving the French crown at this time, Thomas de Conway, a former governor of Pondichéry.[38] De Conway arrived in November 1789. On 31 January the following year, a ship arrived bearing the news that the king, the queen, and the rest of the royal family had been taken to Paris, and that all Frenchmen were now free.

"Civilizing" Slavery:
The Law, Responsibility, and Agency

Underlying the economic, social, physical, and psychological existence of Île de France in the late eighteenth century, as before, was one institution— slavery. Sometimes this looks like a solid, unassailable backbone; sometimes more of a shaky scaffolding. Slavery permeated life on the island and provided a structure to social relations (and not only those between slaves and their masters and mistresses). But simultaneously this "contradictory institution" created instabilities, fragilities, fears, and anxieties. Containing these contradictions was the work of colonialism and, in the latter part of the century in particular, the work of the legal system.[39]

Our access (partial and fragmentary as it is) to a history of the lived experience of slavery is made possible by the creation and survival of legal records, particularly those produced in the last quarter of the century as a result of the administrative and judicial reforms brought in during the period of royal government. Much of the material I draw on for my discussions in the rest of this book derives from the legal records (particularly of criminal procedure) of the period from the 1760s to the 1790s. Ancien régime criminal procedure (unlike English law of the time) required an extremely detailed written record to be produced, from the first investigation into a crime to the last deliberations of the judge, including verbatim (or supposedly verbatim) records of the interrogations of suspects and witnesses. None of this can be taken at face value, least of all in a slave society, but this textual residue is nevertheless too rich in the details of day-to-day life to be discarded.

There is no other source for eighteenth-century Île de France that can give us access to the material and social realities of life for the poorest people on the island, including the slaves. We do not have the slave narratives or the plantation owner's diary[40]—sources that have so enriched our understanding of slavery in the Americas. The most valuable material in these records is often contained within apparently incidental asides and observations, as much as within the central narrative of the alleged crime.[41] The cases are littered with details of meals eaten, with whom and where, with accounts of sociability (even when the central narrative is one of conflict), with lists of items and clothing and the contents of huts. Above all, they are constantly interpolated with renderings of speech, of who said what to whom. These snippets of speech are, as I discuss in a later chapter, deceptively immediate. They are in fact renditions, reordered written versions of speech in an unstable linguistic situation, with multiple opportunities for incomprehension and mistranslation. They are, nevertheless, unique and revealing.

These records reveal the history of slavery in a second, different way. For though there is always an element of chance in the survival of archival records (particularly on a cyclone-prone island), other evidence also points to the growing importance of the legal profession on the island in the last quarter of the century,[42] and in particular of attempts to bring the institution of slavery, and the conflicted relationships that go with it, into the public sphere. In this sense the records of the legal system of this period are records of the changing climate and of an ambition to "civilize" (and therefore to preserve) what was increasingly being seen as an "unnatural" institution.

In theory the institution of slavery was governed, in all French colonies, by its own set of legislation, the Code Noir of 1685, a version of which was promulgated on Île de France in 1723. Under this Code (the contradictions and perversities of which are discussed in Sala-Moulins 1987), though slaves were considered minors under the law for most purposes, in terms of criminal responsibility they were to be treated identically to free persons. Article 25 of the Île de France version read that accused slaves would be judged in the first instance by ordinary judges and with the same formalities as applied to free persons (Noel n.d., 169; Sala-Moulins 1987, 155). In subsequent articles the Code went on both to recommend the harshest of punishments to be meted out to slaves found guilty of assaults on their masters, mistresses, or other free persons, and at the same time to prohibit the unbridled use of force and mutilation by masters against slaves. So Article 26 recommends that slaves who have "hit their master, mistress, the husband of their mistress or their children, causing bleeding, should be punished with death," while Article 38 empowered justice officers to punish, even with death ("depending on the circumstances"), any master or slave commander found guilty of murdering or mutilating a slave. One suspects that this was largely theoretical, however. Other than Poivre's reference to the Code Noir in his address to the colonists, it seems markedly absent in both the correspondence and the legal records of Île de France.[43]

And yet there were two aspects to the Code relevant here. One is the ambition it expressed (among others) to bring the regulation of slavery into the public arena, particularly in the matter of punishment; the other is its explicit assertion that in the area of criminal responsibility the slave lost his or her status as a minor or chattel and was to be treated as a "free person." As Sala-Moulins (1987) points out, in essence this meant that the slave would suffer all the disadvantages and none of the advantages of minor status, and this is obviously true. Nevertheless, there were other ramifications to this position. As Eugene Genovese (1975, 29) has argued in the context of a very different slave regime, the courts had to recognize the humanity and free will of the slave if they were to hold him accountable for criminal and antisocial actions.[44] The attribution of "free will" was, I shall argue, a particularly pronounced feature of the French criminal code through which slaves, like free persons, were prosecuted.

The ambition, evident in the Code Noir, to harness slavery to a legal code, to bring it under the hegemony of the law, becomes a great deal more evident on Île de France from the 1760s onward. A similar tendency is noted by Wayne Dooling (1992) for the Dutch Cape in the same period, and Elizabeth (1989, 766) notes that this was a period of reform on the French Antillean island of Martinique.[45] On Île de France this development was probably the result of a number of factors, some local, some metropolitan in origin. As we have seen from the evidence of the correspondence of the period, on taking control of the islands the Crown also aimed to pursue a program of reform and rationalization—most clearly demonstrated in the appointment of Pierre Poivre as intendant—and the law was an important instrument in this program. Reformist tendencies were not, of course, confined to the colonies. One account of French eighteenth-century history sees this period, particularly the 1770s and 1780s, as dominated by reform initiatives, making the Revolution much less of a revolution (Jones 1995). Second, the growing role and confidence of the legal profession in France in this period (Bell 1994) seems to have been reflected in the colonies, where there was a relative absence of the competing jurisdictions (of Church and aristocracy) evident in the metropole. Third, the increasingly large population of slaves on the island, the continuing problem of maroons, and the presence, particularly during wartime, of thousands of troublesome and rootless soldiers and sailors contributed to the anxiety that had always surrounded the institution of slavery. This anxiety was given a different kind of expression in the latter part of the century by the Enlightenment critics like Bernardin de St. Pierre who argued that slavery was in some essential way "unnatural" and that from this followed the fact that revolt against it was natural.

The presence on the island of a small but growing community of mixed-race *mulâtres* (a term that locally referred to a mixture including "white" blood), some of whom had slave status, some of whom were free, was a constant reminder of the contradictions inherent in the ideology of slavery. Was it not "natural" that the children of white fathers, suffering under the yoke of slavery, should feel a murderous resentment against their fathers/masters? The response of the administration and of an increasingly powerful professional elite to this, and other anxieties, was to make greater efforts to "civilize" the institution. There were no great reforms to the slave system of Île de France during this period; rather it was a question of applying existing laws, of making it clear that the law would prevail. Law, it has been argued, *was* government in France during this period—or rather, the very idea of government evolved out of the function of the judiciary, there being no sense of the separation of powers (Jones 1995, 25). But whereas in pre-Revolutionary France there were multiple and overlapping jurisdictions (including seigneurial courts) and almost any administrative body could operate some kind of tribunal, this was not the case in Île de France. The problem was, however, that slave owners frequently behaved as if they were the equivalent of feudal lords, beyond the law, or operating a law of their own making, and it was this tendency that came under attack.

We should be clear that this use of the law, particularly in the area of regulating slave punishment, was in no simple way the product of a growing Enlightenment sensibility of humanitarianism. It was, as its proponents repeatedly made clear, a matter of survival. Genovese similarly made the case that North American slave owners could see that promoting the law was in their own interests (1975, 41). On Île de France it was often argued that the system had to be seen to be just, even in its brutality, and that individual slave owners had a duty to the wider community to restrain their violent instincts toward their slaves. If they did not, there was no guarantee that the system would survive, for slaves, like free persons, were well able to recognize and respond to an injustice.[46] Here was an attempt to forge and formalize a moral economy of slavery, and an attempt to bring the violence inherent to slave control into the public sphere. Not all slave owners agreed that this was in their interest, as we shall see, and we should certainly not imagine that these efforts brought an end to the acts of violence perpetrated against slaves within their masters' or mistresses' houses.

Though Île de France slavery was not, in this period, characterized by the extremes of social distancing found on plantation regimes, this does not necessarily mean that there were fewer acts of violence. On the contrary, one could argue that the close proximity, even intimacy, between slaves and their owners, combined with a general situation of poverty, was liable to give rise to frequent eruptions of violence. However, there was one important weapon at the disposal of the lawyers: the power of honor and reputation. As many court cases make graphically clear, the relative fluidity and unpredictability of Île de France society made many individuals acutely anxious about their standing and their public reputations.[47] This was true from top to bottom of slave-owning society, from the ranks of the ennobled administrators and decorated war heroes to the lowliest families of "poor whites" and the small but significant group of "free blacks." Issues of honor, as Orlando Patterson (1982) and Kenneth S. Greenburg (1996) have argued in different ways, permeated slave regimes, and that of Île de France was no exception to this.[48] Slaves not only carried and mediated the reputations of their masters, they also in a very real sense *embodied* their masters, much as officers of the administration embodied the king. An offense against a slave, then, was a direct offense against his or her master.[49] But there was a further way in which issues of honor and reputation were mediated by slaves. By the last quarter of the century, if not before, the treatment or mistreatment of slaves itself became a measure of respectability. Slave beating, like wife beating, was not something a respectable man did, and allegations of slave beating made by one neighbor against another were weapons in larger wars of reputation. Those who mistreated their slaves acted, it was said, against the interests of the wider slave-owning society; their reputations were damaged by their lack of restraint and particularly by their direct indulgence in violence. If slavery were to remain intact, the violence that underpinned it would have to be regulated, performed in public and—crucially—executed through the hands of a black man, a slave or former slave himself.

The public spectacles of violence (whipping, branding, executions) that took place on Île de France in the late eighteenth century were certainly not new—they had been a feature of the colony's life since the days of Dutch occupation. But in another sense they were, ironically perhaps, a product of reform. Spectacular they certainly were, and designed to intimidate, but they were not the random acts of brutality and murder that might take place in the confines of the master's house. Furthermore, public acts of punishment were frequently the final outcome of a judicial process that rested on powerful notions of responsibility, agency, and "free will." To this extent the contrast Michel Foucault attempted to draw between the spectacular, oppressive power of the old regime and the "productive" power of the law requires considerable revision. In this vein, and arguing against what he calls the "black legend" of ancien régime law, Richard Mowery Andrews (1994) provides a detailed account of the procedures laid down by the Grand Ordonnance Criminel of 1670, which governed criminal procedure in France (and its colonies) until the Revolution.[50]

"Free Will" and Coercion: Slaves in Court

Andrews argues that a central tenet of ancien régime thinking on crime was that there *was* no crime without malicious intent. A crime was not constituted by an illegal act, but by such an act preceded by a clear intent. That intent had to be discovered and proven if a crime was said to have been committed (Andrews 1994, 1:285). Among the Île de France court cases I examine in subsequent chapters, this search for intent is often very evident—and sometimes pursued in a surprisingly thorough way. Other things followed from this emphasis on intent. One was the notion, upon which it rested, of the existence of an inner disposition in each individual, and hence of a moral existence. The capacity for *dol* (which was clearly distinguished from the concept of *faute*) was an expression of free will, itself a product of the internal struggle within the individual between a sense of conscience and rationality and impulses toward sin and crime. The goal of criminal procedure was to uncover the truth of the crime, the existence or nonexistence of intent, and the nature of that intent. In turn it followed from the emphasis on "inner disposition" that only the perpetrator of an act could really know the truth—only he or she knew, for certain, what their intention had been. This is what Andrews calls the "epistemology of first person authority" (1:442). The best evidence for a crime, then, would come from the accused in the form of a confession, but, as Andrews points out, this legal rigidity on the issue of intent meant that very few defendants confessed—denial was their only real option (1:302).[51]

A slave before the criminal courts of Île de France, then, was conceived of as an individual with an inner disposition, a moral world, intent, and free will. In other words, he or she was a person with agency. Some, not knowing the theories underlying this system, made the mistake of confessing. Surprisingly, perhaps, Île de France judges often went to some lengths to untangle such confessions, sometimes discarding them as false. The accused slave, however, also faced a long, complex, and intimidating procedure and confinement in jail while the process moved from stage to stage. His or her life was at greater risk from the rigors and deprivations of imprisonment (a fact recognized by many slave owners) than from the final outcome of the legal process. But some evidence also points to the jail as being a source of invaluable education in the ways of the French law. There was no defense counsel in this judicial system, and so the accused was in one sense very much on their own in the courtroom. However, if an accused slave was less than fluent in the French creole language, then an interpreter would be present, and these important intermediaries may well have played some role in translating procedure as well as language.[52]

In the Preparatory Instruction, the information-gathering part of the process, the suspects were questioned in isolation. They were not told of the charges against them but were questioned on the apparent facts of the crime and the material evidence. Being "in the dark" was supposed to deprive the suspect of the opportunity for deception. The judge was to watch the suspect carefully, observing facial expressions, for example. As Andrews remarks, the whole mise-en-scène simulated a religious confessional, with which a very small minority of slaves may have been familiar. In the context of a slave society, one can imagine this experience as being more than intimidating, and possibly terrifying.

The next stage of proceedings was the Definitive Instruction, in which the suspect was "confronted" by each witness (individually) and by the witnesses' statements. Each of these staged "confrontations" was recorded in detail, word for word (in theory at least), and later the written record would be presented to the prosecutor. The defendant was given a final opportunity to speak, and then the judge would review the accumulated written evidence. This might be, and often was, weighty. It included the first notification of the alleged crime made to the police or prosecutor, the record of the preliminary investigations (which might include surgeons' reports, for example), the written depositions of the witnesses, the written reports of the "confrontations," the defendant's final statement in writing, and the presiding judge's conclusions. Judgment was given by a panel of three judges and, if the defendant was found guilty, a sentence was passed. However, this was frequently not the end of the case, because appeal to a higher court (in this case the island's Conseil Supérieur) was automatic under this system and not infrequently resulted in a modification, if not an overturning, of the sentence. As I argue in later chapters, the island's culture of conflict and intrigue meant that individual members of the judiciary were frequently involved in personal feuds with each other that could never be entirely excluded from the court-room procedures.

Surprisingly, perhaps, the form and processes of these legal proce-dures as laid down in legal manuals such as that by Jousse (1771) appear to have been followed rigorously in the cases I have examined, even when these primarily concern slaves. Of course, I have no proof that this was always the case, and one must assume that some processes were fore-shortened, abbreviated, and the records falsified and destroyed. Indeed, in a significant number of cases I have been unable to ascertain the final outcome.[53] Similarly, to describe these procedures and processes is in no way to deny either the radical power asymmetry of the courtroom in which a slave faced the bewigged judge, nor to claim that the process was necessarily "fair." Perhaps these cases are better viewed as self-conscious performances on the part of the legal profession, and though their writ-ten records are frequently exhaustively detailed and full of examples of recorded speech, they remain highly crafted texts, "scripts in the theatre of authority," as Muir and Ruggiero put it (1994). More importantly, we cannot know what kind of intimidation, physical and psychological, might have been brought to bear on a slave suspect outside the court-room.

I am not arguing, then, that justice necessarily ruled in the trials of slaves on Île de France, but I am arguing that the form and practice of the law were both constitutive of, and to some degree reflected, changing perceptions of slavery and the slave. In particular, the judicial system treated the slave as an individual with free will, agency, and an inner life and "disposition." Slaves, in other words, were subjects.

In theoretical discussions on the operation of power, slavery as an institution is frequently treated as a kind of excluded "other," an other that we know (it consists of chains and restraints), and which we there-fore need not interrogate. Foucault, for example, explicitly argued that slavery was *not* a power relationship in his terms, since it did not feature free subjects: "Power is exercised only over free subjects, and only insofar as they *are* free. By this we mean individual or collective subjects who are faced with a field of possibilities in which several ways of behaving, several relations and diverse comportments may be realized. Where the determining factors saturate the whole there is no relationship of power: slavery is not a power relationship when man is in chains" (quoted in McNay 1994, 127).

Historians of slavery know, however, that despite slaves not being free, slavery was often a complex and contradictory power relationship, because slaves constantly exceeded their position as property and objects of exchange. They were inescapably persons as well as "things," and this was the "problem" with slavery, as both David Brion Davis and Sydney Mintz long ago reminded us (Davis 1970; Mintz 1974). On Île de France, late-eighteenth-century efforts to police and sustain a slave system have provided us with a historical record of the constant provocations of this complex institution.[54]

Chapter Four

ROOTS AND ROUTES:

ETHNICITY WITHOUT ORIGINS

*I*n April 1777 a slave in Port Louis was about to be flogged on the orders of his master.[1] The flogging was to be carried out not by the master himself, but by his slave "commander." Such was the practice of respectable slave owners in late-eighteenth-century Île de France. The flogging was punishment for the slave's alleged four-day-long unauthorized absence, or *petit marronnage*. The slave's name was Adonis, and he was originally from Madagascar. A small crowd had gathered to watch the event. Adonis was tied to a scaffold and the commander prepared to flog him, but having raised his whip to do so, he paused, because (as he was to explain later) he had caught sight of something odd. Two small packets, wrapped in blue linen, were just visible in Adonis's shirtsleeves. The commander called a halt to the flogging, untied Adonis, removed the small packets, and opened them on the spot. The small crowd watched as the packets were unwrapped. They could see that one contained a substance rather like sand; the other, what looked like two small pieces of wood. The commander interrogated Adonis. What, he asked, were these substances, and what had he intended to do with them? Later a number of witnesses would apparently recall Adonis's reply: the sandlike substance was to be placed in his master's drinking water; the pieces of wood were to be ground up and placed in his food.

Adonis's master was Nicolas Lambert, director of the island's Imprimerie Royale (royal printing press). Lambert, born in Paris in 1741, had taken over this role in 1770. He died on the island in 1806 (Toussaint 1969, 12–21). Lambert was told of these events and in turn informed the *procureur-général*, or public prosecutor. The prosecutor was told that there was "reasonable suspicion" that the substances found in the small blue packets might be capable of producing "detrimental effects" if placed in a *ragôut* or similar "vehicle." He was also told that Adonis was known to be friendly with a king's slave named Diamante, and that it was from Diamante that he may have obtained these substances. The prosecutor ordered the police to search Diamante's hut, which they did the following day, finding more small packages similar to those found on Adonis, containing sandlike substances and pieces of wood and roots, some ground into powder—all of this characteristic, so it was said, of "dangerous and criminal usage." The prosecutor was impressed. Action would have to be taken because, as he put it, "nothing is more essential to the security of the habitants of this colony than to prevent, through swift response and example, the possibility of similar machinations against the life of citizens."

French judicial procedure was clear on matters of suspected poisoning, and the public prosecutor appears to have followed this carefully (Jousse 1771, 4:41–50; Laingui and Lebigre 1979, 11:156–158; Andrews 1994, vol. 1). And so the first thing he did was to appoint a committee of apothecaries and surgeons from among the island's practitioners to investigate the substances found in Adonis's shirtsleeves and in Diamante's hut. French law put its faith in science on this point. The island's experts eventually reported back that their investigations had been inconclusive and that they would need to carry out experiments on a live animal. On 6 June they were given a dog for this purpose, which was to be kept within the confines of the prison.

Adonis and the dog were now being held in the same prison in Port Louis. Adonis was brought from custody there to face his first interrogation by the judge. The criminal procedure of the ancien régime was, as we have seen, essentially inquisitorial, its avowed aim to arrive at the "truth," as in a confessional. Under this system the prosecutor was not permitted to interrogate the suspect—this was done by the judge.[2] The interrogation began.

Was it true, the judge asked, that when he, Adonis, had been attached to the scaffolding to receive his punishment he had had, in the sleeves of his shirt, small packets containing sand and roots? Yes, Adonis had replied. For what purpose, he was then asked, were the contents of these packets intended? Adonis replied that they had been given to him by a slave named Diamante to be used for protection against the flogging he had been about to receive. Was it not true, asked the judge, that at the moment at which he had been cut down from the scaffold, he had said that he had intended to mix the sand and the powder together and to infuse the mixture in his master's drinking water? And had he not also said that the pieces of wood were to be ground up and put in his food? To this Adonis replied that he had said only that the ingredients were destined to be placed in his master's drinking water. What effect, he was asked, was this infusion intended to have? Adonis replied that Diamante had assured him that if he put the powder in his master's drinking water he would avoid the flogging. So, he was asked, had he ever actually put powder in his master's drinking water? Yes, he replied, he had done so once. Was he aware of the names, properties, and qualities of the pieces of wood? No, answered Adonis, he was not. Had Diamante not warned him that the packets he had given him contained poison? (This, in fact, had not yet been confirmed.) No, Adonis replied, he had told him only that if he placed these powders in his master's drinking water he would not be flogged. But, the judge went on, was it not true that, when he was cut down from the scaffold, he had said that the powders were intended for poisoning his master? Yes, Adonis replied, he had said that, because he was a hard master who mistreated him to excess. Was it not the case then, he was asked, that he had not been telling the truth when he had said that the contents of the packets were intended only to prevent the flogging, to avoid the punishment? To this Adonis replied that in saying that he was going to put the powder in his master's water in order not to be flogged, what he had meant was that the effect of these powders would be that his master would die. Adonis, it appeared, was confessing to the attempted murder of his master: a confession which, if believed, would inevitably lead to his execution.

On the same day, Diamante was brought in for interrogation. He was judged to understand and speak very little French and so was provided with an interpreter, Nicolas L'Éveille, a "free black" soldier of Malagasy origin. Through the interpreter, Diamante said that he was a Malagasy of the "Ambolambe" caste (on which more later), that he was about forty years old, and a slave of the king's. He knew Adonis from Madagascar, he said, and saw him regularly, every Saturday. In fact, he went on, Adonis was the son of his sister. Asked whether he had given Adonis the sand and the pieces of wood, Diamante replied that he had given him the sand, but not the pieces of wood. For what purposes, he was asked, were these substances intended? Diamante replied that he had given them to his nephew to enable him to find a cooking pot that had gone missing in his master's house. How, asked the judge, might the sand help to find the lost cooking pot? Because, answered Diamante, the ingredients incorporated a charm that acted to entice the thief into the open. The judge persisted. Had he not, in fact, given these drugs to Adonis for the purpose of poisoning his master? No, replied Diamante, he had given them to him to help him find the cooking pot.

Diamante was next shown the powders and pieces of wood found in Adonis's shirtsleeves and asked if he recognized these. Yes, he said, he did recognize some of the pieces of wood: this was the kind of wood he cut in the bush at Paille (on the hillsides behind Port Louis), the sort he had learned to identify in Madagascar. How had he acquired this knowledge, he was asked—was he some kind of specialist? No, replied Diamante, in Madagascar he had been a cultivator, but he had learned about the qualities of plants and trees from his elders. Asked again whether it was not the case that he had given these ingredients to Adonis with the express purpose of poisoning his master, he replied again in the negative, saying that he had given them to him for the purpose of finding the cooking pot. Did he not know that these ingredients, if taken internally, might be damaging to health? No, he replied, he did not know of any damaging effects of these ingredients.

Both Diamante and Adonis were remanded in custody. Meanwhile, the prosecutor had been waiting for the results of the experiment on the dog. On 14 June the jailer reported that the dog was still healthy and showing no ill effects from its diet of roots and wood. But the jail was a notoriously unhealthy place for humans. Diamante died there on 20 August.

On 8 October the court reconvened and, following procedure, Adonis was reexamined. He had now to confront witnesses, including his master, Lambert, and bystanders at the flogging scene. He repeated that he had intended not to poison his master, but simply to frighten him, believing that in this way he could avoid the flogging. The record of the interrogation of 6 June was read to him and he was asked to confirm the answers he had given on that date. Adonis listened and then said that everything he had been reported to have said on that day was true, except for the answers to three questions, and these he would like to correct (in fact, the record has him correcting only one). He said that when he had been taken off the scaffold he had not said that the small packets found on him were intended for poisoning his master, but only for frightening him. "I am a child," he told the judge, "and I was frightened and thought that I had to reply like that," whereas "in truth," he added, he had never had the intention of poisoning his master, but only of escaping the beating, just as Diamante had promised he would.

Indeed, Adonis *had* so far escaped the beating, so perhaps there was something in Diamante's potion. Evidently this defense was not in the end accepted, because Adonis was found guilty of "receiving and keeping drugs with the intention of poisoning or harming his master" and was sentenced not to death as he might have expected to have been, but to the gallows in perpetuity. But appeal was automatic under this system, and when the case was reexamined, doubt was cast not on Adonis's testimony, but, surprisingly, on that of his master, Lambert.[3] Adonis was still declared guilty of "receiving and harboring drugs and ingredients with the intention of harming his master," but his sentence was now reduced to three years in chains. By the standards of the day and the place he had come off very lightly indeed, though surviving (if survive he did) three years of hard labor would have been no mean feat.

The emphasis on intent and confession within this criminal legal system assumed a number of things about agency, knowledge, and subjectivity that seem apparently in contradiction with the state of slavery, with its presumed loss of agency, its nonbeing. Adonis has already demonstrated to us (and to the judge) that questions of intent and agency are not straightforward. Adonis "confesses," perhaps under duress, though to what exactly is not clear. What does confession mean when truth is open to interpretation? If we are to believe the witnesses to the event (the slave commander, a "free black" woman, a creole woman slave, and Xavier, another of Lambert's slaves) Adonis confessed readily, on the spot, when the blue packets were first found, to intending to use the substances in his master's water. Under examination he provides two rather different interpretations of his own confession in rapid succession. First he insists that his intention, in using these substances, had been simply to avoid the flogging; next, when asked whether he had not, in fact, intended to "do away" with his master, he concurs, arguing that

Lambert was a hard master who mistreated him. When the apparent contradiction between these two statements is pointed out to him, he has another answer—Adonis is having to do some swift thinking on his feet here about the logic of the French courtroom. He points out ("No, *don't*," I wanted to advise him from afar) that there *is* no contradiction between his statements, since by poisoning his master he would also avoid the flogging. He seems now to have confessed with his eyes open.

We must of course assume that coercion, physical or psychological or both, lay behind much of this. Adonis, no matter whether he was "in truth" innocent or guilty, clearly felt that he was supposed to confess to something, and perhaps that confession would ensure forgiveness and protection. This, after all, was the message of the Catholic faith to which some slaves on the island had been exposed, and in fact the Lazarist priests often alluded to the apparent popularity of confession among slaves. Confession may also have been a feature (but we do not know this for certain) in systems of justice in Malagasy societies, just as it was in some African societies. Confessing, and thereby throwing yourself on the mercy of your "protector" who was also your "prosecutor," may, in some circumstances, have been a more effective tactic than denial. Indeed, this is implicitly how Adonis, after a period of education in jail, explains his own earlier confession. His admission of guilt, he says, had been due to fear, he was a mere "child," and so on. No wonder that the judge seems to be struggling to interpret the evidence of confession, for the law demanded (even, it appears, in the case of a slave) proof of intent. But what, exactly, had Adonis known of the content of the packets, and what had his intent been? Then there was Diamante, more consistent in his account in some ways, but nevertheless confusing matters still further. Diamante was an older man, the uncle, and though he had been on the island longer than Adonis, he apparently spoke little French creole. Diamante admitted to a lay knowledge of herbalism, acquired from his elders in Madagascar; he made excursions into the bush behind Port Louis to collect specimens of wood. It is tempting to imagine that Diamante cut a more "traditional" figure in the courtroom. In any event, his insistence that the blue packets were designed to save Adonis from the flogging by "smelling out" the thief of a cooking pot (despite the fact that he is the only witness to mention such a theft) was such as to encourage this view of him.

One can thus read this case as archetypically "colonial," in more than one way. It can be read as the meeting (or nonmeeting) of two radically different worlds in the courtroom, in which one actor has the power of life or death over the other. The judge, who possesses this power of life and death, both as a judge and as a white man facing a slave, nevertheless feels constrained to proceed on the basis of reason and the quest for truth. The defendant, seemingly unaware of the rules of the game of reason, confesses to his intent to poison his master—a crime punishable (even in a nonslave context) by the most gruesome form of death.[4] The judge can see, however, that the slave may genuinely believe in "magic." Indeed, it is a mark of his difference, of his being a slave, that he should do so. The belief in magic cannot be ignored—it too must be subjected to reasoning. An innocent belief in magic and an absence of reasoning would, if only he knew it, have been Adonis's strongest line of defense. And perhaps he *did* know this, at least after a spell in prison.

If Adonis did know this—that a defense based on cultural difference, ignorance, or misunderstanding was possibly his best line of defense— then another colonial reading of this case suggests itself. This reading resonates with theories of colonial mimicry originally outlined by Homi Bhabha and now the subject of a considerable literature in the field of postcolonial studies.[5] Considering the mimetic possibilities in this court encounter does not lead us, however, to any fixed interpretation, but rather reinforces the sense of contingency and complexity suggested by the archival record. If Adonis, after a period in prison, is in some sense "acting out," performing the role of the "native" (of which Île de France, of course, has none) in the guise of a slave, this is neither necessarily a sign of his total subjugation to the script of colonialism, nor necessarily a sign of his successful subversion of that script.[6] Even within this archly formal courtroom setting, there simply is no one script.

And what of the judge? The judge is the expert in the rules of encounter in the courtroom. But though he has the considerable advantage of acquaintance with legal grammar and syntax, nevertheless he too is unable to control the script. In this particular case, it seems that the judge is himself struggling with at least two possible scripts, which, though not necessarily in contradiction with one another, might still require a degree of manipulation in order not to appear to be so. The first script is that of the application of reason through the theory and procedure of the law. Adonis may be a slave, but his intent still needs to be divined. The law's tools of divination mirror those of Diamante: experts are ordered to experiment on a dog, and Lambert's "evidence" is somehow divined to be unsafe and is ruled out of the script. But the judge seems to be working simultaneously with another script—that of difference and unreason. Faced with Adonis and Diamante, he is faced with men who are both slaves and Malagasies—their ethnic identity has been noted and marked.

Malagasies were known on the island for their apparently intense interest in magic, divination, herbalism, and all things uncanny. This was part and parcel of their ethnic identification on Île de France and partly accounts for the frequency with which they were accused of the crime of poisoning. Their use of magic was, as Diamante seems to demonstrate, and as the early-nineteenth-century writer Jacques Milbert indicates, also a real source of power: "Thanks to their talismans," wrote Milbert, "they believe themselves to be protected against every kind of accident, and attribute to them the power to obtain any desired object, the preservation of a good master, or a favorable change in their state" (1812, 2:164). Magic protected against the misfortune of slavery. In this second script, the judge's role is to attempt to comprehend the reasoning of unreason; asking what *exactly* had been Adonis's intention involves him in an encounter with a supposedly very different worldview. In fact, he needs to work with this second script in order to satisfy the demands of the first. So, he must ask himself, did Diamante really believe that the roots and powder would "sniff out" the thief of a cooking pot, and by what means (magic, murder, or both) did Adonis hope to avoid the flogging?

But magic works only if you believe in it, and there is a further dimension here that reminds us of the dangers of assuming anything of the content of the "colonial." Poisoning does seem in some ways to be the colonial crime par excellence, and tales of poisoning abound from all over the colonial world. This is a crime of stealth, a crime of the powerless. On the French Antillean island of Martinique in the same period, anxiety over poisoning (by slaves of their masters, their masters' livestock, and each other) was so great that the authorities had prohibited slaves from practicing any form of herbalism and alleged cases of poisoning were dealt with extremely severely.[7] There was no equivalent panic on Île de France. Nevertheless, Adonis's case, like other poisoning cases, serves to highlight one of the contradictions of slavery, for Adonis was a domestic slave whose role imposed a physical proximity with his master and, in some cases, an intimacy. Adonis was part of the household, and he may not only have had access to his master's food and drink, but have cooked and served it. No wonder that in France, then, poisoning had been a female crime, something that wives, in particular, did to their husbands. As a betrayal of intimacy it was also considered a crime like no other, a "form of homicide more criminal than that committed through the sword, for in the latter case one can usually defend oneself, whereas the former always involves treachery, and is often committed by those one suspects least" (Jousse 1771, 4:41; see also Laingui and Lebigre 1979, 1:156–158).

But the judge also came from a metropolitan society in which reason vied with unreason, and, crucially, the judge and the slaves before him in the courtroom inhabited, together, the shared and altogether nontraditional and complex world of Île de France.[8] Rural France, at least, was home to a lively magical tradition, and in the late seventeenth and eighteenth centuries[9] the French legal profession was still struggling to establish a watertight distinction between poisoning (a heinous crime, full of sly intent and only too much reason) and sorcery (the world of the irrational, the erroneous, the confused and mistaken) (Jousse 1771). Some of Adonis's and Diamante's claims, then, may not have appeared particularly strange to the judge, nor specifically Malagasy in their content. And, furthermore, he was obliged to take them seriously in applying his own reason. The crucial belief was that of the judge—if he believed that the Malagasies before him were steeped in magic, just as many French peasants were steeped in magic, then Adonis's performance of the innocent ("I am a child, and I was frightened") would not be misplaced.

In the end Adonis *is* found guilty, though not sentenced to death—a fact implying some doubt about his guilt, some fuzziness in the line between guilt and innocence. And then, at appeal, his sentence is further reduced thanks to some problem with his master Lambert's evidence. This seems extraordinary, and one can only assume that, as so often was the case on Île de France, there was some other underlying dispute between Lambert and the lawyers, in which the poisoning case became embroiled. But this we cannot know.

Roots and "Roots"

The world of the Île de France courtroom, then, was both a world of radical difference and of a meeting of minds, but the differences and the meetings did not always follow the same pattern. For a moment let us stand in the place of the judge and ask what *exactly* was in those blue packets Adonis had up his shirtsleeves. Let us ask a "roots" question. What did Adonis bring with him from Madagascar?

Cultures are not, of course, packets of roots, wrapped up and hidden in shirtsleeves, and in any case, slaves did not always have shirtsleeves, real or metaphorical, in which to hide anything they brought from home. One important version of the history of slavery features the middle passage as a deep dark hole, a rupture, a trauma that caused the erasure of the past, the erasure of origins, the loss of memory and identity. Survival as a slave, in this version, depends absolutely on forgetting, not remembering, but this is an involuntary forgetting, the product of violence, a symptom of trauma.

However, the literature on trauma tells us that amnesia is not its only possible manifestation, and that the individual and collective meaning given to trauma varies, depending on the context. So, for example, while survivors of childhood sexual abuse are frequently diagnosed as suffering from the suppression and repression of their trauma ("recovering" the memory of it being integral to their healing), survivors of the Holocaust often describe themselves as invaded, overwhelmed by too many memories, unable to allow the normal process of forgetting, which is integral to memory itself, to take place.[10]

The question of cultural "survivals" and transformation under slavery has exercised scholars from Melville Herskovits on, and is the subject of a rich comparative literature that very recently has begun to include studies from Mauritius.[11] We know that those who survived the trauma of the middle passage did create new worlds, albeit painfully, which to varying degrees included or incorporated, in one form or another, a memory of their homes, their origins. The work on cultural transformation in the diaspora tells us this. It tells us, for example, that fragments of African cultures live on, in a very real way, in the Americas, and that sometimes these fragments are transformed into "Africa," a powerful symbolic presence in the face of oppression. The important question, of course, is how to interpret this phenomenon, this "survival" and transformation, and, equally importantly, its absence.

The first, most obvious, and most important point to note is that slave regimes and the experience of slavery in the eighteenth and nineteenth centuries were immensely variable,[12] and that following from this was considerable variation in the degree to which any social memory of "home" could be produced and reproduced. Variability characterized slavery even within a particular region, such as North America. Despite a shared legal framework and many other common historical factors, there was no one, completely generalizable experience of the North American plantation regime. As much recent research has shown, the choice of crop—and the labor regime that accompanied each crop—was one very important factor (Berlin and Morgan 1993; Morgan 1998). Labor regimes may not be completely determining, but they clearly have profound social and cultural consequences, as we shall see. Tobacco and sugar, for example, make different demands. The gender and generational division of labor might have an important effect on slave family life. The extent to which slaves were self-provisioning (Berlin and Morgan 1991), or were hired out, was variable and significant. Moving into a wider comparative perspective, the most frequently noted and thoroughly analyzed difference is that between the demographic regimes of the Caribbean sugar islands, and that of the North American tobacco plantations. There are differences between slave societies dominated by large, sometimes absentee owners, and those dominated by small resident ones. Following from this are differences in the degree of social distance between slave owner and slave. There are of course significant differences between urban and agricultural slavery, even within the same region. The slave experience in colonial Louisiana, for example, was not a completely uniform one (Hall 1992).

Last, but not least, is the question of the histories and identities African (and in the case of Île de France, Malagasy and Indian) slaves brought with them. Here the nature and organization of the slave trade are clearly important. Some slave-owning societies drew on multiple and varied sources for their slaves, while others relied more heavily on one or two areas of slave export. Gwendolyn Hall describes a situation in colonial Louisiana in which at least two-thirds of African slaves came from Senegambia, and from a limited number of cultural groups there. This allows her to argue that the "Louisiana experience calls into question the common assumption that African slaves could not regroup themselves in language and social communities derived from the sending cultures" (1992, 159).

Louisiana, like Île de France, was a French possession in the first half of the eighteenth century, and there is much in the situation described by Hall (including the legal framework) that resonates with the Île de France experience. But in terms of the sources of slaves and the degree of cultural homogeneity among them, the two places could hardly be more different. As we have already noted, slaves imported to Île de France in the eighteenth century came from a wide variety of sources, and though Malagasies dominated in the period up to 1769 (constituting roughly 70 percent of imports) and Eastern Africans from 1770 to 1810 (around 60 percent), these figures, as Richard Allen (2001) points out, disguise a more complex story. Île de France was unusual in having a significant minority of slaves from India—more than reached Île Bourbon in the same period (Allen 2001, 2002a). The small population of West African slaves was, as we have noted, socially and economically significant. Furthermore, the generic term *Mozambiques*, used to describe slaves exported from the coast of East Africa, disguised the very diverse origins of this group (Alpers 2001).

The degree of cultural and ethnic diversity (or homogeneity) among slaves in any given place must, of course, be important, but this is only one factor in the creation of the new culture. As Philip Morgan writes in his study of black culture in eighteenth-century Chesapeake Bay and the South Carolina and Georgia Low Country, "the creation of a coherent culture was the most important act of resistance" of a slave community (1998, xxii). But, as he also points out, this process (if and when it occurred) was full of contradictions. The Chesapeake area produced tobacco, but it was also characterized by a degree of economic diversity and a varied work regime. Here slaves tended to live in small quarters, practiced crafts, and were surrounded by whites. The Low Country, by contrast, was archetypal plantation country. The work regime here was so harsh that the slave population did not reproduce itself until the second half of the eighteenth century. Slaves here lived at a greater physical and social distance from whites, who were fewer in number than in the Chesapeake. They had a greater chance of staying on one plantation or in one neighborhood throughout their lives, and of developing a distinct black culture. Morgan concludes that "material relations and communal autonomy appear to have been inversely related in these two regions" (101).

Île de France in the eighteenth century may have shared some of the characteristics of the diversified economy of the Chesapeake, but in terms of its demography it was probably more like the Low Country plantation country, with its very slow rate of slave reproduction. Demographic creolization came late to Île de France, where harsh material conditions and undernutrition dominated the lives of both slaves and "poor whites." Population growth rested on continued slave imports, and herein lies another contradiction. While the constant arrival of new slaves must have kept the memory of "home" (Africa, Madagascar, and India) alive, the high death rates and low rates of natural increase probably made the creation and reproduction of a distinct slave culture very difficult. As Richard Price has written, with reference to the Americas, "while the kinds of principles that structured the social and cultural worlds of early Afro-Americans, and the processes of institution building may have been broadly similar throughout the hemisphere, the relative importance of particular principles and of particular processes in any particular place differed considerable according to a number of variables" (1979, 144).

The packets of roots that Diamante had given Adonis and which he kept up his shirtsleeves clearly are important. They may be important because they really did protect him against the violence of his master and of slavery, and they may have been important as a kind a mnemonic device, keeping alive the memory of Madagascar. But the roots work only when they are mixed with food and water, because they are ingredients in a set of *practices*; culture is practice, not packets, and can live only when practiced and shared. Adonis and Diamante shared the roots, shared the practices, and enacted them together. The opportunity to practice or perform must be central to any understanding of "cultural survivals," but simultaneously, every performance, and particularly a performance in a new setting, transforms the object and subject of the practice. Herein lie the multiple and ever-changing roots of a creolized culture.

Adonis and Diamante's "roots" lay in the complex, layered, and already creolized culture of Madagascar.[13] There can be no simple tale of origins here, as arguably there never is. Stephan Palmié has recently made this point very forcefully, arguing against what he calls the "theme park approach" to African source cultures (Palmié 2002a, 159). It is legitimate, however, to ask some "roots"-type questions, not least because the alternative would, arguably, contribute further to the erasure in Mauritian culture and society of the contribution of thousands of slaves like Adonis and Diamante who came from Madagascar and Africa. Slaves were never *just* slaves on Île de France; they were identified, in part, through an ascribed ethnicity. Their "traditions" were invented simultaneously with their being deprived of their histories. The procedure in the courtroom makes this clear—and reflects a wider practice of ethnic pigeonholing.[14] Since slave traders, slave owners, and colonial administrators believed that they knew and could recognize, distinct attributes in their invented ethnicities, these categories assumed their own reality. In the courtroom, Adonis and Diamante were not just slaves, they were Malgaches. Furthermore, Diamante was a slave belonging to the king (arguably a kind of ethnic category in its own way), and he was, in what we take to be his own words, an "Ambolambe." The court would have been satisfied with "Malgache" as a response to the question of which caste or ethnic group he belonged to, but occasionally slaves offered their own, more specific answers. But what did "Ambolambe" mean? Tracing the genesis of Diamante's answer takes us into the complex history of Madagascar.

The Malgaches on Île de France came from the *grande île*, as it was known, a source not only of slaves but also of foodstuffs, and the object of French envy.[15] Despite doomed colonizing enterprises, the French had still not given up their attempts at colonial domination of Madagascar in the eighteenth century.[16] Indeed, at the time of Adonis's and Diamante's trials, the French were employing as their agent in Madagascar a Polish count, Count Benyowsky, in an attempt to extend their influence there.[17] Madagascar was the stuff of colonial dreams (and nightmares) and retained its fascination to outsiders through the nineteenth century and into the twentieth. Fascination produces fantasy, and Madagascar, real or imagined has it all, from Indonesian boatmen to "Arab" sailors and traders; it has "light-skinned" people with "straight" hair and "dark-skinned" people with "woolly" hair; it has its own unique language; it has a script—it has beautiful princesses and bloodthirsty monarchs, pirates, astrologers, lemurs, delicate textiles, elaborate mortuary rites, and famous anthropologists to document them.[18]

This fascination with the cultural and "racial'" complexity of Madagascar is evident from eighteenth-century and early-nineteenth-century written accounts of Malagasy slave culture on Île de France. The painter and traveler Jacques Milbert, for example, wrote that the population of Madagascar was made up of "a combination of several peoples (*nations*)," and that Malagasy material culture (as it manifested itself on Île de France) was evidence of a "high degree of intelligence" (1812, 2:165). He describes the clothing and jewelry worn by Malagasies on Île de France, their elaborate hair braiding,[19] their attachment to their "talismans," their carved *sagayes*. He mentions, in addition, two distinct Malagasy groups on the island—the free "Marmites" (of whom more later), who were traders in slaves and foodstuffs, tall and "without a trace of negroid features of their neighbors of the African coast"; and the Muslims, "who practice circumcision." Reflecting prevailing notions of cultural hierarchies, Milbert argued that the "advanced" nature of Malagasy culture could be accounted for by their having been "enlightened" through contact with the Arabs. Bernardin de St. Pierre was similarly impressed, both by the "non-negroid" features of many Malagasy slaves ("These people do not have a nose as squashed nor the skin as black as the negroes from Guinea" [2002, 128]) and by their sensitivity in "matters of honor and gratitude." Yet this admiration for aspects of Malagasy culture was always balanced by a frisson of fear—it was Malagasy slaves who were held to be the most prone to escape and become maroons (a belief not entirely borne out by the available statistics on *marronnage*),[20] it was Malagasies who set sail in boats bound for their homeland (sometimes successfully), and it was Malagasy women who were most often accused of aborting or killing their babies. Malagasies, it was thought, did not like being subject to slavery and would do almost anything to escape. This earned them a degree of respect.

Importantly, Madagascar was recognized to have "aristocracies" into which Europeans sometimes married for strategic and other reasons.[21] One such aristocrat became a prominent figure on Île de France in the 1740s: Princess Betsy, whose story indicates the role Madagascar played in the French imagination.

In a letter home in 1745, Baron Grant, a French habitant on Île de France, recounted a story that was rapidly taking the shape of a myth (Grant 1801, 220–221). According to Grant, a French man of noble origin, M. Grenville de Forval, had been doing business in Madagascar when he became the subject of a plot. Unbeknownst to him, a local chief with whom he had been negotiating planned to kill him. He learned of the plot when he "received an unexpected visit from a most beautiful woman, a native of the island, who after a short apology for her intrusion, expressed her concern that so fine a white man as himself should be murdered. . . . The sooty lady, who appeared to interest herself so much in his welfare, was the daughter of a King and known by the title of Princess Betsy."

She had heard, apparently, of a plan to kill him, but she would tell him details of this only under one condition. This condition was that he should take her with him to Île de France and make her his wife: "I will sacrifice for you the throne of my father, which is my inheritance. I will abandon my country, my friends, my customs and that liberty which is so dear to me. My relations, who will consider me dishonored, will detest me, and if you leave me to their vengeance, I shall be reduced to slavery which, to me, would be a thousand times worse than death."

Whether or not Princess Betsy actually said these words, what is relevant here is the ascription to her of an innate sense of honor and nobility, a fear of the loss of freedom. De Forval, according to Grant, agreed to her condition, escaped death and Madagascar, and brought Princess Betsy back with him to Île de France, where "in spite of the remonstrances of his friends, he lives happily with her." As Grant makes clear, there *were* objections to her because "her colour was certainly displeasing to the white people and her education did not qualify her to be a companion to such a man as her husband." However, she did have some compensating characteristics: "Her figure was fine, her air noble, and all her actions partook of the dignity of one who was born to command." She was, in other words, of the right social class, even if she was the wrong color. From this point on, Grant's description of her becomes more complex:

> She was a real Amazon, and the dress she chose was that which has since received a similar name. She never walked out but that she was followed by a slave, and armed with a fowling-piece, which she knew how to employ with great dexterity, and would defend herself with equal courage if she were attacked. She was nimble as a deer, though stately in her demeanour, but with her husband as gentle and submissive as the most affectionate of slaves. She behaved with her inferiors with equal dignity and kindness, and she never went to the most distant part of the island . . . but on foot, she nevertheless adopted the elegancies and behaviour with great facility, and her society is very pleasant and full of vivacity.

Princess Betsy was clearly a skilful diplomat, successfully walking a tightrope in Île de France elite society. She was "naturally" noble, yet she knew her place; she was "born to command" and was accompanied at all times by her slave, but she was also a "gentle and submissive" slave to her husband; she walked everywhere (while elite white women would have been carried in palanquins), but she did so without sacrificing "elegance." There is more than a hint of androgyny in Grant's description: she was an

"Amazon" (one would like to know what her "Amazonian" dress, which started a fashion, looked like), she went armed (albeit only with a small fowling-piece), and she knew how to defend herself. She was everything —black, but not too black, noble (yet submissive when appropriate), feminine and masculine. She was a powerful figure through which the French represented Madagascar to themselves.

In fact, Princess "Betsy," as we know from other sources, was the daughter of Ratsimilaho (Larson 2000, 62), the famous king of the Betsimisaraka people, whom she succeeded five years after Grant wrote his description. As the *Dictionary of Mauritian Biography* points out, this made her the granddaughter of a pirate, Tom Tew. Her reign as queen was compromised by her close relations with the French, and she faced a major revolt by her people that led her into permanent exile on Île de France, where she acquired property, was baptized and naturalized, and died in 1792.[22]

Milbert was right in his assertion that Malagasy culture was a combination or amalgam of influences. It was in fact a complex, historically layered and unique amalgam of influences from Africa, Southeast Asia, South Asia, Arabia, and Europe (Evers and Spindler, 1995). It was a culture of long-term creolization, and far from static—particularly in the eighteenth century. In the words of the historian Pier Larson, "There were no 'traditional' social structures in late eighteenth century highland Madagascar" (2000, 115). This was a period in which an internally generated process of political centralization in Madagascar was being intensified through the presence of foreigners, the stimulus of the slave trade, and the supply of firearms to Malagasy rulers. It was a period of ethnic and political transformation, in which weaker groups were being absorbed by the more powerful, sometimes peaceably, but much more frequently through force.

Long-distance trade in general, and the slave trade in particular, had a long history in Madagascar. Though the European powers of the eighteenth century might like to think of the Indian Ocean as their "theater," in truth they are a footnote to a much longer history.[23] For some time Madagascar had been both an importer and exporter of slaves. In the seventeenth century, for example, Malagasies were exported as slaves to the Persian Gulf, to Batavia, to Pondichéry and to the Americas (where they were apparently valued for the skill as rice cultivators; see Gomez 1998), as well as to the Dutch colony of Mauritius and to the Cape; at the same time Africans were being imported from the Swahili coast to form a sizeable community on the northwest coast of the island.[24] Larson has shown that in the first two-thirds of the eighteenth century most of the Malagasy slaves exported to Île de France came from the eastern coastal strip, victims of conflicts among coastal chiefdoms. External trade here, as on the African continent in this period, was a critical element in local politics. In this case it played a role in the rise of the Betsimisaraka chiefly confederation. But political conflict and increased demand for slaves did not always and everywhere have identical effects, as Larson shows. In this case, escalating conflict in the eastern region in the late eighteenth century led chiefs to hold on to slaves as a form of ransom, rather than to sell them. French traders and their intermediaries now moved further inland to the densely populated highlands. Here competing sovereigns were seeking to expand their kingdoms and increase their wealth. Conflict led to the taking of captives who, rather than being retained, were readily sold, by the thousands, to slave traders. By 1777, when Adonis and Diamante came to court, Larson estimates that some two-thirds of the slaves exported from the east coast came, like them, from the highlands.

In the nineteenth century, the highlands from which so many of the slaves were drawn would become synonymous with the Merina kingdom, but this was a process still under way in the late eighteenth century. Diamante represents this process in a way, since he identifies himself (or, possibly, is identified by the Malagasy courtroom interpreter) as an Ambolambe. Examining what this ethnic "root" or ethnonym means is revealing, not only of Malagasy history in this period, but of the complexities of following a "roots" route in the history of slavery.

Ambolambe (or, more accurately, *Amboalambo*) designated an ethnic group that would later form a part of the Merina kingdom (Larson 1996, 549–550). But the nature of this ethnicity is obscure. It appears to have been a term used by lowland groups to designate highlanders and may have had derogatory overtones (Larson 2000, 24). It is possible that the court interpreter, Nicolas L'Éveille, ascribed this identity to Diamante, though it is equally possible that this was a self-ascription. Not everyone agrees that *Amboalambo* had negative overtones—it might also be a term designating an itinerant group of merchants. An eighteenth-century source (Nicolas Mayeur) refers to the Amboalambo as synonymous with the Hova.[25] But this does not help a great deal, since the term *Hova* presents its own interpretive problems (Larson 2000, 24–25).

These questions seem important if we want to reconstruct something of the "packet" of cultural practices with which the slaves Adonis and Diamante arrived on Île de France. Since the Amboalambo would later form part of the Merina kingdom, and since the practices of the Merina in the nineteenth century are very well documented, the temptation is to project backward some of the remarkable features of Merina culture and society and ascribe them to the earlier groups from which the kingdom was constructed. But anthropologists and historians of Madagascar have convincingly argued that some of the features of the Merina kingdom (and indeed, those of other groups such as the Sakalava) may not have been age-old practices, but rather *responses* to the depredations and excesses of the slave trade in precisely the period we are dealing with here.[26] This makes it hazardous to guess at the content of the Amboalambo ethnicity. The "theme-park" approach to this history will not work (Palmié 2002, 159). In a revised account, then, slavery becomes integral to any analysis of cultural "roots," not only because slavery may have contributed to the destruction of certain key features of society, and to cultural amnesia about others, but also because slavery and the slave trade may have been central to the creation and construction of the cultural "roots" with which Adonis, Diamante, and others traveled.[27] This, as we shall see, is true of other parts of the slave-exporting world in this period, and not only of Madagascar.[28]

The society or societies from which Adonis and Diamante came were dynamic and complex. An interaction of internal and external factors had produced warfare, political centralization, and ethnic re-creation. The slave trade was both cause and consequence of this process. Scholars of Madagascar are somewhat divided on the extent of social hierarchy and rigidity within Malagasy society, and over how far our perception of this is colored by European observers' fascination with this feature.[29] In highland Madagascar, "kingdoms and chiefdoms, social rank, descent, judicial and religious office, debt, gender and generation formed dense and cross-cutting networks of patronage, obligation and deference" (Larson 2000, 89). But there is great diversity within Madagascar, and some Malagasy societies are determinedly egalitarian and nonhierarchical.[30] Following from this, Malagasy models of personhood and agency range from the highly inclusive and fluid to the most rigid and castelike (Middleton 1999). Equally disputed is the question of how far social hierarchies were constructed around and marked by a "racial" discourse. In the Malagasy language, *mainty* (a word that can be translated as "black") apparently equates directly with servant or slave (*andevo*) status (Ramanantsoa Ramarcel 1997; Randriamaro 1997).[31] Whether marked by "blackness" or not, slaves of African origin occupied an ambiguous position within Malagasy society by the nineteenth century, as evidenced by the history of the Makua communities on the island.

There are layers of African influence in Malagasy society, some very long-term (the earliest Southeast Asian settlers undoubtedly passed through the East African coast) and some more recent. The extent and importance of the African heritage is a subject of dispute,[32] but interaction with the societies of the East African coast was a constant of Malagasy history. Among the more recent African immigrants are groups of Makua, who probably first came as slaves in the seventeenth century (Dina 1997; Alpers 2001), becoming, by the nineteenth century, a clan of the Sakalava people, and still evident as distinct communities today. According to Dina, the position of Sakalava "masters" toward the Makua changed depending on circumstance—at times they were assimilated, at other times (such as during a succession dispute) their difference was remembered and marked. Some were sold into the highlands, where they became more generally and generically known as Masombiky (or Mozambiques); others were kept at court, constituting a kind of praetorian guard and benefiting from a number of privileges. This oscillation between assimilation and distancing, and the ambiguous position of the Makua slave, probably became less ambiguous in the nineteenth century when, in Merina society at least, more impregnable barriers to social mobility began to be erected. According to Françoise Raison-Jourde, this increasing social rigidity (formalized by statute in some cases) was masked by the language of kinship and family applied to the condition of slavery: "The slaves saw then their theoretical social nothingness robed and veiled in a 'parentalization' that transformed them into protected and potentially disobedient children" (1997, 121; Evers 1995). When he referred to himself as a "child" in relation to the judge, Adonis was making use of this mask of kinship through infantilization. Whether the judge would have understood or been susceptible to this appeal, we do not know.

Kinship, in the form of belonging to a lineage, was, at least by the nineteenth century, central to Malagasy notions of autonomy, freedom, and the very concept of being a person. This was true of many African societies, too, and its relevance for our understanding of African forms of slavery has been widely discussed (Kopytoff and Miers 1977; Lovejoy 1983; Falola and Lovejoy 1994; Glassmann 1995). Tellingly, Makua slaves apparently referred to themselves as "those who did not know their maternal uncles" (Dina 1997, 162), a reference both to the loss of kinship continuity implicit in slavery, and to the continued importance to them (in memory at least) of matrilineality. In a sense this sums up the tragic contradiction in which they found themselves—they had forgotten the names of their maternal uncles, but they still remembered that knowing the name of your maternal uncle was important.[33]

Makua slaves also, of course, turned up as "Mozambiques" on Île de France, directly imported from the East African coast (though it is also possible that some Makua came in the guise of "Malgaches").[34] Makua may have been stereotyped as "blue," which also translates as "black," and as *mainty*, which, in an elaboration of meaning can be translated as *les grains de riz qui connaissent le coeur des marmites* (the grains of rice which have come to know the bottom of the cooking pots). And this brings us to another feature of the experience of Malagasy slaves on Île de France in the eighteenth century: the continual traffic between that island and the "grand île."

On Île de France the word *marmite* not only meant "cooking pot," but also referred to a social group—Malagasy traders in slaves and other commodities. These *Marmites* were intermediaries in the trade with Madagascar and perhaps also acted as independent traders. Milbert saw them around on Île de France and referred to them as "valets" of Europeans (1812, 2:165). They are also referred to more casually (and perhaps therefore more reliably) in police reports.[35] By the nineteenth century, the term *maromita* on Madagascar apparently referred to slaves who were used as porters. These maromita developed a collective identity and sense of community, practicing a kind of blood brotherhood that compensated for their lack of ancestral links (Campbell 1980, 348–350). In the eighteenth century, it was not only the *Marmites* who moved between the two islands. Malagasy slaves frequently stole boats and set sail for their birth island, sometimes taking other, non-Malagasy slaves with them.

Enslavement, for some, was a repeated process. In 1790, for example, the slave ship *La Fitte* was trading at Rangaravan on the coast of Madagascar. A group of coastal Malagasies (referred to in the report as *noirs de la côte*) approached the captain with captives (two "Mozambiques" and two "Malgaches"), which they sold to him. No sooner had he paid for them, however, than the captain was informed by his Marmites that the "Mozambique" slaves were speaking French. When interrogated, the "Mozambiques" claimed that they had been abducted from Île de France by fellow slaves, who were Malagasies and who had murdered their master and stolen his boat. They declared themselves "happy" to be returned to their original masters.[36] This constant traffic (both voluntary and involuntary), the presence on Île de France of Marmites, and of other Malagasies of free birth (figures such as Princess Betsy, the Merina King, Andrianampoinimerina,[37] and famous interpreters such as Nicolas Mayeur), combined with the French fascination with the island of Madagascar, meant that Adonis and Diamante were probably never without news of their birth island and its politics. The high death rate among Île de France slaves also may have had paradoxical effects on their ability to keep in touch with their "roots," ever-changing as they were. Each boatload brought another group of people like Adonis and Diamante with their packets of "roots" ready to put into practice given the opportunity; each boatload brought news and reminders, and the potential to keep Madagascar alive in this new place.[38]

We will never know exactly what was in the "packets" Adonis and Diamante brought with them, but we do know enough to make some generalizations. As Paul Lovejoy and David Trotman have recently argued about the Atlantic world of slavery, Africans brought with them into slavery experiences and "expectations" that may have helped shaped their experience of the New World.[39] In the case of Adonis and Diamante, we know that they came from an island with a complex and varied culture composed of many different elements, some completely naturalized, some of which retained their distinctiveness. This included a highly developed and sophisticated material culture. They came from a society in which slavery, if not yet a "total social fact," was certainly an integral part. This does not in any sense mean that they were familiar with or easily habituated to the new kind of slavery to which they were subjected on Île de France, but it is an important fact nevertheless. Related to the prevalence of slavery (but not coextensive with it) was the fact that some Malagasy societies displayed a very acute consciousness of social distinction, difference, and hierarchy. Related to this was the importance of kinship, of knowledge and acknowledgment of one's ancestors. This may both have made enslavement particularly painful (Malagasy slaves were, it was said, terrified of dying away from their kin and the tombs of their ancestors) and have simultaneously made it survivable, since Malagasy slaves almost certainly brought their ancestors with them in the form of spirits.[40]

Rice in the Cooking Pot

Though Madagascar is in many ways unique, this story of complexity and of prior creolization is, to a greater or lesser degree, true of many of the regions from which slaves were exported to Île de France in the eighteenth century—the Swahili coast of East Africa, the south of India, the west coast of Africa.[41] These were all areas of long-term cultural exchange and interaction. They were also areas in which ethnic identities (never a simple matter) might at the same time be clearly marked (sometimes physically on the body, in the form of scarification) and fluid and transformable. Within a lifetime, as we know from the life histories of slaves in Africa, one individual could be captured, partially assimilated into a family, sold again, assimilated again, exported, treated at one moment as little more than a trade good, at another as a cherished member of an adoptive community. Such transformations, we should always remember, were imposed on slaves. This is not the place in which to celebrate the fluidity of identities and *creolité*, but a place in which to document the often painful process of identification and disidentification that was central to the condition of slavery.

As in the case of Malagasy slaves, in the case of West African slaves on Île de France ethnicity was complex, both at its origins on the continent, and in its transformations under slavery. Slaves of West African origin, as we have seen, formed a significant proportion of the total slave population in the early part of the century, and were favored as Company and then royal slaves. The Lazarist priest Caulier in 1772 divided them into five categories: "Guinées, Joloffs, Bambaras, Senegaliens, Widaliens."[42] Earlier correspondence from the 1730s to 1750s mentions "Wolofs," "Bambaras," and "Guinées" (which sometimes appears as a generic term for West Africans). In his account of the evolution of the French creole language on the island, Philip Baker mentions that by the time of the 1761 census, the terms *Bambara* and *Wolof* had disappeared, to be replaced by *Guinée* (Baker and Corne 1982, 180). Yet as late as 1802, Milbert described a group of "Wolof" slaves, complete with body markings: a large sun shape tattooed on the stomach (1812, 11:163). Milbert is generally held to be mistaken, since no "Wolof" slaves had been imported for some time, but this depends on how one regards the possibilities for reproduction and reinvention of ethnicities on the island.

Caulier's list of what he calls "tribes" or "castes" includes some that are simply designations of a general region, or the port of export. *Widaliens*, for example, refers to the port of Ouidah in Dahomey, and *Guinées* could mean any slave exported from the Guinée coast. We are left, then, with two apparently more exact ethnic labels: *Wolof* and *Bambara*. But, predictably perhaps, neither of these labels can be relied upon to lead us to an ethnic or cultural "root"—they lead us, rather, to a process.

The present-day Bambara occupy the upper Niger in Mali, and there is a significant literature on their history and culture. But as both Philip Curtin (1975) and, more recently, Peter Caron (Caron 1997; see also Berlin 1996) have argued, in the context of the eighteenth-century slave trade, *Bambara* could mean a great number of things. In Senegambian French of the eighteenth century it sometimes designated those who spoke Malinke, or those from the interior (particularly if they performed the role of soldiers); it might mean that they were ethnically Bambara, or that they were captives of the Bambara from other ethnic groups. *Bambara* might also refer generally to non-Muslims. Caron goes further, arguing that *Bambara* in the eighteenth century sometimes simply designated "slave" (Caron 1997, 100); this was the use it often had, apparently, on the island of Gorée, one of the major slave export ports for Île de France. Caron believes it likely, in fact, that many "Bambara" were not from "up country" at all, but were of littoral Senegambian origin and possible former slaves of the Fulbe.[43]

To a lesser degree the same complications arise in trying to locate the origins of the "Wolof" slaves, which the Company brought to Île de France and who were given a particular role and status within the slave regime there. There is no shortage of information on the nature of Wolof polity and society in the seventeenth and eighteenth centuries and, thanks to the work of historians, we also have sophisticated analyses of change within that society and the effects of the slave trade (Curtin 1975, Barry 1988, Searing 1993). As in the case of the "Bambara," however, it seems likely that many of the "Wolof" slaves on Île de France were captives from other groups—the Sereer, for example, or more generally, coastal peoples. Whether or not the "Bambara" and the "Wolof" of Île de France were Bambara and Wolof, what we can say with some certainty is that they came from a region with a long history of statecraft, of Islamic influence, some from societies that displayed intricate systems of social stratification and which, in the eighteenth century, experienced (either as aggressors or as victims) a high degree of military conflict. In this context ethnicity was only one part of a complex jigsaw of social differentiation.

Wolof society, for example, exhibited a tripartite division between the freeborn, those who were members of specific "castes," and slaves, but Barry (1988) and others have argued that this was a feature of most Senegambian societies, irrespective of ethnicity. The Wolof caste system displayed a classic combination of discrimination, taboo, and ambiguity. Hence members of the blacksmith caste were regarded as both powerful and a source of danger. Though technically caste members occupied a rung in the social ladder beneath that of all free persons, in practice the situation was more complex. In some circumstances the lower echelons of the free population, consisting of poorer peasants, had fewer social privileges than caste members. Similarly, within the category of slave there was also a hierarchy, with war captives lying at the bottom. The upper echelons of the slave category, the royal slaves, were a privileged and potentially powerful group, just as the equivalent group was in some Malagasy states. There was also a strong warrior tradition in Senegambia, which gave rise in the eighteenth century to the Wolof autocratic and militaristic *ceddo* regimes (themselves in part a consequence of the effects of the slave trade). Though conflict might be ethnicized in this region, often it is difficult, if not impossible, to disentangle this from religious conflict. Jihads and conflicts between Moslems and non-Moslems constituted one of the dynamics producing slaves to be sold to the French. In this context ethnic identities might follow from rather than be prior to religious identifications. In any case, the two were so closely connected that the term *Bambara*, for example, might designate a non-Muslim. Add to the religious differences and religious hierarchies an age-grade system and a kinship system, and one can begin to think that the Wolof might have regarded the society of ancien régime France as simple and egalitarian in its structure.

The French were not, of course, the first Europeans to have engaged with the peoples of Senegambia. The earlier Portuguese presence there in the seventeenth century had produced a significant Afro-Portuguese elite and groups specialized in the Atlantic trade (Curtin 1975, Berlin 1996). The French presence in its turn also produced an important Afro-French creole community, which would evolve further under colonial rule in the nineteenth century (Biondi 1987). The French in Senegambia helped create specialist occupational groups, some of which later found their way to Île de France. The *laptots*, for example, were specialist sailors, normally domestic slaves owned by the wealthy of St. Louis and rented out. According to Curtin, the word derives from the Wolof for sailor, but in time it shifted to mean any African who worked for the Europeans (Curtin 1975, 114). Pierre-Félix David, who was governor of Île de France in the 1740s, had previously been governor of Senegal and was keen to exploit this group in his new setting.[44]

Similar processes had been at work on the southern coast of India, from which a small but significant minority of Île de France slaves were drawn. Here there had been centuries of international traffic and interaction (Bayly 1989); here too, religious identities were important. Slaves from south India were usually referred to on Île de France as Malabars, which might also imply that they were Muslims. Another group, the Lascars, included both free and unfree.[45] In early-eighteenth-century Île de France "Lascar" was both an occupational and a religious category. As we have seen, the first "Lascars" to arrive on the island were not slaves, but technically free Muslim sailors imported by governor Labourdonnais in the 1730s as skilled alternatives to more expensive French labor. Their insistence on practicing their religion caused deep offense to the clergy on the island, but Labourdonnais and subsequent governors valued them highly and defended their right to a degree of religious freedom.[46] The colonial commentator Moreau de St. Méry, however, was insistent that *Lascar* was "the name of a profession and not of a People," comparing them, tellingly, to the "Jews of Europe." But "Lascar" was in fact a category originating in an earlier period of interaction between the peoples of India and Europeans, in this case the Portuguese. Arab traders and navigators, supported by west Asian trading peoples, had spread the Sufi tradition of the Islamic faith along the southern coast of India from the eighth or ninth centuries A.D., while elite groups of Sunni Muslims dominated the maritime towns and trading centers of the region (Bayly 1989, 73–79). When, from the late fifteenth century, the Portuguese founded their trading stations and settlements on the coast of South India, they found Asian Muslims dominating trade in conjunction with ruling Hindus. Groups such as the Lascars were the product of this and earlier interactions—they arrived into the new context of French eighteenth-century colonialism with a long and varied history behind them.

In addition to the Muslim Lascars, there may well have been Christians among the early Indians recruited or enslaved to work on Île de France (Carter 1988–1989, 242; Moutou 1996). Christianity in South India also predated the Portuguese by many centuries, and these Syrian Christian communities were obvious, though contested, allies of the Portuguese (Bayly 1989, chap. 7). More straightforwardly the product of Portuguese influence in South India was another group that also cropped up in Île de France—the so-called Topas. The Topas, or Topasses, were a Eurasian population, mostly of the Catholic faith, and mostly of mixed Portuguese and Tamil origin. They had a reputation for military prowess and featured noticeably in the armies of southern India (Bayly 1989, 395; Weber 1993).

Taken together, the histories of Madagascar, Senegambia, and southern India suggest the complex cultural "roots" of many of the slaves of Île de France. All of these regions of export had been affected by layers of external influence (most notably Arab and Portuguese, but also, in the case of Madagascar, the multicultural pirates), and out of these interactions had emerged some social groups (e.g., the Laptots, Lascars, and Topas) with specialized roles in trade, particularly in seafaring. The Islamic religion was an important (but not uniform) presence in all of these regions, and religious identities were as important as, or coterminous with, ethnic identities. All of these regions exhibited great social complexity and a layering of influences, some of which had become naturalized locally (such as Islam, and possibly Hinduism in Madagascar) and some which retained the label of foreign. Many of these societies were characterized by strong notions of social hierarchy. Of course, the caste systems of India, Madagascar, and Senegambia are not easily comparable, and indeed, this feature of these societies may well have been exaggerated by later commentators, but they do remind us that slaves came with their own sets of perceptions of superiority/inferiority, of inclusion and exclusion, of difference (sometimes marked on the body), of the legitimate and illegitimate exercise of power. In some cases the ambiguous institution of slavery was central to this. West African and Malagasy came from societies in which slave status could produce both social stigma and social advantages. Though there were many ambiguities in the system of slavery that would dominate them in Île de France, this was not one of them—social stigma was not accompanied by power.

One of the most important features of the slave population of Île de France was its diversity. While some slaves, as I have indicated, came from societies that were themselves diverse, stratified, and historically multi-layered, others, we must assume, were from more remote and isolated parts of the African interior. This is probably most true of some of those who were known generically as the Mozambiques and whose origins have been recently explored in a series of papers by Ned Alpers.[47] Certainly the trade in African slaves from East Central Africa had ancient roots (Ewald 2000), and the Swahili coast was nothing if not cosmopolitan, with a very long history of cultural interaction. But some of the Makua, Yao, Maravi, Sena or Makonde chained in slave ships bound for Île de France came from relatively remote agricultural communities in the interior. Isolation is a relative concept. Historians of this part of Africa have gone to some lengths to demonstrate that there was movement, change, and process in these areas for centuries before the arrival of nineteenth-century commentators, yet there is no denying the many social and political differences between, for example, the decentralized matrilineal communities of the Nyanja (remnants of the Maravi Empire) and the highly stratified polities of, for example, the Wolof. A symptom of this relative isolation is the lack of written documentation for some of these areas until well into the nineteenth century. The slave trade was a brutal method of rapid integration into the world economy, and into the world of documentation. It is ironic, perhaps, that in his earlier pioneering work on the history of this region, Ned Alpers used the evidence collected from Mozambique slaves on Mauritius in the nineteenth century to reconstruct a picture of society and economy in the African interior from which they had been taken (Alpers 1975, 10–11).

Tracing the roots of Mozambique slaves is just as hazardous as it is for any other group.[48] What we can say, however, with a degree of certainty, is that many would have come from largely agricultural, largely matrilineal, and largely politically decentralized societies that were caught up in the conflicts generated by the slave trade and the advent of firearms. They also came from societies in which forms of bondage and pawnship were certainly known, but in which social hierarchies were in general much less marked than they were, for example, in parts of Senegambia or Madagascar.

Like all the other groups of slaves, the Mozambiques came with their own discourses of freedom, of servitude and subordination, inseparable from discourses of gender, of kinship, of political authority and religion. The Mozambiques also came from societies characterized by the push and pull of assimilation and fissure, by both the marking of difference and its elision. We know, for example, that the Yao, the foremost slave traders (along with the Makua) were a newish ethnicity in the eighteenth century, probably formed from elements of the old Maravi kingdom as it pushed east into Makua/Lomwe territory in present-day Mozambique (Alpers 1975; Vaughan 2000). The Yao distinguished themselves from the Nyanja, the Lomwe, the Makua, and other groups in the region. Oral testimony tells us that they traded with the coast, built square houses, and wore different clothes from other groups. But this was not an ethnic group with rigid boundaries—Nyanja and others "became" Yao, through intermarriage and through attachment to a powerful chief, through pawnship and bondage.

Here as elsewhere in the slave-exporting areas, there was a preexisting moral world of subordination, a set of discourses that legitimated the exercise of authority by one person over others. To differing degrees the slave trade and the militarization of politics that often went with it both fed on and radically distorted this morality: it fed on preexisting notions of hierarchy and the ultimate subordination of the individual to the life of the group; at the same time, the violence and greed associated with the trade distorted the countervailing tendency of all these societies toward assimilation. The "morality of slavery," the discourses that determined how some categories of person would be both subordinated and assimilated, while others would be subordinated and then elevated, and yet others subordinated and sold—these moral discourses, presumably never static, were inevitably thrown into greater contention by the export trade and the dictates of the market. African societies here as elsewhere wrestled with the huge moral dilemmas the slave trade and conflict and violence brought with them. Larson (2000) has argued that this internal debate on slavery and critique of the use and abuse of power was inherent to the politics of central Madagascar, and much African politics of the period can be interpreted in the same light.

Nothing in the cultural roots of slaves could have prepared them, however, for the horrors of the export trade. As the trader Brugevin recognized (see preface), the Yao of the East African interior, among whom there were many slave traders, when captured viewed the sight of a white man with such dread and terror that frequently they died even before they could be packed on disease-ridden ships. Those who made it through the horrors of the middle passage arrived on the island with a close knowledge of fear. Diamante's roots and powders were medicines against fear.

Roots in Action, Ethnicity in Process

One should not underestimate the influence of ethnicity on the lives of Africans in the Americas. But historians cannot invent ethnicities to distort the lens through which we must necessarily view early African captives. (Caron 1997, 106)

Whatever the internal politics of the societies from which they came, once captured, sold and exported, individual slaves faced a new situation, one in which, we must assume, their own moral discourses on slavery were subordinated and, perhaps, silenced. Nevertheless, it must be important to our imaginings of this new situation that we bear in mind that the cultural roots with which slaves came to Île de France included a package of practices around questions of subordination and the marking of differences and, on the other side of the coin, assimilation and accommodation.

African and Malagasy slaves, for example, in confronting each other on the island may have confronted radical differences and also have identified common characteristics. So too, Bambara slaves who, it seems likely, were non-Muslims, confronted the Muslim Wolofs, with whom they had shared a history of conflict. Nyanja or Maravi slaves from the Lake Nyasa region shared a new generic designation, "Mozambiques," with a group, the Yao, who would previously have been known to them less as slaves than as slave raiders. Between Yao and Nyanja in East and Central Africa, there were very close cultural affinities, including a clan system, enabling intermarriage and assimilation. But at the same time, in the context of the slave trade, there were sufficient markers of difference between them to justify, in some circumstances, the Yao in selling rather than assimilating their Nyanja captives. We do not know if, once on the island, the Muslim Wolofs found any cultural affinity with the Muslim Lascars from southern India, or whether other markers of difference, as well as the slave regime itself, prevented such identification. Neither do we know whether and how "Makua" slaves from Mozambique may have interacted with slaves of Makua ethnicity from Madagascar.

We do have, however, a few glimpses from the documentary record of ethnicity in action. For the most part, the record reveals that slaves of all origins and ethnicities lived and worked side by side—though, as I have already shown, there were some specialist groups (Wolof and Lascars, for example) whose somewhat separate identities were encouraged by the administration. But living together out of necessity rather than choice can of course bring its own tensions—this was hardly the "melting pot" of multiculturalist dreams. So, for example, the Lazarist priests (perhaps unreliably, but it should be noted nonetheless) alleged that there were tensions between Malagasy slaves and West African "Guinées": "The blacks of Madagascar cannot bear those of Guinée. It is believed that they will destroy each other."[49] More reliable, because more incidental, are snatches from court cases of the period. Malagasy slaves when captured as maroons often referred, very deliberately it seems, to their original Malagasy names and, in one case, to the "religion of my country." We know little about the choice of sexual and marriage partners among slaves (though there is more that could be done with existing records), but the Mozambique slave Pèdre, when accused of poisoning, certainly attempted to employ ethnicity in his defense. Pèdre denied that he had poisoned either Jean (a "creole" slave—meaning born on the island), or Jean's partner, Annette (a Malagasy) because he was jealous of their relationship, and of Jean's position as slave commander. Annette had apparently muttered the words "Pèdre Mozambique" and "patattes" (a reference to the supposed poisoned food she had eaten) on her deathbed. Pèdre was found guilty and sentenced to be strangled and then burned (note the difference between his fate and that of Adonis in the same year), but his last, unsuccessful, line of defense had been this: "He had had nothing against Jean," he said, "from the moment he had come to the habitation. He had never had any women other than those from his own country, and had never sought to have Annette, who was a Malagasy."[50]

This may have been both mischievous and desperate as a defense, but the fact that Pèdre thought it a plausible argument is itself significant. More mischievous and more successful was Cherubin, a Malagasy slave who, during the Revolutionary years, was accused of threatening various whites with a stick. Denying that he had had a stick in his hand, Cherubin declared to the Tribunal d'Appel that "No, he had had nothing but a small piece of bamboo which served as a Malagasy violin." He was found not guilty and freed.[51]

Meanwhile the slave system and the slow process of creolization proceeded. Some differences were elided, original languages lost; other differences were invented; cultural attributes were ascribed and renamed. I end with one example. Almost every eighteenth-century visitor commented on the Malagasies' apparently peculiar and particular fondness for amulets, which the French called *gris-gris*. But the entomology of *gris-gris* takes us on a tour that extends farther than Madagascar and back in time. *Gris-gris*, or *gri gri*, appears in a French dictionary first in 1557, referring to an evil spirit (from Guinée), then in 1637 as an idol representing the devil, and by 1637 as "un petit objet magique."[52] The word comes, almost certainly, from a West African language, but on Île de France, it acquires a Malagasy identity. This is creole culture in the making.

Chapter Five

One September morning in 1778, three soldiers were patrolling the salt pans on the edge of Port Louis when they spotted a "white object" floating close to the shore.[1] Bringing it to land, they soon realized that what they had found was not just a "white object" but a "white baby," wrapped in cloth. They reported this to their officers, who in turn reported it to the public prosecutor, who in turn instructed two judges to investigate. They were Nicolas Barbé de Marbois (who also featured in the case of Adonis and Diamante) and Jean Pierre Auffray, both eminent lawyers.[2] They arrived on the scene and reported that the body was that of a white baby girl (*une petite fille blanche*); she was lying on her back, wrapped in old pieces of cloth but otherwise naked, her hands and feet tied together. There were bruises on her thighs. Proper procedure demanded that the body be examined in situ by a surgeon. Benôit Gouly (who was later to play an important part in the island's Revolutionary politics) was called, but did not arrive immediately, and so the body was carried to the confines of the jail nearby. Gouly examined it in the evening. It was dark. A lamp was fetched. Gouly judged the baby to be "white," reckoned it to have been about one month old, and on the evidence of the pallor of the face and the lips, and the blood he found in the mouth, he concluded that the baby had been drowned alive within the previous twenty-four hours.

A white baby, drowned alive on the salt pans, occasioned a bit of a stir.

A few months earlier, in July 1778, the island's highest court (the Conseil Supérieur) had, "in the interest of laws of religion and of the state," reissued the seventeenth-century French regulations against abortion and infanticide, reminding islanders that the penalty for both was death.[3] As the prosecutor put it, a white baby found drowned, its hands and legs tied, taken together with the surgeon's report was enough to indicate a "horrific offense, and one calling for the application of the full severity of the law." Within two days, through the power of gossip, some suspects had been found.

Marie Louise was a Malagasy woman who lived within the confines of the jail. She was the slave of M. Blancheteste, the jailer, who often features in documentation of this period as a figure around whom much happens.[4] Marie Louise had probably seen the baby's body being brought to the jail for examination. At any event, she had a story to tell the investigating judge. The previous evening, she said, she and her friend Suzanne (also a Malagasy) had been eating their meal in Suzanne's hut when they had been interrupted by a woman whom Marie Louise described (with or without prompting we cannot know) as a *mulâtresse libre*. In the evolving racial terminology of the island, this indicated that the woman was both of free status and of "mixed" blood (part of that mixture being white). The recording of racial status was not unusual, but certainly not regular in Île de France documentation of this period. Racial categories were far from fixed, and the self-consciousness of those of part-white origin was in its early infancy. Race was marked when it mattered, and in this case it appeared to matter.

Marie Louise said that although she was acquainted with this mulâtresse libre, she did not know her name. This seems a little implausible given the small society in which the women of Port Louis lived, but, as we shall see, names were slippery commodities. Though she had not known her name, Marie Louise did know that the woman had given birth some eight days previously, and so she asked after the baby. The woman told her that her baby was dead, that a slave belonging to the king, whose name she did not know but who was jealous of her, had come and taken the baby while she was asleep and then had drowned it. "I did not ask her any more questions," said Marie Louise to the judge, "but hurried to tell my master what I had learned." And so M. Blancheteste had learned from his slave an identity, a possible or partial identity for the dead white baby.

Suzanne's story was slightly different. She was described as a *négresse*

FIGURE 2. The salt pans in Port Louis. From *Voyage pittoresque a l'Île de France*, by Jacques G. Milbert, 1812. Bodleian Library, University of Oxford, N 2.16. Art Seld. Plt. 39

de bazard (market slave) belonging to M. St Martin. She was one of the many slaves on the island whose official home was on a rural habitation (in this case in the region of Plaines Wilhems at the center of the island) but who spent most of her time in the Camp des Noirs in Port Louis, where she had a hut and from which she ran a small business for her master. Theoretically the Camp des Noirs was home to "free blacks" only, but in practice many slaves lived there, as did poorer whites and soldiers and sailors. The late-eighteenth-century attempts by Intendant Poivre and others to enforce residential segregation in Port Louis appear to have had little real effect. Suzanne said that she had been having dinner with Marie Louise when a mulâtresse had come to visit. She did not know her name, but she knew that she lived with a soldier. She had asked after the woman's baby, and she had replied that a slave woman called Catherine and a king's slave whose name she did not know, had come and stolen the child.

Though neither Marie Louise nor Suzanne had revealed the identity of the mulâtresse libre, mother of the baby stolen or drowned, it cannot have been too difficult to find someone like her. A woman was summoned to give evidence the same day. Her name was Thérèse. Thérèse may have been a mulâtresse libre to Marie Louise and Suzanne, but the lawyers described her as a *négresse Bengalie affranchie*—a freed slave of Bengali origin.[5] She had been freed, she said, by her former owner, now lover, Pautru, a soldier. She was about twenty years old. She said that nine days previously she had given birth to a baby, which was the "product" of

A Baby in the Salt Pans ❧ 125

her relationship with Pautru, but that after four days the baby had fallen sick with the "cramp" and had died, at four in the morning, in the arms of its father. The father of the baby, whom Thérèse refers to as Pautru, is identified in the records as Sebastien Aupot, a grenadier around fifty years old. No one's identity seems straightforward in late-eighteenth-century Port Louis.

Aupot, alias Pautru, said that on the sixth of the month he had asked permission from his superiors to spend the night with the woman whom he referred to confusingly as "Suzanne Henriette," but who was also known, he says, by the name of Thérèse. He described her as his freed slave, a *négresse bengalie*, who is also the "wife" of a man named Pauldrin, a *noir libre de détachement*. This meant that Pauldrin was one of those freed slaves of the king whom Governor Labourdonnais had first armed in the 1730s in his "guerre intestine" with the maroon slaves of the interior. Pauldrin was a maroon hunter. Sebastien Aupot said that a few days previously Thérèse had given birth to a baby girl, which he described as being *de couleur blanchâtre* (a "white" baby has now become a "whitish" baby), and that when he arrived at the hut the baby had seemed well, but later had begun to tremble all over and then had suffered a cramp and a closing up of the throat.[6] He had done what he could to help the baby, but seeing eventually that he could not save her, he had anointed her with holy water he found in the hut (a practice of which the Lazarist priests despaired and disapproved)[7] and that, after receiving what he called this "spiritual aid," the baby had died in his arms. He had placed the body on a chest and at about five-thirty in the morning had left for work. After work he had gone to see a carpenter, Maurice Bouton, to order a small coffin, but during his absence the négresses libres, the free black women of the neighborhood, had apparently come to visit the new mother and, finding the baby dead, had wrapped it in a shroud and had given it to a woman called Catherine, a *négresse de journée* (a slave hired out by the day) and to a male slave whose name he did not know, without waiting for the coffin. The two slaves were to have taken the body to the church and then for burial. Aupot had checked with the parish priest. The priest did indeed have a record of the death of the baby whose body, following custom, had been carried by him to the cross, but he did not know what had happened to the body after this.

Those whom Aupot described as the *négresses libres du voisinage*[8] were then brought to give evidence, along with Catherine, the slave woman to whom the body of the baby had apparently been entrusted. One négresse libre was Marie Signari, described as a midwife, of South Indian origin (of the Malabar caste) and aged around fifty years. She said that about ten days previously she had assisted Thérèse at the delivery of a baby. Thérèse, she said, was the wife of a "free black" called Paul (but also known as Sansouccy), but that three days later the baby had developed "cramp" and the next morning had died. She had then given to a "free black" called Pierre a piece of paper on which were written the names of the baby's mother and father, and she had told him to take the body to the church for burial. Agathe, a free woman of around seventy years old described as being of Chinese origin (*Chinoise de Nation*)[9] was also asked to give evidence. She said that as far as she could remember, the previous Monday she had gone to the hut of Thérèse, a free black woman, who had given birth some four days previously. She had found the baby dead, lying on a chest. She had dressed it in pieces of an old shirt which she had torn up for the purpose, and she had tied its hands and feet with bits of cloth. The body had then been given to Catherine, and to a king's slave of Mozambique caste, whom she described as a "real brute," to be taken to the priest and then to be buried.

Catherine, described as a slave of Bengali origin belonging to Louisa, a free black woman, was around twenty years old. She said that the previous day she had been called to the hut of Thérèse, whose baby had just died, and there Marie Signari had given her a ticket to present to the priests, along with the baby's body. She fulfilled her commission, she said, having taken the body to the church and then as far as the Corps de la Bute. From there she had indicated to the *noir Mozambique* (whose name she did not know) the route to the cemetery, and then she had gone back to work.

The case was dropped. In the estimation of the prosecutor, there was no case to be answered, there was no infanticide. If there was no case to be answered, the story of the enfant blanchâtre found dead in the salt pans nevertheless poses some questions—questions about mothers, fathers, and families, questions that point to what I call the family secrets of slavery.[10]

Babies and the Family Secrets of Slavery

A "white object" spotted by a group of soldiers is next recognized or misrecognized as a dead "white" baby. But new babies pose a challenge to every fantasy of racial fixity. "Black" babies have white feet and "white" babies can turn black. Newly born, the race of the baby is indeterminate, as is its social body. Thérèse's baby girl is a case in point. In a gruesome exercise of his professional expertise, the surgeon Benoit Gouly examines the body under the light of a lamp and pronounces it to be white. It is likely the whiteness of the baby that caused a stir in the first place. The demographic facts of Île de France made white babies a relative rarity[11] and, in any case, any homicide of a white in a nervous slave-owning society is a serious matter. This is not to say that the island's authorities were unconcerned by matters of infanticide, abortion, or infertility among the black population (they were, as we shall see), but life was exceptionally hard for the poor of Port Louis and the rate of neonatal mortality among the slave population in particular, but also for others, would have been very high. This fact (and the dangers of childbirth more generally) was implicitly recognized by the island's priests, who had adapted the usual churching ceremony for Christian mothers to include those whose babies had died: "Though this ceremony is intended more for women whose babies have been baptized than for those who have had the misfortune to lose their baby in the process of bringing them into the world, if the latter present themselves they should not be turned away, this ceremony being also established to give thanks to God for having preserved them during the labor of a dangerous childbirth."[12] But most slave mothers were not Christians (though a higher percentage of "free black" women probably were),[13] and it seems likely that corpses of many black babies did not find their way to the church, or to the cemetery, nor give rise to criminal investigations. So this assumed *délit atroce* was assumed to have been committed against an assumed white baby.

But as the days of preliminary investigation pass, so Thérèse's baby grows darker, as indeed does Thérèse herself. The baby is described by its father (whom we assume to be white through the absence of a sign of whiteness or blackness)[14] as *blanchâtre* (whitish, off-white), and although Thérèse is described by the two Malagasy women who first tell their stories as a mulâtresse, that is not how the authorities describe her. To them she is specifically a négresse Bengalie affranchie. The very cumbersomeness of this description is telling, incorporating three axes of ascribed identity—the racial (négresse), the ethnic (she is a "Bengalie") and the civil (she is an affranchie, neither a slave nor a freeborn person). The strained specificity of this labeling gives us a clue to the complexity and fluidity of life in Port Louis. Names seem peculiarly slippery in this case, but having more than one name was something all slaves experienced, and may not have been unusual among the French population either. One of the ironies of the slave regime was that, through its renaming and labeling practices, it institutionalized an instability of identity that contributed to problems of control. In this case double or multiple names adhere to both slave and free: Aupot is also Pautru; Thérèse is also Suzanne Henriette, and Paul is Pauldrin and Sansouccy. Only two characters in this small drama remain entirely nameless—the noir Mozambique who is the last person to be seen with the baby's body, and the baby herself, too young to have been named.

In all likelihood the prosecutor was right. Though we can never be certain, it is likely that Thérèse's baby was neither murdered nor abandoned. She had been welcomed into the tough world of the Camp des Noirs by a Malabar midwife; she had been nursed during her short illness by her mother and her father, and her small body had been laid out by an elderly Chinese woman. From their multiple cultural resources, the women of the Camp des Noirs had evolved a system of sorts to deal with both the birth and the death of a baby. But finally her body had been dumped, perhaps by a slave too tired or too disaffected to carry it the final distance to the cemetery.

There is a moment when the story of Thérèse's baby looks as if it might exemplify what has been called the oedipal drama of slavery.[15] In this version of Freud's Oedipus complex, the white master comes to represent the father and to possess a phallic power denied to the male slave. In what has been described as the "primal scene" of slavery, reenacted in many ex-slave narratives (that of Frederick Douglass among others), the male slave looks on, helplessly, as a slave woman (perhaps his mother, or his wife, or his aunt) is beaten, and with the beating, explicitly or implicitly, is enacted the master's sexual access to the female slave. Disempowered, unable to rescue the woman, the slave man is left symbolically castrated. As Gwen Bergner puts it in her critical discussion of masculinity under slavery, in this whipping scene, "slavery and femininity seem to correspond, as do freedom and masculinity." The slave position is, then, a "feminine" position, and in order to achieve manhood, the male slave must identify with the master/father, and in the process with "whiteness," forsaking his own race, represented by his mother (Bergner 1998, 253–254). As Bergner and others[16] have pointed out, this is highly problematic as an account of the formative moment of the construction of the slave psyche, not least because it is formulated from an ideal male position. Nevertheless, there may have been some part of this story being enacted in the case of Thérèse's baby. Thérèse's white master becomes her lover and the father of her child, combining paternity and sexual control with the patriarchal principle already overdetermined in the role of master. Whether his freeing of her makes any difference to his relationship with her we do not know. Thérèse's "husband" (Paul or Pauldrin or Sansouccy) has clearly been displaced as the lover/father. This was the version of the story the Malagasy slave, Suzanne, imagined, fantasized, or possibly maliciously invented—that the baby had been stolen and drowned by a slave (though Paul was in fact an ex-slave) suffering from jealousy and, we might imagine, emasculation.

This is a powerful theme, and one that recurs in other stories from the Île de France archive. But there is more than one family drama of slavery, not just one psychic or social script, not just one set of identifications. The white father/master/lover might, symbolically, appear all-powerful, but the logic of slavery also ordains that the baby will, socially, take the color and the status of its mother. The slave child, male or female, has no claim on the master/father, nor any direct relation to him.[17] The white father, in fact, must disavow his paternity, refuse to be the "real" father, in order to keep the larger patriarchal system intact, along with the fantasy of pristine whiteness.[18] In order to keep the family of slavery intact, the slave father must be denied the symbolic role of father, but by the same token the master must deny his paternity of the mixed-race child, leaving the black mother as both the most vulnerable and simultaneously the most powerful figure in the family drama.[19]

In this particular case, however, we are reminded that individuals do not always enact dominant social scripts. Perhaps it is because Sebastien Aupot is a lower-class "white," or perhaps it is just because of who he is, but though he hardly has time to either fulfill or neglect the role of "real" father toward Thérèse's baby, he certainly shows signs of being tempted to play the part. He seeks permission from his superiors to spend the night with Thérèse (there was a regulation forbidding whites from residing in the Camp des Noirs, honored more often in its breach than in its observance), he tends the baby in her brief illness, he commissions a small coffin from a carpenter. He appears to imagine himself to be a father—not just *the* father—of this small family born of slavery. His position as lover of his slave and father of her child, though theoretically somewhat transgressive, was (as numerous observers repeatedly pointed out) hardly unusual on the island. Indeed, the great founding patriarch of the colony, advocate of the white family and importer of Breton girls, Labourdonnais, had himself fathered illegitimate children on the island. "One imagines with difficulty," writes the Mauritian historian Marcelle Lagesse, "that M. de Labourdonnais was the father of two natural children, but the facts are there" (1987b).

Other master/fathers did, however, follow the social script of disavowal and denial of their paternity, or at the very least attempted to do so. Collectively the white masters had an interest in keeping what Vergès (1999, 9) calls "le secret de la famille," keeping the very evident fact of métissage at bay. The recognition of paternity, after all, not only was the recognition of kinship and alliance, but also brought with it the presumption of economic responsibilities. And it was not only men who disavowed their children, but women sometimes did too. Despite the evidence of community among the women of Thérèse's neighborhood and the creation of a kind of kinship between them, many slave mothers lacked the quality and consistency of female support, which they might have expected in the societies from which they had been removed. There were plenty of abandoned babies in Île de France.[20] Of course, abandoned babies were notoriously common in eighteenth-century France at this time (Hufton 1974; Sussman 1982), and so this is far from being a phenomenon unique to the colonies. But such records as there are indicate that it was not unusual for a single white man to wake in the morning to confront a screaming bundle on his doorstep. In April 1776, for example, Anthoine Ezeard, a captain of infantry, was woken at dawn by his slave Suzanne, who said that she had found on the doorstep a newborn baby girl in a straw basket. Many such babies no doubt were left to die—the records tell us only of those who lived, or who lived a little longer. Ezeard may have been the biological father, or he may have been thought of as a sympathetic person; at any rate, he declared himself "moved to pity" by the sight of the baby, found a wet nurse, and declared to the authorities his intention of caring for the child.[21] In this case there is no surgeon to act as expert witness to tell us the "color" of the child. While it is the very absence of a sign that, in the case of an adult like Sebastien Aupot, signals his "whiteness," in the case of a baby the reverse operates. Abandonment probably matters more to the authorities if the baby is white, but since, as we have seen, the color of a newborn baby is unstable, whiteness cannot be assumed, but must be signaled and fixed with a label.

The local priests also frequently ended up holding the baby. In October 1775, the *prefet apostolique* Francois Contenot had been presented with a newborn baby by Marion Henry, whom he described as a *négresse nourrice esclave*—a woman slave specifically employed to be a wet nurse. She told him that she had been given the baby by an "unknown person" and that she believed it to be unbaptized.[22] The priests undertook to care for the baby. Families were improvised, parenting was improvised, presumably drawing on the traditions of extended kinship slaves brought with them from societies in which fertility and the possession of children were vitally important. But extreme poverty also gave rise to extreme instability and uncertainty for many children. Orphaned or abandoned babies might be passed from hand to hand, breast to breast, and only if they were lucky would they find themselves fostered by someone with both the means and the inclination to parent a child born to another. In 1777 René Mezereon, described as a mulatto tinsmith living in Port Louis, came to tell the police a long and complicated story, recorded in breathless tones by a barely literate clerk.[23] He said that six months previously Rose, wife of a slave, Lazare, and living in the Camp des Noirs, had engaged him (along with a mulatto woman named Geneviève Castare) to present for baptism a newborn baby girl whom Rose said was the daughter of Soffie, a "free black" woman also living in the Camp des Noirs. Mezereon said that the identity of the child's father had not been known, but that a few days later he had heard from a "Sir" who was a surgeon aboard the (fortuitously named) ship *Le Père de Famille* that the father was one Contono, a merchant who had left for India. Later he had learned from Rose that the baby was now living with a Mme. Avrille, who had received a sum of two hundred livres, and that he believed that this money had been paid to her by Monsieur Gallinez, captain of a ship that had arrived from France. Clearly Mezereon was hinting at some wrongdoing, but the Île de France authorities, possibly having problems in deciphering this complex story of paternity and fostering, took no action. This baby was a lucky one, for she was enmeshed in a social web that included "free blacks" and wealthier merchants and ships' captains who, even if not biologically related, felt some kind of obligation to her.

No doubt many such children were completely assimilated into their adoptive families, but there were circumstances in which their status might be revealed as highly ambiguous, and in which the relationship between family and slavery was called into question. In September 1785, for example, Jeanette, who was described as a négresse aged twelve or thirteen, arrived at the police station in Port Louis to complain of the treatment meted out to her by Marie Joseph, a "free black" woman with whom she had lived since she had been very small.[24] Marie Joseph, she said, was treating her "like a slave" and had even threatened to sell her. Marie Joseph was brought in for questioning, and her indignation at this accusation echoes through the pages of the police report. She said that some years previously she had been in Pondichéry, in southern India, with a Monsieur Bourdier, a doctor, when a dying man named Tinjou, who had been a soldier in the Battaillon de l'Inde, had asked her to take care of his child "à peine sortie du premier age." Wishing to calm the poor man (who died shortly afterward), she had agreed voluntarily to do so, and for no reward, for the child had no resources other than those which she herself had furnished out of charity. She had raised Jeanette, she said, as her own child, and had only ever punished her in this spirit, but for the past few years the child had become uncontrollable, a "libertine" and a thief, and she had been obliged to discipline her. Her aim, she went on, was to marry her off advantageously as soon as possible.

Jeanette clearly believed in the distinction between adoptee and slave, between mother and mistress, and indeed these distinctions would become increasingly important during the Revolutionary years, but they were not yet, in any sense, self-evident. Her adoptive mother, she complained, was treating her "like a slave." Unfortunately for Jeanette, and for others like her, the "family," whether biologically constituted or not, was not the fantasy haven from the harsh world of slavery. Life was more complex than this; relationships of domination and exploitation were hardly confined to the institution of slavery. The further irony is that, technically at least, had Jeanette indeed been a slave, then Marie Joseph may have had a case to answer under the regulations governing slavery (though in practice very few slave complaints against masters and mistresses were successful). But Marie Joseph was an adoptive mother, and mothers were expected to punish their children.

The state did sometimes intervene in family relationships, however, in much the same way as it sometimes intervened in those between master and slave—that is, when public order was threatened. Cases involved both free blacks and whites. The same police records show, for example, the women in the family of a free black blacksmith complaining of his violent and drunken behavior. He was eventually deported to the Seychelles, from which he originally came.[25] In 1786 a judge, Brunel, interrogated François, "free black," who was accused of assaulting Brigitte, a "free black woman" in Port Louis. François, it turned out, had a wife on the other side of the island in Port Bourbon. Brunel pressed him on why he was not living with his wife, to which he replied that he did not get along with his father-in-law. He was ordered to return home.[26] In 1775 a Mme. Lorson complained of having been beaten by her husband (her complaint was registered) and a M. Pineaux was arrested for ill treatment of his wife and for refusing to give her her belongings (which included a slave). Complaints were not confined to those of wives against husbands, however. In 1776, the husband of Femme Reginbart complained of the behavior of his wife, who was living with a naval officer on a habitation. She had a history, allegedly, of "bad conduct," of "derangement," and especially of "galanterie." The judge, M. Porcher de la Serré, decided that it was necessary to "make an example" of the woman, who was deported to France, where she was to be confined to a convent.[27] In 1775 one Mezereon (possibly the same man as had reported on the baby) came to the police to complain that his wife had been unfaithful and had infected him with a disease. The judge ordered that the two should remain separated.[28]

There may have been an excessive number of abandoned babies on Île de France, but this does not indicate an abundance of babies. Birth rates, particularly in the slave community, were almost certainly very low. The slave population of Île de France grew nearly sixfold between 1746 and 1767 (from a mere 2,533 to 15,027).[29] It continued to grow substantially in the latter part of the century, reaching 49,080 in 1797. Demographic information is both scarce and unreliable (apart from anything else, taxation on the basis of slave ownership almost guaranteed this inaccuracy) but there is enough to indicate that the growth in slave numbers was largely due to continuous importation, rather than to natural growth.[30] Even by the miserable standards of the rest of the slave world at the time,[31] the implications of the demography of Île de France are shocking. It is not necessarily the case that Île de France slave owners were more brutal than others—though brutality and ill treatment were common—it is rather that many of them were poor, and their slaves shared in this general poverty. One small indication of this was given by Pierre Poivre as intendant in 1768, when he remarked that some slaves on the island had not received clothes for six years, and that indeed most of the colonists lacked shirts for themselves, their wives, and children.[32] Two years earlier the head of the Catholic Church on the island, M. Le Borgne, wrote that he was inundated by the poor and starving: "I have nothing to give them, but can only add my tears to theirs."[33] Malnutrition must have been a constant feature of slave life, for though La Bourdonnais's introduction of manioc had been significant, the island never produced enough food and remained subject to serious dearth throughout the century. Malnutrition contributed both to high mortality rates and to low fertility. It was an important factor in susceptibility to disease, of which there was much, ranging from periodic epidemics of smallpox (some of which themselves had serious demographic effects) to the more chronic diseases of poverty, such as scurvy. Sexually transmitted diseases were also common, again contributing to low fertility rates, and though hospitals had existed to treat slaves since the time of Labourdonnais, it was debatable whether one was more likely to survive in them or out of them. One eminent doctor who had worked on the island implied the latter.[34] Slaves must have relied to some degree on their own medical knowledge and practices, for which, unfortunately, we have scant records, though we do know that such practices have survived in creolized form (Sussman 1980). But perhaps the most significant factor making for low fertility among the slave population was its highly unequal sex ratio. This was a very male community: in 1776, for example, there was a total of 7,772 adult women slaves on the island to 12,346 adult male slaves.[35]

The importance of encouraging slave reproduction, and thus the importance of women, was explicitly acknowledged by administrators throughout the century but did not for the most part translate into practice. In a long anonymous mémoire, a visitor to the island in 1763 bemoaned the treatment of slave women and argued for incentives to be given for slaves to reproduce. He had seen, he said, slave women subjected to the most "painful" labor at the port, work that must "stand in the way of propagation." He emphasized the importance of marrying slaves to each other and compensating them for the birth of children. Those with six live children would earn an extra two days off per month; twelve live children would guarantee the freedom of their mother and father and of any children born subsequently.[36] For the most part we can be certain that such advice was not followed, but the story in this, as in so many other dimensions, was nevertheless a differentiated one.

There was a small but significant group of large slaveholders on the island—administrators, former administrators, military men, merchants with large habitations in addition to their town houses. Some actively encouraged family formation among their slaves. In 1775 the bankruptcy and sale of a large forge owned by two Frenchmen (Count Rostaing and his business partner, Hermans) occasioned the enumeration of the establishment's slave population (which had earlier been badly hit by a small-pox epidemic). The form that the list takes is significant, for some are listed in family groups. The creole slave Pierre, for example (a "good worker"), lived with his mother Phenace (a Malagasy), her husband Ladouceur (also a Malagasy), his eleven-year-old brother, Bernard, his pregnant sister Geneviève, her husband (an Indian horse groom, La-croix), and their one-year-old son, Jean-Jacques. This was followed, however, by lists of single slaves.[37]

Another wealthy habitant, Baron Grant de Vaux, also claimed to have encouraged slave marriages and family formation on his estate. He emphasized the affective role of the slave family ("they are generally fond of each other and discover the most tender affection for their children"), while also revealing its utilitarian dimension. When slaves misbehave, he wrote, it is the slave commander who punishes them with a whip, but "if the wife should be guilty the whip is consigned to the husband, who may correct her" (Grant 1801, 210). This other version of the "family drama" of slavery, in which the master directly exploits slave masculinity and gender inequality, is familiar from other parts of the world of slavery. Handing the whip to the slave husband was a powerful symbolic act. Not only did it allow the white master to remove himself from the direct violence of slavery (an issue that becomes increasingly important on Île de France) but it also allowed him, should he wish, to step in and "save" the woman from her husband's beating.[38] This was slavery at its most perverse. In this version of the primal whipping scene, it is the master who looks on, willing the slave to beat his own wife for him. Finally, though, he asserts his patriarchal authority over the slave man, inter-venes, and rescues his property before too much harm can be done.

Among the king's slaves, as I have already indicated, certain groups were favored, among them the West African Wolofs, Guinées, and Bam-baras. Governor David had been particularly keen on encouraging family formation among this group, and this policy appears to have been continued. At the government's Jardin de Roi (the botanical garden famously founded by Pierre Poivre), for example, in 1772 there were eighty-eight slaves listed as working on the garden. Of these a small minority were enumerated as members of family groups. There were six families listed, all of the Guinée caste. Given that the importation of Guinées had almost certainly ceased by this stage, many of these slaves would have been born on the island and therefore would have been, in the technical language of slavery, creoles. Their special status appears to have given them the opportunity not only to live in families, but also to reproduce themselves socially as a distinct group—though as we have seen, what *Guinées* actually meant is hard to know. They included Pierrot, a slave commander, who was listed as head of a family comprising himself, his wife (a laundress), their son Jean (the deputy commander), their daughter Marie Thomas (a laundress and seamstress) and two grandchildren, Jean-Louis and Felicité. But other "family" groups look rather more complex and intriguing, hinting at the improvisation that must have been so much a part of slave life. The sixth Guinée family listed, for example, was said to be headed by the gardener Rama,[39] his wife Catherine, their daughter Marie, and finally Savoir, a Malabar. Families, no doubt, included non–biologically related people, just as they might in Africa; families could be constructed and kin invented, if slaves were given the opportunity to do so. Many were not. Following the Jardin de Roi's list of families was a more typical enumeration of the remaining slaves: 23 noirs mozambiques, 5 négresses mozambiques (note the disproportion among the sexes), 17 noirs malgaches, 12 négresses malgaches, and three Bambaras.[40]

Treating one's slaves well and keeping them alive (referred to at the time as *la préservation des noirs)* was not only economically rational, but also gave the slaveholder a good feeling. Apologists for slavery commenting on the regime on Île de France pointed to good practice, of course, and no doubt embellished it. The Code Noir did in fact make provision for slave family life, but there is no evidence that this was ever enforced. One of the many mémoirists of the period made a further argument for encouraging slave reproduction. In contrast to the Malagasies who found it hard to forget their homes and often tried to escape there, creole slaves, born on the island, had nowhere else to go to, and, crucially, no *memory* of anywhere else, or any state other than slavery: "They know no other country than the island, no other state but servitude. If they run away from time to time it is because this country does not give them recognition, but treats them just like the others."[41] Good slaveholders, he went on, were few and far between on the island, but he had seen two habitations that qualified as such. On these slaves were kept in families, and each *père de famille* was given a small plot on which, on Sundays and feast days, he could cultivate his vegetables. The demarcation of this plot with a dry stone wall apparently made him feel that he had his own "little district" and was head of his own ménage. Slaves treated in this way were, he argued, comparable to the peasants of Denmark, Russia, and Poland and developed a deep affection for their homes. Similar arguments and schemes to encourage slave reproduction were made in the French Antilles at this time, where reproduction rates were also low (Moitt 2001, 94).

The same writer, however, had been equally struck by the multitude of abandoned children on the island, who had nowhere to live and often survived through prostitution. For while all might agree that it was in the interests of the community of slave owners to treat their slaves well, enable their family lives, encourage them to reproduce, allow slave mothers time off to feed their babies, and so on, there were other imperatives operating for the smaller, poorer slave owners who dominated numerically. Among them, the day-to-day drive to derive some kind of income from their slaves might override any longer-term rational calculation of the benefits that could be accrued from slave maternalism. Moitt argues for the French Antilles that slaveholders might deplore the low fertility of slave women, "but economic calculations took precedence over the lives of slaves" (2001, 93).

This was a fact known only too well by Marianne, a Bengali slave belonging to a Malabar mason named Sobria. She came to the police in Port Louis in 1790 to lodge a complaint.[42] Like so many other slaves in the town, she was sent out each day by her master to sell her labor. This arrangement might, on occasions, contribute to a slave's upward mobility —there were slaves on the island who became owners of property and purchased their freedom by this means. But this depended on the degree of control exercised by the slave owner and the kind of skills possessed by the slave. Crucially, Marianne had a small baby. The baby, she said, impeded her work and so she could not earn the 40 sols a day demanded of her by Sobria. Worse, the baby cried all the time from hunger and she had nothing to give it—her milk had dried up and her master gave her only one bowl of rice per week. Sobria was not around to defend himself against these charges, but his brother appeared before the police to do so. Whether we think his defense credible or not, the form it takes is telling: he said that his brother never forced her to go out to work. Far from this, he had persisted in trying to persuade her to stay at home and look after the needs of the house, but she had consistently refused to do this, and instead had gone running about, and in three weeks had brought only in 20 livres. As for her milk, she had never really had any, despite the food that she had been provided with, and so the child had had to be fed with sago and milk obtained from the wet nurses of the neighborhood.

Cynical as this defense appears to be, it does indicate that by the time of the Revolution, at least, there existed a discourse on the "proper" treatment of nursing slave women. Marianne, we assume, was aware of this when she made the courageous move of bringing her complaint. She was rebutted with the accusation that she was a bad mother. There was no uniform view of slave mothers on Île de France, though not infrequently slave women (and particularly Malagasy slave women) were alleged to practice abortion, infanticide, and the neglect of their children.[43] Induced abortion as well as frequent accidental abortion was likely to have been part of the experience of many slave women, but by the last quarter of the eighteenth century none of the accounts we have of slave maternity can be divorced from the larger debates around the morality and viability of the slave regime itself. The "bad slave mother" could be employed on both sides of the slavery debate, either embedded in the antislavery argument (life for the slave woman is so miserable that she must deny her natural instincts and refuse to bring a child into the world), or it could be mobilized in the defense of slavery (slave women are not human—they lack maternal instinct and even kill their own babies). Motherhood was always about more than reproduction.

From the time of the Dutch onward, it was always alleged that maroon slave women callously killed or abandoned their babies. This may well have been partially true, but it was also part of the maroon myth, repeated to each visitor to the island, as a reminder that at the heart of the island lay a dark and dangerous center. The three Lazarist priests on their way to China in 1732 repeated it: "They [the maroons] have wives, but it is their practice to kill their babies who might impede their flight or reveal them through their cries."[44] In some accounts, however, maroon women are seen as victims of male violence (de la Caille 1763, 1776). In this version fear and horror were focused on the male maroon, whose alleged ruthlessness extended to killing any babies born within his band. This version emerges, as one might expect, from trials of maroon women.[45] In 1746, for example, three women were arrested who had been part of a band of maroons in the mountains behind Grand Port in the southeast. They were Monique (a Mozambique), and two Malagasy women, Marie and Louison (who had also kept her Malagasy name, Fonavola). Monique said that she had not joined the group voluntarily but had been abducted one day when she had been collecting wild greens with her baby on her back. Quinga, a maroon armed with three assegais, had taken her by force into the woods, where she watched "with sadness as he speared her baby to death."[46] A few years later there was considerable excitement on the island over the existence of a maroon band allegedly led by "La Grande Barbe"—a super masculinist antihero. One of the women members of the group, Magdalene Marena, was caught and brought to trial in July 1751. She said that she had been forcibly abducted from her master's habitation by La Grande Barbe and others. She had been pregnant at the time and gave birth in the woods. La Grande Barbe and another man, Ziramby, had killed the baby and thrown its body away.[47]

Whether slave mothers could be "good" mothers or not was a question that mattered in more ways than one. It mattered because the colony needed to reproduce its slave population, it mattered because it was a symbolically powerful issue in the debates around slavery, and it mattered to many white families directly, because slave women nursed their babies.

Black Breasts, White Milk

A few years before Thérèse's baby was found in the salt pans, the engineer/botanist/novelist and Enlightenment figure Bernardin de St. Pierre,[48] had visited the island. An outspoken critic of slavery and friend of Rousseau, Bernardin de St. Pierre was representative of French elite sensibilities of the latter part of the eighteenth century. His extraordinarily best-selling novel set on the island, *Paul et Virginie* (see Racault 1986; Reid 1993, chap. 3; Hunt 1992, chap. 2), would have much of Europe's reading public in tears, and subsequent French visitors to the island frequently broke down at the sight of the sites of the novel's tragedy. But, as we have seen, before writing *Paul et Virginie*, St. Pierre had published an earlier account of his visit to Île de France (Bernardin de St. Pierre, [1773] 2002). A striking figure in this account is that of the white creole matriarch.[49]

Arriving at the habitation of M. Le Normand[50] in 1775, St. Pierre was struck by the simplicity of the white family's existence and, above all, by the virtues of Mme. Le Normand who, despite coming from a "good family" in France, seemed content with her new, simpler life on the island: "The air of contentment and the good nature of this young mother of a family seemed to make all who got close to her happy. She was breast-feeding one of her infants: the four others stood round her, playful and content" (Bernardin de St. Pierre 2002, 158).

In fact, as we shall see, all was far from idyllic in the larger slave-owning Le Normand household, but nothing at this moment detracted from Bernardin de St. Pierre's rapture at the sight of the white breast. Mme. Le Normand's virtuousness as a breast-feeding mother will not have been lost on the French reading public of the time. All great Enlightenment figures of the late eighteenth century followed Rousseau in extolling the virtues of the mother's breast and opposing the practice of wet nursing (Fairchilds 1984, chap. 7; Donzelot 1979; Jacobus 1995, chap. 10; Sussman 1982), and spurting breasts would feature centrally in Revolutionary iconography. The promotion of the mother's breast was in part a response to the appallingly high infant mortality rates in France, but it was also part of a pre-Revolutionary critique of the overindulged aristocratic woman who denied "nature" (Reid 1993, Hunt 1992). Bernardin de St. Pierre's white colonial woman, living in the midst of nature, dressed simply in her cotton from India and nursing her own children, was apparently the antithesis of the overindulged metropolitan woman, denying her own biological functions as a mother and callously risking the lives of her babies at the hands and breasts of working-class wet nurses.

In fact, so taken was Bernardin de St. Pierre by this vision of the white colonial matriarch that in *Paul et Virginie* he wrote the father out of the text completely and centered his story on two single women and their children, Paul and Virginie, who together constitute a new kind of family (Reid 1993, Hunt 1992), the antithesis of the patriarchal version of old-regime nobility, with its concern for alliances and inheritance and its lack of sentimentality. *Paul et Virginie* went into dozens of editions and became one of the period's greatest best-sellers. It was, as Reid has put it, a "lachrymose" novel (1993, 106), and fans delighted in recounting how they had cried from beginning to end, but particularly at the end, with the tragic death of Virginie. It is not surprising, then, that after the novel's publication a *Paul et Virginie* quality enters many visitors' accounts of Île de France, with eulogies both to the island's physical beauty and to the white creole matriarch.[51] This was an image of fecundity and wholesomeness.[52] The painter Milbert, for example, described the white creole woman as having a "natural beauty, developed by the salubrity of the climate" (1812, 11:158). The fair sex, wrote Jacques Arago, another early-nineteenth-century visitor to the island, "are very handsome . . . the girls are brought up in the sentiments of modesty which heighten the lustre of their charms" (Arago 1823, 124). White creole girls, he added, reached maturity at a very early age (Milbert also noted this): the women were fruitful, with instances being known of their bearing twenty-five children (Arago 1823, 135). The white creole mother was also a tender and indulgent mother; her children were allowed to run free, they were unswaddled in babyhood, and enjoyed an unusual proximity to the "bounties of the natural environment."

Bernardin de St. Pierre's choice of the island as the setting for his romantic novel is, in fact, a little ironic. Demographically, the white mother was a rarity.[53] The white family, in fact, was in trouble. Half a century after Labourdonnais's attempts to root the *colon* family form on the island through the importation of Breton girls and their instruction in the arts of marriage and domesticity, this was still, by and large, a society of single men. The white creole mother was, in fact, a more common feature on neighboring Île Bourbon, with its very different social and economic structure. But the Bourbon creoles were perceived as both too "rough" and insufficiently "white" to perform the role which Bernardin de St. Pierre had assigned them and to appeal to metropolitan tastes.

Family, morality, and economy were intimately linked in much eighteenth-century French thought. To the distress of some (including the Lazarist priests and exponents of Physiocracy, such as Pierre Poivre), the wealth of the island remained firmly located in its trade and in its military and naval functions, rather than in its agricultural resources. It was therefore a very male place, and a male place at war for large stretches of the century. Frenchmen still left their wives in France, despite decades of administrative attempts to encourage the settlement of whole families. Some were completely abandoned by their husbands, as attested to by the frequency of appeals to the Ministère de la Marine, and even to the king himself, by wives of colonial adventurers. Some men, as we have seen, were simply too poor either to return to France or to remit any money to their families there. Other cases were more complex and were not confined to the poor. Guillaume Desranges de Richeteau, for example, was an inspector of police and lawyer on the island in the 1760s and 1770s who had originally gone there to join his brother. In 1773 his wife, la dame Blot, wrote to the Ministère de la Marine to say that in the seventeen years her husband had been in the colony she had received no help from him, despite her poor health. In fact, she did not even know if he was alive, because he had not responded to her request to send her a *certificat de vie*.[54] The wife of Claude Horque was in much worse circumstances. She and her children were reduced to begging around the Hôtel de Praslin in Paris, where she spent her time attempting to get aid from the famous duc de Praslin. Claude Horque was a worker who had been recruited to go to Île de France in 1770. She had no means by which to join him there, was destitute, and by 1785 had come to believe that he might be dead. He was, in fact, alive and well, according to the island's administrators. They reported that he had been making a good living from the lucrative business of buying goods from the estates of the deceased and then selling them. Perhaps to soften the blow, the administrators suggested that the island's economy had recently been depressed, and this might account for why Mme. Horque had not heard from her husband.[55] In fact Horque, otherwise known as "Champagne," was one of very few slave owners successfully prosecuted for cruelty to a slave. Horque, who described himself as a "merchant and a bourgeois," had not only beaten his Indian slave François, but also tied him to the chimney and lit a fire under him. He was fined and François was confiscated.[56]

The white family then, was relatively rare, and even where it existed, often incomplete: incomplete because of high mortality rates, and incomplete because men as well as women were often absent, either at war or on business. In this respect Bernardin de St. Pierre's fantasy matriarchal unit bore some relation to reality, for though there were always many more men than women on the island, nevertheless there were a lot of fathers missing. White women, both elite and poor, were often left in control of households, habitations, workshops and, of course, slaves.

The 1776 census of Moka district gives us some sense of the composition of households in what was a rural district (and thus more "female" than Port Louis and its surroundings). Of the sixty-seven habitations surveyed, fourteen had no white members, being run by absentees; twenty-five resembled a conjugal unit (man and wife), sometimes with children, always with slaves; eighteen had no white women in them, but were headed by single men, either alone or in twos or threes, and ten were headed by women, having no adult white male members other than, on occasion, a white male worker.[57] In her memoirs, the aristocratic Mme. Journel remembered that at the death of her father from tetanus, her mother, previously depicted as weak and unworldly, immediately took over the running of their large habitation, setting about building bridges, workshops, mills and houses: "Very few habitations were managed as ingeniously as this one; my mother calculated that the loss of a minute on the part of each slave added up to hours of lost work and she allocated work accordingly, minimizing unnecessary acts" (Journel 1940, 37). Economic necessity and the conditions of colonial life, then, ensured that the progress of new ideals of femininity and of family life, as extolled by the Enlightenment thinkers, would make slow progress on the island. That such ideals were clearly in circulation and not just the stuff of novels is evident from the proposal (which, however, never came to fruition) for a girls' boarding school. The sisters Poupelain placed great emphasis on modesty, on the preservation of the girls' innocence, and on the practice of body maintenance. Care was to be taken to protect the girls from exposure not only to the opposite sex, but to older women and to the "inappropriate" behavior of the slaves who would be the school's domestic workers.[58]

In practice, however, most girls, if they stayed and married on the island, would find themselves heavily involved in the running of households and business enterprises, and of course, the management of their slaves. Married women had a clear interest in the preservation and generation of family wealth, not least because under family law (which for whites and "free blacks" was the Custom of Paris) they retained independent rights to a portion of any property they brought to a marriage (Lebrun 1998; Mousnier 1979, chap. 2). With high death rates, remarriages were common. Wills, testaments, and guardianship arrangements not only kept the island's large population of lawyers in business, but also attest to the central importance of property and business enterprises in elite family life, made more complex by the colonial setting and often enduring family ties to the metropole. The family of the lineage and of alliance appears to have been very alive within the wide-flung French colonial system. Colonial positions often ran in the family, and colonial business enterprises frequently went hand in hand with marriage alliances. At the same time, however, because merchant wealth was so dispersed and often disputed, dramatic reversals of fortune were not uncommon, helped by the fractiousness of the island's elite and the ruthlessness of individuals in plotting the downfall of their rivals.

White women's involvement in the management of wealth, including that invested in slaves, did not meet with universal approval. In the eyes of some, it detracted from their "natural" femininity. At the beginning of the nineteenth century Arago would write that though he admired the "fair sex" of white society on Île de France, "I should like, however, rather less *decision* in their gait, I should prefer a little more *timidity*." And though Bernardin de St. Pierre would have the white matriarch at the center of his colonial romance, on an earlier visit to the island he had become decidedly queasy when faced with the real-life figure of what he called a "War Goddess Bellona." Her story, and Bernardin de St. Pierre's reaction to her, is revealing.

His encounter with the woman he refers to as Mme. V*** comes soon after his horrified description of an expedition to capture maroon slaves. Encountering a troop of armed "blacks" on the road, he soon realized that they had been sent out by the police to catch maroons. They showed him their booty. They had killed one man, whose talisman (*gris-gris*) they showed him—and which, Bernardin de St. Pierre remarked, looked very much like a rosary. But the real horror was to come. A captured woman, who seemed "overwhelmed with grief," was carrying a bag on her back: "I opened it and was appalled, alas, to find a man's head inside! The beautiful scenery vanished, and I was faced with a land of abominations" (Bernardin de St. Pierre [1773] 2002, 161). The poor woman, added Bernardin de St. Pierre, might perhaps be carrying the head of her lover.

Recoiling from this horrific spectacle, Bernardin de St. Pierre continued on his way. In the southeast of the island he stopped at the house of a wealthy habitant, whose name was V***. He was abroad, but his wife was there, a "large, gaunt Creole, who walked about barefoot, as was the custom of the country."

> When I entered her room, I found her surrounded by five or six daughters and as many mastiffs which nearly strangled my dog. They were kicked out of doors, and Mme de la V*** posted a naked black woman, clothed only in a ragged petticoat, to keep watch on them. After some small talk, one of the dogs found a way to get into the room

and the uproar began again. Mme de la V . . . held an electric ray's prickly tail in her hand and whipped the slave's naked shoulder with it, leaving a long weal. . . . This lady told me that she had narrowly escaped drowning when she went out in a pirogue to harpoon a turtle on the reef. She would also go off into the forest to hunt runaway slaves: she was proud of herself, but told me that the governor had reproached her for hunting deer, which is forbidden. (Bernardin de St. Pierre 2002, 167)

Mme. de la V*** was in fact separated from her husband and ran her habitation completely independently, along with a band of slaves she had trained in the art of "maroon hunting" (Lagesse 1987, 8–9). The contrast between Bernardin de St. Pierre's description of this "creole" woman and his idyllic portrayal of Mme. Le Normand, breast-feeding and surrounded by her children, is striking. Here was a "real" creole woman (unlike Mme. le Normand, who came from France), and Bernardin de St. Pierre did not like what he saw. Mme. de la V*** could not be the virtuous matriarch of his dreams because she was corrupted by slavery, and her violence violated the ideals of gender difference. In fact, violence also permeated the life of the Le Normand family, but perhaps Bernardin de St. Pierre did not know this. In 1776 six of the slaves of the household approached the police, complaining of cruelty at the hands of their master. Domingue alleged that he gave them no time off, fed them badly, beat them continually and, around a year previously, had even murdered a slave. Janetton gave the same story.[59] In 1791 (by which time he was mayor of Rivière Noire), his slaves are still complaining. Sophie, for example, had run away because, in her words, "She would rather go to Madagascar with other slaves who had formed a plan, than stay at Le Normand's."[60] The crucial difference, of course, between the Le Normand and Victoire households was that in the former the violence against slaves was allegedly perpetrated only by a man, while in the latter, a woman not only participated in it, but relished it.

All was not well in the white family, and Bernardin de St. Pierre knew this. Not only was the white creole mother a rarity, but she did not always breast-feed her own babies, employing slave women as wet nurses. The white family could not survive without the sustenance provided by slavery. Echoing common views of the time (which extended well beyond the slave-owning world), Bernardin de St. Pierre argued that white babies would inevitably imbibe the "vices of the negro woman" with their milk. What the wet-nursing slaves thought about milk and its qualities we do not know, though we do know that in some African societies breast milk was thought to transmit many qualities, including those of kinship. Neither can we know (though we might imagine) how slave wet nurses felt about sustaining their masters' families, possibly at the expense of their own babies; though for reasons of self-interest, their masters and mistresses may well have ensured that they were reasonably well fed. We do know that sometimes performing the role of the dedicated wet nurse earned women slaves their freedom. In 1781, for example, an ex-slave named Henriette went to one of the island's lawyers to confirm the freedom accorded to her and her children by her former owner. According to the manumission document, her mistress had granted Henriette her freedom for having "nourished" her two children. She had also freed Henriette's children (a girl and a boy), whom she described as *frères de lait* of her own children, indicating that some notional bond of kinship had been established through the sharing of the breast.[61]

Though we should be careful not to impose a post-Freudian script on this phenomenon, the figure of the slave woman as both wet nurse and object of sexual desire was clearly a troubling one to visitors like Bernardin de St. Pierre.[62] Others were more explicit than he about the feelings aroused by the subjugated slave's breast. Milbert, always prone to flights of fancy, was much taken by the figure of an Indian woman slave who had been sent by her master (who was also her lover) to deliver to him (significantly perhaps), a jug of milk:

> She was a young and beautiful Indian who, for several years, had enabled this habitant to forget the tedium of bachelorhood. It is rare to see, even among the most beautiful women of Europe, such an attractive person. She carried in her arms a young child, to whom she had no inhibitions in offering the breast, in front of me. There was no veil to hide my view of her charms; their beauty was not the effect of any disguise or posture. . . . This Indian had skin which was white rather than bronze: just one thing diminished for me the admiration into which my first view of her had thrown me: her deformed bare feet were a reminder that this woman, whom one wanted to adore like a god, groaned under the yoke of slavery and the whims of an absolute master. (1812, 11:171–172)

Milbert, in this characteristically florid and voyeuristic passage, invites us to identify with both his desire and his disgust. The woman is sent by her master to give him milk. The woman offers her breast to her baby without embarrassment; Milbert sees it as being offered to him. She is unveiled, her beauty is without "disguise," and her charms are laid bare. She is so perfect, in fact, that she almost becomes white. But Milbert's reverie is brought to an abrupt halt by the sight of her feet, bare, deformed, the symptom of her condition of slavery, her complete submission to her master/lover. She is not perfect at all; she is tainted by slavery. She is the lover of her master, she is the carrier of milk, she is nursemaid to her (and very probably her master's) baby.

Keeping the system of slavery intact required collective work on the part of slave owners. Some of this work took place at the level of the law, in the public sphere in the policing and "civilizing" of slavery, and the attempts to subjugate the individual slave owner's desires to the common slave owners' good. But there was a psychic life to slavery, just as there is a psychic life to all power relations (Butler 1997), and here I refer less to the psychological and social creation of subjection, discussed by Butler, and more to the psychological problem of domination. The problem of domination was this: slavery was a system of dependency sustained through the exercise of power. By dependency I mean not the dependency of the slave on his or her master, their "attachment to subjection," but, more problematically, the dependency of the master on the slave. The slave owner exercised his power (backed up by violence) to maintain control over the slave's labor, and in the process, to maintain his own dependence on the slave. Slave ownership was, as we shall see, fundamental to the construction of the free male subject—male subjectivity rested on dependence on another, the slave. Faced with the slave mother/wet nurse, the problematic nature of this dependency was writ large. She was a reminder that the white slave-owning family could not feed itself, that its patriarchal head could not provide for it. In Hegelian terms, through this labor she placed her "signature" on the object—in this case the master's child.[63]

The family and lineage were the dominant models for control, the hierarchical extraction of labor and reproduction, not only in the lives of French colonists, but (with significant variations, of course) in the societies of Africa, Madagascar, and India from which slaves were drawn. But there is more to lineage and family than this. The lineage is the social site in which individuals locate their past (through the ancestors and their spirits) and their future (through reproduction, inheritance, and the passing on of "blood"). The family (large, small, conjugal, and extended) is the site of affective ties, as well as of control, the site of relationships between men and women, parents and children, which are fundamental, powerful, and frequently dangerous, because families are places where processes of exchange take place between differently gendered individuals and different groups. Here some of the most intimate and violent exchanges take place in sexual relations, in the processes of birth and death, symbolized by the shedding and exchange of fluids: semen, blood, milk.[64] In the context of a slave society, these fluids were continually exchanged across the porous dividing line between master and slave—the white man's semen, the slave woman's milk and her blood.

Slavery on Île de France, as in very many other places, was built on an idealized patriarchal family form. It was an institution continuous with, not radically apart from, the other dominant forms of society. In the case of this French island, at the apex was the king, beneath him the pseudo-feudal authority of first the Company and then the royal administrators, and beneath them, ideally, a community of slave owners, wielding patriarchal authority over their immediate families and their slaves. This "family of slavery" and its "economy of kinship" was certainly a cynical one, deliberately manipulated for benefit of the slave owner, sometimes through a denial of the importance of affective relationships among slaves, sometimes through their generation and distortion. But cynical manipulation was not the complete story—this was a realm that constantly threatened to subvert the patriarchal order, a realm in which desires were not always easily either repressed or ordered. Slave-owning society, then, went through many contortions in an attempt to contain the contradictions. As we have seen, the overarching structure of the family of slavery was patriarchal, with the master controlling both his own family and that of his slaves and placing the male slave either in a kind of "feminine" position, or in that of a minor. Yet when it came to the "real" biological paternal relations between many masters and their female slaves' children, these had to be denied in order for the larger patriarchy to survive. There could be no question of patriliny here—a matrilineal kinship system was obligatory within the slave family. A slave child was born of its mother alone, and this made the slave mother simultaneously extremely vulnerable and potentially exceptionally potent

FIGURE 3. Frontispiece from *Paul et Virginie*, by Jacques-Henri
Bernardin de St. Pierre, 1799. Bodleian Library, University
of Oxford, Vet. A5 f. 2588

—a potency enhanced when, as a wet nurse, she sustained not only her
black or mixed-race baby, but the white baby too.

Bernardin de St. Pierre, apparently uneasy and queasy around all this,
went to enormous lengths in *Paul et Virginie* to invent a family form and
economy that were self-sustaining. The results are interesting. His two
white matriarchs lived as a unit without men, sustaining each other and
nursing each other's babies. And Paul and Virginie, brought up as brother
and sister, nursed at the same breasts, become the ideal conjugal couple,
tragically unachieved due to Virginie's "corruption" in France. Incest, he
appears to say, is ideal. But, though they nurse their own babies, the two
white matriarchs are slave owners, albeit apparently generous and benign
ones. Slave ownership and slave control among women also created problems and contradictions for the patriarchal ideal, for here were women
acting as if they were men. Little wonder that Bernardin de St. Pierre was
so disturbed by his encounter with Mme. de la V***, for she was proof that

slavery distorted and corrupted the "proper" roles of men and women. Slave owning, far from enlarging and enhancing the male power of the master, theatened at moments to undermine it by pointing to its fundamental dependency on the other. Slavery threatened to expose "masculinity as masquerade."[65]

Chapter Six

*J*ean Lousteau, clerk to the high court of Île de France, was an exceptionally litigious lawyer on an island of litigious lawyers. He had a number of enemies among fellow members of the colonial elite, and throughout the 1780s was fully occupied in defending his reputation—a defense that took him to Paris and to eventual vindication by the king himself.[1] Nevertheless, he took time, in 1785, to pursue another matter that was very close to home—the escape (*évasion*) of one of his slaves, Jouan. Jouan, he was informed, had been smuggled onto the royal ship *Le Brillant*, bound for Pondichéry, the French possession in southern India.[2]

Lousteau alleged to the police that Jouan had not simply gone missing, but had been abducted or, at the very least, lured away. He knew this because a woman called Modeste had told him. She was a Bengalie slave, he said, belonging to the Lascar fisherman Bacou. And, he went on, there were other potential witnesses too, for a number of people had apparently assisted in Jouan's escape by, for example, moving his belongings from place to place and eventually secreting them on the ship. But he understood that the person who had been central to this évasion had been Bernard, a *créol libre* (that is, a free person born on the island, but later described variously as *Malabar, soi-disant libre* and *Topas libre*).[3] Lousteau wanted Jouan back; he was a skilled carpenter who could earn him a significant sum every month, and Lousteau had been offered (but had refused) the sum of 5,000 livres for him. The loss of Jouan represented, Lousteau said, a serious loss to his (Lousteau's) large family. Lousteau did not mention, but we know from other sources, that he had "lost" valuable slaves before. In 1774 his Malagasy slave La Violette, a horse groom, was shot dead by his neighbor on his habitation at Montagne Longue.[4]

In order to facilitate the search for Jouan, Lousteau provided the following description. He was, he said, easily recognizable.

> He declares that his fugitive slave is of the Lascar caste, a Malabar, dark black in color, short in height, with a handsome, slightly thin face, a gentle appearance, with long hair in a ponytail . . . that he is well dressed, being abundantly endowed with clothes, such as jackets and shorts . . . wearing small gold earrings, a pin with a gold heart on his shirt, and on the arm a mark on the skin which he thinks reads DM. He can be easily recognized by his gentle demeanor and cleanliness.

Lousteau, like any attentive slave owner, knew intimately the qualities, physical and other, of one of his most valued and valuable possessions. Jouan's erstwhile friends provided the authorities with more details. Modeste was the first to be questioned. But before the investigating judge heard what she had to say, they first needed to pin down her identity on a number of different axes (just as they had attempted to do with Thérèse in the case of the baby on the salt pans). Modeste was described cumbersomely, and in a way that perhaps indicated the difficulties the colonial authorities had in conceptualizing and defining the state of slavery among Indian slaves in particular: "Bengalie négresse, concubine of Jouan and so-called slave of Bacou Caremy, free black Lascar, to whom she pays each day the sum of two livres, despite the fact that she claims to have bought her freedom with the help of a certain sailor."

Clearly they did not believe Modeste's assertion that she was free (why else would she be paying Bacou two livres each day?), but they brushed aside this complication for the moment. Modeste said that she and Jouan had been arguing lately and that she had separated from him, and then he had escaped on the *Brillant* with Bernard, free black Topas, cook by profession, with whom he was very close ("très lié avec"). Bernard's departure, she added, had been confirmed by the butcher Bellegarde, who was the former master of Louise, the négresse whom he had married to Bernard. Modeste was particularly concerned about her belongings— clothing and jewelry—which had been in Jouan's chest, secretly removed from her hut in her absence one day.

Five months later Jouan was still missing and Lousteau was becoming more agitated. He reiterated his complaint, with some additions: "My slave, the carpenter Jouan, escaped on the royal vessel *Le Brillant*, which left port on 20 May, and is living in intimacy (*en liaison intime*) with Bernard, *noir Topas*." He went on. This Bernard, he said, had debauched Jouan and arranged his escape on the ship by passing him off as free and by telling people that they were brothers. Jouan, he understood, had been known aboard ship as Joseph and had been taken on as a servant by one of the officers of the Regiment of Île de France with whom he had disembarked at Pondichéry. Meanwhile, he said, Bernard had apparently returned to the island and had been seen around town wearing a hat, a shirt, and a handkerchief, all of which Lousteau recognized as belonging to Jouan, a fact that went to prove the great intimacy (*la grande intimité*) that existed between the two men.

Other witnesses (with what kind of prompting we cannot be sure) reinforced this apparent emphasis on the relationship between the two men. Pierre Moussa, a West African (Bambara) slave belonging to the king, who had been involved in smuggling away Jouan's trunk, said that the two men had lived together in "intelligence" and "amitié" and that they called each other "brothers." Modeste too elaborated her story. She said that Jouan and Bernard had been involved "intimately" for some time. Furthermore, she too had seen Bernard since his return to the island, sporting Jouan's shirt, handkerchief, and even a hat bordered with gold. Lindor, another slave, had known Jouan on the island and had also been on board *Le Brillant*. He had recognized Jouan and asked him what he was doing. He had replied that he was "going to find his freedom." Jouan and Bernard, he added, had lived together and eaten together onboard ship and had called each other "brothers." Lindor had asked Bernard if they were *really* brothers, to which Bernard had replied that they were indeed, from birth. Jouan had given him, Lindor, a blue shirt, in the pocket of which he had found a gold pin with a heart on it.

On 18 October, Bernard was found on the island and arrested, and on 8 November he was interrogated. Described as "noir, soi-disant libre," Malabar, and forty-eight years old, Bernard (who was literate enough to sign his name) said that he lived in the Camp des Yolofs.[5] He admitted having aided Jouan to embark on *Le Brillant*, claiming that he had seen nothing wrong with this, not being acquainted with the ways of the colony.[6] When asked if it was true that he was "tres lié" with Jouan and that they sometimes referred to each other as brothers, he replied that they did sometimes call each other brothers, but in fact he had known Jouan well for only two months.

In December Lousteau, frustrated at the lack of progress in restoring his slave to him, told the authorities that he now had information on Jouan's whereabouts. He was, he had heard, in the employ of a lieutenant of the Regiment of Île de France, one Lieutenant Brousse, who had employed him onboard ship and who continued to employ him in Pondichéry. No doubt, said Lousteau, the lieutenant had believed that Jouan was a free man, but "on this island no black can call himself free who does not have proof of that condition, and it is impudent of him to believe the word of a black man whom he does not know, and thus to compromise the property of the habitants."

The case disappears from view, and we can probably assume that Lousteau lost Jouan for good. Perhaps Jouan did find his freedom back in India (though according to Bernard, he was not happy there). Bernard may have stayed on the island. His name crops up in 1789 in the records of the lawyer Antoine Touraille. By now he is dead, but his daughter by his marriage to Louise (négresse Bengalie) is marrying the son of a Malabar carpenter, and Bellegarde, the butcher and former owner of her mother Louise, is acting as her guardian. She brings to the marriage three slaves and a sum of 4,500 livres.[7]

What do we make of Bernard and Jouan's relationship and the nature of their masculinity? There is, as I have already indicated, a powerful (though challenged) narrative of masculinity under slavery, and this is the narrative of emasculation and symbolic (and sometimes real) castration. The issue of masculinity has come up again more recently in discussions of Fanon's work and his problematic representation of gender and sexuality. In diagnosing and attempting to redress the psychological damage done to men by slavery and colonialism, there has sometimes emerged, as Stuart Hall (1996) has argued, a peculiarly phallocentric and homophobic version of black masculinity. None of this is straightforward, of course, in part because these discussions of gender and sexual identification rest on an application of psychoanalytic theory which presumes that sexual identity takes precedence over all others, including that of "race." Diane Fuss (1995) has raised this problem of the colonial history of psychoanalytic thought, as have, in different ways, Jean Walton (1997), Hortense Spillers (1997) and Kalpana Seshadri-Crooks (1998). But adding one binary (race) to another (sex) does not, as many have noted, quite solve our problem. In fact our problem appears very similar to that faced by the administrators of Île de France, with their lengthy and cumbersome descriptions of the intersection of different axes of identity. Just as Modeste is a "négresse" (denoting possibly, but not definitively, race and legal status), a "Bengalie" (ethnicity), a "so-called slave" and a "concubine," so contemporary theorists struggle to find an elegant description of a complex reality: "Desire is performed within history at the intersections of gender, race, sexuality and class" (Moglen 1997, 204), or "race speaks through multiple discourses that inhabit intersecting axes of relations" (Spillers 1997, 138).

Despite being a slave society, Île de France in the late eighteenth century was not, as I have already indicated, a society overdetermined by ideas of inferiority and superiority as based on physiological differences. But though not overdetermining, race certainly was invoked when required. Lousteau appears to do just this when he argues that "no black can call himself free who does not have proof of that condition." Blackness, he seems to be saying, is at the very least a warning sign. In her study of the Police des Noirs and of ideas of race in late-eighteenth-century France, Sue Peabody has argued that while in the seventeenth and early eighteenth centuries the word *nègre* was most commonly used for "black" in France and denoted both color and slave status, by the later eighteenth century this was increasingly replaced by the word *noir*, signaling color, but allowing for the possibility that some blacks might be of free status (1996, 141n1).[8] But as Peabody also notes, contemporary dictionaries indicate that the word *nègre* was commonly associated with African origins, while Simone Delesalle and Lucette Valensi's survey of eighteenth-century dictionaries shows that sometimes *nègre* could denote "people of Africa" without implying slave status (Delesalle and Valensi 1972).

Not only was there slippage and ambiguity in the usage of racial terminology in metropolitan France at this time, but it is also clear that such terminology could vary from one colonial situation to another. As we have seen, Île de France was unusual in having a slave population drawn from a very wide range of geographical sources, and in particular in having a significant population of slaves of Indian origin living side by side with Indians of free status. The island's own shifting terminology reflected this complex situation: an Indian slave like Jouan would be more likely to be referred to as a noir esclave than as a nègre. Meanwhile, in France, lawyers were also grappling with the complexities of the

French Indian Ocean empire. Peabody discusses the very revealing case of Francisque, a slave from Pondichéry who had been brought to France by his master and then had attempted to evade his control. In the lawsuits that followed, Francisque's legal team argued, among other things, that Francisque, as an Indian, was not covered by the French laws devised for esclaves nègres. They backed this argument up with an elaborate contrast between the supposed barbarity of the African and the civility of Francisque's Indian natal home, drawing on Buffon's climatological theories, which isolated the African as peculiarly suited to slavery. But when it came to the crunch, Francisque's lawyers drew not only on a theory of "civilization," but also on the finer points of physiological differences among "blacks": "Such is Francisque: It suffices to see him to know that he has never spent a day on the burning sands of Guinea or Senegal. It is true that his nose is a bit large, his lips a little fat. But disregarding his color, he looks more European than many Europeans who need only black skin to appear African" (Peabody 1996, 65–66). In 1759 the lawyers won their case and Francisque was deemed a free person.

Clearly Lousteau was determined that no such argument might be made about Jouan, despite the latter's "civility." In fact, it was his very civility that made him such a valuable slave. But it seems that Jouan had precisely succeeded at "passing" for free in Pondichéry.

If Jouan's case points to the complexities of legal status and color, it also hints at other complexities. Were Jouan and Bernard men forging a fictive relationship of brotherhood (not uncommon in slave societies) or were they, perhaps, involved in a homosexual relationship (as implied at certain points in the court record), and if so, would this have been viewed as transgressive? Can we say that sexuality was at issue at all here?

Historians of France argue that it was only in the nineteenth century that the concept of the "homosexual" came into being;[9] however, some have also argued for an important shift having taken place in the late seventeenth and early eighteenth centuries in the conception of male same-sex relationships. The word *pederast* gradually replaced *sodomite* as a descriptive term, and police prosecutions for sodomy decreased.[10] Naval and piratic communities, however, remained associated in French thinking with the practice of sodomy, and this may well have had a resonance on Île de France—host, as we have seen, to thousands of sailors in this period. But in the record of the Jouan and Bernard case neither word is ever used (though, unfortunately, we will never know the words used in the gossip that surrounded the more formal proceedings)—rather, we are presented with ambiguity and ambivalence. At various moments it does appear that both Lousteau and the judge are trying to hint at something. Jouan's former friends and his former lover, Modeste, had remarked on a degree of closeness between him and Bernard that was, perhaps, unusual. Neither Pierre Moussa nor Lindor (both African slaves) seem to have been entirely convinced by the assumption of fraternity. Lousteau, meanwhile, used the verb *débaucher* to describe Bernard's alleged influence over Jouan. This could have sexual connotations, but in the eighteenth century it was a wide term that might be used to mean "lead astray" and (importantly, as we shall see) was commonly employed in cases concerning control over labor.[11]

It is possible, of course, that Jouan and Bernard did have a sexual relationship and were homosexuals avant la lettre. But (and here I deviate from the dominant narrative of the psychic life of slavery) it seems to me very unlikely that French concepts of sexuality, important as they might be, were the only concepts circulating on the island. A less ethnocentric analysis would have to allow for the possibility, at least, that Jouan and Bernard's relationship drew on a long history of male same-sex relationships in the Islamic tradition of India.

Jouan and Bernard, as far as we can tell, came from southern India. That is as much as we know for certain, and therefore, as I have already indicated, we must be wary of inventing their ethnic roots and lapsing into some kind of ethnographic exoticism. The emerging history of masculinities and male sexualities in India is, however, worth signaling, not because of its radical difference to the French history, but because of its parallels and convergences.

Rosalind O'Hanlon, for example, has described the shifting codes of masculinity in the Mughal courts of northern India in the seventeenth and eighteenth centuries (1997, 1999).[12] Among these was the *mirza* tradition. *Mirza'I* derived from the Persian suffix used to indicate princely or noble status. In India, however, it came to be associated with the cultivation of a particular version of masculine gentility and of personal cultivation in the courtly tradition. Manuals of the late seventeenth century defined appropriate conduct for the mirza down to the last detail of dress and deportment. The Indian mirza tradition of this period, as O'Hanlon makes clear, is firmly located within the history of the spread of luxury goods and revolution in consumption—great emphasis was placed on fine dress, food, drink, the etiquette of bathing, the furnishing of a house, the appreciation of gardens, smells, and sounds. But the conduct manuals, while offering advice, also expressed anxiety. The first anxiety concerned the use of the *mirza* "cult" as a mode of social mobility: "Their principal concern," writes O'Hanlon of the authors of these manuals, "is to define the boundaries of the *mirza'I* against upstarts and social inferiors seeking to pass themselves off as *mirza*, but who had no proper understanding of the social and spiritual cultivation that a true *mirza* should possess" (1999, 72).

The second anxiety concerned the boundaries of gender identity and sexuality. The *mirza* was warned that the border between the cultivation of this particular version of elite masculinity and effeminacy was a fragile one. Manliness of this kind was defined by a narcissistic refinement, but the proper distinctions between men and women had somehow to be held in place. Effeminate style and deportment might also be taken to be homoerotic. Contemporary sources apparently point to an inclusive approach to sexual pleasure, despite imperial attempts to distance the court from Mughal traditions of explicit and public homosexual attachment. The expression of same-sex desire remained common but did not necessarily denote any exclusive homosexual identity (O'Hanlon 1999, 80).

Clearly this history is unique in many ways, but it does have some interesting resonances with similar debates in France. There are common themes in the spread of luxury consumption, and anxieties around social mobility, "effeminacy," and sexuality. Michel Rey, in discussing Paris in the first half of the eighteenth century, emphasizes the importance of class to the meaning of certain styles of masculinity:

> To people of the lower class, a noble—powdered, pomaded and refined—was both elegant and effeminate; but that bothered no-one as long as the mode of attire remained faithful to the specific social tradition which its wearer represented. If someone lower on the social scale assumed this costume . . . not only did he betray his social condition, but in addition, his effeminacy, by losing its accepted association with elegance and upper class, became an indication of the wearer's *real* effeminacy. (1987, 189)

At stake, argues Rey, was a "double deception" of both gender and social status.

With some of these issues in mind, we can return to the case of Jouan and Bernard. Perhaps the ambiguity surrounding their relationship can be explained if we allow that sexuality may not have been the main issue here, or at least not an isolable issue. The eighteenth century in France may well, as Foucault argued, have seen the rise of new and specific discourses on sexuality, but their progress (if that is what we can call them) was hardly linear, least of all, perhaps, in a colonial context.[13] What may have been more immediately relevant here were issues of honor and social status. The masculinity at stake, I would argue, is not Bernard's or Jouan's, but Lousteau's.

Lousteau took pride in his slave, Jouan, not only because his skills as a carpenter were of great economic value, but because of his demeanor, his appearance, his elaborate dress. Jouan was an Indian slave and though, as Marina Carter has shown (Carter 1988–1989), many Indian slaves worked side by side with their African and Malagasy counterparts in menial work, the evidence of manumission patterns in particular indicates that some slaves of Indian origin formed a relatively privileged group and were dominant among the ranks of domestic servants of the elite (Allen 1999). We are reminded too that the French possession of Pondichéry to which Jouan and Bernard were heading, and from which they may have previously come, had been, before its near destruction at the hands of the English, a very different colonial city from Port Louis. In his study of the society of Pondichéry in the eighteenth century, Jacques Weber (1993) describes a cosmopolitan city, very much a Franco-Indian creation. This was a slave-owning society (elite families employed slaves of both African and Indian origin), but to a far lesser extent than Île de France. The majority employed domestic servants of free status, albeit of low caste. While the colonists of Île de France had had no "native" society to engage with, this was very far from the case in Pondichéry, where the French were obliged to recognize and work with the complex of caste and other distinctions within the Indian population. Among other distinct groups were the Topas, like Bernard, described by Weber as being heavily influenced by Western culture, subject to French civil law, and dressed distinctly in European clothes with a hat known as *topi* in the Tamoul language, from which their generic name derived (1993, 151). Pondichéry, at its height, had also been the location of sumptuous consumption—of the wealth of Indian textiles and of elaborate locally manufactured furniture, for example. And amid other items of conspicuous display was the liveried domestic servant.

When, in the 1780s, the elite of Île de France began to assume, more confidently, the cultural attributes of a colonial elite, the possession of exotically dressed Indian slaves may have become an important marker of wealth and status. So when Lousteau lost Jouan, he had lost a component of his social capital. For in this particular slave regime it was not always the case that, as Patterson argued (Patterson 1982, 98), the master's sense of reputation and recognition depended on the degradation of his slave— the opposite might be true. What is more important is that Lousteau had lost Jouan to another man—Bernard—who had "seduced" him away, and then to another—Lieutenant Brousse, who had believed him to be free. The problem for Lousteau was not unlike that described by Rey. Jouan's particular kind of masculinity (which depended perhaps on a play on femininity) made him both valuable and dangerous, for if it went "too far" it would enable him to "pass" as free: "On this island," Lousteau had said, "no black man can call himself free who does not have proof of that condition." The deception at work here was peculiar to a slave-owning society. Lousteau's honor was at stake with the loss of Jouan, and Jouan's sexuality was relevant only insofar as it might have played a part in his escape. Sexual desire between men, if it existed in this case, may not have been seen as particularly transgressive. The disruptive desire was Jouan's desire (as described by Lindor) to "find his freedom."

There are other desires in circulation in this story other than sexual desire (if that it is). Lousteau is thinking about the loss of wealth and honor; Modeste may have been sexually jealous—we cannot know for sure, but she seems particularly keen to get her clothing and jewelry back. In fact, in this story, as in many others, intimacy is expressed through the location and lending and giving of material belongings.[14] We know (or we think we know) that Bernard and Jouan are unusually intimate in part because, as both Lousteau and Modeste point out, Bernard returns to the island wearing Jouan's shirt, handkerchief, and gold-bordered hat. Of course, these things may have been given in payment (just as Lindor is possibly paid off by Jouan with the gift of the blue shirt, with its rather suggestive gold heart in the pocket), but witnesses seem inclined to interpret the exchange of goods as a sign of intimacy. Île de France may not have been Paris, but it was a place in which luxury goods both passed through and were, by some, consumed. Alongside the abject poverty, the lack of clothes and food, was continual evidence of wealth and excess. The island imported a range of textiles from both India and France, porcelain from China, and domestic commodities, described by Toussaint as ranging from "feathers for hats and anti-syphilitic balsam, to heavy wardrobes, cabinets and coaches" (Toussaint 1967, 117). There were plenty of opportunities, then, for social and economic distinctions to be marked through dress, bodily management, and domestic furnishings. The vast majority of slaves could play no part in this economy of refinement, but a few, like Jouan, did. Lousteau was proud of his slave's refinement, his clothes, his cleanliness and demeanor, because it reflected well on him—but these very attributes also enabled Jouan to "pass" as free.[15]

Sex and Economics

Economics quite explicitly dominated elite discourses on sexual morality on the island, particularly in the first half of the century: sex and monopoly, sex and usury, sex and production, and sex and free trade were all part of this vocabulary.[16] As we have seen, in the early decades of French rule, as in the Dutch period, a critique of sexual morality (along with the important question of the *distribution des noirs*) was intrinsic to the critique of the elite and its abuse of power. Administrators were portrayed as greedy—greedy for sex, greedy for slaves, attempting to monopolize access to both. In the 1720s, for example, the newly arrived Lazarist priests complained that the immorality of the officers of the Company got in the way of their avowed mission to "give comfort to the poor slaves." The Code Noir, a version of which had been promulgated on the island in 1723, made it clear that responsibility for the moral and religious welfare of slaves lay with their masters. But the priests were persuaded that the morality of the majority of masters was not one to be emulated. They were even more critical of what they saw as officially sponsored immorality. In their view, the attempt to install family life on the island through the importation of Breton girls had backfired disastrously. Both islands, they asserted, had been quite literally infected by them, and worse, senior officers of the Company had actively participated in the spread of this "infection." How, asked one priest, could an officer be regarded as fit to be in a position of authority who, though married, had contracted a venereal disease from one of these girls and then, to make matters worse, had proceeded to marry her to a habitant, whom she also infected?[17]

But if sexual immorality was associated with old-fashioned monopoly and the abuse of power in the first half of the century, the priests found no comfort at all in the liberalization of trade in the second half. In fact, they clearly thought that with the granting of this "freedom" things only became worse.

Even before the introduction of a limited version of free trade in 1769, observers had employed a contrast between the two islands of Île de France and Île Bourbon to illustrate the political economy of debauchery (Racault 1996). For although the islands might both be, in the words of the priests, "two little corners of prostitution and debauchery," one was widely held to be worse than the other. The difference lay, apparently, in their economies, for while Île Bourbon was an island of small producers (who, were it not for the crucial fact of slave ownership, one might be tempted to label "peasants"), Île de France was an island of trade and war, of sailors and soldiers and "get-rich-quick" merchants. It was, as we have seen, a very masculine place, with what to the priests were "regrettable" tendencies, made worse by the liberalization of trade. "It is hardly surprising," wrote Father Teste in 1764, "that men who think only of their fortune are so given to the lowest of vices," adding that "vice is introduced easily here by outsiders, but rather than leaving with them, it spreads and swells."[18] In 1772 Father Caulier wrote, in a similar vein, that things were worse on Île de France than on Île Bourbon due to the "transitory gold-diggers, the sailors, the merchants and the military men, whose morals and religion are, so to speak, already formed in the 'torrid zone' even before they arrive on the island."[19] Just as the island had no "natives," neither, or so it was implied, did it harbor "original sin"—immorality originated elsewhere, either in Europe, or in other parts of the "torrid zone." Bernardin de St. Pierre expressed the same view. Remarking that European women on the island looked with disdain on the creole woman, who herself regards the European as an "adventurer," he went on: "If the state of marriage leads to infidelities, the fault is ours, we who have brought our French morals to an African sky" (2002, 123–124).

Predictably, the priesthood itself was not immune from charges of immorality. In 1759 Father Borgne wrote from Port Louis that "to the shame of our religion there is always a troop of scandals here." Among them was that concerning Père Botrel, a priest from Paris whose letter of "seduction" to a young girl had been intercepted by her parents. Then there was a "certain Père Lambert Cordelier" who was always to be found dead drunk on the streets, and the Abbé Tournillon, who, since he had arrived on the island, was found every night at dances with négresses, and had even caused disturbances in church.[20]

Imported it may have been, but like many things on Île de France, sexual immorality and the discourse surrounding it went "native" quickly, taking forms specific to the island's social and economic makeup. As elsewhere, sexual scandals were simultaneously social commentaries. On one hand, the colonial elite appeared to revel (particularly after the publication of *Paul et Virginie*) in the island's reputation as the site of intense romantic encounters. The legend of Île de France as it emerges in the course of the nineteenth century includes, approvingly, the story of Governor David's romantic exploits (which necessitated the building of a large country house, Le Réduit, for the accommodation of his love affairs), and the great passion (unconsummated, it is implied) of Bernardin de St. Pierre for Mme. Poivre, wife of Intendant Pierre Poivre. Mme. Journel's memoirs also contain accounts of the romantic exploits of the island's colonial male elite.[21] But for St. Pierre, romance was one thing, sexuality another. In *Paul et Virginie,* for example, the "perfect" incestuous love between the two children is shattered by Virginie's sexual awakening, in a famous passage depicting her sexuality as a "strange ailment" by which "her skin took on a yellow tint; her fine blue eyes became shot with black; all her body felt languid and oppressed," she was "filled with fear by these dangerous shadows and by these waters that burn hotter than the sun in the torrid zone." Paul, it appears, did not suffer from an equivalent ailment.

While the elite was not immune from criticism by the priests, more commonly sexual disorder was seen as a vice of the lower classes. The colonial commentator Moreau de St. Méry[22] attributed the "vices" of life on Île de France to the presence of a "multitude" of workers and soldiers and petty traders who "devote their first earnings to the acquisition of a négresse, on the frivolous pretext of some necessary service, but in fact destined for a use against the morals, religion and laws of the country."[23] He goes on, however, to point the finger equally at the population of *femmes libres* (of whom more later) who, "frequently accompanied by the vile products of [their] crimes" and without resources, resort to prostitution to support themselves.

As Ann Stoler has argued (1995), "sexual disorders" were as often *expressions* of the colonial order of things as they were *subversions* of it. Such disorders and illicit desires were as much about bonds as they were about boundaries. All manner of relationships could be accommodated, as long as they did not seriously threaten property or the institution of slavery, or cause larger social order problems. Of course, sometimes they did just that, and it is these cases that found their way into the historical record.

Take, for example, the not untypical case of the lovesick sailor François Bangé (or Béranger). He had been living with Zilia, a young Bengalie slave, fourteen or fifteen years old, whose owner, M. Ravenel, divided his time between a habitation in Trois Ilots and a house in Port Louis. Some three months into the relationship, Bangé had approached M. Ravenel to "ask for mercy" for the girl and offered to buy her. His offer was declined, which angered him, but the two continued to live together and she kept her belongings in his house (which, as we have seen, was considered a sign of trust and intimacy). There is no indication that this arrangement caused any particular problems—presumably Zilia, who was "pretty" and favored by Mme. Ravenel, continued to execute her duties as a domestic slave satisfactorily. Then one day in 1793 Bangé had gone to visit Zilia on Ravenel's habitation, along with a number of friends. In the words of another of Ravenel's slaves, Sophie, the men had "kidnapped" Zilia and taken her away by canoe. A search was mounted in Port Louis. Bangé was spotted coming out of a bar run by Dame Rousseau with four companions and a young girl, heading along the canal toward the Camp des Noirs. The "good citizens" took the girl away and put her in a block for the night, from which she had escaped by morning. Bangé and his friends had meanwhile caused a significant disturbance. When the "good citizens" had attempted to arrest him he had said, "You can do what you like, but I am too attached to the girl to abandon her," adding that he would "cut off their heads like turnips."

Bangé's arrangement with Zilia would hardly have been unusual. Though there were repeatedly reiterated ordinances against whites living in the Camp des Noirs of Port Louis, this rule was largely unenforceable. Zilia's master, M. Ravenel, almost certainly knew that Zilia spent much of her time with Bangé—Bangé had probably said as much when he had asked to buy her. What really caused the problem was her abduction (if that it was) from the habitation. Sophie had indicated that Zilia had not just gone to Port Louis with her lover but had been "kidnapped" by Bangé and his friends. And then, of course, when cornered, Bangé had created a public order problem with his violent resistance and threats to cut off heads. In the context of the Revolutionary years in particular, when everyone was jumpy and when rumors spread of a possible slave rising abetted by sailors and soldiers, it is easy to see why Bangé's behavior might have caused alarm—not because of his infatuation with Zilia, but because of his rebelliousness. What bothered Ravenel, it seems, was not that his slave was living with a sailor, but that the sailor might deprive him of her labor. He was insistent that she was a valuable slave, and that his wife liked her. Just as Jouan meant a great deal to Lousteau, so Zilia meant a great deal to M. and Mme. Ravenel. What Zilia herself might have felt and thought and wanted is a different and more obtuse matter—she might have been a willing participant in her own abduction, or she may have been a victim of violence and rape.

There were, as I have indicated, some very powerful and dominant discourses on sex and sexuality on Île de France. But, as Stoler has argued for other colonial contexts (1995), this is no more a straightforward Foucauldian tale of the production of sexuality as a separate realm than it is a Freudian tale of repression. In fact, it would appear from this history that discourses on colonial sexuality sometimes arose not to displace what Foucault calls the "deployment of alliance," but to reinforce it. Sexual alliances (in addition to formal marriage alliances) could have important material consequences, both negative and positive, for property, inheritance, family reputations and hence jobs, business deals, and social and political advancement. Illicit sex might be the norm for most white men, but it could still be used against them by their enemies on an island where everyone (or so it sometimes appears) was a satirist. We have seen that M. Grenville de Forval lived openly with the Malagasy "Princess Betsy," whose skill at combining an "aristocratic" air with a certain degree of subservience deflected criticism. The authors of the *Dictionary of Mauritian Biography* insist that the story that they married is false, and this may well be important, since marriage would obviously have increased her claims on his wealth. On occasion, however, the anxiety created by such relationships would be sufficiently heightened to find its way into correspondence with Paris.

In 1777 the intendant, Maillart Dumesle, wrote to the Ministère de la Marine of his distress at learning of the marriage of a military officer, M. le Chevalier de Hort, with one Demoiselle Réminac, for "despite this officer's attempts to keep this secret, the public have penetrated something." What the "public" (an interesting term) had "penetrated" was the "secret" of the demoiselle's origins. Her father, it seems, was the offspring of a union in India between a French soldier and a former slave who "owed her liberty and enfranchisement only to her marriage with this soldier." The "public" could not understand, he went on, how M. de Hort could have "lost sight" of the distance that separated him from the woman with whom he had now formed an indissoluble union: "You will judge easily . . . how much respect he has lost in giving his hand and his name to a person, the issue of blood (*issue d'un sang*) which still needs some generations to pass before being counted even as the bottom rank of bourgeois."[24]

Île de France did not go in for the obsessive classification of degrees of blackness which characterized the racial discourse of the Antilles, but there is no denying the anxiety about race that emerges from this unusually explicit statement. Nevertheless, there is no uncomplicated deployment of race. First, the statement invites us to consider the relationship between degrees of blackness and degrees of freedom, for freedom, despite the rhetoric, was always relative. Had Demoiselle Réminiac's grandmother been a "free black" from birth, rather than a slave enfranchised for the purpose of marriage, then, it is implied, this superior status might have somewhat tempered her color, for color was relative too. This could also work the other way around, as we are reminded by no less than the king. In 1766, in a general circular to the colonies, he drew attention to, and expressly forbade, the practice among priests of baptizing "as if free" children born to either gens de couleur or to those of mixed blood (*sang melé*), without first ascertaining their legal status and ensuring that their mothers had been affranchised.[25] Color, the king reminded everyone, was not a reliable indicator of legal status in this case—while Lousteau had argued that being black was at least a sign that a person might not be free.

If both race and legal status were relevant in the case of Demoiselle Réminac and Chevalier de Hort, so was class. Though the use of the phrase *issue de sang* can obviously be taken to refer to "black blood," it might also refer to social origins in a wider sense. We are told that it will take many generations of (implicitly) "whitening" before the Réminac offspring can be admitted to the lower ranks of the bourgeoisie. Transformation of blood is possible, then, if slow. But the concern over blood is also, arguably, a concern over M. le Chevalier de Hort's blood, for the consequence of his marriage might be a severe case of downward mobility among the nobility.[26] Had de Hort been of humbler origins, more proximate to those of his wife, it is unlikely that the proposed union would have produced this flurry of correspondence with Paris. And, of course, had this not been a case of marriage, with all its legal and financial consequences for future generations of the de Hort family and its fortune, it is unlikely that mention would have been made of it at all. Despite the moralizing of the priests and of visiting *philosophes*, concubinage was preferable to unsuitable marriage, for obvious reasons.

Illicit alliances, if they resulted in the birth of children, could create problems for elite families, even when race was not at issue. This seems to have been the case for Sr. Rivaltz de St. Anthoine, a prominent and fractious individual who had, in the late 1760s, been locked in dispute with the governor, Dumas, and found himself exiled for a period to Rodrigues.[27] In 1781 he seemed less concerned with politics and more with disposing, on the part of a friend, of an inconvenient child.[28] Rivaltz de St. Anthoine's friend was Sr. Leroux Kymorseven,[29] another prominent and very wealthy Île de France figure, who had a habitation in Pamplemousses and whom we have met supplying the administration with his own slaves. Working on the habitation as a manager was a young "bourgeois," Matthieu des Landes. Rivaltz de St. Anthoine approached des Landes on a visit to his friend and told him that he had a proposition to make which would ensure that des Landes "made his fortune." Des Landes professed himself deeply honored by his superior's interest and inquired as to what he needed to do. Rivaltz de St. Anthoine then said:

> You saw that small girl who was dining at the table; she is the illegitimate child of M. Leroux Kymorseven and Demoiselle Dupont. I know that your wife gave birth to a baby on board the ship that brought you here from France, some four years ago. That child is now dead; M. Leroux Kymorseven's daughter is about the same age. What you need to do, my dear des Landes, is to declare yourself the father of the girl, who we will pretend is the very same child as that your wife gave birth to onboard ship. In order to execute this in the utmost secrecy, we will go to the parish of Moka to baptize her. I will be the godfather and my daughter the godmother.

Des Landes protested that the child born to his wife had been a boy, and he had a certificate of baptism indicating that. Rivaltz de St. Anthoine argued that this was not a serious problem—all they had to do was to scratch out the word *fils* and put, in its place, the word *fille*. Des Landes said he was worried about the consequences for his other, living child, and his inheritance. Rivaltz de St. Anthoine said that his friend had undertaken to pay des Landes the sum of 12,000 livres and to give him a habitation. This was a generous offer, and des Landes was, in his own words, "seduced" by it. Rivaltz de St. Anthoine then took the baptism certificate, altered it, and at a later date arranged for them to travel to Moka, to a priest with whom he had made the necessary arrangements. The child was baptized as Anthoinette Louise des Landes, the legitimate daughter of Matthieu des Landes and his wife, Marie Veronique Boidec. Des Landes, despite assurances, continued to feel uneasy and confided in his wife. No one had counted on the ferocity of her disapproval. When Rivaltz de St. Anthoine was again visiting his friend on the Pample-mousses habitation she found the two men, argued with them loudly (several witnesses heard the altercation) and threatened to make the matter public. Rivaltz de St. Anthoine threatened her, saying that her husband was disliked by the procureur-général, and that if she made any noise about the affair she would see him carried off to the authorities. Des Landes decided, at this point, to "deposit his fears and his concerns at the breast of the law," arguing that he had been an innocent participant in a maneuver that "did violence to the laws of nature and of the state." The record of the case, unfortunately, stops here.

If sexual "transgression" was part of the "colonial order of things" and mattered only when it threatened relations of property and class, never-theless, by the 1780s, it is beginning to take on a life of its own and to be more closely associated with a discourse on race. The reason for this is easily identified in the emergence of a larger (though still comparatively small) free black population, dominated by women. Sex and race begin now to look like two incestuous siblings, producing offspring from their illicit union.

Love among Slaves

Bernardin de St. Pierre seems not at all sure how to represent the sex-uality of slaves. As an antislavery activist he is drawn to a depiction of slave sexual innocence. In *Paul et Virginie* slave sexuality is, for the most part, contained "within the family," mirroring the relationship between Paul and Virginie. And so Marguerite's worthy Wolof slave, Domingue, is married to Mme. de la Tour's Malagasy slave, Marie. Their ethnicities are different, but they and their owners are part of one "family." In his earlier *Voyage* Bernardin de St. Pierre had portrayed the slaves of the island as seeking love rather than expressing their sexuality. Love among slaves, he implied, was a defense against the melancholy intrinsic to their state. Or, perhaps more accurately, love on the part of *male* slaves was such a defense. It was also a compensation for loss of their mothers: "By temperament, Negroes are naturally playful, but after some time as slaves, they turn melancholic. Only love seems to still conjure away their sorrows. They will do anything to get hold of a woman. If they can choose, they prefer women who have passed the prime of their youth; they say 'they make better soup' " (Bernardin de St. Pierre [1773] 2002, 129).

Bernardin de St. Pierre's male slaves are looking for mothers, and his female slaves are soup-making matriarchs, rather than sexually predatory sirens. He domesticates slave desire and makes love among slaves innocent. Perhaps this was the only comfortable representation for an abolitionist, but it may also have reflected something of the reality of slave life, in which the formation of a household between men and women was as much to do with soup as it was to do with sex. Certainly, his hint that the loss of the mother was at the heart of the melancholy of the slave state has resonances with recent theoretical work on the psychic life of colonialism and slavery (hooks 1996; Moglen 1997).

Even the most moralizing of observers, the Lazarist priests, have relatively little to say about slave sexuality. Father Teste's remarks of 1764 are fairly typical, referring in a matter-of-fact way to the general presence of libertinage among slaves and the lack of attention to these matters by owners.[30] In 1742 another priest, Father Criais (referring probably to Île Bourbon rather than Île de France), argued that immorality among slaves was in part due to their "maldistribution." Occasions arose among the poorer habitants, he said, where there might be five or six négresses to only one noir.[31] Father Caulier explained in 1772 that very few slaves were ever admitted to the Eucharist because they were unwilling to give up their "sinful habits," which were encouraged by the sexes living "pêle-mêle" together.[32] The catechism in the creole language Caulier had written for the islands referred, of course, to sexual morality:

> Do not run around, do not make mischief with girls, and the wives of
> others: do not keep anyone in your hut; do not spoil the households of

others. . . . Do not speak mischief, do not think malicious thoughts, do not take sinful pleasure. . . .

Is the marriage of Christians like the marriages of pagans who leave each other? No. Once married, they never leave each other, unto death. . . .

Married people, men and women live together in peace, with friendship in their heart, listening to the reason of each other, never arguing or fighting or seeking to quarrel. Never run around, either man for his part, or woman for hers, keep faithful, unto death.[33]

The progress of the Catholic faith on the island was, however, so slow in this period that it seems highly unlikely that Christian concepts of marriage and morality influenced more than a small minority of slaves. The priests of the Lazarist order concentrated their attention on Île Bourbon, which they viewed as a more fertile ground for the implantation of Christianity.

Elsewhere in the archive, sexual and romantic relationships between slaves appear only when they create a problem—usually a dispute between men that allegedly has its root in jealousy over a woman. The relative silence around the sexuality of slaves, and particularly of women slaves, contrasts to the noise increasingly evident toward the end of the century around the figure of the "free black" woman. This reminds us of the deeper silence underlining this history. Though between masters and women slaves there may have been long-term and affectionate relationships usually resulting in the manumission of the woman, we must assume that there were many, many more that were nonconsensual and violent. Rape of the woman slave by her master was an act of violence so normalized and so unlikely to create a problem of social order that it could be passed over without comment, though Milbert glimpses it, perhaps, symbolized in the deformed feet of the Indian slave, and Bernardin de St. Pierre employs the desperate figure of the ill-treated woman slave (whom Virginie and Paul "rescue") to allude to it.

Sex between the master and the slave woman was in a sense sex within the family, incest within the fantasy family of slavery, nominally transgressive, but largely undisruptive of the colonial order of things. The woman slave, unlike the "free black" woman or her male counterpart, was not a desiring subject—her sexuality had no separate existence, it was part and parcel of the labor she performed.

Maroons and Masculinity

While rape of slave women by their masters is a deafening silence in the historical record, there is plenty of noise over the alleged sexual ambitions of maroon male slaves. As in the Dutch period, in the French maroon slaves continued to disrupt, to excite the imagination, and to terrify. In reality, as the century wore on and as the spatial colonization of the island was extended and deepened, so the possibility of maroons forming secure, hidden alternative communities in the forests receded. But the French *preferred* to think of "their" maroons as inhabiting this other space, rather than face the fact, increasingly apparent, that many maroons were urban runaways, hiding out in the crowded streets of Port Louis, and sometimes living within earshot of their masters and mistresses.[34] This was, in one sense, a much more threatening prospect.

The Mozambique slave Rose was an example of such an urban maroon. She was arrested in the Camp des Malabars in Port Louis where she had been living with a group of slaves belonging to the king and using her skills as a seamstress to keep herself fed. She had originally been a slave of the Company, but at its dissolution had been sold to a judge, Bois-Martin, and by him to a lawyer, Balu. She said that she had gone maroon at the time of the Fête Bonne Année[35] and, judging by the moon, she said she had been maroon for over a month. Her body was already marked and mutilated with the evidence of previous convictions for marronnage —both her ears had been cut off, and her shoulders were also marked. Now she would have the *fleur de lis* burned onto her left cheek and would be chained "in perpetuity."[36]

Given the common practice of hiring out slaves to work, it was not always clear where the boundary of marronnage lay. Slaves were supposed to carry a permit from their masters and mistresses when they were living and working away from them, but this was largely unenforceable. The supposed marronnage of François in 1790 demonstrates the confusion, which slaves could sometimes use to their advantage. François was a Mozambique slave, who belonged to a woman named Nanette, a créole libre. He had spent some time on the habitation of M. Ceré (the botanist) and then moved on to work for a tanner named Cavallo. The latter had given him board and lodging in return for his harvesting of nuts. Cavallo, denying that he had been harboring a maroon, said that he had employed François because he had shown him a note from Nanette, permitting him to work.[37] And some so-called maroons were simply destitute or lost. Tulip, for example, described as a small Mozambique boy of the Macombe caste, was found wandering in 1776. He knew neither his master nor the district in which he lived, but was later claimed.[38]

These cases may have been fairly typical of maroons of the latter part of the century, but remaining far more prominent in the minds of habitants, administrators, and, possibly, slaves, were the rare large organized groups. Like the Dutch, the French appear to have found some comfort in the idea of conspiracy. They were deeply invested, in fact, in the fantasy that maroon communities were hierarchical, highly organized, ruthless, and plotting to overthrow the entire regime. At the head of the maroon community was the figure of the hypermasculine leader of the "band" who was also, importantly, portrayed as a rapist.

There was no shortage of maroon women who, when arrested, claimed that they had not been voluntary maroons but had been kidnapped by men and taken into the forest against their wishes. Earlier I gave the example of Magdalene Marena, part of the band of La Grande Barbe, who claimed that she had been kidnapped when pregnant and her baby later killed. There were others. Monique, Marie, and Louison had a similar story to tell when they were arrested in a "Camp des Noirs Marons" in the hills behind Grand Port in the southeast of the island in 1746. A habitant whose own woman slave had been kidnapped on the Moka road had orchestrated their arrest. According to him, the camp comprised five newly built huts and contained over twenty maroons. The three women had been taken to Grand Port and placed in the block. They were, it was noted, *chargées de gris-gris*—wearing amulets and charms. Monique, a "Mozambique," when asked why she had gone maroon, replied that she had not done so voluntarily. One day, while collecting wild greens, her baby on her back, she had been captured by Quinga, who was armed with a saber, and who had taken her into the woods. He had taken her child and speared it. Once in the camp she had become Quinga's "wife," but after a month or so he had been killed by another maroon.[39] Louison, a Malagasy, was then interrogated. She was pregnant and said that she had been in the band for some time. Asked if her real name was Louison, she replied that her Malagasy name was Fonavola and that this was the name she used among the maroons, but when with her various masters she was called Louison. Marie, another Malagasy, said that she had not been so long in the camp. She had been kidnapped, she said, at the time when M. de

Labourdonnais had left the island to go to war. All three women denied that they had ever accompanied the men on raids. Their job, they said, had been to stay in the camp.

There were good reasons for women to deny in court that they were voluntary maroons—if convinced of this the judge might drop the charges against them, or at least find them not guilty of the additional crimes (theft, for example) that exacerbated the charge of marronnage. And, as I have indicated, there was a powerful propensity on the part of the French to imagine male maroon leaders as supremely violent men, rapists and pillagers. The other side of this vision, as we have already seen, was a romanticization of the "good maroon," which seems to have assumed a place in Mauritian folklore of the nineteenth century (once slavery had gone, to be replaced by indentured labor). It would seem extremely naïve to adopt a version of this romanticization when reading these cases. Maroon groups emerged out of the violence of slavery and were almost certainly themselves desperate and violent communities. They shared with the society they had temporarily escaped from the marked imbalance of the sexes. Women were a vulnerable minority. Yet maroon groups did not simply mirror the larger society. There is evidence, sparse and fragmentary, that they might create a somewhat different cultural space. Magdalene Marena, the Malagasy maroon whose baby had been killed, spoke of "practicing the religion of her country"; observers commented on the frequent use of charms and amulets by maroons (Monique, Marie, and Louison had been "weighed down" by them), and Louison was not the only captured maroon to refer to her alternative, original name. Marie's assertion that she had gone maroon at the time when Labourdonnais had gone to war was also not untypical. Maroon time may have been different in some ways, but what made maroons such a threat was the fact that they were not, and could never be, completely out of sight or out of time. Moving from one space to another, between forest and habitation and even the town, they kept up to date with the news of the colony. When captured and questioned they often referred to the "time of Labourdonnais," or the "time of Magon," or some other administrator, giving the impression that, from their vantage points in the forested mountains, they could somehow view the comings and goings of the whole island. The interweave between French fantasy and maroon realities was, then, a complex one. Each society in a sense needed the other.

Our most suggestive account of life inside the maroon camp comes from a trial of 1778. Unfortunately (as is often the case) the documentation is in poor condition and incomplete. It centers on the powerful figure of Machabe.[40] Machabe was a Malagasy in his midtwenties and he had gone maroon twice before. He belonged to the estate of the Vergès family, which was held in trust. On this occasion his escape had lasted two years. Or this is what he reckoned, offering the information that when he had first gone into the woods, M. de Ternay had already left the island.[41] He was accused not only of the crime of a repeat of marronnage (*marronnage recidivie*—this would be his third time, warranting the death penalty), but also of attacking and robbing slaves on the highway, of kidnapping several slave women, and, in the words of the judge, of exhibiting the "manifest intention" of similarly kidnapping white women (*les femmes blanches*).

Machabe told the judge that he went maroon because a new commander, Charlot, had been put in charge on the Vergès habitation, and his treatment was very harsh.[42] He had been fishing one day, he said, when he was approached by Cezar, the chief of the maroon band, who greeted him with *salam, salam*,[43] asked him if he was a maroon, and asked if he wanted to join him and others in the woods. He had agreed. The camp, he said, consisted of nine men, including himself, and sometimes some women. Cezar's wife, he offered, had been hanged (presumably for marronnage). He insisted that the men had no guns, but were armed with sabers, that they moved around frequently, and that they lived entirely on wild foods—*choux palmistes* (cabbage palm) and eels which they caught in the rivers. Another captured member of the band, Narcisse, also a Malagasy, said that he had gone maroon because his mistress, the widow Duplessis Campare, made him work beyond his physical capacity. She sent him out to the forest to cut wood, which he was then to sell, bringing her a given amount of money every day. If he failed to achieve this, she "mistreated" him. Rienzaf (this was his Malagasy name; he was otherwise known as Auguste) was arrested at the same time. He had been maroon for three years, driven away by a harsh slave commander. He insisted, however, that he had never been part of the "band" but had lived alone.

The interrogation of maroons followed a basic structure. Machabe, following legal procedure, was being interrogated alone. Later the judge would compare his account to that of others and confront him with witnesses. Machabe denied ever having pillaged cassava, corn, or chickens from the habitations, and said that Cezar the bandleader had never commanded him to do anything bad, except to kidnap women. This had been the fate of three women from the habitation of Sr. Brun. They were called Thérèse, Geneviève, and Babette and were arrested along with the men. Unfortunately most of their evidence is missing. Some has survived, however. Both men and women agreed that, having been seized and taken into the woods, the three women were "distributed" among the men. Machabe, on his own account (and that of the witnesses, including the women) had allocated to himself Geneviève. But, he said, Geneviève was young and very small and had complained that he was too big for her and would hurt her. Babette, her sister, had intervened to protect her. Machabe, apparently insulted by the suggestion that he might have been violent toward the women, offered the following account when confronted with their testimony:

> The accused said that, far from being obliged to use violence against the witness [Babette] and her comrades, the women had, on the contrary, expressed the greatest satisfaction at being at liberty with them in the woods. . . . That the witness lies when she alleges that he had hit her with a stick and had threatened to tie her to a tree and abandon her to all his comrades because she did not want him to sleep with her sister, Geneviève. . . . That he was not so mad that, having a woman, he would wish to share her with others, though it was true that, when the women were being shared out, little Geneviève, who was destined for him, had complained that he was too big for her, and that she would suffer with him, and so, in order to keep everyone happy, he had given her to Dianabe, contenting himself with Babette. The latter, believing that he was being unfaithful with Thérèse, showed signs of jealousy, which displeased him, and he had said to her that between maroons one had to exercise the greatest freedom (*qu'entre marrons on devoit jouir de plus grande liberté*).[44]

Machabe appeared keen to display to the judge something of the character of his masculinist maroon morality. Denying rape, he claimed to have acted in a chivalrous manner (trying to "keep everyone happy") by reallocating the "petite Geneviève" to Dianombe, "who, being smaller, suited her better." He also denied threatening Babette with any kind of gang rape, arguing that he would "be mad," having acquired a woman, to want to share her. At the same time, however, he asserted that sexual freedom (for men, that is) was an intrinsic part of maroon morality. Babette's supposed jealousy had no place in the maroon camp: "Between maroons, the greatest freedom should be enjoyed." Machabe was also in no mood for denial. His comrade, Rienzaf, continued to assert to the court that he had not been part of the "band" and that he had never met Machabe before. In the staged legal confrontation between the two men, Machabe asked, "Why not tell the truth, I know you, you know me . . . the White knows eveything. Why hide?" ("Pourquoi n'a pas dire la verité moi conne toy toy conne moi . . . Blanc conne tout. Pourquoi cacher?").

But the judge, it seems, wanted more, and there is one point on which Machabe would not gratify him. This is the allegation that he had threatened to abduct white women. Asked if he had ever boasted that he would "attack the whites" and kidnap white women, he denied this emphatically, though he said that he knew that this story had gone around the island, because he himself had heard it from a slave woman he had encountered in the woods. Later in the case, the charge was reiterated by a captured maroon woman, Françoise. Machabe again denied it, saying that "he was not so mad as to demand to dine with the Governor, neither had he ever boasted that he would sleep with a white woman if he was lacking a négresse" ("qu'il n'etait pas aussi fou pour dire qu'il iroit demande a dine a M. le Gouverneur et que jamais il ne s'est vante qu'il coucheroit avec une madame blanche lorsque les negresses lui manqueroient").

Machabe denied the charge of grandiosity (I am not so mad as to demand to dine with the governor), and the charge that he threatened to abduct and rape white women. That, he seemed to be saying, is your fantasy, not mine.

Chapter Seven

REPUTATION, RECOGNITION, AND RACE

*I*n 1791, and hence at the beginning of Île de France's years of Revolutionary turmoil, Anthoine Commarond complained to the police that his neighbor was seriously mistreating a slave.[1] Arriving home one evening on the street known as La Chaussée in Port Louis, Commarond was greeted by a young slave girl who told him that her master, and his neighbor, Sr. Beauralet, had sent her out, had chained up her mother, and was threatening to beat the latter when he had finished his supper. Commarond went to bed but was soon disturbed by the sounds of heavy strokes of the cane coming from his neighbor's quarters. The beating, he later said, was so long and so harsh that eventually he felt obliged to knock on the floor, indicating that it should stop. Beauralet did stop for a short while but, Commarond alleged, only to get his breath, and then he had started all over again. The sound of the cane and the cries of the poor woman had eventually forced him to get out of bed and to go downstairs, where he had protested to Beauralet that it was "horrific to mistreat the slave so cruelly and to trouble the rest of his neighbors," adding that he was himself thereby doing the work of a slave and that if the woman had misbehaved there was a police force to pronounce what her punishment should be, a bazaar (the usual site of public punishment), a jail and chains for those it was judged needed to be locked up. But Beauralet was furious at this intervention and this "sound advice" and responded by calling Commarond a *drôle*, a *polisson* (naughty child), and other equally insulting things. Commarond had retreated and gone back to bed, whence he could hear, all night, the crying of the slave woman.

The following morning at six o'clock he arrived at the police station to ask the police to intervene and to prevent Beauralet from punishing his slaves in this way, adding that he (and other neighbors) could testify that Beauralet had a method of tying up his slaves different from that of others: he attached the chain to their hands, hoisted them up toward the ceiling and left them hanging. Beauralet, summoned to the police, appeared unrepentant, telling them that he resented Commarond's interference and asserting that he was "master in his own house." He was particularly annoyed that Commarond had resorted to hanging out of his window and announcing loudly to the neighbors that he, Beauralet, was killing his slaves. But though Beauralet was generally undeterred, he was clearly sufficiently affected by the allegation to be insulted by Commarond's broadcasting of it. In addition, and tellingly, when he gave his own account of the incident to the police he implied that it was not he who had actually beaten the woman, but a slave commander: "I had my black give her a few strokes of the cane while waiting for the police to punish her according to the law."

An allegation of slave beating, made by one slave owner against another, like an allegation of wife beating, had the potential to do damage to that most valuable form of property—reputation. As this case implies, there was a constant tension between the powerful notion of the property owner's exclusive rights over his property (all the more forcefully articulated during the Revolution) and the idea of the public good. As Eugene Genovese put it, the "slave-holding community did not intervene against a brutal master because of moral outrage alone; it intervened to protect its interests" (Genovese 1975, 41).[2] As I discussed in chapter 3, the preservation of the institution of slavery in certain circumstances depended on the curtailment of the property owners' rights, their inclinations, their "inner dispositions," and particularly their violence. This in turn had deep class and racial dimensions—a man who beat his own slave was not only not a "respectable" man, he was also, in a very real sense, not a white man. This is a rather different interpretation of the role of honor than that put forward by Orlando Patterson, who argued that in slave-owning societies the master's honor was nurtured through the degradation of his slave (1982, 98). This may well have been the case in Île de France under some circumstances, but an alternative relationship between honor and mastery is also, very evidently, at work here.

As I have already argued, throughout the second half of the century, the Île de France authorities had attempted to move the disciplining of slaves from the private to the public domain and subject it to the increasingly hegemonic function of the law. Nominally such a function had existed since 1723, with the passage of a version of the seventeenth-century Code Noir, but it is difficult to discern any real effects of this on slave owners. More noticeable, however, is the evolution of a more "homegrown" moral economy of slavery, particularly in the last quarter of the century. As the institution came increasingly under attack from high-profile visitors such as Bernardin de St. Pierre, so the island's administrators and other members of the elite (lawyers included, of course) attempted to "civilize" it in order to preserve it. Though some of the roots of this shift were common, this was not the same phenomenon as the emergence of an ideology of "enlightened paternalism" that has been described for the North American plantation regime in the late eighteenth century.[3] I have already referred to work on South Africa at this time, but exact comparisons are difficult to make, owing to the lack of comparability of historical sources. We do know, however, that the expectation grew on Île de France that "respectable" slave owners did not physically punish slaves themselves but referred them to the island's authorities or, failing that, employed a slave commander to carry out the physical punishment. Beauralet was clearly sufficiently affected by this new moral discourse on punishment to claim that he had, in fact, employed a "black" to beat his slave, though we know this not to have been true. Physical constraint and violence still lay at the heart of this system, but as elsewhere, the violence enacted by slave owner on slave would be displaced onto another slave, or a free black, leaving the master in the role of spectator. To beat one's own slave was a sign not of power, but of weakness. Crucially, it also became a sign of lowly class origins. Of course, this is not to say that elite men and women did not beat their slaves and treat them cruelly—we know that some certainly did—but it is to argue that slave beating became a weapon in the conflicts which characterized the island's class of slave owners and their struggles for recognition.[4] Philip D. Morgan describes a similar phenomenon in late-eighteenth-century Virginia and South Carolina, where members of the elite, having deliberately fostered white lower-class contempt for their slaves, then recoiled in apparent horror at spectacles of violence and the "barbaric" treatment of slaves (1998, 311). Slavery, in order to survive, had to be a total disciplinary institution in a Foucauldian sense—an institution that relied not only on slaves, but also on slave owners disciplining themselves.

Slaves on Île de France then, as elsewhere, frequently acted as conduits for their masters' and mistresses' reputations and as carriers of class conflicts. Île de France society, as will have become apparent by now, was riven with jealousies, host to vicious and enduring disputes, a theater of slander and backbiting. Such disputes ran through all levels of society. Reputation, and the mutual recognition that lay behind it, was an extremely fragile commodity in what was in some senses (and despite its avowed rigidities) a highly mobile society. The economic history of the island in the eighteenth century has yet to be written, and unfortunately we do not have any clear picture of how, in this colonial outpost, the opportunities of trade and war may have accelerated and exaggerated the social mobility that was a feature of metropolitan France in this period. But, as we have seen, money could certainly be made in the Indian Ocean war zone, as many of the island's administrator/entrepreneurs knew very well. How stable these fortunes were, and how far they were translated into social status, is less clear. Volatility is perhaps more evident than stability in the records of the period, with an abundance of bankruptcy cases and incidences of what appears to be extreme downward mobility. Sometimes these cases have clear and direct economic causes, but more often it is difficult, if not impossible, to disentangle economics from reputation and social status.

The maritime colonial economy was certainly volatile and risky, though vast fortunes could be made, and some Île de France families became trading dynasties. Maritime trade was vulnerable to shipwreck, slave revolt, and the depredations of pirates, but investment in local productive activities on the island was also not without considerable risks. The Comte de Rostaing, who had served as a soldier in India under Labourdonnais, invested a considerable amount of money in opening a forge (the Forges de Mondesir) on Île de France—an enterprise for which there was a clear demand, since all the island's ironware had to be imported. He did this in partnership with a man named Hermans, who was clearly of lower social status than himself, and using the inheritance of his wife, who was the daughter of the marquis de Salner. He was, however, mostly an absentee entrepreneur, and in his absence the enterprise foundered and eventually collapsed. Pleading for employment in the Americas in the 1770s, he wrote that the failure of the forges could be put down to the following combination of circumstances: his absence from the island, the misfortunes of the war of 1756, the "maneuvers" of an "unfaithful" associate (clearly referring here to Hermans) and the "partial" judgment of a tribunal.[5] He might have added smallpox to this list of misfortunes, for in fact an epidemic had devastated the slave labor force on his enterprise.

The biographies of many of the island's elite speak to a fluidity we know to have been a feature of this island colony. Distance from France facilitated reinvention of self. The island had always been home or exile to the disowned, disinherited, and disreputable sons of French families for whom a colonial career, far away, appeared to offer a last chance of rehabilitation or (perhaps more likely) a continuation of their former activities away from the gaze of superiors. But fluidity and mobility are only part of the story. The very fact of social fluidity could in itself give rise to anxiety, to a conservative reaction, and to an impulse to reinstate boundaries and proofs of status. As Daniel Roche has put it in analyzing social classifications in France at this time, there was a reality to the Imaginary of orders and privileges, even while these distinctions were being blurred (1998, 398). The island's most prominent professional elite, its lawyers, themselves sometimes the products of social mobility, showed all the signs of the anxiety that accompanied this, and they were continually engaged in disputes over honor and reputation. These disputes could, in themselves, result in economic and social ruin.

Jean Lousteau, whom we have met already pursuing his favored slave Jouan, was involved in many more court cases throughout the 1770s and 1780s. One was a long-running and acrimonious dispute with the judge Pourcher de la Serré. Pourcher de la Serré, according to his personnel records, had been a counselor of the Parlement of Bourgogne before becoming a judge on Île de France in 1772; Lousteau was clerk to the island's high court and had a large legal practice. Lousteau claimed that he had been gravely insulted by Pourcher de la Serré, in the presence of others, with what he called "apostrophes grossières." Among these alleged remarks was the biting comment that "people who are bottle washers in France arrive here and think themselves the equal of their superiors." The altercation and the ensuing scandal were sufficiently prolonged, and the insult regarded by Lousteau as sufficiently damaging, for him to enlist the help of his brother, a merchant in Paris, who wrote to the Ministère de la Marine, "It will not have escaped you that one of the most ancient families, who hold among the best houses in the Province of Bearn, and who feel themselves so wickedly insulted, must obtain a just satisfaction."[6] Lousteau's wife left the island in 1780 to join in her husband's defense in Paris.

In fact, both men had more serious problems. Lousteau, who had been the subject of a long-running fraud and corruption case, alleged that he was being persecuted by the intendant, Denis-Nicolas Foucault, and eventually obtained vindication from the king. Pourcher de la Serré, in 1776, was accused of theft, in what looks like a classic setup,[7] and he spent the rest of his life trying to clear his name. He died a ruined man. In 1785 his widow, Mme. Lancel, outlined her plight to the Ministère de la Marine, requesting a pension. In addition to their other problems, the Pourcher de la Serré family, on their return to France, had been both kidnapped by the English and then shipwrecked off Brittany, losing all their belongings in the process. Pulling at the heartstrings of the Ministère, she finished her letter with the following postscript:

> About four years ago, Monseigneur, I had the honor of presenting to you my son and I told you that since the age of two he had been a volunteer, without appointment. I asked you if you thought it appropriate that he continue to wear the uniform, and you generously told me that I could be judge of that. Now he is nearly nine years old. I am taking the liberty of asking you this question again, and, if it is possible, that he might be given half the pay of a volunteer, to help me with my needs. I can assure you that this child will one day be a brave soldier.[8]

A decade or so earlier, a dispute at the very top of the administration had threatened to rip the island's elite apart. The famously acrimonious relationship between the intendant and botanist, Pierre Poivre, and the commandant general, Dumas,[9] had rippled throughout the entire community, implicating a number of individuals. Among them was Rivaltz de St. Anthoine, whom we have already met attempting to arrange for the "adoption" of his friend's natural child. He was eventually exiled by Dumas for eight months to the even smaller island of Rodrigues, during which period he kept a diary expressing his feelings of injustice and outrage.[10] In 1769, released from captivity, he was in Paris, complaining to the duc de Praslin of his treatment at the hands of Dumas. An anonymous commentator in the Ministère de la Marine attempted to explain the situation that existed on Île de France: "The Rivaltz affair is intimately connected to the troubles of Isle de France and in order to understand it one has to go back to the origins of these troubles . . . Dumas and Poivre were divided against one another almost as soon as they were nominated, and before their departure from France. The jealousy, taking sides, rivalry of powers and especially opposition to authority, led each of them to the greatest excesses." Rivaltz, claiming compensation, argued that the exile had caused him to lose his health and a significant part of his fortune.

For the most part we must assume that the island's elite maintained sufficient unity to preserve the status quo, but their identifications with each other were not accomplished without a great deal of work. Furthermore, the endless disputes inevitably opened up gaps for others to exploit. We do not have the full story behind Adonis's alleged attempt to poison his master, Lambert (see chapter 4 above), and, crucially, we are not told why Lambert's evidence was ruled by the judge to be unsafe. It seems possible, at least, that Lambert was involved in some larger dispute, which led his word to be deemed unreliable—even though it was, in this case, his word against that of a slave.

All the way down the social scale we find the striving for recognition no less acute, bringing individuals and families constantly into conflict with one another. And, to return to the main theme of this chapter, such disputes were, more often than not, played out over the institution of slavery, and over the bodies of slaves. This could take a number of forms. Poivre and Dumas accused each other of appropriating an excessive number of slaves for their own uses, of dressing them in personal liveries and using them to intimidate others. Commarond had implied that Beauralet's treatment of his slave was antisocial (the beatings disturbed the neighbors) and that "respectable" slave owners did not personally punish their slaves. Respectable men did not allow the blood to be on their own hands.

At its simplest, the role of slaves in mediating the social relations of slave owners was as pawns in the game of honor, and as (literal) boundary markers. Somewhat lower down the social scale than Lousteau, St. Rivaltz, and others were the Bouderet and Valton families, involved in a long-running battle of wills.[11] According to the Bouderets, Mme. Valton had sent her slave, Michel, to steal from the Bouderet garden. But the Bouderet's slave, Augustin, had caught Michel in the act. Mme. Valton, apparently "free of all sense of modesty," had come to the aid of Michel and, *comme une furieuse,* had leapt on Augustin and beaten him. As

Bouderet made clear, this attack on his slave was an attack on him, made all the more galling, perhaps, by the fact that the attacker was a woman: "A premeditated murderous act against his own person . . . since she had had the temerity to beat his own slave on his own property, on his own habitation." Bouderet seemed to be experiencing a double assault on his property—an assault on the property of his slave, which took place on his own land. Mme. Valton, meanwhile, will have done her social reputation no good at all by leaping on Augustin.

In yet another case, Jean Lousteau, in 1774, was seeking compensation for another of his slaves, La Violette, who had been shot dead by Lousteau's neighbor in the district of Montagne Longue.[12] Lousteau's argument had a number of interrelated strands. The murder of La Violette, he indicated, represented an assault on Lousteau's property and person, and as such had consequences for the whole of society: "To kill a fellow creature . . . is to weaken property rights, in destroying another's goods, and to violate the principle of all laws in doing to another an act (mal) which one would be angered to receive oneself."

As a member of the legal profession and of the island's elite, it comes as no surprise that Lousteau couches the expression of his loss in terms that emphasized the social good. But though the slave's own loss of life is certainly secondary to Lousteau's loss of a slave, it is not entirely irrelevant. Summing up his complaint, he said that that this was an offense that, "apart from depriving a man of his life, had also gravely threatened the wealth of a proprietor." The unjustified murder of a slave threatened the whole fabric of society. There was, as Lousteau made clear, an etiquette for slave killing, which had not been followed in this case. Crucially, La Violette had been shot in the back, as he fled, and with no evidence that he had actually stolen anything.

Lousteau's complaint refers in part to the long-standing problem of dealing with marronnage, a problem which never disappeared, but which changed in nature over the century, as I have already indicated. While slave owners had a collective interest in marronnage being dealt with severely, as individuals they might feel less happy about their own slaves being shot dead on this pretext.

In 1787 Anthoine de St. Rivaltz (returned from exile in Rodrigues) complained that his slave Noel, had been arrested on suspicion of being a maroon by another slave, named Tranquille, who belonged to his neighbors, the Dureau family.[13] Tranquille had then, allegedly, beheaded Noel.

St. Rivaltz put his case like this. He had been informed, he said, that his Malagasy slave, Noel, aged about eighteen years, and who had been maroon for some time, had been arrested in Plaines Wilhems by Tranquille, a slave of Sr. Dureau, and that a number of people had seen Tranquille apparently leading Noel away, with a cord around his neck. Eager to reclaim his slave, he had rushed to the commune headquarters, assuming that this was where Tranquille had taken him. But the information he received from the officer in charge had "frozen him with horror." He had been told that Noel was dead and his head had been presented to officials of the commune. St. Rivaltz went on to say that, in view of what had previously occurred between Tranquille and his wife, he had grounds to suspect murder.

At the beginning of the year, he said, Tranquille had been on his property in Plaines Wilhems and had arrested one of his domestic slaves, called Jasmin. Jasmin had been released by a white blacksmith named Moraux, and Tranquille had been "furious" to see his "prey," from whom he had hoped to "gain certain benefits," escape from him, and began swearing at those who had come to Jasmin's aid. And so Sr. Moraux had arrested Tranquille and taken him to St. Rivaltz's wife (he being away from the habitation). She, suspecting that Tranquille was drunk, had ordered him to be placed in the block until the following morning. At the crack of dawn, Sr. Dureau had appeared, armed with a gun, and had begun to threaten Mme. St. Rivaltz, and intimidated her so much that she had Tranquille released, rather than having him taken to the police, which is what she had intended. But no sooner had Tranquille been freed than, in the presence of his master, he had begun issuing terrible threats against the St. Rivaltz slaves, swearing to "have their heads" as soon as he found any of them maroon. "In comparing this horrible sermon," St. Rivaltz went on, "with the news of the horrific decapitation of Noel by the same Tranquille, he could not help but see in this barbarous action an odious murder, premeditated over a long period."

Tranquille told the court that he had been leading Noel to the commune headquarters, having found him maroon, when Noel had jumped into a ravine and injured himself, dying later. He was found not guilty, and it is clear from the proceedings of the case that he had been acting, in theory at least, as part of a local detachment established for the chasse des marrons. Finding him not guilty, the judge took the opportunity to remind everyone that they should not shoot at maroons until they had three times shouted the warning "arrêtez," adding that it was forbidden to decapitate the heads of maroons who had died from their wounds or from accident.

There are several dimensions to this case. One is the familiar one of slaves mediating the honor and reputation of their masters (whether their mistresses independently possess honor is another question). St. Rivaltz is affronted by the murder of his slave (albeit one who had for some time been maroon) by the slave of Dureau, with whom he was clearly not on good terms. Dureau, for his part, had clearly been offended by Mme. St. Rivaltz's earlier arrest of Tranquille and had come immediately to his defense (and had not, apparently, intervened when Tranquille had issued his threats and insults). But beyond this is the more complex question of the social sanctioning of Tranquille's violence against another slave, and his identification with this role. As a member of the marechaussée of the district, Tranquille was empowered, in the name of the social good and the maintenance of the institution of slavery, to arrest and even to kill maroon slaves. Just as the individual slave owner was expected to delegate the work of punishment to a black slave commander, so collectively the slave owners of Île de France delegated much of the work of violence associated with the phenomenon of marronnage to other slaves (though in fact the "sport" of maroon hunting continued to attract the participation of slave owners themselves).

So naturalized was violence in this society that it took the sight of a severed head to bring about a sense of reality. Bernardin de St. Pierre had, as we have seen, been traumatized by the sight of the captured maroon woman forced to carry a severed head in a bag on her back; St. Rivaltz represented himself as "frozen with horror" at the news that Noel's head had been delivered to the district headquarters. Arresting a maroon, even shooting and killing him, may have been part of his socially sanctioned work, but his decapitation of Noel (or of Noel's already dead body, if we are to accept the verdict of the court) offended St. Rivaltz and, perhaps, offended society at large. When Tranquille had allegedly threatened to "cut off the heads" of any of St. Rivaltz's slaves whom he found maroon, it was not anticipated that he would actually carry this out. Noel had been maroon for some time, but St. Rivaltz felt the loss of Noel's head as an amputation.

The reputation of the slave owner is, in this case as in others, a central part of the story here. St. Rivaltz is offended, and offended in the name of his wife, as Dureau had earlier been offended, and so it goes on in an apparently endless striving for proper recognition between slave owners, mediated by their slaves, who, at the most extreme, might literally lose their heads for their masters. The question of honor has long been recognized as an important dimension of master-slave relationships. Orlando Patterson used a number of examples to demonstrate that the slave was a proxy for his master's honor, including that of slavery in Kuwait, where "to kill or kidnap a man's slave affects his honor, not so the slaying of his son" (1982, 82). The slave, then, was a commodity and a conduit—both property in and of himself or herself and a carrier of the property of honor.

The honor at stake here is, obviously, male honor, externalized onto the slave, paralleling and sometimes intersecting with the male honor invested in the reputations of wives. The latter, as we have seen, was also at issue in Île de France society (wife beating paralleling slave beating in the reputation stakes), but the central fact of slave ownership added another important dimension, and one which is not easy to unravel. For example, while in general it was probably the case that women in elite Île de France society were, as it has been argued for France,[14] "ineligible" for honor, it is possible that their role as slave owners complicated this picture. St. Rivaltz had been offended by Tranquille via Tranquille's treatment of his wife and then, directly, by his killing of Noel. In this case, Mme. St. Rivaltz was a conduit for her husband's honor, and not in possession of honor herself, but Île de France had numbers of women owning slaves in their own right, begging the question of whether their possession of slaves may also have put them in possession of "masculine" qualities such as honor. Bernardin de St. Pierre had been so offended by the activities of the "maroon-hunting" Mme. de la V*** in part, it would seem, because her "unfeminine" behavior brought into disrepute the collective honor of slave-owning men, distorting and corrupting proper gender roles. Her behavior was proof that slavery was an "unnatural" institution.

But beyond this is another issue raised by Tranquille: the question of his own honor and reputation. So far it would appear that the economy of honor and reputation on Île de France was not only largely a male economy, but also one in which the circuits were well defined. Male slave owners dealt blows to each others' honor via the question of their treatment of slaves, and sometimes via the bodies of their slaves. And, we might imagine, similar, parallel circuits of male honor existed within the slave community—slaves, after all, came from societies that had their own codes of honor (Iliffe 2004). In this case both Noel and Tranquille were Malagasies and may well have had their own scores to settle with each other.[15] The other question, however, is whether and how these circuits defined by the slave/master divide might sometimes overlap, and particularly whether, in the social world of Île de France, slaves might have their reputations, their sense of honor recognized, acknowledged, by slave owners. Slaves, as has been frequently noted, often had the capacity to exceed and complicate their position as objects of exchange and mediation. There is more than a hint that in this case Tranquille's privileged position as a member of the maroon hunt has given him his own sense of honor, which he is at pains to defend. Tranquille's sense of honor is, viewed from outside, a tragic one, deriving as it does from the defense of the collective position of masters over slaves, of which he is one. This identification, this assumption of the "honor" of being a maroon killer, may well derive from an original debasement, an earlier experience of "dishonor" that Patterson sees as inherent to the condition of slavery—but this makes it no less real. The account of the offense to his honor comes, importantly, from St. Rivaltz, whose case against Tranquille rests on the assumption that he had been humiliated by his arrest by Mme. St. Rivaltz and was determined to seek restitution. St. Rivaltz appears to recognize, then, that though Tranquille is a slave, he is a slave with a reputation.

That male slaves might be thought, in certain circumstances, to be in possession of honor and reputation, is also indicated in the following case.

It was September 1777, and one or two o'clock in the afternoon on the Rue des Limittes. Gabriel Francois Chevalier de La Poëze, an employee of the Royal administration, was leaving his house to go back to work.[16] He was carrying his parasol, which, as he later told the police, he carried with him every day. But he found his way partially blocked by a young noir, who was arguing outside his door with a young négresse. He told the young man (whose name he did not know) to leave the girl alone and to get out of his way, but the young man replied "insolently": "What has that got to do with you . . . I want to kiss her,"[17] and in response to that he had hit him twice with his parasol and told him once more to get out of the way. But far from doing this, the young man had in fact menaced him, both with words and his fist, saying, "Come on then, if you are capable, hit me, if you dare." La Poëze had then warned him that if he did not back off he would "go for him," but the "noir" continued to threaten him with his fist, so eventually he had hit him several times with his parasol until eventually he had retreated, and he was able to continue on his way.

La Poëze was indignant, which comes as no surprise. A young slave had, after all, refused to move for him, resisted him, even humiliated him on the street, in front of others (there were witnesses to the event). As he indicated to the police, life in Port Louis for respectable people like himself was made rather disagreeable by this kind of incident: "It is dangerous that slaves should insult and menace whites in this sort of way . . . which occasions every day the most disagreeable and even dangerous scenes for those who are obliged to have dealings with them."

He asked the police to investigate the case, with a view to prosecution. The young noir in question was Joseph, a Mozambique about eighteen years old, and belonging to Sr. Clonard, a lieutenant in the King's fleet. Before La Poëze's case can proceed very far, Sr. Clonard himself attempted to bring about a prosecution—against La Poëze. He stated the case clearly:

> He complains that a certain white had committed an assault on his domestic slave, Joseph [whom he describes not as Mozambique but as Malagasy], who had received a large wound on the head, causing a great loss of blood. And such excesses are all the more worthy of the attention of the law and of reprehension being committed against a slave since they risk that the latter will forget, in those first moments of pain and sensitivity the singular respect which they are obliged to hold for a white.

Clonard was voicing directly what had become a somewhat formulaic statement of the argument for the "civilization" of slavery. Unwarranted violence against a slave, "unjust" treatment, would cause the slave to forget, in those moments of real pain, when the blood was flowing, his essential and inevitable subordination to the white man. The slave's body would, he implied, involuntarily rebel, and the whole edifice of the slave system, with its internalization of subordination, would come tumbling down. The slave owner must discipline himself against the excessive expression of the violence that still inevitably underpinned the regime.

Of course, while Clonard complained self-righteously that the beating of his slave by La Poëze threatened the viability of the slave system, we might suspect that he was also a little personally offended, humiliated, by the assault on his property by another white man. But this was not simply a case of the perceived assault on one slave owner's honor by another through the treatment of a slave.

Under interrogation, Joseph had produced his own account of the incident on the street. He said that he had been on the Rue des Limittes with a woman slave named Perrine, who belonged to Sr. Bellerose, when a "white," whom he did not recognize, had accosted him and asked him what he was doing with the woman and whether she was his wife. He replied that she was indeed his wife, to which the white man had said, "So you sleep with her then," to which he had answered, "Yes." The man then asked him to get out of his way, but Perrine had grabbed him by the shirt and stopped him from doing this, and then the man had begun beating him with a parasol.

The judge, in his interrogation of La Poëze, implied that the latter had, in fact, incited Joseph by addressing unsuitable and improper (and perhaps disrespectful?) questions to him: "Was it not the case that he had asked the slave if the woman was his wife and if he slept with her . . . and therefore was it not the case that this slave's indecent and improper (malhônnete) response to him had in fact been in reply to his improper (malhônnete) question . . . since he had asked the slave if he slept with the woman." Joseph, it is implied here, might be a slave, but he is also a man (albeit a young one). As a man, even though a slave, it was not unreasonable for him to expect a degree of respect on the basis of his masculinity, particularly as it manifested itself in his relationship with (and implied power over) a woman. Joseph, then, was man enough to be capable of feeling insult, and the judge felt it was unwise of La Poëze to have asked him "improper questions," thereby provoking violence. For her part, Perrine, though apparently involved in some kind of argument with Joseph, was nevertheless keen that her man did not cede passage to the abusive white man—she had grabbed Joseph by the shirt and stopped him moving out of the white man's way.

It would be naive, of course, to conclude from this case that any generalized respect was accorded to the "private" sexual lives of slave men. We know that this was not the case. But as an articulation of a kind of principle, the judge's line of questioning is interesting, suggesting that their domination of women was at the center of a kind of male slave subjectivity. Such a formulation, of course, left slave women in a very different position to their menfolk.

Race and (Mis)Recognition

Just a month before the minor fracas created on the street by Joseph's refusal to move for La Poëze, Port Louis had experienced some days of high drama. These were rare moments in which the whole edifice, the scaffolding of the colonial system, rocked and could only be steadied by the erection of a real scaffold. In August 1777 a crowd had gathered to watch the hanging of a man named Benoit Giraud, also known as Hector the Mulatto. When not referred to as a mulatto (which implied that he had mixed, partly white blood), Giraud was described as a freeborn black, from another island on the other side of the French colonial empire, Martinique. More proximately he had come from Paris where, after a spell in the notorious Châtelet prison, he had, to his immense outrage, been exiled to Île de France by order of the Ministère de la Marine. What exactly Giraud was alleged to have done in order to warrant this treatment is far from clear. The correspondence from Paris to the administrators of Île de France simply stated that he was a "dangerous" man, who had made a number of unfounded and defamatory allegations against (unnamed) public figures.[18] The identity of one of these figures, however, was revealed a few months after Giraud arrived on Île de France.

As soon as Giraud had stepped off the boat from Paris in May 1777 he had been placed in chains and confined to prison. On 15 August 1777, in the late afternoon, he and another prisoner, a young boy named Cézar, were digging a trench close to the island's administrative headquarters. Benoit Giraud and Cézar were chained together. At about five o'clock senior government officials walked together across the square, passing close to the trench the two men were digging. Among them were the intendant of the island, M. Maillart Dumesle, and M. Denis-Nicolas Foucault,[19] the intendant-elect, shortly to replace Maillart Dumesle. As they walked past in a group, a number of witnesses saw Benoit Giraud hurl an object in the direction of Foucault, the force of which was deflected by Maillart Dumesle's cane. Having apparently missed his target, Giraud then leapt at Foucault (dragging the unfortunate Cézar with him) and attacked him, physically and verbally. The precise words of the insult reported by witnesses varied somewhat, but most recalled hearing something along the lines of: "You villain, you are the cause of all my misfortunes and you will pay for it." Finally, the other officers pried Giraud away from Foucault and returned him to jail, where his ranting and raving could be heard by all. In his testimony the jailor, M. Blancheteste (who also featured in the case of mistaken infanticide), reported that on being returned to jail and admonished for the terrible thing that he had done, Giraud had replied, "I have only one thing to say—I promised myself that I would do what I did—let them hang me." The next day he stood trial.

Giraud's first examination by the judge followed the prescribed form. His identity must first be established, and so he was asked, essentially, the question "Who are you?" His answer to this apparently simple question is crucial. Giraud stated that he was thirty-seven years of age, that he had been born in Martinique, that he had worked as a domestic servant in Martinique and in Europe, in the service of M. Foucault.[20] He was, he emphasized, of free birth. Asked if he had ever been convicted of a crime, Giraud answered that he had never been subject to a "punition infamante," but that he had spent fifteen days in the Châtelet prison following an argument. A punition infamante was one that involved the loss of civil rights, and in using this term Giraud would appear both to be well versed in French law, and to be asserting that he was a man who had rights to lose.

Giraud never denied that he had thrown something at Foucault—in fact he admitted it readily—but throughout the trial he claimed that the missile was mud, not a rock. In his fury at seeing Foucault, he said, he had picked up whatever was at hand, and this was mud. In fact, he added, he was not entirely sure what he had done the previous day because as soon as he had set eyes on Foucault his "blood had boiled" and he had not known what he was doing or saying. But yes, he added, he had called him a number of names—that he did recall. Asked if he had intended to kill M. Foucault, he replied that he had not, but that given the terrible things that Foucault had done to him, he had wanted to humiliate him. He was certain, he said, that his imprisonment and exile had not been at the orders of the Ministère de la Marine. He demanded justice.

On 18 August Giraud was examined again and confronted with the witnesses. Again he denied throwing a rock, but admitted throwing mud; again he admitted that he had insulted Foucault, but added that this was in response to Foucault's own insults to him—for Foucault, he maintained, had called him his "slave." Asked whether he did not know that Foucault had been named by the king as successor to Maillart Dumesle as Intendant, Giraud replied that he had not known this, and that even if he had been told so he would not have believed it, since Foucault had been dressed in plain gray, not in uniform. Asked whether he was not aware of the laws which ordained that free blacks and liberated slaves show particular respect to whites, Giraud responded that he was familiar with the Code Noir and he had seen the chapter in which it was stated that "noirs mulâtres" enjoyed the same rights and privileges as other free persons. His own case, he went on, was that of a free person who had been insulted by a "bourgeois," for M. Foucault could not be regarded as anything but a bourgeois, having been dressed as one, and not in uniform.

Giraud was found guilty of assault and hanged on the same day. In this case, and unusually, Île de France "justice" worked fast. There was none of the waiting for "expert" deliberation as to whether Adonis's potions were poisons; none of the balancing of reputation and insult that the judge in the La Poëze case felt necessary to add to his conclusion. Writing after the event to the Ministère de la Marine, Maillart Dumesle expressed something of the sense of outrage this case had occasioned. Imagine, he wrote, that even in his final interrogation this man admitted that he knew M. Foucault, and that he had intended to hit him, but continued to argue that as far as he was concerned this was just a quarrel between one free individual and another. "You may well see," he went on, "how these small pretexts can serve as excuses." The case served only to underline (he added) how important it was that officers of the state should bear marks of distinction, especially on this island where the streets were "continually full of slaves, of free black and mulattoes, of workers and foreigners, such that under the pretext of not recognizing an official anything might be thought permissible."

I found no definitive trace of Giraud in the Martinican archives (though the family name was not an uncommon one). But fortunately we do know something of the world from which he came through the work of Yvan Debbasch (1967), Émile Hayot (1971), and Léo Elizabeth (1989). In 1765 there were some 1,871 *libres de couleur* in Martinique, compared to 11,625 whites and nearly 70,000 slaves. By 1775 their number had risen to 2,716, while the population of whites had remained more or less static. Though Île de France had a much smaller population overall, the proportions of libres de couleur to whites was not dissimilar: in 1767 there were 587 *gens de couleur* to 3,163 whites and 15,027 slaves (Allen 1999, chap. 4). The number and economic significance of this population on Île de France would grow significantly toward the end of the century. In Martinique, as in Île de France, this was a disproportionately female community, reflecting the practice of white masters freeing their slave concubines.

Léo Elizabeth has argued that in general persons of mixed race (of which Giraud was one), whether slave or free, were readily absorbed into the extended slave-holding family of Martinique, but that in the second half of the eighteenth century the administration exhibited increasing anxiety over this local liberalism. Yvan Debbasch, describing the situation in the whole of the French Antilles, also sees a hardening of attitudes taking place, particularly in the 1760s and 1770s as concern over "color" wins out over the legal criteria of equality for all who are technically "free." Giraud's anger over his treatment and his reported words of defiance appear to exemplify Debbasch's argument perfectly. In theory, according to the Code Noir, it is only the "affranchi," the manumitted slave, who is obliged to show a "singular respect" for his former master. But, Debbasch argues, in the late 1760s and 1770s this injunction was being extended to mean that all persons of color should demonstrate this "singular respect" to all whites. No wonder that Giraud was so insistent on his freeborn status. According to Debbasch, in the latter half of the eighteenth century this was a lost cause, for "all those not recognized as whites found themselves, in effect, in one and the same class" (1967, 91). This despite the fact that Martinique was the home of Moreau de St. Méry, with his obsessive classification of "degrees" of blackness (Hayot 1971, 61).

Certainly the sumptuary laws enacted in Martinique (of which I can find no equivalent in Île de France) seem to reinforce the view that "color" was winning out over legal status. These laws explicitly prohibited "mulâtres" as well as manumitted slaves and freeborn persons of color from wearing clothing made from expensive material and from displaying any items of luxury—the penalty for infringement was the loss of their freedom. In Martinique anxiety over the loyalty and controllability of the population of "libres" had probably been intensified during the Seven Years' War. Elizabeth quotes a European commentator (Pléville) on the society of Martinique in 1779 who joined what had become a chorus of opinion against "easy" manumission and who wrote of the libres de couleur that they "knew by heart" the works of the antislavery writer Abbé Raynal (Elizabeth 1989, 799).

As Elizabeth argues, however, this was not a straightforward story of the increasing racialization of Martinican society. In the 1770s in particular, some of the anxiety and the hardening of attitudes was coming directly from France, where, as we have seen, in 1777 Louis XVI enacted legislation known as Police des Noirs (Peabody 1996, chap. 7). In the same year the king had reminded colonial administrators that "libres are either manumitted slaves or descendents of manumitted slaves: no matter how distant they are from these origins they always retain the mark (tâche) of slavery and are unfit for public office" (Elizabeth 1989, 712). The realities of colonial life, however, often mitigated against this kind of hard and fast position. For one thing, libres de couleur formed an important component of the militia in Martinique and Île de France, as elsewhere.[21]

In this context it seems that the timing of Giraud's exile to Île de France may not have been accidental. We do not know when he left Martinique, but he may well have been witness to or victim of increasing efforts by the administration there in the late 1760s and 1770s to divide the population by color above legal status. Whatever the nature of his original dispute with Foucault, his time in France would seem to have coincided with the increasing crackdown on blacks in the kingdom, culminating in the 1777 Police des Noirs. The drama enacted during Giraud's trial, then, was less about racial attitudes on Île de France than it was about racial attitudes in metropolitan France.

We can be reasonably certain that Frantz Fanon had never heard of Benoit Giraud, the trace of whose existence is deeply buried in the archive of Île de France. But it is tempting to speculate on what, two hundred years on, one famous Martinican would have made of another less famous one.[22] Identity and identification, as Fanon reminds us, and as Diane Fuss has recently reiterated (1995), has a colonial history, and often a painful one, we might add. Giraud's story is in part a story of the impossible struggle for recognition, yet it is perhaps not quite the story that Fanon would have told.

Fanon's formulation of the position of the "Negro" as he presents it in *Black Skins, White Masks* is engraved in a number of his more famous and unforgettable phrases: "The Negro is comparison"; he is "sealed into crushing objecthood," the "black man must be black in relation to the white man," and so on. The primary psychological dynamic of the colonial situation, then, is one of "othering"—the black man becomes the repository of the white man (and woman's) projections, of the most fundamental feelings of hatred and desire. And, so Fanon would appear to be saying, the black man is paralyzed by these projections—paralyzed by the white child's shout of "look, a Negro!" paralyzed in the cinema by the reflection of Tarzan (this, in one of Fanon's striking footnotes), "stricken and immobilized" by white psychic needs and desires over which he has no control. The black man has no independent existence; he does not exist, says Fanon, except via the white man's gaze. The colonial relation is not, in this part of Fanon's work, a dialectical relation, it is a one-way projection. If such a formulation can be made for the colonial situation of Algeria, or for Fanon's own Martinique, then, one might imagine, it would be all the more applicable to a society dominated by the institution of slavery.

Recent scholars have gone further, reformulating Fanon's own formulation and giving it a Lacanian hue.[23] This interpretation is perhaps yet more devastating, going beyond the psychology of projection and "othering" into the realms of the impossibility of subjectivity itself. Fanon's argument, it is said, implies that the psychic violence of colonialism extends to exclude the black "man" from coming into being for himself. He is so thoroughly othered that he never experiences the internal split Lacan saw as the essential ingredient of entry into subjectivity.[24] Yet, as Fuss reminds us, theories of the subject from Hegel through psychoanalysis have their own, albeit often disguised, colonial histories. Fanon was in some senses brilliant at playing with and subverting this heritage, but in other ways (particularly, as many writers have pointed out, in his views on sexuality and gender) tragically caught within its web.

Let us look again at the minor eruption created by Giraud in the society of Île de France, and at the conflict between him and Foucault. What would Fanon have made of this, and, indeed, what would a confrontation between Giraud and a later Foucault have looked like? What, finally, can Giraud tell us about agency in a colonial situation?

Perhaps one of the most compelling aspects of the figure of Giraud as it emerges from the pages of the archive is the ringing evidence of his anger—his boiling blood, as he puts it. This is an anger not unlike that which rings through *Black Skins, White Masks,* a defiance reminiscent of that of Antigone.[25] Giraud is angry because he believes himself to be unjustly treated, and most importantly because he is not being recognized for who he is—a man, born into freedom, with the same rights as other free persons. His resistance to being treated as a slave, even named as a slave by Foucault, makes his "blood boil," and he is happy for everyone to know this. In this case confession is almost certainly genuine, not coerced, and confession is an opportunity for him to assert, in public, to officers of the state, to the law, that he has been misrecognized. He thinks that there is a mistake, that if he can only get to the top of the system, the mistake will be rectified. For Giraud, this is a case of mistaken identity, of the yawning gap (the split) that opened up, as he dug in the trench, between his self—a free man, a man with rights—and the distorted reflection of this in the faces of the officers of the administration. For them he was, at that moment at least, another black man in a trench.

Giraud both experiences and resists the kind of violent projection and othering so vividly described by Fanon. He does this from the basis of knowing who he is, of thinking he knows who he is, of having a "fictive" sense of self. He resists, refuses to be the "black man," still less the "slave," because he knows that he is a free man. And he is willing to die for this. Giraud is a man who refuses to be "sealed in a crushing objecthood," who refuses to respond to the cry, "Look, a Negro!" except by hurling a missile. Symbolically he refuses to be tied to Cézar, who is a slave, but of course he is tied to him physically, which in a sense sums up his dilemma.

It would seem then that Giraud is hardly a man denied a subject position, or a self. And yet there appear to be real limitations to the political potential of Giraud's subjectivity and to his agency. In the context in which we meet him, the dominant feature of Giraud's subjectivity is that it is resistant, created to a large extent by the psychological and physical violence of colonialism. Further, his refusal to be the black man (as synonymous with slave) is made possible only by his insistence on being something else—a mulâtre at one moment, and more consistently, a freeborn person. For Giraud, while race, he insists, is more than black and white (he stands between), freedom is, and must be, a black-and-white issue. One binary division replaces another. There is little display here of the sometimes playful, sometimes subversive "colonial mimicry" of which Homi Bhabha writes (1984).

As Giraud learns to his cost (and where Bhabha may be relevant), the most powerful feature of the colonial system (and perhaps of many political systems) is its ability to combine an apparent fixity with a more complex, more all-encompassing flexibility. The fixed objects are certainly there—represented by the chains with which he is tied and the gallows to which he is led—but this is also a social and political system able to mobilize strategically, and sometimes no doubt unconsciously, a complex set of definitions and identifications, and not to be confined to one dimension. In Foucauldian terms, it combines the repressive power of the chains and the ritual execution with a web of more "productive" power in which Giraud is necessarily enmeshed. Giraud's belief in the concept of "freedom" and the simple distinction between slave and free is a mistaken one. He may well be able to throw the law at the representatives of the system, by quoting the Code Noir and referring to a punition infamante, but the law was never as simple as that. As Butler argues for Antigone, so one could also argue that Giraud "cannot make [his] claim outside the language of the state, but neither can the claim [he] wants to make be fully assimilated by the state" (2000, 28).

It is not simply that Giraud's rights are being denied because he is black and a troublemaker, it is, more generally, that in French eighteenth-century law freedom was a relative, not an absolute condition, and rights were manipulable. Everything did, indeed, depend on "who you were," but who you were in the eyes of the law was a great deal more complex than the interdependent ideologies of freedom and slavery implied. Under ancien régime criminal law, for example, there were seven "circumstances of the person" or of the offense that could be taken to aggravate culpability and to increase penal severity. A number of them might have applied in this case: "Rank and social condition, if the offended was infamous"; "if the victim was an illustrious personage"; "if the crime was committed in a public square"; "if the crime was committed by assault or surprise . . . or with blatant scandal" (Andrews 1994, 1:498). The regime, then, had no need to invoke "race" at all, in the way that Giraud attempted to invoke it by referring to the specific rights of mulâtres like himself.

Caught though he is in a web, Giraud does have the capacity to disturb and disrupt in his struggle to the death. This disruptive capacity is based less on his impressive if ultimately hopeless struggle for recognition, and more on his refusal to recognize the other, in the form of the white man. Giraud plays them at their own game. He confesses, apparently readily, to his assault on Foucault but, in his defense, or in mitigation, asserts that there was no way he could have recognized him for what he was—a representative of the king—since he was wearing no uniform. Foucault, he asserts, was simply a bourgeois like him; his whiteness, Giraud implied, was not relevant, was unrecognizable without the uniform. Whiteness needed to be marked—or, to put it another way, he could not be expected to recognize Foucault without his clothes on. Giraud's refusal to respond to the equivalent of "Look, a Negro!" is combined, then, with his refusal to say "Look, a white man!"

Giraud needles and disturbs with this line. The colonial masters could deal with his resistance to being wrongly identified as a slave/black man, but they could not so easily deal with his refusal to recognize the white man. Or so it seems from Maillart Dumesle's reaction. His defense of misrecognition might be an "excuse" based on a "small pretext," but Dumesle concluded that one of the lessons of the case was that officers of the state should bear their "marks of distinction," for this was indeed a place in which the streets were "continually full of slaves, free blacks and mulattoes, of workers and foreigners, such that under the pretext of not recognizing an official, anything might be thought permissible." The white man was a white man only when he had the right clothes on.[26]

Slavery, Recognition, and Subjection

In her discussion of Hegel in *The Psychic Life of Power*, Judith Butler avoids the use of the terms *master* and *slave* and replaces them with the terms *lord* and *bondsman*—perhaps more accurate, certainly less charged in the context of the postslavery society of America. Hegel's use of the master/slave duo as the archetype of power relations is perhaps unfortunate for scholars of slavery since, in one sense, it deprives us of a language in which to talk about the relations of slavery. Yet the questions raised by Hegel and by social and psychoanalytic theory since Hegel are essential to our understanding of the dynamics of slave societies.

Slavery was an enormously variable institution, and so no one account of these dynamics will ever be satisfactory. In the case of eighteenth-century Île de France, a preplantation economy and a society composed for the most part of smaller slave owners and their slaves, these dynamics, social and interpersonal, were complex and worthy of consideration. For Michel Foucault, a slave society, one saturated by physical repression, is not one in which "power relations" in his sense operate at all (McNay 1994, 127). Power relations, according to this theory, rest on an element of freedom, allowing a push and pull between freedom and constraint, and a process of "permanent provocation," of guerrilla warfare between the "recalcitrance of will and the intransigence of freedom." Slaves in Île de France were often in chains, often forced to submit totally to the wills of their masters, mistresses, and slave commanders, often humiliated, debased, murdered, and decapitated. The violence of slavery was always present, even when disguised and displaced. The violence (not the slaves themselves) was what the reformers of the slave system attempted to externalize, to disown, to exclude. Judith Butler argues that all subjects are created via the exclusion of others, through the creation of abject, deauthorized subjects, and "populations erased from view" (Butler 1992). But if exclusion was at work here, it was not in any simple sense directed as slaves, or even at the population of maroon slaves, whom we have seen were invested with agency. The violence (and not the slaves themselves) was what the reformers of the slave system attempted to externalize, disown, and exclude. But like all attempted exclusions, this was never entirely successful. In psychic terms, writes Jessica Benjamin, "all exclusion is an illusion" (1998, 102), and this was certainly true of the attempt to "other" violence, which continually reappeared as the "real" in the form of the severed head of Noel that caused St. Rivaltz to "freeze in horror."

The slave owners of Île de France could not completely exclude or deauthor their slaves, because they needed them, not just as objects, but also as subjects. They exercised their power to maintain their own state of dependence. In some sense, then, they reached the kind of impasse described by Hegel in his description of this "archetypal" relationship. If we accept that these relationships were not simply ones of othering, then we can begin to think about the complicated ways in which slaves did sometimes become subjects, and we can then address the question of the exercise of power and the power of subjection under slavery.

Chapter Eight

SPEAKING SLAVERY: LANGUAGE AND LOSS

*I*n all likelihood we would never have met Joseph, the Malagasy slave, had he not been involved in a fracas on the street with the white man La Poëze.[1] And because of the nature of their dispute, and the inquiry which followed from it, we not only encounter Joseph, we also "hear" him—the documentary record provides us with fragments of Joseph's speech, the spoken words of a slave.

In the last chapter I read this case, including the words allegedly spoken by Joseph, to explore questions of reputation and honor. But Joseph's words are also significant in their own right, for they are some of the earliest recorded words of Île de France creole. Young Joseph cannot have known that his words, spoken in anger, would in the late twentieth century constitute evidence in the field of creole linguistics and would be examined and reexamined by experts in this field.

In this chapter I explore questions of language as an aspect of the subjective experience of slavery. We cannot, of course, have direct access to this experience but can only hazard some guesses at it on the basis of what the historical record has left us—a partial residue. In other chapters I have very largely confined myself to discussing the eighteenth-century records, avoiding the practice of projecting backward from later evidence. However, in the case of the question of language as addressed in this chapter, I have regarded a certain amount of this as unavoidable—for though languages are always evolving and changing, they are also a kind of archaeological residue of the past. While nineteenth- and twentieth-century Mauritian creole were and are not the same as the eighteenth-century language, they do contain within them evidence of that earlier period of linguistic evolution. But for now, let us return to the more direct, if fragmentary, eighteenth-century evidence.

Joseph's words are part of this evidence for eighteenth-century speech, and the eminent French linguist Robert Chaudenson has used the very same record of this in his analysis of the origins of Mauritian creole. Joseph's linguistic habits, his syntax, become grist to the mill of a linguistic debate. Joseph becomes the quintessential creole speaker.

What Joseph allegedly said, as reported in Chaudenson's reading of the case, is contained within the following set of statements:

> Ayant demandé à ce noir pouquoi il inquiétait cette négresse, le noir lui répondit: quesque cela te fout, moi voulé baiser ly.
> Ce noir se sentant frappé lui dit en menaçant du poing pourquoy toi battre moi qui toi faire moi.
> Toi va paye moi ça, avances si tu l'oses.
> Viens si tu es capable qui toi faire battre moi.
> Qui toi vouler faire moi, battre si toi oser.
> Moi voulé baiser ça négresse la. (Chaudenson 1981, 78)[2]

Joseph's "speech," then, constitutes a series of moments in which we apparently have direct access to the evolving language of Île de France creole, as spoken by a slave.

But things are more complicated than this. A written text is a written text, even when apparently reporting direct speech. In particular, court records are court records, highly structured rerenderings of events and, as many social historians have pointed out, they have obvious biases—the judicial process itself limits what can be asked and what can be said; judicial texts serve as scripts in what Muir and Ruggiero call a "theater of authority" (1994), all speech within them is conditioned by fear of punishment, of torture, of death.[3]

On the other hand, as I have already indicated, French criminal procedure of the eighteenth century placed enormous emphasis on intent, motivation, and inner disposition. Confession was regarded as the only true evidence (the connection with Christian theories of moral personality is clear here)—only the perpetrator of a crime really knew what he or she had intended. From this followed an emphasis on speech, on the exact words that might act as a key to intent. The evidence given by slaves did, on occasion at least, seem to matter—the exact words spoken on this occasion and that, the intent behind the words, and their "real" meaning (translators were used for those deemed not fluent in the creole language —another complication). Reported speech from the court record, then, hedged around, interspersed with silences (which, of course, are missing from the record), committed to paper, cannot be dismissed entirely; it can mean something, if we read it carefully. As it happens, my reading of the evidence of Joseph's "speech" would be rather different from Chaudenson's.

The case, as we have seen, centered around a contretemps on the street between the white man La Poëze and the young slave Joseph. La Poëze came out of his house to find Joseph and his girlfriend Perrine blocking his route. He asked Joseph to stand aside, which Joseph refused to do, at which point an argument developed that ended with La Poëze hitting Joseph on the head with his cane and drawing blood. The words spoken mattered to the court, because, as the judge eventually concluded, La Poëze had provoked Joseph through his insulting and indecent references to Perrine. Joseph, the judge decided, had been insulted. The record of the case does indeed contain some of Joseph's reporting of his own words on that occasion, but some of the examples of Joseph's speech used by Chaudenson are, in fact, words spoken by his adversary, La Poëze, reporting to the judge what he alleged Joseph had said during the encounter. And so it is, in fact, La Poëze speaking, mimicking, rerendering Joseph's creole when he says, "Quesque cela te fout, moi voulé baiser ly . . . viens, si tu es capable, qui toi faire battre moi . . . avances si tu l'oses."

Chaudenson cites other examples of early creole speech, many of them also from the court records. The earliest is dated 1734, and is another case in which, in fact, one witness is reporting the speech of another: "Il auroit apercu un noir qui etoit blessé et qui auroit dit moy fini mouri . . . et le dit enfant fu sakabar" (He saw a slave who was wounded and said, I am going to die . . . and the child will be shut up) (Chaudenson 1981, 77). Or, later in the century, this reported response of a slave to a master who was accusing him of laziness: "Moi vieux, Monsieur, moi malade, vendez-moi" (I am old, Monsieur, I am sick, sell me) (Chaudenson 1981, 78).

Chaudenson takes other examples (which he acknowledges to be less reliable) from published accounts by colonists and travelers. The colonist Baron Grant wrote in a letter home in 1749 that his slaves said "in their corrupted French: Ca blanc la li beaucoup malin, li couri beaucoup dans la mer-haut." Bernardin de St. Pierre in his *Voyage* reported the following conversation, juxtaposing French and creole: "Le patron me dit dans son mauvais patois: Ca n'a pas bon Monsié. Je lui demandais s'il y avoit quelque danger, il me répondit 'S'il nous n'a pas gané malheur, ca bon.' " (The skipper told me in his poor patois: "That's not good sir. I asked him if there was any danger, he answered, 'If no harm comes to us, that's good.' ")

The linguistic debate to which all of this evidence is substance is an important one concerning the origins and development of Île de France creole. Robert Chaudenson argued in 1974 that Île de France creole derived largely from "Bourbonnais"—that is, from the creole or patois which had developed on neighboring Île Bourbon from the seventeenth century and which was exported to Île de France with the first group of settlers in the years 1715–1720 (Chaudenson 1974). Philip Baker and Chris Corne (1982) dispute Chaudenson's account of the origins and nature of Île de France creole.[4] They focus on what they see as the formative years in the evolution of the language—that is, between 1721 and about 1750. Drawing on (among other data) a painstakingly detailed reconstruction of evidence relating to the origins of the earliest inhabitants (both slave and free), they argue that Chaudenson has exaggerated the "Bourbonnais" influence on the formation of the language.

Île de France creole, in Baker and Corne's account, was created out of the following formative inputs: more or less standard French "written if not actually spoken by administrators," regional dialects of the eighteenth century (Breton being perhaps the most evident), and various non-French languages spoken by slaves and others. Among the latter they emphasize the importance, in the earlier part of the eighteenth century, of West African languages such as Wolof, Fon,[5] and Bambara, as well as of Bengali, Tamil, and Malagasy. By 1749, they argue, the basic elements of the language were in place and Île de France creole had acquired its unique character. The foreign-born slave, according to Baker, "could identify Mauritian creole as his target language and reach that target" (1982, 120). Île de France creole had become a *langue d'arrivée*.[6] Furthermore, this new language incorporated, at a "deep structural level," much that was of African linguistic origin. Baker and Corne conclude, then, that "Île de France Creole belongs, if not to the mainstream, then to an important tributary of 'Afro-French' " (1982, 127). They suggest that though the bulk of the vocabulary of Île de France creole may have its roots in French or French dialects (there seems little dispute about this), the grammar, the syntax, and the "deep structure" have their origins elsewhere—specifically in the elsewhere from which the earliest slaves were drawn, West Africa, Madagascar, and parts of India.[7]

This has engendered heated academic debate, with words flying in a number of different directions.[8] In part it has hinged on linguistic technicalities that are hard for the nonexpert to master, but more obviously it is a political debate relating directly to the definition of "culture" in contemporary Mauritius, and particularly to the subordinate position of the present-day Creole population, the real and symbolic descendants of slavery. To put it at its simplest, the linguists' debate is a debate about who made the creole language—the slaves or their masters, the Africans or the French. In contemporary Mauritius, as I have already argued, Creoles are defined by their "lack": their "lack" of a "real" culture, their "lack" of a "real" history, since in a sense nothing created on the island is regarded as real. All Mauritians, whatever their backgrounds, speak the island's creole language, but many groups have retained and revived other languages— the "Francos" their standard French, and a variety of Indian languages among those of South Asian origin, and Chinese dialects among the Chinese minority (not to mention, of course, the official language of English). Only the Creoles speak only creole, and this in one sense places them in the position of Derrida's monolinguals.[9] While their slave ancestors had a *langue de départ* (and possibly more than one) and acquired a *langue d'arrivée* they have only one language and therefore, in Derrida's terms, they are deprived of all language. On the other hand, this one language contains within it very many others.

What does it mean to say that the "deep structural" and grammatical features of the language are of African origin?[10] It would be nice to think that French colonial administrators and slave owners were subject to a kind of linguistic colonialism on the part of their slaves—that they spoke, despite themselves, and even when uttering apparently French words, an African language. Whether the language can rightly be called Afro-French and therefore unconsciously, and almost despite itself, continues to contain and express the experience of the earliest slaves is hard to say. For the very different context of the American South, Philip Morgan has grappled with the same question (1998, 560–580). If Creole languages have an African-derived grammar and a European-derived vocabulary, what does this mean for the experience of slave speakers of the language? Morgan argues tentatively that this African-derived grammar was one feature contributing to Africans being "less powerless in their linguistic encounters with Europeans than their slavery might imply," and he goes on, rather more speculatively, to assert that "Africans were able to strip away a European morphological system and recast it in a familiar mold. They grafted a European vocabulary onto West African grammatical structures that had much in common" (1998, 561–562). But this kind of argument makes a number of assumptions about the relationship between language, culture, and consciousness. In particular it implies that grammar, being "deeper" and more "structural" than vocabulary, contains within it some kind of African cultural essence, which survives the trauma of enslavement. Such assumptions must surely remain speculative.[11]

It is equally hard to assess Baker's other claim about Mauritian Creole: that the language had acquired its unique character, had become an identifiable langue d'arrivée, by a precise date, 1749. What we can say is that even if this langue d'arrivée had arrived by this date, the island's speech, its daily babble, would have been marked by a continuing and continually changing linguistic diversity. The small elite French population talked among themselves on a continuum of more or less standard French (still an unstable language in the metropole at this time) and regional dialects, and a version of the island's creole to their slaves. The large numbers of sailors and soldiers (often of very multicultural origins, despite being employed by the French navy) spoke a nautical patois, and some, at least (according to one fragmented account) appear not to have spoken any French at all.[12] Newly arrived slaves, in all their linguistic and cultural diversity, certainly would have had to learn fast the island's creole in order just to survive, but the presence of translators on the island testifies to the fact that language acquisition is not automatic. In addition, the appallingly high mortality rates among the slave population imply (apart from many other things) that no sooner had one generation of slaves learned the new language then they were dead—ceding their place to a new boatload with their own langues de départ.

We cannot really know to what extent "mother tongues" survived, if only for short periods, or to what extent bilingualism or multilingualism may have characterized the slave experience. Slaves on Île de France came from a bewildering diversity of linguistic backgrounds in East and West Africa, Madagascar, and India. We certainly cannot make any assumptions about mutual intelligibility among the slave community. On the other hand, there were probably some counterbalancing factors. The very complexity of the African linguistic situation, for example, meant that Africans were familiar with the experience of encountering foreign languages and often adept at acquiring some degree of fluency in them. Furthermore, by the eighteenth century (and for West Africa, much earlier) trading languages and coastal "pidgins" were an important feature of the linguistic environment. So, for example, we might speculate that some East Africans may have shared some knowledge of Swahili, even if their "mother" tongues were not mutually intelligible.

Once on the island, whatever their backgrounds, slaves had, of necessity, to communicate with each other and with their masters. Linguists have models for this process of linguistic creolization, but they sometimes appear to raise more questions than they answer.[13] The classical (but now much disputed) model proposes that under particular social circumstances (including those of the slave trade) the "target" language (in practice, the language of the socially and economically dominant group—the traders or colonizers) undergoes a simplification and takes the form of a "pidgin." This "pidgin" will be a second (or perhaps third or fourth) language for its speakers. But, in certain situations, the children born to these pidgin speakers will have no language other than the "pidgin." Once it becomes the primary language of a community, the "pidgin" undergoes a reverse development of becoming more complex, more expansive, in a process known as creolization. A creole language is the outcome of this process, and for Île de France, Baker sees it as having its origins in the first generation of children born to the island's slaves (those 465 children whose births were recorded between 1727 and 1738). If Baker is correct about the influence of West African languages in the early, formative period of the development of creole, this would accord to some degree with what we know about the privileged position of some West African slaves (Wolofs in particular) in the early slave system, their somewhat more balanced sex ratio, and their greater ability to form endogamous family groups. But much else we do not know and, as another analyst of creole languages has pointed out, Baker and Corne's model can be read as reductionist, not fully taking into account the complexity of Île de France society (Valdman 1992). Given high mortality rates, and the continued influx of newly acquired slaves, we must assume that the sedimentation of the island's creole was a slow and hesitant process and that other languages would have been heard on the streets and habitations.

Creole, Créolité, and Slavery: Later Evidence

Île de France creole may have acquired its own identity by the middle of the eighteenth century, but there was certainly a moment in the late nineteenth century when some Mauritians (now under British rule, of course) felt that "their" creole language was in danger of being lost. In 1880 the Mauritian linguist and folklorist Charles Baissac produced an interesting study of what he called the *patois créole*.[14] By this time the island had been subject to another major social and cultural change, with the massive immigration of Indian indentured laborers imported to work on the sugarcane fields. Baissac feared that the "old" creole would be swamped, lost in this new wave of immigrants, and that the stories, traditions, and folktales that had evolved with slavery would be forgotten.

Baissac's study displays more than a little romanticism. For him, the real creole language, the real creole culture, was dying with the last of the emancipated slaves—always represented as a venerable, but somewhat patronized old man. Colored though it is by a number of late-nineteenth-century preoccupations (not least the French-Mauritian experience of being colonized themselves by the British), Baissac's study is nevertheless an interesting one.

To begin with, he has an evocative way of describing the coexistence of stability and instability in the creole language, its openness and closure. Creole, he writes, is a language "ready for any transaction, any compromise, any concession." Its vocabulary is open to "all imports" and its syntax ("si syntaxe il y a," if there is a syntax) bends itself this way and that, cedes to what he calls the "violence of the foreigner." And yet the creole language also knows itself and can come home to itself: "Creole allows anything to be said, recognizes everything. But after all its capitulations on the public stage, it comes back home, shuts its door, resumes its personality, its individual originality, so qualité même as it says" (Baissac 1880, vii).

Baissac is clear that the creole language was the creation of the island's slaves: "It is the slaves who created the creole language," he writes, "and it is easy to prove this." The proof, according to Baissac, lies not in the grammar and syntax—since he is not even sure that there is any—but in turns of phrase that for him represent the residues of the social relations of slavery. Mistrust, he argues, is central to these: "The creole never says *regarder* [look] but always *guetter* [look out for], that is to say, to look

with a forethought of mistrust. . . . In the same way, *chercher* [to look for]
is always *roder* [to prowl, to hang out] since, for the white, the black was
always a prowler" (Baissac 1880, xii).

And so on. Unlike modern linguists, Baissac sees the vocabulary of the
language as more telling than its grammar. But the most suggestive part
of Baissac's analysis is his account of the birth of the creole language in
the trauma of slavery. Loss, he appears to argue, is at the heart of the
creole language: the loss, for example, of the verb *to be*, the resistance of
silence:

> Out of the barbarism from which the slave traders seized them,
> brusquely removed by slavery into a world of new ideas contained
> within the French language, the slaves resolutely closed their eyes and
> their ears, and beyond the tight realm of the material world they
> wished only to ignore everything, feeling themselves incapable of un-
> derstanding anything. Abstraction in particular found them invinci-
> bly rebellious, to the point that the abstract verb par excellence, the
> verb *être*, to be, does not exist in creole, so that it is impossible to say
> *Dieu est*—God exists. Descartes was lucky to have had another lan-
> guage at his service—*je pense, donc je suis* becomes *mo mazine . . .* he
> would have been cut short and we would not have had the Discourse
> on Method. (viii–ix)

In his discussion of the "mutisme" of slavery, Baissac anticipates by a
century the work of the cultural and literary theorists of créolité—the
French Antillean writers Edouard Glissant, Patrick Chamoiseau, Raphael
Confiant, and Jean Bernabé, and, in a somewhat different vein, their
fellow Martinican Frantz Fanon.[15] Glissant (1991) traces the source of this
mutisme. He argues, as have others, that the "rupture" of slavery, the
moment of trauma (which some locate in the Middle Passage), meant
that African slaves lost their mother tongues, at least as functional, day-
to-day languages. Insofar as these languages survived, they did so, he says,
largely through their endowment with quasi-religious significance—they
became fetishized. The power of this linguistic fetish (the name of a god,
an utterance of a spirit, the incantation) lay, argues Glissant, in its near
incomprehensibility, even to its speakers. For Glissant, then, opacity and
mutisme are important resources of cultural resistance for the slave—all
the more so because the creole language is known to both master and
slave (Britton 1999, 18). The very fact of mutual intelligibility meant that

slaves developed their own particular usage of creole, as well as their own ruses of camouflage. Creole speech is in fact a screen—creole is "polysonic vertigo" (Bernabé, Chamoiseau, and Confiant 1993, 99).

Baissac for his part appears to think that the creole language talks more to loss than to liberation. Not only, as he indicates, is there no *to be* in creole, there is also no *I* only *me*—hence "je pense, donc je suis," becomes truncated to "mo mazine." Mauritian creole speakers, Baissac appears to argue, make no distinction between subject and object. What, if anything, does this mean in terms of our understanding of slave subjectivity and agency? The French legal system, as I have already indicated, clearly imagined slaves as having agency, inner dispositions, "first persons." In the courtroom the accused slave was unable to say "Yes, I did it" or "No, I didn't do it"—only the equivalent of "Me do it" or "Me no do it." In her suggestive article, Rhonda Cobham-Sander (1995) discusses the absent "I" in present-day Jamaican English. A young man, Colin Ferguson, is in court accused of murder, which he denies: "Me nevah do a ting." Yes, says Cobham-Sander, *me* never does "do a ting," only *I* can do that. The creole speaker, ventures Cobham-Sander, is somewhat "psychotic," for, according to Lacan, a subject enters the symbolic order only when he (it is he) inserts himself into the language as *I* and thereby becomes a speaking subject. If she were right, it would cast a lot of doubt on my interpretation of slave subjectivity, because there could be none. Acknowledging the limits of her argument, Cobham-Sanders goes on to concede that "everyone is perfectly aware that the creole 'me' is capable of agency, responsibility and love," but argues, nevertheless, that the historical memory of trauma produced the absent *I*.

The apparent absence of the *I* in creole languages is intriguing,[16] but creole speakers do, in fact (and of course), make distinctions between subject and object, and there is no easy interpretation of this and other aspects of language created under slavery. Jacques Lacan describes all subjects as "slaves of language" (1982, 148), and this Lacanian model of alienation in language is reiterated by Jacques Derrida (1998), who, in his account of language and colonialism in North Africa, insists that all culture is "colonial." If we understand that all subjects are necessarily alienated by the "otherness" of language, the suggestion is that the violence of slavery produced a kind of double alienation represented by the creole language (though this is not what Derrida is suggesting). Not everyone believes that creole languages are liberating in their essential panglossian origins—some stress their limitations, and their origins in the erasure of identities (Metellus 1998). Baissac, who clearly was not a Lacanian and had not read Derrida, is also struck by the absences and mutisms of the language, features he attributes to the Middle Passage. A picture emerges from Baissac of both loss and confusion—the blanking out that sometimes goes with a traumatic event,[17] and the confusion caused by forcible entry into a completely different world. Yet out of this arise a language and an oral tradition that Baissac appears to celebrate, and the anticipated loss of which he guards against by writing it down.[18]

We may not agree that all subjects are equally alienated within the "colonialism" of language. Britton, in her discussion of Glissant's work, argues that the lack of a language is not "just a question of missing items," but more radically, of the fact that "the language they do use is experienced by them as lack, blighted by a kind of nothingness" (Britton 1999, 43). But Derrida and others are surely right to assert that mastery over language is a fantasy. Whether or not we accept Baker and Corne's view that Île de France creole was and is in a sense more African than it is French, it is clear that the "masters" of the island could never completely have command of a language that, even if it was a langue d'arrivée by the mid–eighteenth century, nevertheless remained an unstable one, continually added to by the babble of new arrivals, and containing many spaces for innovation, inversion, and (possibly) subversion. Slaves on Île de France may largely have lost their "mother tongues," but it seems likely that even within the medium of French creole they would have been able to move between registers and "code switch."[19] This was predominantly an oral culture (though the written word was also making its mark, as we shall see)—and as an oral culture and largely unwritten language, it was particularly hard for anyone to control.

Riddling and Other Word Games

Eighteenth-century travelers in Île de France remarked on the popularity among slaves of certain cultural forms. Milbert, in the early years of the nineteenth century, mentioned the practice of "charades" (1812, 1:270), and though he gives no detailed account of this, we can assume that it involved a degree of mimicry noted in many other parts of the slave world (see Burton 1997). The performative aspect of charades may also, to some degree, have circumvented any problem with language and linguistic intelligibility. Singing and dancing were also central to slave culture, forms that could also easily be turned to social commentary. Milbert again noted the practice of slaves singing as they carried their masters and mistresses in palanquins: "It is easy to recognize on the roads the approach of a rich colon by the songs with which the slaves who carry him relieve the fatigue of the journey" (1812, 11:155). By the early nineteenth century a syncretic dance form—the sega—had also come into being.[20] But there was another aspect of slave culture suggestive of linguistic exploration and agility: the practice of riddling. Many of the island's slaves came from riddling cultures in Africa, Madagascar, and the Indian subcontinent.[21] There do not appear to be any recorded riddles dating from the eighteenth century, but Baissac made a collection of them in the nineteenth, including the following:

> *Mo maison est peinte en jaune, a l'interieur j'ai une bande de petits mozambiques? —Une papaye mure.* (My house is painted yellow, inside is a group of young Mozambicans —A ripe papaya.)
> *Du blanc dans du très noir? —Le riz dans la marmite.* (Something white inside something very black? —Rice in a cooking pot.)
> *Maman guinée joue du violon, tous les blancs dansent? —La marmite de riz sur le feu.* (A Guinée mama plays the violin and all the whites dance? —The cooking pot of rice on the fire.)

More recently the Mauritian-born novelist Le Clézio has also documented Mauritian riddles (or *sirandanes,* as they are known), many of which are identical to those collected by Baissac. Riddles are, according to Le Clézio, also "mots clés," key words, which "permit the memory to open and reveal a hidden treasure." Sometimes, he argues, their message is particularly mysterious and suggestive, as in this riddle commentary on kinship: *Ki ser mo papa napa mo matant? —Disan.* (Who is sister of my father, but is not my aunt? —Blood) (Le Clézio and Le Clézio 1990, 18).

In his exhaustive analysis of the riddles collected by Baissac, Philip Baker has traced their origins variously to Europe and Africa (Baker 2003). African and Malagasy slaves brought riddles with them to the island, as did the French colonists and workers. African and European riddles met on the island and were part of a mutually constituted world. There are two aspects of riddling I would like to discuss here: first, the internal structure of riddles and its play on strangeness and familiarity; second, the dialogic character of the act of riddling.

The internal structure of riddles is a play on the strange and the familiar. Riddles first render the familiar unfamiliar and uncanny (the cooking pot becomes the Guinée mama), before rerevealing, in the answer, the familiar (the Guinée mama turns out to be nothing more than a cooking pot). They have a transformative potential and, like poetry, work through processes of condensation and displacement.[22] They superimpose the unknown on the known and "reveal in a brief flash an excluded cosmos, a non-world or topsy-turvy world lurking just beneath or within our ordered one" (Hasan-Rokem and Shulman 1996, 4). The metaphor of which riddles are an example works, writes Lacan, by setting a "creative spark," which "flashes between the two signifiers, one of which has taken the place of the other in the signifying chain" (1982, 157). Riddles do set up, if only very temporarily and conditionally, an alternative reality, an extraordinary metaphoric relationship that in day-to-day life would seem impossible, even mad. They work only by being allowed to exist in relative autonomy from the everyday world of cognitive categories and the usual relationships among them. But unlike a fantasy or illusion that might go on and on, the riddle leaves you in this alternative world only very briefly before bringing you back to earth—it's only a cooking pot! The riddles slaves brought with them, then, not only constituted part of their memory of "home," but also, in their very structure, enacted the experience of displacement.

Riddles are not only a quintessentially oral form, they are also inescapably social and dialogic. It takes two to riddle. In each riddle confrontation there is a self and an other, a testing of strangeness and familiarity, a test of how far the two of you share the same world, the same understanding (Handelman 1996, Cohen 1996). There is also a learning process. Over time you learn the knack, and many of the answers. Repeating the strangeness of the riddle gives you control over it, rather like the child who likes to hear a frightening story again and again. The fearful is turned into the familiar (you see, you knew it really, you just did not recognize your own answer). If we imagine the practice of riddling in a multilingual slave society, with all its disconnections and incomprehensions, we can see it as a way of creating a common language—but, crucially, only via a detour through the strangeness of the uncanny.

Île de France in the eighteenth century was, by and large, an oral culture (though literacy played an increasingly important role, as we shall see), and one whose creole speakers ranged from halting to fluent. Plays on words, both structured as in riddling, and more accidental (the result of incomprehension and metonymic association), were in all likelihood a marked feature of the linguistic life of the island. But the slave experience of language was not a continual play on words, nor was it necessarily subversive of the power relations of the slave system. Metonymy might, after all, be the residue of painful incomprehension, and riddles do not allow one to live in a fantasy world for very long. One visitor to Île de France claimed to have heard slaves articulate a very pessimistic view of language. In this account, the possession of language and not its lack is regarded as a source of oppression: "The monkeys are so similar to man in their intelligence and their organization that the slaves call them lazy men. As they say in their jargon: "Ca petit di monde la na pas voulé palé pour na pas travaillé"—those little people there, they do not want to speak because they do not want to work" (Milbert 1812, 240–241).

I have tried simply to suggest ways in which our understanding of the experience of slavery is both mediated by language and might be affected by an examination of the particular characteristics of the language that evolved during this period. But we certainly cannot hear this eighteenth-century creole in its different registers—and since phonemics are such an important part of these language cultures, this is a major problem. Our only access to the oral is, in this case, via a detour through the written. And Île de France was not without the written word.

Language and Belief, Catholicism and Orality

Here as elsewhere in the colonial world, missionaries were important agents, if not in the construction of, then certainly in attempts to fix and render written previously unwritten languages. Priests worried about language, and for good reason.

Four priests of the order of St. Lazare were among the first French functionaries to arrive on Île de France from Île Bourbon in 1721. The Lazarists had been employed by the Compagnie des Indes in Madagascar from the mid–seventeenth century, and in Île Bourbon from 1712. The early years of their mission on Île de France were rocky, to say the least. Their relations with officials frequently broke down amid mutual re-crimination, and this was to remain a feature of their mission throughout the century.[23] In 1780, for example, the governor and intendant (Souillac and Foucault) were writing to the Ministère de la Marine that "the spirit of ferment which activates the missionaries of this island reproduces itself from time to time, and it seems that these priests appear to be quiet for a period only in order to have the opportunity to get their breath."[24] This fractiousness, and their very small numbers, means that we should not exaggerate their impact, least of all on the slave population. They were obliged, however, to work among this population, in part because the island's 1723 version of the Code Noir specified this.[25] Bernardin de St. Pierre regarded this mission as particularly cynical, writing, "It was not enough for these wretches to be bound to the meanness and cruelty of depraved landowners, but they also had to be the toys of their sophistry. Theologians assure us that slaves in this life will find some kind of spiritual freedom. But most are bought at an age when they cannot learn French and missionaries do not learn their language" (2002, 132).

The impact of the Lazarists, and hence of Christianity (no other "cultes" being permitted in the French colonies), on the slaves of Île de France was, one must assume, very limited. The very paucity of evidence of the religious lives of slaves is telling. There are no lengthy accounts of slave spirituality such as exist for the Protestant context of North America, and only slight hints of the slave reinterpretation of Catholic ritual that took place elsewhere.[26] We know little, then, of this potentially important dimension of the slave experience.

The best informed, or at least the most reflective, of the small group of Lazarist priests who wrote on Île de France in the mid– to late eighteenth century was Father Philippe-Albert Caulier.[27] Caulier worked on Île Bourbon and paid no more than brief visits to the neighboring island, but his observations on language and religious practice are unusually detailed. Listing the dozens of ethnic groups represented in the slave population of Île de France, he described the linguistic situation as a "multitude bigarée," adding that it would "take a second Pentecost to be able to speak all the barbarous languages needed in urgent cases."[28] There were plenty of "urgent cases," and this is what drove the priests to address the subject of language directly. New slaves frequently arrived off the slave ships close to death. The priests were anxious to baptize them, but were equally anxious not to render this sacrament meaningless through the absence of a common language. For arriving Malagasies (the Lazarists had had a long relationship with Madagascar) they used interpreters, of whom we know there were numbers on the island. In 1763 the priests were issued with the following instructions on how to proceed in these circumstances:

> As for adults arriving sick, if they are in danger, and especially in near danger of death, an interpreter must be employed to instruct them in the principal mysteries of the religion, on the necessity of baptism if they are to be saved; to bring them to ask God for forgiveness of their sins. . . . But since one finds very few interpreters capable of making these truths understood, it is expedient to arm oneself with a notebook in which they are expressed in the Malagasy language, to guide and aid the interpreters in helping these poor moribunds to understand.[29]

The oral skills of the interpreters, then, were to be supplemented with the written word of the essentials of the faith, in a notebook, in the Malagasy language. And when necessary, the priests would themselves attempt some words in the slaves' languages: "On balboutie comme on peut en leur langue," wrote Caulier.[30]

Beyond these "urgent" cases, however, the emphasis was to be on teaching potential converts the "rudiments" of the French language; this had to precede any preparation for baptism: "Above all, one must force them to 'jargon' in our French."[31] Caulier, while ready to admit to the limitations language imposed on the priests' mission among slaves, went on to argue that more important than the lack of language were the "repugnance" and "indolence" slaves demonstrated toward religious matters. The result was that "out of a hundred slaves taken at random, one would not find six who could correctly recite the *ornison dominicale*, even fewer the salutation, symbol and commandments, fewer still who would understand what they were reciting."

Though language might be a problem for the priests' mission among the island's slaves, their illiteracy was not; the practices they attempted to put in place were oral and performative. These centered on the catechism. In France, especially from the seventeenth century, there was a similar emphasis on the catechism in missionary enterprises among peasants and Breton "savages." But the vehicle for instruction was the printed catechism, which spread rapidly, not only as a book of religion, but also as a reading manual (Brodeur and Caulier 1997, Croix 1997). Implied was the inseparability of literacy from religious instruction—and from authority. In the eighteenth century the printed catechism would become a symbol of papal authority.

In Île de France, by contrast, the catechism was not to be read by slaves, but to be recited. This was a faith of the spoken word, but a spoken word that would be carefully directed, rehearsed, and ideally committed to memory. The priest alone would recite the demands, always in the same terms, and he would then accompany the respondents in their responses, word for word, attempting all the while to render their pronunciation less "crude." There were limits to this faith in orality, however. The power of the church hierarchy and desire for conformity meant that it was important to put in writing exactly how this oral practice should be conducted: "To avoid any singularity . . . it is necessary that newly arrived [priests] should have in writing, a directory to guide them, a kind of manual."[32]

Ideally the written version would be not in French, but in some version of the slaves' own languages. Father Caulier produced two of these translated catechisms—one in a version of Malagasy, and the other in a version of the creole.[33] The latter is in a version of the creole of Île Bourbon, not that of Île de France, though Caulier clearly intended it for use on both islands. We have no evidence that it was used, but it is an interesting document nevertheless.

Language difficulties and pronunciation should not, wrote Caulier, be allowed to get in the way of the transmission of the elements of the faith. Neither should incomprehension. When Malagasy slaves say "tsi fante (non intelligo)," one should not desist, he wrote, but repeat and repeat the principal points of doctrine. Incomprehension, went on Caulier, could have a number of causes—perhaps the evangelist had not quite "caught their accent," but more likely, slaves had never before heard talk of religion; it was a "completely new language to them."[34]

As Caulier makes clear, then, for the missionaries, language was inseparable from concepts, from "truths." There could be no randomness in the use of words here (no play with metonymy), but a careful adherence to a script, the only copy of which would be in the possession of the priest. Somehow, through repetition of the words, over and over, the concepts would finally lodge themselves in the minds of the slaves. This, in fact, may not have been such a strange idea to many slaves who came from cultures in which just this kind of repetition was central to religion and ritual. In many ritual circumstances in Africa, for example, participants would not be expected to understand every word or gesture, but they would be expected to utter and enact. Meaning would be revealed later, not through any direct explication, but slowly, perhaps over years, through repeated participation and by association. Slaves on Île de France came from a variety of religious backgrounds in Africa, Madagascar, and India. Though the priests frequently pronounced that they had no religious beliefs, and therefore they were working on a "blank slate," this clearly was not the case. We know, for example, that some of the enslaved of Indian origin (as well as those of free birth) were practicing Muslims, since this created periodic problems for the relationship between the administration and the priests. We also know that others from southern India (and possibly from farther afield) were Christians.[35] These groups find their way into the documentation because they are seen as having identifiable (if problematic) religious beliefs; many more, of course, arrived with beliefs and practices which were categorized not as religion, but as "superstition." Unfortunately, we have very little detailed evidence of these beliefs and practices of slaves in the eighteenth century, nor do we know much of their interpretation of Christianity, and so it is impossible to construct a picture of this crucial aspect of slave life, other than through the eyes of the priests themselves, and the occasional observations of visitors.[36]

The catechism is dialogic in form and therefore bears a superficial resemblance to the riddle. But while the riddle makes a detour through the strange and uncanny only to return to the everyday and the familiar, the catechism does not appear to offer the same everyday sort of reassurance that the strange is the familiar in disguise. Rather, everything is a bit strange and remains that way. The following is a short abstract from Caulier's "Petit Catechisme . . . tourné au style des esclaves nègres":

DEMANDE (D): Où qu'il est bon Dieu? [Where is the good God?]
RÉPONSE (R): Bon Dieu l'est partout, au Ciel, icy même, li voir à nous la nouïct cõe lé jour. [The Good God is everywhere, in the sky, even here, he watches over us night and well as day].
D: A cause donc nous y ne voit pas Bon Dieu? [Why cannot we see the Good God?]
R: à cause qu'ili etre un espirit, ça que note zieux ne peut pas voir. [Because he is a spirit, something our eyes cannot see.]
D: Bon Dieu n'en a un corps? [Does the Good God have a body?]
R: Non va. [No.]

D: Nous y peut cacher nous autes du Bon Dieu? [Can we hide our-
selves from the Good God?]

R: Non va. Li est partout, li voir tout, tout ça que nou i pense, tout ça
que nou i fait, li entend li acoute tout ça que nou i dit. [No. He is
everywhere, he sees everything, everything that we think, everything we do, and hears everything that we say].

Not all the concepts contained in the questions and answers of the
catechism would have been strange to respondents. Slaves, we can assume, lived with the reality of a spirit world, though concepts of original
sin (and of the Trinity, explained at length in other parts of the catechism) may have been rather more remote. Most strikingly, the language
of slavery permeated the catechism Caulier devised (though of course
this language was present in the French and Latin versions of the same
period and was not "invented" for this context):

D: A cause Fils de Dieu se faire homme? [Why did the Son of God
make himself into a man?]

R: Pou rachiter à nous tretous pauvres Saclaves du peché, pou em-
pêcher que nous aller en Enfer, et pou gagner à nous Paradis. [To
redeem us poor slaves from sin, to prevent us from going to Hell
and to gain us Heaven.]

D: Est'ce que nous tertous venir au monde, Saclaves, du Diab et du
Peché? [Do we all come into the world as slaves of the Devil and of
Sin?]

R: Ouï, nous venir au monde Saclaves ça même, à cause grand Peché
d'adam, premier Pere à nous. [Yes, we all come into the world as
slaves, because of the great sin of Adam, our first Father.]

D: Comment que N. Sgr Jesus-Christ fini racheter à nous autres? Li
fini racheter avec Piastres? [How does Jesus Christ redeem us? Does
he redeem us with piastres?]

R: Non va. Li racheter à nous par son sang, par la mort, li fini souffri et
mouri pour nous. [No, he redeems us with his blood, by his death,
he suffered and died for us.]

On Île de France the word *racheter* had a specific meaning, which
referred to manumission. One could buy oneself out of slavery, or could
be bought out of slavery by another person, and *racheter* was the word
used to describe this process. We do not know whether slaves found the

words of the catechism powerful, but there is some evidence that they developed what became, for the priests at least, a rather embarrassing enthusiasm for confession.[37] Priests commented on, and attempted to avoid, an unseemly scramble for confession at the beginning of Lent, for example.[38] Words appeared to have the power to save, to redeem, to transact within the economy of sin and slavery. In his (controversial) analysis of the psychodynamics of orality, Walter Ong argued that in all oral cultures words have this kind of power, that far from being "tags," their utterance in and of itself can make things happen (Ong 1982, chap. 3). It may sometimes have seemed this way, for the priests also noted that on occasion sick and dying slaves refused to be baptized because they had witnessed so many deaths apparently following directly from the ceremony,[39] as if the words themselves had caused the death. Baissac also alludes to the power of the word in his brief discussion of the language of witchcraft and sorcery. This vocabulary, he argues, is large: while the word *yangue* refers to sorcery in general, there were always ways of referring more explicitly to the form this took. These included the use of drugs ("Li ti drogue moi"), or bad wishes ("Liti mete lequer av moi"), and of words themselves: "Lite mete la bouce av moi" (1880, xxxiv).

While Catholic missionaries did not expose slaves to the written word, their practices worked in the interstices of written and oral. Words were performed in church rituals that also frequently reinscribed the political and social hierarchy. Slaves were rarely admitted to the Holy Communion, but they could not have failed to have witnessed this ceremony, and priests did their best to "inspire in them a desire for the celestial food."[40] The colonies celebrated fewer saint days than did metropolitan France, thanks to a special dispensation from the Pope, who had agreed, in 1728, that "too many [fêtes] occasioned grave inconvenience, either by the scandals which resulted, the negligence of observation, or disorders."[41] Nevertheless, such saint days and festivals as were observed provided graphic performances of the connections between temporal and spiritual power. Priests were reminded of the importance of rank when it came to the distribution of Communion bread and other aspects of church ritual: "Following the advice of our Superiors . . . it is important to act with circumspection and a wise deference, not only toward the Governor, but in proportion also to the Counselors and Chief of the districts. . . . Besides, the people have need of this unspoken lesson in order to repress the license with which they are apt to censor and even to declare against their spiritual and temporal superiors."[42] The celebration of the festival of St. Louis provided a particularly elaborate display of the temporal order, culminating in a grand ball for the island's elite (Chelin 1988); death was a constant reminder of inequalities, with the church distinguishing clearly between slave and free, treating the former not as adults but as the equivalent of freeborn children, and burying them in a separate cemetery. If not all slaves could catch the precise meaning of the words the priests recited to them, they could hardly fail to catch some of the meaning of the enactments which accompanied these words.

Satirizing the Colony in Print

We must assume that only a very small percentage of the island's population was literate by the mid– to late eighteenth century,[43] but the small reading public was an active one (Caudron 1996). A printing press was introduced onto the island in 1768 (an early date for the colonies) and between that date and 1800, it produced nearly three hundred items, including newspapers, almanacs, and books. From 1773 to the end of the century, there was always at least one locally produced newspaper in circulation, and sometimes two (Toussaint 1951; Caudron 1996). Some members of the elite had very large book collections, which come to light in the documentation of the period, either through sales or in wills. These collections were not dissimilar to those of their metropolitan contemporaries, encyclopedic in nature and containing many multivolumed works. Of the 159 identifiable volumes possessed by one M. Lezongard, for example, 30 comprised the works of Voltaire (Caudron 1990, 183). The wealthier habitants of the colony apparently read philosophy (Voltaire, Montesquieu, Raynal, Helvetius, Locke, Rousseau), scientific and practical works (Buffon, Bernardin de St. Pierre, works on geography, medicine, finance, navigation), and novels, poetry, and dramatic works.

Book ownership was almost certainly confined to a very small elite, but while noting this it is important to bear two other facts in mind. First, reading and writing are not the same thing. I have no evidence from the legal records of slaves being able to sign their names (though a few "free blacks" could do this, and the number who could probably was growing), but this does not necessarily mean that they would have been unable to decipher a written note, for example. Not all slaves came from societies without scripts—the important minority of Indian slaves clearly did not.

In addition to this, it is clear that the written word in Île de France was a very social word—frequently read out, sung, and posted on trees and walls, or circulated by hand. The oral and the written were in constant exchange with each other.[44] So, for instance, many of the examples of defamation that came to the authorities' attention had a written component, and perhaps the writing made them all the more powerful. In 1779 the officer in charge of the royal printing press on the island was reminded that he needed permission before he printed anything. In this respect the situation on the island was a microcosmic version of that in metropolitan France, where the authorities were engaged in attempting to control the circulation of an increasing volume of "clandestine" literature in this period (Darnton 1995, 1997). More often, of course, the written word was handwritten, and not always in anything resembling "standard" French. These were not attempts like those of the missionaries to deliberately produce a creole text, but there was a creole continuum in writing, just as there was in speech.[45]

A typical case was the complaint made by Louis Bergicourt (a noir libre) in his name and in the names of his wife Marie and his three sisters-in-law.[46] The complaint was against the Goy brothers and a surgeon named Moutou (a name indicating Indian origin). They, allegedly, had sung an "obscene and defamatory" song both at the door of the church and outside Bergicourt's house. For those who had missed these performances, they had produced a written version, which they posted on Bergicourt's door, and which had been copied and circulated.

Performance must have been a common feature of the insult culture of the island, though this aspect is almost entirely written out of the written record. In addition to the slave creole practices of riddling and charades, and the performance of songs and of the sega dance, Port Louis also boasted a theater, founded in 1754 (Chelin 1954) in which, judging by the police reports, performativity was as much a feature of the audience as it was of the cast.[47] Midnight mass and the *jours gras* of carnival time also caused the authorities some anxiety. Police were present at the mass to "prevent disorders" and to arrest any individuals who were "conducting themselves scandalously or with irreverence,"[48] while at carnival time police were ordered to patrol the streets and allow to move around freely all who were masked and dressed "decently," but to arrest those who were dressed in ecclesiastical robes, or who were committing disorders.[49] By the time of the Revolution there was also a visiting opera troupe. Joseph

Laglaine, a naval surgeon with a theatrical bent, arrived on the island in 1788 and set about raising subscriptions for a theatrical troupe. Having raised sufficient money, he set off for France and returned with recruits in 1790, when he set about building a *salle de spectacle*, which was inaugurated in July of that year. With the help of the musician D'Amouroux, the *troupe dramatique* evolved into a *troupe d'opera*, but it was so decimated by the smallpox epidemic in 1792 that it ceased to exist.[50]

The evidence for a culture of performance does not in any sense imply that life on the streets of Port Louis was one long entertainment, but it does suggest modes of communication not entirely dependent on a shared language, let alone literacy.[51] Social critique could also be given a particular edge when rendered into the written word. One example comes from 1778, when a placard was nailed to the church door in Port Louis. The document is in poor condition, but appears to read as follows:

NOTICE
The office of Gossip is still at the house of Reneaut, hatmaker and bankrupt, whose wife is in Paris. Or, failing that, in the houses of Moriniere and Planche. It is in these abominable houses that the reputations and virtue of the most established are destroyed.
   Table of the honest notables who are in the office:
   Reneaut—the "sparkling."
   Faquin.
   Lima—the drôle.
   Apendu l'ecluse—the insolent armourer.
   Etienne—"W" on his shoulder.
   Barre the idiot without education.
   De sauce—preacher at the junior [seminary?].
   Commarond—tavern keeper, crazy.
   Jumel—spiritual apothecary.[52]

Though the placard was regarded by the authorities as slanderous, it was, in addition, clearly a comment and criticism of other authors of slander, naming them and their "headquarters." This twist seems to have been facilitated by the use of writing, for the placard took the form of a "Notice," handwritten and in less than standard French, but masquerading, nevertheless, as an official document.

   More elaborate still was a case in 1775 of an "outrage against morality" that, in what appears in itself to be a commentary on literacy, took the form of the spurious "Catalog of the Books Which Compose the Library of Isle de France"[53] Handwritten copies of this catalog were circulating on the island and were also being read out loud for the benefit, one supposes, of those who could not read. The public prosecutor was clear that this was a serious attack on public morality: "Nothing is more dangerous in a society than public pests who trouble the repose, the order and the harmony in attacking others with a piquant and murderous irony. . . . they malign the honor, the principles, the sentiments, and the morals of the most respectable persons and citizens." He went on: "There is in circulation a handwritten document titled *catalogue des livres*, which one might call a bloody satire, or infamy, containing calomnies and implicit defamations. . . . a few days ago an individual, wearing the dress of the bourgeois, and a large blond wig, with great lines on his face, read this same libelous document out publicly, to a full assembly."

The copy of this *satire sanglante*, which has survived in the Mauritian archives, is, unfortunately, in poor condition, but the general gist is clear. It consisted of a list of phantom publications authored by well-known characters on the island (including members of the government):

"The art of governing men and doing it . . ." a treatise on truth and the art of appearing natural, by Maillard Dumesle.[54]
"The seeker after the spirit" by M. Bailly, under commission.
"How to make a book," by M. Thomas, naval scribe.
"Love of war with . . . the authority of naïveté and simplicity" by master Guillame, Captain of the Bulot.
"How to have children" by M. Launay, augmented by M. . . .
"A new method of conserving the teeth" by M. Dupleix.
"The embarrassment of riches" by M. Payot.

Literacy, limited though it was, did appear to be giving the island's authorities some cause for concern by the time of the Revolution. In the heated atmosphere of 1792, when events in St. Domingue were very much on the minds of the island's new revolutionary government, the literacy of the lower orders, particularly of the "free black" population, induced some anxiety. In June 1792 the procureur-général spent some time reassuring members of the Directoire that a document circulating on the island was not, in fact, an incitement to black revolution:

Monsieur Perichon informed the Mayor (of Port Louis) that his *maî-tre d'hôtel*, a free black, had received a document, the substance of which was that the gens de couleur in America were in possession of all the rights of free men, thanks to the courage they had displayed in going to war with the Whites, and that those of Isle de France should imitate them. . . .

After several inquiries I found that the piece of paper in the hands of M. Perichon's maître d'hôtel was nothing other than a copy of the agreement made between Whites and gens de couleur in the America, and can be found in all the public papers distributed in this colony.[55]

There was no real threat of revolt from the "free blacks" of Île de France, but the Procureur's reassurances nevertheless appear rather naive in a society in which the written and oral were so imbricated. He had read the document and knew it to be "innocent," but a literate or semiliterate maître d'hôtel might well have endowed it with a different tone or even have changed its content entirely.

We enter into language, we do not master it. Slaves arriving on Île de France entered into an unstable language. All languages are unstable, of course, but entering a particularly unstable language situation such as characterized Île de France in the eighteenth century presented both constraints and opportunities: instability and mutism can be inter-preted in different ways.

The first generation of slaves kept a memory of their mother tongues, their langues de départ, even if many of them were never afforded the opportunity to share and pass this language on. The second or third generation of slaves born on the island would have had no such recourse to another language—they (and some of the free black population) were in the situation described by Derrida for the monolingual. They had nowhere to go, no recourse to a fantasy language homeland, no langues de départ. Yet their language, the creole language, contained within it traces of both these multiple "mother tongues" and the absences and scars sustained in the violent passage from here to there.

Meanwhile, as the century progressed, so script and scraps of paper assumed more significance. Slaves carried scribbled notes from their masters and mistresses authorizing them to work away from home; news-papers were posted, circulated, read aloud; financial transactions (large and small) were noted and inscribed; the death of Thérèse's baby, and other babies like her, was committed to writing by the priest. Lawyers recorded the speech of individuals like Joseph and left the record on which much of this book is based. Perhaps the most symbolically significant act of writing, however, was the manumission document—an act of writing through which the slave was transformed into a free person. Once manumitted, the "free black," even when illiterate, entered the world of lawyers and writing. This was a community committed to the legal forms that not only provided proof of status, but authorized the sale of property, defined the terms of marriage, recorded the wills of the dying. Most free blacks, even at the end of the century, were unable to sign their names, but they could make and did make their marks on documents invested with great importance.

A Postscript: The Language of the Spirits

Though we have very little evidence for the spiritual lives of slaves on eighteenth-century Île de France, we do know from other sources that many African and Malagasy slaves came from societies in which kinship between the living and the dead was a fundamental fact of life. The fact that Malagasy maroons often stole boats and set sail for their homeland, for example, was widely, and perhaps correctly, attributed to their fear of dying away from home and of not being buried with their ancestors. Physical dislocation was a fundamental of slavery, as was the dislocation of the kinship group and, as I have indicated in this chapter, linguistic loss as well as linguistic creation. But I began to think again about this and about the Île de France "creole" slave sailors who accompanied the slave traders on their trips to Madagascar and the African coast, when I read Michael Lambek's 1998 account of one spirit medium in northern Madagascar, whom he witnessed in a trance in 1994. Among the spirits who emerge from time to time into the present of this area are those of French and Creole sailors of the precolonial period—the period of the slave trade. Possessed by one such sailor, the medium switches from Malagasy into French. Through the medium of French the medium reflects on Madagascar, speaking of his own nation as a "partial outsider."

I have no direct experience of spirit mediumship in Mauritius, but in one interview with an elderly creole man in the south of the island, I was told that the ancestral spirits of slaves arrived by ship from over the ocean. When these spirits possessed an individual it was essential, he said, that the name of the ancestor be called up, recognized, and then the spirit would speak. "What language do these spirits speak?" I asked. "Greek," he replied and, tired of my questions, refused to elaborate.[56] While the languages of Africa and Madagascar may have been lost to the living in Mauritius, perhaps they live on in the "Greek" speech of ancestral spirits that periodically erupt disruptively into their lives. Likewise, though the slave trade has long gone from northern Madagascar, the spirits of the creole sailors are still there, still speaking French.

Chapter Nine

MÉTISSAGE AND REVOLUTION

*I*n late December 1793 the procureur-général of the island's new Revolutionary administration was approached by two citizens requesting him to investigate the circumstances existing in the house of one Citizen Letimié, a member of the island's new Colonial Assembly.[1] The procureur reported his investigation to the meeting of the island's Directoire on 21 December:

> Two individuals (*particuliers*) of this town told me that Citoyen Letimié, member of the Colonial Assembly, daily invites a black to his table, eats and drinks familiarly with him, and that this black who can be considered (*rangé*) by his color as belonging to a class distinct from that of Whites, wears no sign characteristic of liberty (which some among them enjoy); that he is dressed in a shirt and short of blue cloth, that he wears, in a word, the livery of slavery, with no indication that he shares the prerogatives of the freeborn man.

The procureur investigated and was told by Citizen Letimié that:

> the black in question was the head of a large family, and had been enfranchised a long time ago; that from the moment that he had given him his freedom, he had grown closer to him, not recognizing any difference between one man and another when both, though of different colors, resemble each other in the qualities of the heart, their probity, their humanity, the generosity of their sentiments; that this man had acquired an honest fortune . . . that since he had been free, he

and his family, he had eaten with Letimié, not just over the last two weeks, but for more than two years, not just alone, but with two of his children; that this man is a worker by profession, that he usually comes in from work at the hours of dinner or supper, which accounts for why he does not wear his uniform of the Garde Nationale at the table . . . that he [Letimié] was surprised that the internal regime of his house had for so long been ignored since, having nothing to hide, he always dined and supped with the windows of the dining room open.[2]

By late 1793 the anxieties expressed by the two citizens of Port Louis about their fellow-citizen's guest at table were hardly politically correct. The procureur-général, though he had seen fit to investigate, quotes approvingly Lemitié's indignant response. His former slave had every right to dine at his table, they were equals though of "different colors." He had nothing to hide, his windows were wide open, and his dinner guest had no need to dress for the occasion—he was a free man. But clearly some whites still worried about slaves passing as free. Free blacks, either freeborn or affranchised slaves, had always been caught in the web of this anxiety. In this case, the two vigilant citizens argued that since the man who was Letimié's dinner guest was black and therefore not white, the least one could expect was that he would sport some sign of his free status, rather than continue, confusingly, to dress in the "livery of slavery."

One might argue that, since he was clearly making no attempt to dress as a free man, this might be a clear indication that he was a free man. "Passing," after all, was necessary only if one had something to hide. Jean Lousteau, as we have seen, argued that his slave Jouan had done precisely this when he escaped on the *Brillant*, and, with his fine clothing and jewelry and manners, had deceived Lieutenant Brousse into thinking that he was a free man. Benoit Giraud had used in his defense the mirroring argument that he had had no way of knowing that Foucault was a representative of the king, since he bore no marks of office. Though indignant at this response, Maillart Dumesle had been forced to admit that things were confusing in Port Louis, where the streets were "continually full of slaves, of free blacks and mulattoes, or workers and foreigners, such that under the pretext of not recognizing an official anything might be thought permissible." Benoit Giraud attempted, unsuccessfully, to apply to whites the rule which was applied to blacks, the insistence that they needed proof of their status. Sometimes having such proof, however, could backfire, as it did on Jean Toinette. Slaves selling items at the bazaar were required to carry notes from their masters or mistresses authenticating that such items were not stolen. In 1791, Jean Toinette, described as a "noir créol libre" (a free black born on the island) when accused of selling a stolen silver fork, produced in his defense a note giving him permission to sell it. His accuser retorted that "he could not then be free, or he would not be carrying such a note."[3]

News of the Revolution arrived on the island in January 1790.[4] The white population almost immediately divided itself into two factions. The conservatives, appealing above all to the need to maintain order (and beyond this, the status quo) favored doing nothing until clearer instructions were received from the metropole, while others grasped immediately the implications and the opportunities implied by the news. The governor, Thomas de Conway,[5] gave in to the most immediate demand, which was to create a Colonial Assembly, the island's first stab at some kind of representative government. But just how representative was, of course, immediately an issue—only white male property owners were accorded the right to elect members. When it met for the first time in April 1790, it looked like, and was, an assembly of the island's wealthy white elite—habitants, rich merchants, lawyers, military officers. Nevertheless, its very existence began a process with a momentum of its own, and meanwhile, out on the streets, the "rabble" expressed their enthusiasm for the new dispensation by wearing the *cocade*. In May 1790 police measures were tightened in response to rumors that sailors were planning to supply arms to the island's slaves (North-Coombes 2000, 10).

Much of 1791 was taken up with constitutional matters. As yet there had been no major disturbances on the island. If there was no bloodbath, there was enough happening on Île de France after 1790 to account for repeated appeals for the need to keep order, particularly the patriarchal order of slavery, in place. In 1792 smallpox (introduced via a boatload of Indian slaves delivered to the Monneron establishment) swept the island, wiping out thousands of slaves and necessitating an embargo on external relations (Vaughan 2000). The small island turned in on itself, colonists squabbled over whether their newfound liberties gave them the right to inoculate their slaves, or the right to refuse inoculation. Food supplies ran low, and the government was crippled. Isolation increased suspicion that English spies and anti-Revolutionaries lurked in every doorway. News had already reached the island of the slave insurrection in St. Domingue. The year 1793 brought the rise of the Sans-Culottes (locally known as La Chaumière), news of the declaration of war, and finally that of the execution of the king. The ever-present threat to the Colonial Assembly was that the mass of soldiers and sailors (to whom appeals to the sanctity of property rang rather hollow) might make common cause with blood-thirsty slaves. In November 1794, with the news of the fall of Robespierre, the Colonial Assembly closed the Chaumière clubs and exiled the island's leading Jacobins to France. But Jacobin sympathies remained strong on the island, particularly among the "poor whites" of Port Louis and in the Regiments of Île de France (the 107th) and Pondichéry (the 108th). On 4 February 1794, the Convention in Paris abolished slavery. Colonists learned of this "with stupefaction" in August that year, but the text of the decree did not arrive until September 1795. Throughout this period the island was troubled by maroon slaves who, in all likelihood, were seizing the opportunities provided by a degree of disorder and confusion. The importance of the maintenance of order was constantly reiterated by members of the Assembly and by emissaries from France. Le Boucher, a *commissaire civil* sent from Paris in 1792, wrote that on the island there were many enemies of good order, for whom the words "Revolution, Liberty, and Patriotism" meant little but were frequently on their lips. "Revolution," he reminded Paris, ought to be synonymous with "good order": "Here, as in France, the Revolution (that is to say public order, for the Revolution having been achieved, good order must be the result), the Revolution has two sorts of enemies."[6]

The Assembly spent much time discussing the 1794 decree abolishing slavery and reasserting its position that such a move would be disastrous and would end in civil war. Jean-Jacques Rousseau's comments on serf-dom in Poland came in useful and were much quoted: "I would fear," he had written, "the vices and cowardice of the serfs. . . . Freedom is a juicy food, but a rich one. . . . To free the people . . . is a great and beautiful undertaking, but a bold and dangerous one which should not be at-tempted without consideration."[7] This was in May 1796. Following shortly afterward was the most famous event of the Revolutionary years on Île de France, and one unlikely to have escaped the attention of the island's free blacks and slaves. In June, two agents of the Directoire, Baco and Burnel (the latter had previously lived and worked on the island as a journalist), arrived, accompanied by boatloads of soldiers. Sent by the Directoire to enforce the 1794 decree abolishing slavery, their presence aroused fierce sentiments among the colonists, and after a show of local military strength they were dispatched back onboard ship.[8] The system of slavery remained intact and the island's colonists were now articulating, much more clearly, their defense of the institution. It was, as North-Coombes has argued (2000) an increasingly and explicitly racist ideology that was being articulated. As Burnel put it, the premise of their arguments was that "a black man was not a man like them." At the same time, however, the Revolutionary years saw increasing numbers of manumissions in an attempt, perhaps, to mollify the slave population, while public pronouncements simultaneously revealed a hardening of attitudes.

Occasional moments of high political drama took place against a background of financial and subsistence crises, naval blockades, and the threat of an English invasion. The atmosphere of crisis also encouraged theatricality. How, one wonders, did slaves watching from the sidelines read Revolutionary dress conventions? In 1794, for example, their mistresses were urged to coif their hair in a mélange of red, white, and blue (Pitot 1899, 172). The Festival of Federation was first celebrated on the island on 14 July 1793, with an orderly procession in the Champ de Mars and the singing of the Marseillaise (d'Unienville 1982, 183–184). But the island's Sans-Culottes had adopted other Revolutionary festivals, which in the colonial context appear to have presented a less orderly, more bizarre spectacle.[9] The five-day-long celebration at the end of the Republican year, which consisted of the Festival of Virtues, the Festival of the Harvest, the Festival of the Grape Harvest, the Festival of the Death of the Last Tyrant, and the Festival of Innocence, featured colonists (and their wives and daughters) in a variety of unfamiliar guises. The bacchanalian Festival of the Grape Harvest, for example, starred two *citoyennes*, wives of prominent members of the bourgeoisie (according to Pitot), enacting scenes of debauchery. "Innocence," meanwhile, was represented by a small white girl, clothed simply in a white tunic and bedecked with flowers, who, as Pitot dryly remarks, was exposed too long to the cold and died the next day. Islanders also celebrated the Festival of Reason, parading the wife of a prominent member of the Assembly, dressed as Minerve. Île de France slaves, so many of whom had been forcibly renamed after Greek gods, were now being exposed to a full range of classical allusions.

The Revolution was a spectacle, but its effects were far from revolutionary for the island's population of slaves, ushering in, as it did, a more conservative, repressive, and exploitative Napoleonic order.[10] Post-Revolutionary Île de France would see an intensification of the regime of slavery. But this is not the full story. Revolutionary ideology brought into sharp relief questions of color and citizenship. Though the colonists of Île de France successfully held out against any abolition of slavery, and though they were spared a slave insurrection, they could not completely ignore the issues raised by the rhetoric of freedom. Both the allegation against Citizen Letimié and his vigorous response to it were part of the same current, as we shall see.

While the colonists of Île de France would stand famously fast against abolition, their leaders presented a liberal face when it came to the issue of the rights of free blacks, now increasingly referred to as *gens de couleur*. Almost as soon as news of the Revolution reached the island, the gens de couleur petitioned the Assembly asking for their own primary assembly from which they could elect representatives. Similar demands were being made by gens de couleur in the French Antillean islands and in the French Indian possession of Pondichéry.[11] Presumably the island's gens de couleur had heard news from Paris of the campaign in favor of the rights of gens de couleur that had been undertaken by the Amis des Noirs, and of the delegation of "Les Mulâtres de Paris" that had gone to the National Assembly in October 1789, demanding six seats (Bénot 1989). For the time being the Île de France white elite held back, arguing that they had no authority to confer these rights. The gens de couleur waited patiently, intent, as they would be throughout this period, to demonstrate that they were, above all, loyal and law-abiding. In order to understand the less than revolutionary politics of this group, we need to recall their social origins and composition, and also their economic role within the colony.

The evolution of the free black population of Île de France has been described in detail by Richard Allen (1999) and by Musleem Jumeer (1984). There were two original components of this community: manumitted slaves and their descendants, and freeborn immigrants and their freeborn descendants. Manumission rates in Île de France were certainly not high. Allen calculates that even in the late eighteenth and early nineteenth centuries they amounted to no more than 0.2 percent a year (1999, 83). This was, then, a small community, though a growing one. In 1767 there were only 587 "free blacks," compared with 3,163 whites and 15,027 slaves. By 1806, however, their numbers had overtaken those of the white population: there were now 7,154 gens de couleur to 6,798 whites and 60,646 slaves (Allen 1999, 82). As we have seen, not everyone had an equal chance of being manumitted. Both slaves of Indian origin and those who were creoles (that is, born on the island) had a greater chance of being freed than did members of other groups, and free women outnumbered men by a significant degree, such that, by the end of the century, the free black population contained twice as many women as men (Allen 1999, chap. 4). As elsewhere, many women were freed because they had become their masters' lovers, and in particular because they had borne their children. The free black population, then, was one closely associated with (though not synonymous with) the anxiety-ridden issue of métissage (Vergès 1999), and though the category of "free blacks" certainly had legal and administrative significance, this was not a homogenous community. Differences and commonalities coexisted, as is indicated by the strained and unstable terminology applied to members of this community.[12] The existence of free blacks was the visible manifestation of the process of demographic and cultural creolization the colony had been undergoing since its inception, and the unevenness of this process was reflected in the composition of this community.

Freeborn blacks, albeit in small numbers, had played an important part on the island at least from Labourdonnais's time, as we have seen. He and his successors had depended heavily on the labor of freeborn Lascar sailors from southern India, and of Malabars. In addition, there were those (like Bernard, whom we met earlier) who were designated Topas (or Topazes), coming from mixed-race, Portuguese-influenced communities in South India (Taffin 1996, Weber 1993). Even within an apparently discrete community, however, there could be complexities. Jumeer points out, for example, that some of the Lascars normally assumed to be Muslims were in fact Christians, speaking Portuguese as well as Urdu (Jumeer 1984, 357). And from Madagascar, in addition to the slaves, came freeborn intermediaries and interpreters. Much has to be guessed at, deduced, from the unstable terminology of race and ethnicity that characterized the island. Those who were, at the beginning of the century, labeled *affranchis*, later came to be called *noirs libres*. Someone of Malagasy origin referred to as a noir libre malgache would, according to Jumeer, be understood to be an affranchi, whereas a noir libre de Madagascar was one of free birth (1984, 24). These distinctions might not matter a great deal in everyday life, but on occasion they could be important. As we have seen, the scandal of the marriage of Reminiac centered not only on the fact that she was "black" to some degree, but that her lineage of freedom was not deep—her mother having been an affranchie. The fact that some of the colonies' free blacks were of mixed blood (referred to in Île de France frequently as mulattoes or mulâtres) only made things more difficult. My impression (and it can be only an impression) is that reference to "mixed blood" increased over the century, reflecting an increasing perception of its significance. The Revolution would enhance this trend. The whole question of legal and racial status, and the relationship between them, troubled the French colonial empire in the second half of the eighteenth century.[13] In 1766, for example, the king reminded priests in his colonies that children born of gens de couleur or of sang-melé should not be baptized as free persons unless they had proof of their mother's affranchissement.[14] To qualify as freeborn demanded proof that both one's parents were free—a degree of white blood did not confer this right. In addition, the existence of a community of nonwhites in France (including a high proportion of those from the Indian Ocean; see Boulle 1996) had led in 1777 to the promulgation of a new law that attempted to ban entrance to France of "Blacks, mulâtres and gens de couleur" (Boulle 1996, Peabody 1996).

In the documentation of the latter part of the century, free blacks on Île de France might be referred to in a number of different ways. The most common would be simply as noir libre, or négresse libre, though this might be followed by affranchi de . . . , and the name of the former master or mistress. Some individuals were designated créol (créole) libre, indicating that they had been born on the island or (toward the end of the century) indicating that they were not perceived as having any particular ethnicity. Significantly, in the case of free blacks of Indian origin (who, by the end of the century made up about 40 percent of this community; see Jumeer 1984, 105), some indication of their supposed ethnicity might be given. For example, "Marie Francoise bengalie libre," "Francois Lascard libre," "Catherine malabard libre" or "Bernard Topas libre." Some of these individuals would undoubtedly have been "creoles" but the (no doubt inconsistent) addition of an ethnic tag is significant. Among the slave population, as we have seen, such tags were applied to everyone, in the form of a "caste" designation—Malgache, Mozambique, Guinée, and occasionally more specific references to their origins were used. But once affranchised, individuals of African or Malagasy origin ceased to have any ethnicity attached to them—they became noirs or négresses libres, or, if of subsequent generations, créols libres. Very occasionally West African origin would be signaled, for example in a case in 1793 in which Martin Biram was referred to as "citoyen de couleur, originaire de Guinée, libre en vertu d'affranchissment."[15] With the Revolution came the terminology of *gens de couleur* replacing *noirs libres* and then, with the acquisition of civil rights, *citoyens libres*.

Visitors certainly made much of the ethnic distinctions within the community of noirs libres. Many of these descriptions (perhaps Jacques Milbert's in particular) seem designed to appeal to the reader's taste for the exotic, but they are significant nevertheless. Bernardin de St. Pierre described the community of "Malabards," residents of the Camp des Noirs in Port Louis, as a "mild and gentle people from Pondichéry" composed of servants and skilled workers who had been engaged to work on the island for a number of years. A 1791 map of Port Louis shows five apparently distinct residential areas for free people of color: Camp des Malabars et Lascars, Camp des Iolofs [Wolofs]; Camp des Malgaches, and Camp des Noirs Libres.[16] Though there is sufficient evidence of residential fluidity in Port Louis for us to doubt whether the populations of these districts were as distinct as they appeared on the map, nevertheless the very existence of these designations at this time indicates perceived, if not actual, differences within the free black community.

Distinctions of dress were noted by many visitors. So-called Malabar men are described as wearing turbans, long muslin gowns, and an assortment of jewelry, including earrings and bracelets. Milbert, characteristically, focused his description of the Malabar community on its women members (1812, 11:71–72), of which more later. He also described the existence of a "Camp des Malabards" outside the small town of Pamplemousses, to the north of Port Louis:

> I stopped for some time to consider these natives of the coast of India: their houses, which I entered, displayed not the slightest luxury, but neither did they present any aspect of poverty. All were kept very clean; the masters of the houses, their wives and their children were dressed in the superb white muslin of India, which would be envied by the most elegant of French women. The Malabar women, overloaded with rings, gold and silver bracelets, more rings on each toe, their heads embellished more by their beautiful black hair than by the gold

and jewels with which it is intertwined, have a noble bearing and features which, by the regularity, make them resemble Greek and Roman women. Their husbands largely exercise the professions of mason, carpenters and worker. (1:217)

Whatever their original ethnic and caste origins (which were undoubtedly mixed; see Jumeer 1984), the Malabar community clearly forged a separate identity within the free black population. Jumeer describes how, in the 1770s, assemblies of Malabars in the Camp des Malabards in Port Louis began to come to the attention of the police. The spontaneous development of a form of community justice (which included corporal punishment) within the camp gave rise to some dissension and eventually brought about the intervention of the authorities. Their response, however, was not to attempt to suppress this form of community rule but to better control it, through the creation in 1784 of the post of "Chef des Malabards" (Jumeer 1984, 251–254). In 1790, when a census of the free black population was conducted, the administration divided the community into two halves: Malabars and Lascars were to be enumerated separately from all the other noirs et négresses libres (314). Clearly not everyone felt comfortable about the degree of cultural and administrative independence accorded to free blacks of Indian origin. In 1793, for example, fifteen citizens petitioned the Assembly, demanding that Malabars should either abandon their ethnic costume or be treated as foreigners (d'Unienville 1982, 59). The Assembly refused to act on this, but the issue was raised again later in the year. By the turn of the century, Jumeer argues, a conflict was beginning to develop between the Malabar community and those gens de couleur who did not share their ethnicity, and whose cultural affinities were with the white population. In 1803 this group argued for the limitation of the powers of what had now become the "Chef des Malabards et des Lascars" (308).

The Lascar community was founded, as we have seen, by the first sailors imported onto the island in the 1730s, and it grew with the growth of the maritime economy between the 1760s and 1780s. Though by no means all Lascars were either free or Muslims, nevertheless, the Islamic faith to a large degree defined them and, according to Jumeer, imposed on them something of a clandestine existence. Lascars, according to Jumeer, would be among the first to take the opportunity of the new Revolutionary laws of civil status to register notarial acts. Jumeer has uncovered evidence for the existence of Lascar priests and argues that members of this community signed their names in the Urdu language (even when their origins were southern Indian).

There were other freeborn persons on the island who probably did not form an integral part of the free black community but would have had dealings with them. The most distinct as a group were the free Malagasies known as Marmites, intermediaries in the slave and other trades with Madagascar, and often employed as interpreters. Milbert described in detail their dress and hairstyles (1812, 11:165). Like the members of the Indian communities, these and other elite Malagasies brought with them cloth, jewelry, and other admired items of personal adornment that appear to have brought them to the attention of observers like Milbert. During the Revolution, anxieties surfaced over the relationships between Marmites and slaves of Malagasy origin and the question of allegiance. A watch was kept over them by the island's authorities, and they were required to wear their "native costume" in order to make them more easily recognizable (d'Unienville 1975, 66). While Malabars were regarded as suspect by some on account of their ethnic dress, Marmites caused anxiety if they abandoned it.

Though ethnic and religious distinctions clearly existed, and were important, within the free black community, there is also plenty of evidence that they were not hard and fast. Perhaps the very fact of fluidity and créolité caused some members of the Malabar and Lascar communities in particular to place additional emphasis on their distinct cultural identities. There may well have been a degree of deliberate endogamy practiced within these groups (indeed, that is the impression gained from a reading of the records of *notaires* in this period),[17] but this could never be complete, in part because of the imbalance of the sexes within the free black population (though we should note polygyny may well have existed and, as Richard Allen (2002b) notes, a significant number of free black households were matrifocal). Members of the free black community married among themselves and across "ethnic" lines, and these ethnic lines may have been additionally blurred by the fact that some of the offspring of free black women were identified as mulâtres. Being a mulatto or mulâtre did not necessarily mean that one would renounce the cultural and ethnic identity of one's mother—many Malabars were probably of mixed race—but there may have been some incentives to do so, or at least to mix that allegiance with one to the dominant "white" culture.

If gens de couleur were not a completely unified group, they did have one important feature in common: their stake in property ownership. Land grants made to gens de couleur began to increase in the 1770s, many to men who were noirs de détachement ("maroon hunters"). As Allen makes clear, the majority of these grants were small, and this was far from a wealthy community, but notarial acts demonstrate that these investments were highly significant, both economically and socially. By the end of the century the volume of private transactions involving gens de couleur had increased significantly, and it would appear that some members, at least, of this community were becoming more able to mobilize capital. If investment in housing, land, and household goods was significant, so too of course was slave ownership. In 1776 the 475 households of gens de couleurs owned a total of 623 slaves, though only seven of these households owned more than ten slaves (Allen 1999, 90–91). Femmes de couleur, who dominated the community numerically, depended more heavily on renting out their slaves in order to subsist. As Allen points out, in some cases slaves may well have been a very marginal resource for these households, and even a liability. The argument that the political conservatism of the island's gens de couleur can be explained by their investment in the system of slavery certainly has some merit, but it is not straightforward. Perhaps equally significant to the politics of the period was the economic marginality of the majority of this population (Allen 2002b). Though there were certainly some wealthy members of the free black population, by and large they do not appear to have posed much of an economic threat to the colony's whites. This, and their internal ethnic divisions, may have distinguished them from their Antillean counterparts.

The extension of the rights of citizenship to the gens de couleur would eventually be granted by the National Assembly in Paris in May 1791, an occasion at which the Île de France deputy, Pierre Anthoine Monneron, delivered a passionate speech in their favor. Monneron, a member of the island's most successful merchant family (Butel 1996), a family whose fortunes rested firmly in their participation in the slave trade, was a man of the world. The gens de couleur of Île de France, he argued, had shown admirable restraint but could not be expected to wait forever. Why, he demanded to know, did a free France hold out against according them rights, when the English, the Spanish, and the Portuguese had done so? Indeed, he went on (to a reported mixture of applause and murmurs), in

1775 a mulâtre had been a mayor in Senegal when it was ruled by the English, and in Portuguese colonies white and black priests and municipal officers worked side by side. He ended, however, with a threat: "In effect," he said, "it is easy to envisage a time when the gens de couleur will be numerous enough to say to the Europeans: 'Go back to your country if you persist in contesting our rights of man: you are visitors on our soil. . . . while we multiply in this climate following the commandments of the creator, in a climate that providence has created for us, and with such a progression as necessarily leads you to be dependent on us; if you want to uphold a privilege which contrasts with the most sound rules of morality and eternal justice' " (d'Unienville 1975, 158).

This was, in many ways, an extraordinary statement from the representative of Île de France, for in it Monneron appeared to argue that the gens de couleur were, in a sense, the "natives" of the island, and with certain moral rights attached to that status. Monneron's comments need to be understood not only in terms of Revolutionary politics, but also against the background of the real increase in numbers and political consciousness of the island's small population of gens de couleur. Lurking in the background, of course, was the much larger and (for the colonists) literally terrifying question of the abolition of slavery. Île de France might appear liberal on the question of the rights of gens de couleur but would hold out famously against the liberation of slaves. Perhaps, as North-Coombes has argued (2000), the elite's liberal attitude to gens de couleur was part of a conscious strategy to "keep them on board" on the question of abolition.

Attitudes toward free blacks or gens de couleur on Île de France were not consistently liberal on Île de France and were never without contradictions, but it is noticeable that most of the evidence for anxiety about this community comes from the reports of visitors, rather than from residents. Some thirty years earlier a visitor to the island, M. Courcy, in a mémoire to the Ministère de la Marine, argued that there were "prodigious" numbers of them (in fact they were a small community) and, mirroring Monneron's later argument, that they should be "sent home" (Courcy seemed to believe that "home" was Madagascar). Though M. Courcy worried that free blacks would soon outnumber whites, he did acknowledge that they could be usefully employed in the chasse des marons.[18] In fact, some free blacks owed their freedom to the performance of this service, and their use as soldiers, particularly in the guerre intestine against maroons, remained important. In 1785 there were four companies of noirs libres employed and paid for the capture of maroons. Some commentators felt that greater use could be made of this group, implying that their loyalty was not in question. One M. Houbert, for example, argued that they should be formed into a proper "troupe de couleur," since many of them were excellent soldiers. "They are all," he wrote, "animated by the patriotic zeal which is natural in the creole."[19]

There is little doubt that the events of the Revolution enhanced the status of free blacks or gens de couleur on the island and contributed to their political consciousness as a group. The Revolutionary years see gens de couleur exercising their new civil rights and standing up for these rights, but this was not an uncomplicated consciousness, as is demonstrated by the following small incident.

In March 1792 a free black woman came to lodge a complaint with the mayor and municipal authorities of Port Louis.[20] She gave her name as Toinette Gabriel Marie Marguerite but was also known as Marguerite Marier. She was described as a créole libre. She said that two days previously she had been involved in a court case with a Sr. Brizard, which she had lost. She was in the environs of the court when Sr. Brizard had come out very happy with the judgment, which had gone in his favor and against her. He had then, she said, addressed her saying: "B . . . g . . . sse[21] you have been caught out, you thought you would get to punish Perrine [the négresse whom he was protecting] and it is you now who will get it, because I am going to put you in chains at my house and burn you slowly to death."

Marguerite told the officers that "upset at losing her case, and offended by these comments, she had allowed herself to respond, at which he had beaten her with his cane, knocked her down and kicked her." At this treatment she had said to him "there is justice for whites as well as for blacks, and I will demand it." He had replied that "she was lucky that he did not have his sword on him, or he would have passed it through her body." Then, she said, a M. Brunel, officer in the merchant marine, who was with Brizard, had said to him "are you going to allow this négresse to talk to you like this?" and then he had set about threatening her. She had said to Brunel that if it were daytime he would not be doing this because "I am a négresse and incapable of vengeance." He had then kicked her and punched her and finally called the guard, who had taken her to prison, where she was forced to spend the night.

Brizard meanwhile had made his own complaint to the police on the morning after the event. He said that the previous evening he had been leaving the court where he had been pleading in the case regarding the freedom of an affranchie of Sr. Marier, and was accompanied by his lawyer and three other men, when he was surprised to see Marguerite Marier among the crowd. She had descended rapidly toward his house, shouting that she would get her vengeance. At this his companions had quickly run to his house to prevent him from being exposed to such a disagreeable scene, but this had not stopped the négresse from making efforts to get into his house, and indeed she would have succeeded had his companions, seeing him in danger of being insulted in his own house, not succeeded in stopping her. The said négresse had than "vomited" a thousand insults at him, even going as far as to *tutoyer* him.[22] Brizard demanded that action be taken against this woman to prevent him being insulted by this négresse and her "adherents."

Marguerite, when told of Brizard's account of events, was outraged. It was not true, she said, that she had threatened vengeance, neither had she been near Brizard's house, but was at the gate of the court with her granddaughter when she had been insulted by him. She was, she told the officers of the municipality, "a poor unfortunate whom he had wanted to burn to death."

Marguerite had displayed a mixture of defiance and deference. She was a free woman, a créole libre who was apparently disputing the affranchissement of her former slave Perrine. Perrine was being supported and protected by a white man. Marguerite was bitter that she had lost her case, but more angered still when her adversary, in public and amid a phalanx of other white men, had insulted and mistreated her. Justice, she asserted, was for both blacks and whites, and she would seek it. Brizard for his part felt insulted by Marguerite, whom, though he knew her to be free and a slave owner, he referred to as if she were a slave herself, calling her a négresse. His friends may have encouraged him in thinking that to be insulted publicly by a black woman (of whatever legal status) was an outrage. The free black woman and the white man for a moment stood face to face in confrontation over the question of a slave, both appealing to their senses of honor. At one point, however, Marguerite refers to herself as a négresse, incapable of vengeance and, she implies, worthy of protection. In the end the white men win and she is carted off to prison for the night to prevent any further offense to Brizard's honor. This did not prevent her, however, from lodging a complaint with the authorities the following morning.

The island's gens de couleur had acquired rights, but these were rights which necessarily rested on, and perhaps enhanced, the distinction between slave and free. We do not know the details of Marguerite's case with Sr. Brizard, but it is clear that the dispute over her former slave allowed him to take a high moral position. At the same time, however, there is little doubt that Brizard and his friends found Marguerite's assertiveness offensive—she might be a free person with rights, but she was also a woman and a "black." Ultimately, when tempers became frayed, she was nothing more than a négresse.

"Free blacks" would always be just that—technically free, but inescapably black—and might (it was thought) at any moment make common cause with mutinous slaves. News of events on St. Domingue would appear to bear this theory out. These fears did not go away, despite conspicuous displays of loyalty and patience on the part of the gens de couleur of Île de France, who, it was said, offered during this period to go on the offensive against maroon slaves without reward. In An 4, for example, in the wake of both events in St. Domingue and the Convention's surprise announcement of the abolition of slavery, General Magallon, who would later become governor of the island, wrote that though the gens de couleur of Île de France were for the most part "content with their sort and had no pronounced passion other than that for women," nevertheless it was "only too proven that he [the free black] might lose himself in the responsibilities of the citizen, take liberty to mean license . . . and end by plunging the sword into the breasts of the very nation which had adopted him and which only wanted to secure his happiness."[23] The image was one of parricide, powerful in a Revolution marked by the execution of the king, but there was a day-to-day reality to this fear of the "ungrateful" and ultimately murderous free black, because no discussion of this group could be completely divorced from the issue of métissage.

Métissage and the Confusion of the Colonial Family

In her study of neighboring La Réunion (formerly Île Bourbon), Françoise Vergès argued that métissage was, in the European imaginary, a site of both fascination and repulsion: "Thinking métissage requires accepting a genealogy . . . a past of rape, violence and complicity" (1999, 11). This was part of the history of slavery which the dominant discourses on sexuality, romantic love, and maternity (which I have described in earlier chapters) attempted to pass over quickly. There is relatively little mention of métissage in the pre-Revolutionary documentation for Île de France, and none of the obsessive characterization and categorization of this group that went on in the French Antilles. Mention might be made of the "mixed blood" of an individual (by which was always meant a proportion of white blood), but this was far from consistent. Benoit Giraud was a mulâtre, but he came from the Antilles and insisted on this particular status. We can have no idea what proportion of the island's free blacks, or indeed its slaves, were "mulâtres" in the eighteenth century, and perhaps this is because it was not viewed as significant. Yet by the last quarter of the century there is some indication of a creeping anxiety. Île de France was not cut off from the rest of the colonial world—many of its colonists and administrators had close family and institutional links to other regions, and this was an age that valued highly the intellectual work of comparison. Around 1780, for example, the famous colonial jurist and commentator from St. Domingue Moreau de St. Méry reflected on the situation on Île de France and Île Bourbon. Though his "Reflections" do not necessarily reflect local opinion, they do represent currents of thought to which inhabitants of Île de France were exposed. Moreau de St. Méry, famous for his elaborate classification of degrees of race mixture, argued that the dangerous *mélange de couleur* was not so advanced on Île de France as to be irreparable:

> It is generally recognized that mulâtres born either free or of slave [mothers] have bad inclinations and unite the vices of both whites and blacks; further, there is in the soul of every white a contempt for all mixed blood, of whatever degree. It is therefore important that the Government always acknowledge a distinction between the two colors, and even their nuances, and it would be better still to make a total separation between them. Île de France for a long time preserved its purity and was without mélange, and the little mixed blood which has slipped in there is not numerous and without any [inconvenience?] could, I believe, be sent back to Île Bourbon, from which the majority have come, and where circumstances forced a blind eye to mixed alliances.

Moreau de St. Méry was wrong about the origins of the island's mulâtre population, but his theory provided him with an apparently simple solution to the problem their existence posed. He reserved his most florid language for the free black woman, whom he saw as responsible for the creation of this unnerving and dangerous mixture of blood. She had, according to him, earned her freedom through licentiousness and continued in this "disorder" after manumission. She could be seen on the island accompanied by her children, whom he described as the "vile productions of her crime" and as "equivocal beings, as much in their state as in their color" who, though they "might now arouse compassion from the Government" would, before long, "excite other sentiments."[24]

Familial language was central to the political discourse of the French Revolution (Hunt 1992) and, as Vergès (1999) has shown, took on new meanings in the context of a slave society. Most colonists of Île de France could identify the patriarchal order of the ancien régime as oppressive—this had been a powerful theme throughout the eighteenth century. Personified in the masculine, bewigged figures of ruthless governors such as Dumas, its systems of justice were viewed as arbitrary. Venality and greed characterized the colonial system as a whole, as well as its individual representatives; trade never really was "free," despite some gestures in that direction, and royal officials were seen to grow fat on their privileged access to it. In particular the distribution of slaves remained a constant source of friction, and even Pierre Poivre, a man with distinct antislavery sentiments, could be accused of keeping the "best" slaves to himself. But though most colonists might relish the symbolic if not the real execution of the oppressive and distant patriarch, the substitution of this order with one of "fraternity" was hardly straightforward, for it was not easy to apply this concept to the fundamental social and economic institution of society—slavery. No wonder then that the familial metaphors of Île de France Revolutionary years were distinctly mixed ones. In 1792, for example, the island's deputies to the National Assembly were instructed to express to the president the islanders' "extreme emotion" and gratitude for the "paternal letter" he had addressed to them. In addition, they were to tell France that "the immense distance that separated them only added to the brilliant affection which we have for her . . . That we have never, and will never have any other interests than those which tie us to the tender Mother."[25] Though the central appeal was now for loyalty toward this "Mother," from time to time it seemed that a firm paternal hand was still required: "I believe," wrote Magallon, in An 4, "that the moment has come when the Government, through certain paternal measures . . . can inspire great sentiments in these men."[26]

Beneath and in the interstices of this rhetoric were the real colonial relationships of kin and family and slavery. The Mère Patrie, as Vergès has argued, was a fictional, imaginary parent, a distant mother both protective and castrating (1999, 3–4). The real families and the real parents of Île de France were more complex, a heterogeneous mixture of family forms and absences, as we have seen. There was the often incomplete white family, the usually unachieved slave family, the improvised family of foster parents and neighbors, and the female-dominated family of the gens de couleur. In addition there were the pre-Revolutionary brotherhoods of the business partnerships and the institutionalized brotherhoods of ship life and warfare. Unspoken and underlying the increasingly evident fact of métissage was the reality of violence and rape. Loss and disavowal were integral parts of this family system: the white father, in theory at least, would disavow his son or daughter, whose consequent sense of resentment and wish for revenge were viewed as "natural." In the colonial version of the "family romance," it was the ungrateful mulâtre who murdered his father, while his sister, the mulâtresse, contented herself with the seduction of the next generation of white men. Both, if not out for revenge, were out for an inheritance, and fears of this operated in the day-to-day lives of colonists. Sometimes, as we have seen, the claim took the form of a screaming baby left abandoned on the doorstep. Or the claim might come later. In 1793, for example, a butcher named Pierre Godin died.[27] He had been in a long-standing business partnership with another man, Noël Froment. Neither man could write or do accounts, and at Godin's death it was suspected that his natural children (referred to as une fille naturelle and a noir libre), apparently more literate and numerate than their father and his friend, had made off with much of the inheritance. Froment meanwhile appealed to another familial concept— that of fraternity. He and Godin, he argued, had enjoyed an association of "perfect fraternity, founded on confidence and reciprocal friendship, the most solid bases of all society": more reliable, he implied, than the vagaries of "blood."

Godin's children had the status of free persons, but this was not true of all mulâtres and mulâtresses. The currents of the Revolution appear to have enhanced disquiet at the existence of slaves of "mixed blood," for the

FIGURE 4. The church of Pamplemousses. From *Voyage pittoresque a l'Île de France*, by Jacques G. Milbert, 1812. Bodleian Library, University of Oxford, N 2.16. Art Seld. Plt. 26

combination of unfree status with a proportion of "white" blood had always been regarded as somewhat contradictory, even to those who believed wholeheartedly in the ideology of slavery. Containing these contradictions became increasingly difficult, particularly given the social proximity of many slaves with freeborn persons.

In 1792, in the small town of Pamplemousses, a habitant, M. Rigal, told the municipal authorities that he had gone into a small bar run by a slave woman to drink with a fellow citizen, M. Renard. Also in the bar was Charlot, whom he described as a mulâtre esclave (in other words, a slave, but recognized as having some white blood). According to Rigal, Charlot had said to him that he "wanted to drink with the whites," to which Rigal had replied that he must know that "his condition as a slave made this impossible." Rigal, intending to leave, had then made to pay for his drink when, with no warning, he was hit between the eyes by Charlot. He had been knocked out for a while, he said, and had been bleeding too much to make an arrest of the slave, who had immediately fled. He asked for Charlot to be punished according to the full force of the law and with no concessions (*adoucissements*). He also demanded that the slave woman, who was infringing the law by running a bar in a district other than that of her master, be punished.

This woman was Rosette, around forty years old and described as a Bengalie slave belonging to a M. Roblet who lived in Port Louis. She ran the bar for him in Pamplemousses, where she lived with Charlot. Her version of events was slightly different. She said that M. Rigal and M. Renard had come to drink eau-de-vie in her bar and, finding Charlot also there, Rigal had said to him, "You are drinking alone," to which Charlot had said that "this was just as well because they would not want to drink with him," at which more words were exchanged and Charlot, who was drunk, had hit Rigal and made his nose bleed. After hearing the evidence, the procureur of the commune (Magon) concluded that it was clear that the mulâtre named Charlot had committed a battery (*voie de fait*), which would be grave in any circumstances but when committed by a slave against a white "becomes a terrible attack, the punishment of which knows virtually no limits under the law." He went on, however, to voice some other considerations:

> The justice due to this citizen, the reparation which he claims, are joined to the interests of society which demands that such disorders be severely punished. However . . . it is in the spirit of the magistracy that he should examine any circumstances and considerations that might be attenuating, and certainly he should not fail to examine them when it appears from the testimony of the bar-keeper that the mulâtre was drunk . . . and it might be reasonable to believe that a slave who commits such an act was perhaps not in a tranquil or cold-blooded state, rather that he was moved by some cause, some strange force. On the other hand, I cannot help but have a thought, only a supplementary one certainly, but one which I feel must have a place here, despite the fact that it is perhaps not of a nature to influence my judgment. I ask myself whether there might exist, among certain whites, a kindness, an ease of character which might in certain circumstances lead them to forget something of the distance which separates them from the other color (*la couleur opposée*), a momentary and accidental complacency, which does not constitute any excuse for the guilty, but in which it is not impossible that a black might mistakenly perceive either an encouragement or a pretext.

Though Magon claimed that these considerations would not affect his judgment at all, the sentence he handed down (which consisted of a public beating, three Sundays in a row, outside the door of the church) was seen by the commune's citizens as offensively lenient, and they appealed to a higher authority. Magon's argument concerned the obligation on the white man to maintain a social distance from the "other color," lest the "other color" mistakenly conclude that intimacy were possible. The argument was a familiar one, as was the slippage in argument between reference to slave status and reference to "color." While Rigal reported himself as having referred to Charlot's slave status as the factor that made drinking with him impossible (though we also know that black and white, slave and free drank together all the time in the bars of Île de France), Magon referred not to legal status but to the two "opposing colors." But Charlot is also referred to throughout this case not simply as a slave, and not simply as black, but specifically as a mulâtre. Perhaps, it is implied, this particular condition made it all the more important that he should not have been encouraged to fraternize, perhaps it accounted for what Perrine reported to be his resentful words, perhaps it accounted for what Magon described as a "strange force" that moved him to punch Rigal on the nose.

The free black Marguerite and the mulâtre esclave Charlot had both publicly vented an anger that, in the context of the Revolution, was perhaps less easy to dismiss than before. They were punished, but their very existence remained disturbing. Meanwhile, less loudly, in lawyers' offices in Port Louis, some of the most poignant moments of the "family romance" of slavery were being recorded.

Manumission documents are largely formulaic, and in the Revolutionary period the formula shifted. Most notably, a number of gens de couleur (mostly women) presented themselves to lawyers wishing to manumit slaves who were also their family members, often their own children. When a slave was manumitted, their master or mistress was obliged to demonstrate that he or she would not, as a free person, be a burden on the authorities. In order to do this, they would donate an amount of money, a small piece of property, and more often than not, human property, to the former slave. Ownership of a slave was a mark of one's freedom and, ironically, of one's "self-sufficiency." Within an instant the slave became a slave owner. But sometimes the slave so donated would in fact be the child or the sister or brother of the slave being manumitted. Children became the slaves of their mothers. Though it is hard to know how much Revolutionary rhetoric filtered down to slaves, and in what form, manumission records of this period certainly contain new words expressing what were perhaps not new sentiments, but at least sentiments previously without legal expression. Rosette, in 1793, freeing

Victoire, declared (through a lawyer of course) that she considered that "maternal attachment cannot endure slavery";[28] Jeanneton also freed her son, Jean Pierre, "in consideration of her maternal attachment";[29] Margueritte freed eight-year-old Melanie, who, she said, was "her daughter and nevertheless her slave";[30] and Marie Rose declared that Zaire, though her slave, was really her daughter, something "she had never declared to anyone before."[31] To many of these newly freed children were given, of course, slaves—Marie Rose, for example, gave Zaire a fifteen-year-old Mozambique boy. Meanwhile Bail, a Lascar diver, in 1792 freed his wife with the following words:

> He said that during the thirty-seven years that he had been in this colony he had always worked with a great deal of effort and difficulty, and today, if he possessed anything, he owed it to the work, activity and great economy of Marie Louise, his Bengalie slave, with whom he had lived since he first arrived on the island and whom, after the laws of his own country, he had always regarded as his wife, despite the fact that he had bought her . . . he would have allowed her to stay in the state of slavery, but helped by the counsel of wise people he had come to recognize that it was necessary to assure her of tranquility by procuring her freedom.[32]

Wife and slave, daughter and slave are now words placed in opposition to one another, like freedom and slavery. Whether or not Bail had actually "bought" his wife in India, the new languages of freedom circulating during the Revolutionary years appear to have made him feel that his contract with her detracted from the affection and gratitude he felt toward her. With the Revolution some contradictions had emerged from the shadows and stared everyone in the face: femmes de couleur found their children (some of whom would have been mulâtres) to be their slaves and freed them, giving them, in turn, their own slaves.

Meanwhile enthusiastic promoters of the Revolutionary fraternal order desperately tried to draw a fast line around the band of brothers, a line that would definitively exclude slaves but would have to include those who, by some good fortune, had found themselves freed. In one of their appeals against the abolition of slavery, the slave owners of Île de France appeared to imply that slaves were not worthy of the state of freedom since they came from Africa, the site of the most primitive forms of patriarchal servitude, where only the women hoed the land, while the men hunted animals and "sometimes other men, either to satisfy their hunger or to satisfy the caprice of some chief whose fortune rests on nothing other than the trade in captives."[33]

Once again the figure of the hypermasculine maroon reared its head, all the more potent now amid fears of a bloodbath. The maroons were real—two large bands under "Alexandre" and "Jean-Louis" were captured. The colonists reminded Paris that these men were ruthless in their intentions, as much toward those of their own color as toward whites. There was no need, they wrote, for the colonists of Île de France to look to America for examples of monstrosity, since Alexandre and Jean-Louis had provided them on their doorstep: "When these monsters, torch in hand, spread through the countryside, is the cottage of the black man, of their comrade, any more respected than the house of the white? Are they not equally prey to the arsonist? Is it not through the rape of the femme de couleur and over the body of the child, its throat slit, that they embolden themselves for even headier pleasures?"[34]

Maroons were men without familial sentiment: they were, in fact, a nightmare version of the Revolutionary band of brothers outside patriarchal control. Having done away with the father, the slave master, they would rape and pillage and destroy even their own. Appeals to the tender metropolitan mother would have no effect on such men. Slavery, it was concluded, was the only possible family form for a colony.

Chapter Ten

*I*n 1826 a census of slaves was carried out on what was now the British colony of Mauritius. This was not a mere counting of heads: slave owners were instructed to supply both the first name by which a slave was "habitually known" and a second name, if they had one. The Order-in-Council for the registration of slaves explicitly acknowledged that some slaves' family names would be unknown to their masters. Under such circumstances "a name such as the proprietor, or person making out the census list, shall deem proper to place there to serve for a surname, which surname the said slave and his descendants, whether legitimate or natural, shall bear in the future."[1]

The invention of surnames was not the only naming practice revealed by the 1826 census. One owner recorded the names of his entire workforce as follows: "Le Bon, La Sourde, Imbécile, Vache, Capricieuse, Lundi, Mardi, Mercredi, Jeudi, Vendredi, Samedi, Dimanche, Janvier, Février, Mars, Avril, Mai, and Juin." Another submitted the names of his kitchen slaves as "Salade, Asperge, Carote, Navet, Choux, Oignon and Rave" (Barker 1996, 57). These patterns were repeated over and over again. Some slave owners, it would appear, had no knowledge of the names by which their slaves lived. But registration demanded names, and so they "named" them. One proprietor in Rivière Rempart supplied the following: "Al, Bal, Cal, Dal, Fal, Gal, Hal, Tal, Mal, Nal and Pal."

If names mean anything at all, then the results of this survey are telling. As Anthony Barker has noted, it is highly unlikely that many of

FIGURE 5. A "romantic landscape." From *Voyage pittoresque a l'Île de France*, by Jacques G. Milbert, 1812. Bodleian Library, University of Oxford, N 2.16. Art Seld. Plt. 20

these names (either the demeaning "Imbécile" or the anonymous "Al") would have been adopted and used by slaves themselves. They may be significant nevertheless. A high proportion of the slave "names" of 1826 are demeaning, denigrating, or crudely objectifying and dehumanizing: they carry all those qualities we habitually associate with the state of slavery at its worst. If slaves were unlikely to have known themselves by such names, these names do appear to say something about the psychology of slave owners.

Slave owners in eighteenth-century Île de France, as we have seen, were often brutal and violent toward their slaves, but they could not erase them from their consciousness. The "psychic life of power," to use Judith Butler's phrase (1997) could not be ignored. In previous chapters I have attempted to convey some sense of the complex, conflictual engagement between self and other at the heart of the master-slave relationship in this particular slave-owning society. The community of slave owners on the island was far from being a "natural" one. It was a community deeply divided by status, class, and, with the slow emergence of a free black population, by race. Slaves were not necessarily protected by the struggles over status and reputation that dominated the social existence of slave owners, but they were highly relevant to them. In most of the cases I have examined (and one must acknowledge again that court cases are not representative of anything but themselves) slaves were important not only as objects of such struggles, but also as their subjects. This is not surprising. Small-scale slave ownership sometimes necessitated a degree of identification, even intimacy, between master and slave. This is not to imply that such relationships were cozy or benign, for closeness could itself breed violence, and, as many writers on slavery have pointed out, it also mitigated against the creation of any kind of autonomous slave culture. But these were, nevertheless, relationships that rested on a degree of mutual knowledge. It would be very unlikely that an owner of four or five slaves would name them after the letters of the alphabet or the days of the week, in part because this would simply not be functional. In order to make optimal use of his or her slaves, such an owner would need both to foster individual aptitudes and qualities, and also to encourage flexibility in labor roles. Knowing your slaves was important, and when you knew your slaves you were involved in some kind of engagement with them.

The simplest explanation for the changes that had occasioned the alphabetization of slave identities by 1826 can be summed up in one word: sugar. In the early nineteenth century the island underwent a remarkable transformation into a sugar colony, and many of the features of sugar slavery found elsewhere in the world were reproduced here as the fields of cane came to dominate the romantic landscape of *Paul et Virginie*. By the time of emancipation in 1835, Mauritius was one of the largest slave colonies in the British Empire and had achieved a certain notoriety for the cruelty of its slave regime (Barker 1996, 1). But there were political factors at work too, many of them related to the legacy of the Revolutionary years and the peculiar nature of the British colonial regime on Mauritius. Let us backtrack, then, to the crucial decades of the 1790s and 1800s.

Île de France, as we have seen, passed most of the Revolutionary years in splendid isolation from the metropole. Its critical strategic position meant that the authorities in France were forced to tolerate the colonists' intransigence on matters such as the abolition of slavery, and in any case the state of war rendered the exercise of external authority difficult, if not impossible. The Revolutionary politics of the island were complex, however, and full of intrigue, reflecting the deep divisions within Île de France colonial society and the island's ambivalent relationship with France. As we have seen, Île de France deputies to the National Assembly supported the campaign for the rights of gens de couleur, and though the news of the St. Domingue revolution did induce considerable anxiety among some of the island's colonists, the general tone of the reaction was along the lines of "It cannot happen here." Years later, however, members of the same colonial families would cite St. Domingue unceasingly in their stand against the second abolition of slavery. It was on the question of abolition that Île de France colonists were most clearly united. They opposed it in 1794; they would oppose it again in the lead-up to 1835.

After they had succeeded in expelling the agents of the Directoire (in 1796), and with news of Jacobin control of the Convention, the island's politics took a somewhat more radical turn, leading some families to flee into exile.[2] The main sources of opposition to the island's colonial elite came from the *petits blancs* of Port Louis, now allied with sailors from France. In 1798 soldiers of the 107th and 108th Regiments were accused of fomenting revolt among the slave population. The revolt failed to materialize and the Colonial Assembly stood its ground, backed up by a locally recruited national guard. Despite their exercise of de facto political autonomy, members of the Colonial Assembly continued to profess deep attachment to France and always attempted to justify their actions in the eyes of the metropolitan government. Colonial radicalism was tempered, we must assume, by fear of retribution and by the close bonds of family and business that continued to tie so many individuals to the metropole. In any case, the powers in France had not given up on the idea of reasserting their authority over the Indian Ocean islands. As late as 1799 they were considering this, but financial constraints and the burdens of war (including, from 1798, the Egyptian campaign) made this impracticable. Furthermore, the fact that Île de France colonists were so busy arming privateers against English ships meant that, unruly as they were, they remained more of an asset than a liability to the French.

War might have contributed to the relative isolation of the colony from metropolitan control in this period, but this does not imply other kinds of isolation. War certainly disrupted the growing slave trade with the East African coast, and Indian Ocean commerce more generally, but it did not bring it to a halt. This was, in Vijaya Teelock's words, a "free-for-all" period, with French, Portuguese, Brazilians, and Americans competing for slaves, some of which were destined for Île de France, others for Brazil. Continuing the role it had acquired from the 1780s, Revolutionary Île de France was the hub for a great deal of intercontinental commerce. In 1796, for example, the American ships *Active* and *Deque* arrived in Île de France hoping to buy slaves in return for Spanish currency, as did a Spanish ship from Buenos Aires (Teelock 1999a, 7). Paul Butel's recent work provides more evidence for this thriving commerce, much of it conducted on behalf of Bordelais merchants by neutral, especially American, intermediaries. Analyzing the correspondence of Louis Monneron and of the Couve de Murville family (both prominent Île de France merchants), he demonstrates that Indian Ocean commerce (with Île de France at its center) grew in the Revolutionary period and continued growing after 1802.[3] Privateering was another profitable activity of the Revolutionary years in which many Île de France colonists invested heavily. All in all, this period saw an extension of developments that had begun in the 1780s—Île de France and its colonists were now more heavily involved than ever in both Indian Ocean commerce and intercontinental commerce, including, crucially, that in slaves. Furthermore, increased French commercial interest in Île de France, combined with the profits of privateering, was helping to finance the island's nascent sugar industry. The collapse of sugar production in St. Domingue had also helped. Land under sugar on Île de France expanded from 400 hectares in 1789 to a peak of 6,000 hectares in 1803 and, according to North-Coombes, much of this expansion was capitalized by the privateering cruises that set off from Port Louis in this period. In the process, Île de France planters were becoming increasingly indebted to merchant creditors, but inflation (caused by the periodic injections of booty and the overissue of paper money by the Colonial Assembly) made repayments more feasible (North-Coombes 2000, 11). Finally the island seemed to have arrived at a situation in which commerce (and the by-products of war) was financing agricultural production.

In the next decade, under the Napoleonic regime (1802–1810), the island's elite, aided by administrators from France, elaborated a self-serving, explicitly racist ideology, turned back the clock on a number of social issues, and institutionalized a harsher slave regime. The labor demands of sugar are part of the explanation here, but we can trace some of these attitudes back to the Revolutionary years, when the Île de France colonists had been forced to articulate their opposition to the 1794 decree abolishing slavery. Though the manumission rate increased during the

Revolution, and though gens de couleurs had won some significant concessions, this did not prevent members of the Colonial Assembly from expressing, more clearly than ever, the view that slavery was completely indispensable to the colonial economy, that blacks alone were suited to perform manual labor in the tropics, and that coercion was essential to keep them at work given their innate taste for idleness. While some elements of this argument had been circulating since the very beginnings of the colony's existence, from the 1790s onward they began to cohere in response to the threat of abolition.[4]

What followed in the first two decades of the nineteenth century was nevertheless extraordinary. Though, as I have argued in earlier chapters, it would be a mistake to portray eighteenth-century Île de France slavery as a benign regime, slaves who had the misfortune to arrive on the island as it was expanding its sugar industry would experience something more akin to chattel slavery than anything that had come before, and this was backed up by legal, institutional, and ideological changes. The reaffirmation of slavery began under Decaen's governorship in 1802, which in turn reflected Napoleon's own views on slavery and those of Forfait, minister of marine and colonies from 1799. Decaen was instructed not only to uphold slavery, but also to "maintain with care the distance between the colors on which the colonial regime rests" (North-Coombes 1978, 139). He was aided in this task by a reactionary commisary of justice, Pierre Crespin, who had lived on the island since 1790. Among other retrograde policies that emphasized the position of slaves as chattels, Crespin reduced their legal protection.

Under ancien régime criminal law, as we have seen, slaves suspected of crimes were prosecuted under exactly the same procedures as applied to the freeborn or manumitted. Much of my reconstruction of the social world of slavery has relied on the records produced by these procedures. Arguing that public debate of slave misdeeds was as much a threat to the social order as the crimes themselves, Crespin put an end to this system. Under a law of 3 December 1803, slaves were tried in "abbreviated" fashion before special tribunals meeting behind closed doors, and consisting of nine members, three of whom were "proprietor-colonists" (North-Coombes 1978, 140). It is clear that this move did not go ahead without criticism and opposition. North-Coombes cites those of subprefect Marchant of neighboring Île Bourbon: "One would be mistaken to think that the investigation of the misdeeds of slaves requires less research, less expertise than misdeeds arising from other causes; it matters to society that slaves should not feel that they can obtain impunity as a result of the weakness of a tribunal, and also that they should not doubt the safety of a verdict finding them innocent" (North-Coombes 1978, 140; my translation).

Other reactionary reforms followed. Manumission rates dropped in part as a result of a law of 1804 that made the procedure costly and bureaucratic and conditional on a long period of service. Crespin did not believe that manumitted slaves could ever be fully assimilated into free society and placed further legal disabilities in the way of such a possibility. If the acquisition of freedom meant less than it had before, the corollary to this was an increase in explicitly racial discourse and discrimination. Many of the legal and constitutional gains made by the island's gens de couleur were reversed and would remain this way well into the period of British rule. In 1805, for example, the civil code was redivided to provide separate legal systems for slaves, gens de couleur, and whites and legal obstacles were placed in the way of the disposal of property between these groups (Carter 1998a, 15). Yet, as Richard Allen has shown, the gens de couleur were by the end of the first decade of the nineteenth century "an integral part of the island's economic landscape," owning more than 7 percent of all inventoried land and nearly 15 percent of the colony's slaves (1999, 96). By 1825 they were even more entrenched, owning more slaves than ever and capitalizing on the development of the sugar industry by moving into agricultural production and meeting the increased demand for foodstuffs.

The early nineteenth century is one of the better studied periods of Mauritian history, benefiting from important work by Anthony Barker (1996), Richard Allen (1999), Vijaya Teelock (1998; 1999b), Marina Carter (1993, 1998a), and emerging new work on apprenticeship by Satyendra Peerthum.[5] Some significant questions remain, but collectively these works point to the interaction of economic and political factors that combined to transform Mauritian society, even before the radical changes attendant on abolition and the importation of hundreds of thousands of Indian indentured laborers.

In 1810 the British captured Île Bourbon,[6] and from there Île de France. This was not without a struggle, however—the French forces had rebuffed an earlier attempt at invasion at the Battle of Grand Port. British interests at this point were largely strategic, since the famous *guerre de course* (privateering) operating out of Île de France was proving enormously expensive to them. The French on the island may have felt humiliated at their reduction from colonial rulers to colonial subjects, but the terms under which the British "annexed" Île de France were hardly oppressive to them. The British instituted a kind of indirect rule that formally recognized French law and custom and informally devolved power into the hands of the French elite. As Barker has put it, once this recognition had been granted, "the choices facing a British governor and his handful of assistants were comfortable acquiescence in inefficient oligarchical rule or constant conflict in pursuit of reform" (Barker 1996, 3–4). Robert Farquhar, governor almost continually from 1810 to 1822, chose the former strategy, but conflict with the French would come, and once again it was over the issue of slavery.

Though the British had abolished the slave trade in 1807, policing this ban in the western Indian Ocean proved difficult. Now, with their policy of expedient coexistence with the French planters and merchants on Mauritius, British policy toward the slave trade displayed more ambivalence than ever. Farquhar attempted unsuccessfully to persuade London to grant the Mauritians an exemption from the 1807 law prohibiting British subjects from engaging in the trade. There is little doubt, though, that he and his colleagues were aware that the abolition of the slave trade would lead eventually to the abolition of slavery, and he began exploring the uses of technically nonslave labor. This included convicts transported from India (Anderson 2000, Carter and Gerbeau 1989, Barker 1996) and a particularly tragic group of enslaved Africans who had been "rescued" by Royal Navy patrols in the Indian Ocean, only to be sentenced to a period of "apprenticeship" (for which read servitude) on Mauritius.[7] But despite this search for alternative sources of labor, recent scholarship points decisively to a large illegal slave trade thriving during Farquhar's governorship (Allen 2001, Barker 1996).

In economic terms the first decade or so of British rule was not an easy one for the French on the island, despite the concessions they had obtained from their colonial overlords. Allen (2001) argues that there was a significant flight of capital after the British takeover, and this, combined with the application of the Navigation Acts in 1815, undercut the commercial activity which, as we have seen, had become so central to the island's economy since the 1780s. British investment at this point was minimal, and the 1819–1820 cholera epidemic devastated the slave population. But if Allen is right, the demand for slaves remained high during this period of economic downturn. He argues that contemporaries' estimates of 30,000 to 50,000 illegally imported slaves landing on the island between 1811 and the early 1820s were not far wrong. Some three-quarters of the slaves came from Madagascar (despite diplomatic efforts to cut off supply at its source there), the remaining quarter from Eastern Africa. The extent to which Farquhar and his colleagues actually participated in this trade, as opposed to turning a blind eye to it, is still a subject of some dispute (Allen 2001; Barker 1996, chapter 3), but its existence and extent are not.

Things began to shift, in rather contradictory ways, after the 1825 act equalizing the sugar tariff in the British Empire. This paved the way for a rapid takeoff of the nascent Mauritian sugar industry. Sugar was grown on largely French-owned estates on the island but backed by significant amounts of British credit. With nearly all the crop going to London, the colony's economic dependence on Britain, argues Barker, was "almost complete" (1996, 5). One of the paradoxes of this situation was that Mauritius came increasingly under the heavy scrutiny of British abolitionists, and one of the results of this was that, just as sugar took off, the supply of illegal slaves dried up. The illegal trade had, according to Allen, stopped by 1827, and this was not unconnected with the arrival on the island the previous year of the Commission of Eastern Inquiry, charged with examining all aspects of the administration of British possessions in the region acquired during the Napoleonic Wars. They reported in 1828, commenting extensively on slavery and the illegal slave trade. In 1829 the slave protection system applied to all British slave colonies, was put into effect in Mauritius.

Mauritian planters were now well and truly in the abolitionists' limelight, as Barker has shown (1996), and allegations of atrocities committed against slaves were numerous. There is little doubt that many of these allegations were well founded, but it is also clear that Mauritian slavery and Mauritian planters were coming to assume a symbolic role within British abolitionist discourse as the epitome of evil. In addition many members of the British administration were heavily invested in the island's sugar industry, making them at the very least complicit in the system. British rule in early-nineteenth-century Mauritius was characterized by an astounding level of hypocrisy.

Two related developments came to dominate the political economy of the island in the 1820s. First, the rapid development of the sugar industry, combined with the drying up of the supply of illegal slaves, led to a radical reorganization of existing slave labor on the island. Second, as both Vijaya Teelock (1998) and M. D. North-Coombes (2000) have argued, the island's francophone elite began to assume all the qualities of a classic oligarchy, united not only by their shared economic interests, but also by their resistance to British interference in their affairs and the threat (the second time round) of abolition.

The efficient production of sugar, as we know from the work of Sidney Mintz and others, implies a very specific and thoroughly modern exploitation of labor, sometimes described as the "factory in the fields" (Mintz 1985; Palmié 2002a, 41; Berlin and Morgan 1993). The transformation of slavery on Mauritius in this period is a reminder, if we needed one, of the centrality of labor regimes to any history of slavery. Sugar came late to Mauritius, as it did to Cuba, but in both cases a slave system emerged that was only too familiar from an earlier period of Caribbean history (Knight 1970, Teelock 1998, Barker 1996). What this meant in practice on Mauritius has been described by both Vijaya Teelock (1998) and Anthony Barker (1996). Sugar was most profitably grown on large estates employing steam- and water-powered mills. The logic of the "factory in the fields" was that these voracious eaters had to be kept fed by a constant supply of cut canes. As the area under sugar production on Mauritius increased from 10,908 arpents in 1808 to 48,163 arpents in 1830,[8] so more and more of this land came to be consolidated into large estates with large slave populations. This consolidation (rather than any independent shift in planters' attitudes) probably accounts for what I referred to at the beginning of this chapter as the "alphabetization" of slaves. In practice this also involved a large volume of sales of slaves within the island, from the less productive districts in the south to the center of sugar production in the north, and from smaller slave owners to the larger planters (Barker 1996).

It would be wrong, however, to conceive of this as one large and decisive shift, and one set of slave sales. The frantic boom in the Mauritian sugar industry after 1825 was rapidly followed by a slump in 1829, occasioning bankruptcies, more sales, and further consolidation. Mauritian slaves were now not only likely to be subjected to the harsh labor regime of sugar production (work gangs, task work, longer hours, and the increased exploitation of female and child labor), but might also expect to be bought and sold, their family lives (if they had such a thing) disrupted in the process (Teelock 1998, Barker 1996). Another, related feature of this regime was its extensive use of hired labor. So-called personal slaves comprised 42.5 percent of privately owned slaves by 1832. This category consisted largely of slaves who were hired out as agricultural laborers, increasing the flexibility of the labor force overall and allowing individual planters to deploy their labor efficiently. Hiring out slaves was nothing new on Mauritius, as we have seen, though now the context for this hiring out had changed. Teelock argues convincingly that these "unattached" field slaves, with no permanent home, were the worst off of all (1998, 131).

The introduction of the slave protection system in 1829 did little or nothing to regulate, let alone improve conditions for slaves on Mauritius, but it did have two other important consequences. First, this office (combined with the activities of the abolitionists) produced detailed documentation of the nature of the labor regime, the alleged cruelties of slave owners, and the resistance all of this generated on the part of slaves. Second, this intervention helped harden the attitudes of the French planters, bringing them into direct conflict with the British and in the process (as in the 1790s) forcing them to articulate directly their defense of slavery. The French on Île de France may not have always been united as colonizers, but they found it easier to achieve unity as the colonized subjects of British overlords. In 1827 the leading French planters formed the Comité Colonial under the leadership of Adrian d'Epinay. In their opposition to the policy of slave protection and "amelioration," this group produced a lengthy and detailed defense of slavery, referring repeatedly to events in St. Domingue. All of the 229 petitions they produced gave an unfavorable assessment of slave "character" and presented an alarmist vision of the consequences of abolition (North-Coombes 1978, 145). As Barker has pointed out, this group went on to organize a boycott of legal cases initiated by the Protector of Slaves, refused to pay taxes and formed themselves into an armed civil guard nine hundred strong, without any interference from the governor of the day, Sir Charles Colville (1996, 6). Perhaps their status as a colonized group spurred them on, in addition to their economic interests. The end result was a level of opposition to reform that went further than anything produced by their West Indian counterparts.

Matters eventually came to a head with the appointment of an Englishman, John Jeremie, to the office of procureur-général. This office was the apex of the French legal and administrative system, which the British had preserved when they took over the island. The Comité Colonial members were incensed: Jeremie was not only an Englishman, he was also an abolitionist (Barker 1996, 6; Burroughs 1976). A general strike and demonstrations forced Jeremie to flee the island. He was later reinstalled, only to be expelled again. His views on the French Mauritian elite were, as one might imagine, scathing.

Abolition came in on 1 February 1835. The slave owners of Mauritius were generously compensated, and the liberated slaves now began their six-year term of "apprenticeship." As Satyendra Peerthum has shown (2000), many did not wait this long but, capitalizing on the shortage of skilled labor, accumulated wages and bought their own freedom. In any case, Mauritian planters were already in pursuit of alternative forms of labor to work the sugar fields. For this they turned to India. Between 1834 and 1839, 25,468 Indian indentured laborers entered the colony. In 1839, in the wake of criticism that this was a disguised form of the slave trade, the traffic was temporarily halted. It resumed, however, on a large scale in 1842, and in the next quarter-century 340,718 Indians were landed on Mauritius under the immigration scheme, of which only around 87,000 eventually returned to India.[9] The island's social and demographic landscape had been dramatically altered.

The Contradictions of "Creolization" (Again)

Bernardin de St. Pierre's landscape of Île de France was a social landscape as much as a physical one, and a social landscape marred by the scars of slavery. If it had not been for that blot, Île de France society would have been, for this romantic, an idyll of what we would now call "multiculturalism"—the kind of multiculturalism of which many present-day Mauritians are so proud and which advertises the island in the tourist brochures. At no point in its history could Mauritian society be characterized simply as the "voices of men of different nations in the same landscape," living out their traditions of origin in peaceful coexistence, not least because that blot on the landscape, slavery, was to have lasting consequences. Yet neither has Mauritius in any simple way exemplified the later and equally romantic vision of the Antillean architects of créolité and their portrait of a society in which difference and otherness are subsumed by one shared creole culture (Glissant 1981; Bernabé, Chamoiseau, and Confiant 1989; Britton 1999). Throughout its history Mauritian society has experienced the push and pull of cultural synthesis and internal division, or, in the culinary terms often favored by commentators on the island, the difference between soup and stir-fry. Above all, we should not forget that these simultaneous processes took place in the context of the violent struggles produced by systems of forced migration and labor. As Stephan Palmié has argued for another part of the ex-slave world, "Historically, the unstable and fluid Caribbean hybridities and syntheses that nowadays so capture our interest and imagination were achieved at a gruelling price" (2002b, 32). One might add that the "prices" paid by different groups in this process were not uniform—and perhaps not even commensurate.

As we have seen, for much of the eighteenth century Île de France can be characterized by the poverty in which the vast majority of its inhabitants lived and by the instability of its population. The latter was a function both of very high mortality rates and of the island's role as a strategic base rather than as a site of colonial production, a fact which also had the consequence that the French colonial elite was relatively slow to sediment. For the whole of the eighteenth century and well into the nineteenth, white men far outnumbered women, making the creation of the ideal white creole family a slow process.[10] Bernardin de St. Pierre's portrayal of the white creole matriarch obscured the reality of a sexual economy based on concubinage. Slavery provided a central—if not *the* central—structuring principle to this society, but slavery itself was a highly diverse institution here, with slave experiences ranging from the collective grueling manual labor of many of the Company (and later king's) slaves on the island's infrastructure and fortifications, to the harsh but semi-independent existence of the many slaves who belonged to small-scale owners. The origins of the slave population were peculiarly diverse and, in the preplantation era, the opportunities for the creation of a distinct slave culture, limited. There are hints of such a culture among maroon bands, but these were relatively small in number and size. There is plenty of evidence for what the French called marronnage, but most of this took the form of individuals escaping for days or weeks from particularly harsh treatment—taking a break from slavery. In reality the maroon was more likely to be hiring out his or her labor in town than foraging and plotting in the forests.

There can be little doubt (and it comes as no surprise) that the dominant culture of eighteenth-century Île de France was some version of French culture. French colonial society on the island was deeply divided, as we have seen, but this fact may have enhanced rather than detracted from the value of certain kinds of metropolitan cultural and social capital. Even when times were hard, the colonists of Île de France were paying for ships' holds to be filled with furniture, fashions, and food from the metropole. At the same time, however, they were importing Indian textiles for their own use, as well as for re-export. This was French culture with an orientalist flavor, though Port Louis never resembled Pondichéry, where a distinct Franco-Indian style had developed and where the French were obliged to engage with a complex local society. It seems likely that subordinate members of this highly stratified society sought to emulate aspects of French culture and appropriate it. Some slave dances mimicked formal eighteenth-century French forms, and some of the better-off slaves and free blacks wore "European" forms of dress. And yet, the evidence is always contradictory.

As we have seen, some groups within the slave and free black populations seem to have forged distinct identities for themselves—helped on, always, by a degree of recognition by the colonial authorities. These included the Lascar seamen, the West African Guinées and Wolofs, and the Malabars. Jouan, the Malabar slave whose case I discussed in chapter 6 flaunted his Indian style of dress; some Malagasy retained their distinct form of hairdressing. As I have argued (and as many others have argued for other contexts), the existence of such apparently distinct categories among the enslaved population does not indicate any straightforward transfer of African or Indian cultures to this new environment. All of these categories were reinventions, though this is not to deny their reality. The question of how to conceptualize these complex processes of "cultural transfer" in the New World has been the subject of an extensive literature from the work of Melville Herskovits onward (Herskovits 1941, Mintz and Price 1976), recently revisited at length in the work of Stephan Palmié (2002a, 2002b). Palmié makes a powerful critique of what he calls the theme-park approach to the study of African American religious traditions (2002, 159). What is perhaps most striking about the historical record for Île de France in the period of slavery is the relative absence of material on African and Malagasy cultural practices, particularly in the realm of religion.[11] It would be difficult to take a theme-park approach to this history, even if one was so inclined.

Whether we should conclude from this that African cultural practices in particular were effectively erased by the eighteenth-century system of slavery is another question. It would certainly be reasonable to conclude this, given the relative silence of the historical record on this subject combined with the relative absence of (consciously articulated) African cultural features in contemporary Mauritius.[12] As I have already indicated, there are many aspects of Île de France slavery that may have made it difficult for African and Malagasy slaves in particular to successfully re-create in this "new world" a lasting legacy of the worlds they had left behind. But this is not the same as arguing that African and Malagasy practices and languages were absent from the streets and plantations of eighteenth- and early-nineteenth-century Mauritius. The basic brutal demographic facts mean that we have to find some other way of imagining this world. New slaves arrived continually to replace those who had died, and we now know that this process carried on into the first two decades of the nineteenth century. Roger Bastide long ago pointed out the importance of this process in his study of slave religion in Brazil: "Time, in the long run, would erode all [African-derived] traditions, however firmly anchored in the new habitat. But the slave trade continuously renewed the sources of life by establishing continuous contact between old slaves, or their sons, and the new arrivals" (1978, 47).

Direct evidence for this "renewal" of Africa on Mauritian soil in the nineteenth century is provided by the extraordinary work of a French ethnologist, Eugène de Froberville (1847; see Alpers 2003). De Froberville's research into the "customs and traditions" of the Makua people was conducted not in their native Mozambique, but in Mauritius and Île Bourbon, among slaves of Makua origin. He interviewed more than three hundred, fifty of which were newly imported slaves,[13] constructed thirty-one vocabularies, and went home with masks and busts as evidence of their physical appearance. The evidence they provided de Froberville of the East African world from which they had come is striking for its detail and immediacy, and also for the fact that much of their folklore was apparently marked by the experience of the slave trade. De Froberville's interest in their modes of physical adornment (body tattoos, earrings, nose studs and lip plugs) also reminds us that first-generation African slaves carried on their bodies not only the brand marks of slavery but also those of their previous lives.

Nineteenth-century Mauritius may have had a more "African" atmosphere than we have been led to think, though this is best thought of in terms not of cultural survivals, but rather of the incorporation of African and Malagasy elements into the evolving new creolized culture, in which all groups participated to one degree or another. As I have indicated, this was not a linear process.

The new creolized culture of the island that evolved in the course of the eighteenth century was, then, always accompanied by the counter-vailing process by which some groups successfully carved out a place in which to express difference. Clearly the population of French masters did this, though it is also the case that lower class whites in Port Louis shared in an urban and seafaring culture of cosmopolitan origins. Some slaves and free blacks of Indian origin also managed this, though there is simultaneously plenty of evidence for their absorption into a shared hybrid culture through intermarriage with slaves and free blacks of African and Malagasy origin (Carter 1998a, 1–30). The lives of people of Indian origin on Île de France could take a number of trajectories. Jumeer cites examples of some Indians who had been baptized into the Catholic faith, but who continued to practice their Hindu or Muslim faith (1984, 459–460). Studies of the late-eighteenth-century free black population indicate that this was far from being a homogeneous community, and this was truer still for the nineteenth century.

The nineteenth century saw a series of major upheavals, as we have seen. Sugar, abolition, and Indian indentured labor each successively had far-reaching effects, all taking place under the political overlordship of the British administration. In this period questions of racial identity also come more clearly to the fore. As Nancy Stepan (1982) and others have argued, the achievement of abolition did not signal the end of racism, far from it, and this was as true of Mauritius as anywhere else. Whereas late-eighteenth-century observers like Bernardin de St. Pierre might remark, with pleasure, on the diversity of the island's population, mid- to late-nineteenth-century writers were more likely to comment anxiously, in explicitly racial terms, on the island's population of "mongrels" and "half-castes" and the alleged horrors of métissage.[14]

If the transformation of the island into a sugar colony had been a traumatic time for the island's slaves, abolition in 1835 did not mark the end of the trauma. The so-called apprenticeship system tied slaves to their former owners in theory for a maximum period of six years, though apprenticeship was in fact ended in 1839. In Mauritius, as elsewhere, plantation owners and administrators characterized the ex-slave population as a problem, fulfilling all the prophecies of the proslavery lobby: give them freedom and they will avoid labor at all cost. Work by Richard Allen on the economic fate of the ex-slave population indicates a complex set of circumstances that, in the end, resulted in the relative marginalization of many ex-slaves from the Mauritian economy. Ex-slaves (or, more accurately, ex-apprentices) certainly voted with their feet and abandoned the plantations. This much of the common characterization of them was true. Ex-slaves had no desire to work for their ex-masters and attempts to compel them to do so failed (in part due to the intervention of the Colonial Office under abolitionist scrutiny) (Allen 1999, 109). According to the 1851 census, only 4,461 of the 48,330 ex-apprentices and their descendants lived or worked on sugar estates. What former slaves wanted, more than anything, was land of their own, which they would labor on their own account, and this some of them managed to achieve, if only temporarily. Some squatted on unoccupied land; the better off purchased plots, often in close proximity to the plantations. Others moved to remoter parts of the coast where they could acquire small plots of land and combine agricultural production with fishing.

In the years that followed the ending of apprenticeship, then, it seems that the former slave population was beginning to establish itself as a community of smallholders, growing food for their own consumption and for the market, and supplementing this with some wage employment. This is a broad pattern of development familiar from other parts of the ex-slave world (Craton 1992, Sheridan 1993, Engerman 1992, Hall 1978). But the evidence for this period, as Richard Allen points out, is patchy and contradictory. The former slave population was an aging one, and still with marked disparities in its sex ratio. Allen's account implies that the very instability of this social group bred in some of them a desire for respectability, which in turn entailed the withdrawal of women from employment, which itself in turn deprived them of an important source of capital accumulation.[15] Some aspects of this period remain unclear, but what we do know is that by the late 1840s many of the ex-apprentices were being forced, by economic circumstances, to sell their pieces of land. The number of ex-apprentice landowners may have fallen by as much as two-thirds by the end of the 1840s.

In anticipation of the abolition of slavery, the planters of Mauritius turned to India for their labor. The first wave of privately recruited Indian labor arrived between 1834 and 1838—a total of nearly 24,000 Indian laborers landed on the island over these four years. This already constituted a major change in the island's demography.[16]

The important story of the fate of the ex-apprentices has been relatively neglected by historians of Mauritius—though we do have Allen's pathbreaking work, and more scholarship is in progress. This neglect mirrors events on the ground in the mid–nineteenth century, when the ex-apprentices virtually disappear from the record (they cease to be enumerated separately in 1861) as all official attention is focused on the phenomenon of Indian immigration. Crucial to any understanding of this period is the fact that the importation of Indian indentured labor, in very large numbers, followed hard on the heels of abolition. This would not have mattered to the ex-slave population if they had been more successful in their strategy of small-scale landownership, off-farm employment, and capital accumulation. But in practice it further contributed to their marginalization from the engine of the Mauritian economy.

Amid humanitarian protests that indentured labor was nothing more than a new form of slavery, Indian immigration to Mauritius was suspended in 1838, but renewed again in 1842. By 1871 Indian immigrants comprised more than two-thirds of the island's population. The allegation that this was "slavery in disguise" was not without foundation. Indian immigrants were destined for the harsh regime of the sugar fields, where by 1846 they were providing 96 percent of the labor (Allen 1999, 59). In the first two decades at least, Indian immigrants experienced severe exploitation, and ruling-class attitudes toward them were denigrating in a fashion only too reminiscent of slavery (Ly-Tio-Fane Pineo 1984; Carter 1995, 1996). Their sheer numbers and the impoverished backgrounds from which they came created fears of "vagrancy" and lawlessness. The marked imbalance of the sex ratio among the new immigrants helped to fuel these fears. In 1838 only 2 percent of Indian immigrants were women, and although this issue was addressed by government regulation from 1855, sex ratios remained unbalanced to some degree throughout the nineteenth century (Allen 1999, 58). Allen argues that the nature and dynamics of nineteenth-century labor relations on the island after 1834 illustrate both continuities and differences with the pre-emancipation period, and this seems a judicious assessment. Though we should not exaggerate the importance of legal distinctions, nevertheless it made a difference that Indian indentured laborers were conceived of as free persons under the law. Unlike slaves, they had entered into contracts, at the end of which they were free to leave for home if they wished.

Most did not, in fact, choose to leave at the end of their contracts. The story of Indian indentured labor is in part a story of how a population of desperately poor and servile laborers carved out a central role for itself in the island's economy as independent landowners, traders, and businessmen. To some extent this was achieved at the expense of the ex-apprentices, who had had insufficient time and resources to consolidate their position as small-scale landholders. The first wave of Indian immigrants began moving onto the land in the 1840s and 1850s, once they had completed their contracts. They also moved heavily into the growing service sector of the economy as "peddlars," "hawkers," shopkeepers, laundrymen, and women (Allen 1999, 148). These sources of nonagricultural income presumably helped them to accumulate sufficient capital to acquire land, but perhaps more important still were the sources of credit that became available to this group. Marina Carter and James Ny Foong Kwong argue that the presence on the island of a large and active business community of Indian origins ensured that the system of indenture "did not operate simply as a European-sponsored importation of a non-white workforce" (Carter and Kwong 1998, 49), and Richard Allen details the impressive business careers of members of this group (1999, 153–160). By the 1870s Indian traders and merchants formed a dense network over the island, providing "the foundation for a network of credit services which reached from Port Louis into the smallest hamlet in the most remote part of the island" (182). Sources of credit were available, then, to facilitate what is known in Mauritian historiography as the *grand morcellement*.

This process of the subdivision of large estates began around 1875 and gathered momentum with the severe agricultural crisis of the 1880s. Foremost among the investors in land were members of the Indian immigrant population: by 1900, Allen argues, Indians accounted for a third of all property changing hands (1999, 144). Until the 1880s most settlement of former indentured laborers had taken place in close proximity to the sugar estates; from the 1880s more and more Indians were living in rural villages away from the sugar estates (North-Coombes 2000, 95). This was in part a response to changes in the organization of sugar production, and particularly of the milling process. Declining sugar prices drove smaller millers out of business, and increasingly the process was centralized in a small number of highly capitalized and more efficient mills. The corollary to the centralization of milling was the decentralization of sugar production. Small cane growers, many located away from the estates, now produced an increasing proportion of the crop. Though the old planter class looked on this process with some alarm, the small Indian grower remained by and large subordinated to large propertied and milling interests, in fact, and life for the small grower was frequently tough.

The indenture system and the subsequent growth of Indian land-ownership had an important sociocultural dimension in addition to its far-reaching economic significance. The Indian indentured population was, overall, heterogeneous in origins, but within this heterogeneity there were opportunities for the re-creation of social bonds and identities. Unlike slaves, indentured laborers were often recruited en masse from particular villages in India, to which they sometimes retained close bonds. Place of origin seems to have been a key factor in determining settlement patterns on the island. The villages of laborers and former laborers were, to some extent at least, language and cultural communities. This was by no means a simple process, as historians of Indian immigration to Mauritius have shown. Rather it entailed a great deal of reinvention. Caste and religious distinctions, for example, continued to be significant, but only in interaction with other factors. New identities were created out of fragments of the old, and some Indian men married outside their ethnic group altogether, their families becoming "creolized" in the process. But overall the consensus seems to be that the organization of labor recruitment, and particularly its concentration among large kin groups from particular villages, provided a basis from which indentured laborers could create communities that consciously retained the memory of their origins, of a time and place before migration.

This appeal to premigration origins was not a strategy available to the island's population of gens de couleur, who, by the last quarter of the century, were increasingly referred to as "Creoles." This group was, however, the product of a shared history: the history of eighteenth-century slavery, of manumission, of the struggle to gain or maintain the status of free person. As a group, gens de couleur began the nineteenth century with a collective political cause: to do away with the legal disabilities and restrictions reimposed on them by the Napoleonic regime and carried over into the British period. At the legal level this was finally achieved in 1829, though many discriminatory practices remained as Mauritian society became more rather than less race-conscious. Among the political leaders of this struggle for full equality was Rémy Ollier (Vanmeerbeck 1865, Prosper 1995, Arno and Orian 1986). Ollier was born in 1816, the son of an enfranchised slave and of a former artillery captain. After a limited formal education and a spell as an apprentice to a harness maker, he went on to found a small school in Port Louis and then, in 1843, the newspaper *La Sentinelle de Maurice*, which became the organ of his community. Ollier's politics were complex, reflecting in part a search for recognition by a community that now faced not only discrimination from whites, but also the challenges presented by the abolition of slavery and the beginnings of Indian immigration.

Ollier argued passionately for equality with whites, but not for a negation of difference:

> We *do not want to make ourselves white* (*blanchir*). We are the equals of whites in terms of our rights, and if Mauritius closes her ears to our complaints, London will listen to them. . . . we are the equals of the whites in our hearts and in our intelligence, and if we are not the equals of the whites in terms of education and customs, tomorrow we will sacrifice everything to acquire these customs and education. Those are the prerogatives of which we are envious. But the color of the skin? Origins? What rubbish![17]

Ollier's defiant denial of the significance of skin color was of course partly a reflection of the very importance accorded to this "sign" in nineteenth-century Mauritius. Indeed, while Ollier passionately argued for the unity of "people of color," no matter what their origins, he often distinguished in his writings between so-called mulâtres (those with some assumed white blood) and the hommes de couleur.

In their historical-sociological study of Mauritius, Arno and Orian argue that this period after the end of slavery was one marked by social "anomie." Slavery, the only stable structuring principle of Mauritian society, had gone, leaving a "relational void" (1986, 64). They go on to argue that the response of social groups to this prospect of greater equality and social mobility was to somewhat desperately redefine themselves and put up the barriers to entry: "A game of reciprocal anxieties was from now on decisive. Wavering was no longer possible, the previous flexibility in social relations had now to disappear, the urgency of closure now affirmed itself" (67).

This "closure" was, they argue, particularly marked among the gens de couleur, whose social position was threatened both by emancipation and by Indian immigration. One sign of this was a move away from matrifocality within the gens de couleur community, greater control over women's sexuality in particular, and a new emphasis on respectability, marriage, and morality (67). Arno and Orian's work is largely neglected by historians of Mauritius.[18] Their kind of social-psychological analysis is more commonplace in neighboring Réunion and in the francophone islands of the Antilles and fits uneasily with the empirical anglophone tradition that dominates Mauritian studies. Certainly one might disagree with elements of their analysis and with its emphasis. For example, they almost certainly underestimate the importance of class, and particularly the dimensions of common experience and interests that drew together Indian laborers and ex-apprentices. Their theory probably leads them to exaggerate the degree to which hommes de couleur struggled to distinguish themselves from ex-apprentices. In fact there are large gaps in our knowledge here, for though Richard Allen has reconstructed some aspects of the history of this community, their political, ideological, and cultural development awaits a full account. In particular the development and spread of the Catholic mission enterprise in the nineteenth century was undoubtedly of key importance in the formation of what came to be called "Creole" identity.[19]

And yet it is impossible to read mid- to late-nineteenth-century sources on Mauritius without being struck by some of the obsessions Arno and Orian identify in order to construct their theory of the "battle against anomie." How far these concerns were those of Mauritians themselves, how far they reflected the anxieties of (mostly British) observers, is hard to tell, but they are inescapable. A concern with the minutiae of racial difference is the most obvious. In midcentury the Scottish missionary Patrick Beaton remarked on the "antipathy" among whites against the "smallest admixture of African blood" as amounting to a "positive passion" (1859). It seems that "whiteness" was being more closely defined, and sexual relations between whites and gens de couleur more subject than ever to censure. Race "admixture" was a concern among liberal critics of the island's regime, as much as for more conservative observers. Jean-Joseph Le Brun, for example, had arrived on the island in 1814 to work for the London Missionary Society, to champion the cause of the slaves and gens de couleur. Le Brun was horrified by what he represented as the unbridled promiscuity of the femmes de couleur and, like many others, believed that mixed-race children were bound to seek bloody revenge against their white fathers. His response to this was to advocate much stricter laws against miscegenation.[20]

Meanwhile, despite their common political objectives, gens de couleur were themselves divided in ways which indicate the complex cross-cutting axes of race, ethnicity, and class, and more generally the low esteem in which the "African element" was held. This prejudice was, according to Anthony Barker, only too evident in the correspondence of Governor Cole in the 1820s, and he also cites the comments of a long-term British resident who noted in 1826 that locally born gens de couleur, no matter "how fair and respectable," were segregated in the theater in Port Louis "while Indian country-born half-castes have an unqualified privilege to sit where they please—however dark they may be" (Barker 1999, 141). Skin color, as these comments make clear, was by no means all-determining—an Indian origin apparently acted as a compensating force. These remarks predate, of course, the arrival of Indian immigrants in large numbers. Indian immigrants, as we have seen, attracted many of the deeply denigrating representations previously reserved for slaves, but there is some evidence that within the community of gens de couleur "Indian blood" was more highly valued than "African blood." At least, this is what observers would lead us to believe. By the late nineteenth century, race theory had evolved to such a degree that Hervé de Rauville[21] (admittedly farther to the right than most), could confidently assert that it was important to make a distinction between what he called the métis Indien and the mulâtre africain—the latter being an inferior type. His argument was based on the theory that Hindus were Aryans and that therefore any homme de couleur of Hindu origin was not, properly speaking, of mixed race (de Rauville 1908, 140–141).

This is not a simple story of the denigration of all things African, however. The late-nineteenth-century linguist and folklorist Charles Baissac expressed a wave of nostalgia for the "vrai creol noir" whose cultural influence was being "drowned out" by the sheer numbers of Indian immigrants combined with the desire to forget the painful humiliations of slavery. On the former Baissac expressed common prejudices; on the latter phenomenon, he wrote:

The words "slave" and "master," which recall an odious past, have disappeared from their lips, and if you hear an old man say "*momete*" to a White when he wants a favor, this will not be because he has forgotten, but because the urgency of his need has led him to employ the vocabulary of the old days. In place of the word "*maître*" has been substituted that of "*borzois*"—to such a degree that horses and dogs no longer have "*maîtres*," but now "*borzois*." (Baissac 1880)

Emancipation, Baissac argued (as have Arno and Orian), marked an attempt to eradicate the memory of slavery, to eliminate it from the language. But slavery and the struggles against it constituted the only common history binding together gens de couleur and ex-apprentices— all those who would later come to be known as "Creoles." This might not have mattered but for the fact that, simultaneously, members of the heterogeneous community of Indians were successfully building new identities on the basis of real and reimagined common origins. The game of multiculturalism had begun, and the Creole population, dispossessed by the twin processes of enslavement and emancipation, would lose.

Notes

Preface

1   This was the Duc de La Rochefoucauld-Liancourt. Debien speculates that the Société des Amis des Noirs may have played a role in its production (92).

2   Brugevin's account suggests the possibility that slaves may have suspected that they were being poisoned: "Ces hommes sont ennemis de tous médicaments composés et qu'ils ne les prennent qu'avec le plus grand dégoût" (109).

Chapter 1: In the Beginning

1   Throughout the nineteenth century, and for most of the twentieth, the Mauritian economy was based on sugar monocropping. More recently, however, it has undergone a rapid industrialization, focused on the manufacture and export of textiles. Tourism is also an important component of the new economy. On the political economy of sugar, see North-Coombes 2000; for a critical analysis of postindependence Mauritius political economy, see Durand and Durand 1975; and for a discussion of recent economic development, see Dommen and Dommen 1999.

2   On the *longue durée* of Indian Ocean history, see especially Chaudhuri 1985 and 1990.

3   I discuss the question of identity without origins in chapter 4. This aspect of "creolization" is also analyzed in the literature of the Antillean *creolité* movement, which I refer to in chapter 8 (see Glissant 1981).

4   At independence in 1968, communal tensions were seen as a major worry for the new nation, along with population pressure, poverty, and the island's dependence on sugar; see Titmuss 1968 and Benedict 1965. These pessimistic predictions were not fulfilled, and the specter of serious communal conflict has receded, at least for the time being. Problems remain, however, not least the economic, political, and social marginalization of the Creole community (those largely descended from slaves and ex-slaves), in addition to the dissatisfactions of the

Muslim community and the threat posed by versions of Hindu fundamentalism. On recent Mauritian politics and the question of ethnicity and nationhood, see Simmons 1982; Rajabally 1997, Eriksen 1998, 1999; Arno and Orian 1986; Miles 1999; Teelock 1999b.

5 The exact number of "Creoles" on the island is a matter of some dispute, since they are enumerated not as a separate group but as part of a category labelled "General Population," which includes whites and others. In 1996, of an estimated total population of 1,140,256, around 27 percent were Creoles.

6 This issue is not, of course, unique to Mauritius, but it takes a particular form there. Wider questions of the culture of "creolization," of identities that do not depend on "origins," have been discussed most notably by Antillean intellectuals and writers such as Edouard Glissant and Patrick Chamoiseau. See Glissant 1981 and Chamoiseau, Confiant, and Bernabé 1989. See also discussions in Britton 1999; Benitez-Rojo 1996; Burton 1997; Vergès 2000; Bongie 1998; and Balutansky and Sourieau 1998. For issues of "authenticity" in areas with a native population, see Thomas 1997.

7 On the instability and "invention" of islands, see proceedings of the conference Islands: Histories and Representations, University of Kent, Canterbury, April 1998, edited by R. Edmund and forthcoming from Cambridge University Press.

8 For an examination of the history of extinction on Mauritius, see Grove 1995 and Taub 2000.

9 This term was used in a recent conference on the Dutch period in Mauritius, held at the Mahatma Gandhi Institute, Moka, Mauritius. For a discussion of the "virtual reality" of the dodo and its iconography, see van den Heuvel 2000.

10 The account that follows is as unstable as any other. I have drawn on two accounts based on a reading of the Dutch archives in both the Cape and the Netherlands: Moree 1998 and Liebbrandt 1896. In addition I have drawn on the work of the nineteenth-century Mauritian historian Albert Pitot (1905). See also recent work on the Dutch period by Jocelyn Chan Low (2000) and Daniel Sleigh (2000).

11 This story is told by Pitot (1905, 32) and, more elaborately and self-consciously, by de Rauville (1889, chap. 10). De Rauville is explicit about the "legendary" nature of his account: "Souvent au cours de ses récherches l'historien releve une série de circonstances touchant des faits dignes d'être relatés, mais qu'il ne peut relier entre eux faute de documents—c'est ce qui m'est arrivé; j'ai trouvé, tant de vieilles traditions de l'Île de France que dans les circonstances racontées incidemment par des voyageurs qu'n'y attachaient pas d'importance, des fragments d'episodes historiques et des relations de moeurs non sans intêret" (preface).

12 The historian of Dutch Mauritius Perry Moree disagrees with my interpretation, arguing from his reading of the primary sources that "François," as he was known, was almost certainly alone on the island (e-mail communication to author, 2 December 2001).

13 Moree lists a number of calls on the island by the Dutch in this period (1998, 16).

14 On Simon van de Stel's career, see Grove 1995, 142–143.

15 See, in particular, Larson 2000 and Barendse 1995, describing the evolution of the

slave trade on Madagascar in the seventeenth century and its relationship to political conflict. Malagasy slaves were used in this period by the Omanis, but also in Batavia and Pondichéry. They would later also be found in the Americas. Madagascar became both an exporter and an importer of slaves—a fact that in itself hints at the complexity of this history. See also Campbell 1989; Deschamps 1960; Kent 1970. I discuss Madagascar in more detail in chapter 4.

16 For a particularly telling example of the latter, see the story of "La Legende de Sacalavou" in de Rauville 1889.

17 As Governor Deodati remarked in 1698, "They have to wear heavy irons when working in the forest and consequently do very little."

18 This comes from the Dolphin Account in Barnwell 1948, 32. See also this letter from Mauritius to Batavia, 2 July 1694: "Eleven years ago some slaves escaped, and because of the impenetrable forests could never be recaptured. Some children have been born to them, and they have made the roads very unsafe . . . Last year they even set fire to the house situated five hours west of the Lodge" (Liebbrandt 1896, 27).

19 Representations and fantasies of maroons can be theorized in psychoanalytic terms of exclusion. Jessica Benjamin argues "exclusion is a term that can only mean to psychically 'relocate.' . . . Excluded refers to that which is repudiated, cast out of the self, abjected, in order to shore up the subject's identity, not truly the outside other" (1998, 103). Certainly maroon fears and fantasies seem, on the surface, to fit this general theory, but maroons were, as we have seen, subject to both exclusion *and* a degree of identification, albeit a kind of nostalgic identification that disguised the violence of encounter with them. See Fuss 1995 for a discussion of theories of identification. On the repositories of fear, see Phillips 1995.

20 See translated documents in Leibbrandt 1896, 412; and Barnwell 1948, 91; and the account given in Pitot 1905, 327.

21 On French colonial policy in the ancien régime, see Mayer, Tarrade, Rey-Goldzeiger, and Thobie 1991, Lokke 1932, Cornevin and Cornevin 1990, Priestley 1939, and Saintoyant 1929. On the Compagnie des Indes, see Boudriot 1983 and Haudrère 1989.

22 I do not deal in any detail with the history of Île Bourbon, though initially the two islands were administered jointly, and trade and communication between them remain important to any understanding of this period. On Île Bourbon, see Rosset 1967 and Azema 1859.

23 For the disputed history of this second prise de possession, see Amadée Nagapen's account (1990).

24 This is quoted in Ly-Tio-Fane Pineo's history of Île de France in the period 1715–1746 (1993), which I have drawn on extensively. See also Lagesse 1972. Lougnon (1933) produced a valuable summary of correspondence of this period, and I have also consulted original documentation in the Archives Nationales in Paris; AN: Fond des Colonies: c4/1, Correspondance de l'Île de France 1714–1732. The following account draws on all of these sources.

25 In his careful account of the peopling of the island in this period in Baker and Corne 1982, Philip Baker argues that there would have been no maroons left over from the period of Dutch occupation—but I am not clear how we can know this.

26 This list is in Baker and Corne 1982, 143. See also Bourde de la Rogerie 1934. A detailed account of the first habitants of Île de France is also given by Anthoine Chelin ([1949] 1987), and of the first European women by Marcelle Lagesse (1988).

27 Archives de la Congrégation de la Mission (formerly the Lazarist order), Paris: Receuil 1504, f. 27: Lettre écrite par un missionaire, Bourbon 1739.

28 See the copy of these instructions in Ly-Tio-Fane Pineo 1993 (290–291).

29 For this purpose he was supplied by the Company with a detailed model of a land concession: AN: C4/1: 1721.

30 AN: C4/1: de Nyon to Compagnie, 22 September 1724.

31 Freud's description of "typical" phobias includes thunderstorms and vermin attacks (1993, 42).

32 AN: C4/1, 1730, M. Le Noir, Gouverneur de Pondichéry: renseignements sur les Îles de France et de Bourbon.

33 AN: C4/1; Pitot 1899, 5.

34 AN: C4/1, 1730, Mémoire concernant le gouvernement de M. de Maupin.

35 A form of punishment in which the naked victim was lowered onto a sharp-sided wooden "horse," sometimes called "Judas cradle" or "witch's cradle" in English.

36 Congrégation de la Mission 1504, f. 83: Borthon and Igou, 10 November 1728.

37 AN: C4/1, 1729, Extrait de la lettre de la Compagnie à M. de Maupin, 24 September 1729.

38 AN: C4/1, 1730, Mémoire concernant le gouvernement de M. de Maupin.

39 AN: C4/86, 1731.

40 The *Méduse* arrived from Juda with 178 slaves; see Baker and Corne 1983, 181.

41 AN: C4/1: 20 December 1732, Affaire relative du libelle de M. Teinturier de Gennincourt; January 1732, Requêtes au Roi par M. Teinturier de Gennincourt.

42 AN: C/4, 6 October 1730, Extrait de la lettre du Conseil de Île de France sur l'état de cette isle.

43 For a discussion of this issue as it relates to French possessions in India, see Haudrère 1993, 46.

Chapter 2: Engineering a Colony, 1735–1767

1 See the discussion of his role in this novel in Bongie 1998, 112–113.

2 Obvious comparisons (there are many) include, within the French empire, Louisburg (Johnston 2001), Pondichéry (Vincent 1993) and the port towns of the Antilles islands (Butel 2002; Pérotin-Dumon 2000). Another comparison is with Cape Town in this period (Worden 2000).

3 The real jewel in the crown of the French colonial empire was St. Domingue (McClellan 1992). Indeed, as McClellan shows, St. Domingue was not only hugely dominant within the French empire in this period but was also a significant pivot

of the entire world economy. In 1776 it produced more wealth than the whole of the Spanish Empire in the Americas. Anne Pérotin-Dumon's recent work (2000) on urban Guadeloupe in the seventeenth and eighteenth centuries provides a useful comparison with Port Louis. On Martinique in this period, see Elizabeth 1989, and on slavery in the Antilles more generally, Debien 1974. Crucially, Île de France was not a sugar colony in the eighteenth century, and thus the particular demands of sugar production were absent (Schwartz 1992). This would all change, however, at the beginning of the nineteenth century.

4   Archives d'Outre-Mer, Aix-en-Provence (hereafter AOM): DFC IV: Mémoires/10: Île de France: pièce 38, June 1752.

5   On the development of the engineering profession in this period, see Picon 1992 and, in the colonial empire, McClellan 1992.

6   AOM: DFC IV: Mémoires/10: Île de France: dossier 25, 1738.

7   One of Labourdonnais's first tasks was road building, much of it using corvée slave labor. Building roads and introducing carts allowed him to free a significant amount of slave labor and also to reduce the price of building materials, such as wood and sand, procured on the island.

8   I discuss the origins of this group more fully in chapter 4. In Pondichéry, meanwhile, Labourdonnais is credited with having introduced black (cafres) soldiers with a reputation for bravery (Weber 1993, 151).

9   The possible comparisons are many and include examples as far-flung as Cape Town (Shell 1994, Worden 1985) and colonial Peru (Bowser 1974). On labor regimes more generally, see Berlin and Morgan 1993.

10   For a discussion of the meaning of these ethnic designations, see chapter 4.

11   Conseil Supérieur de Île Bourbon to the Company, 25 November 1736, in Lougnon 1933, 62.

12   On Bambara seamen in the Atlantic world, see Bolster 1997, 62–63.

13   AN: C4/86: 1 September 1738, État Général des Esclaves appartenants à La Compagnie.

14   AOM: DFC IV: Mémoires 10: pièce 28: État de la depense des ouvriers qui sont employés aux travaux de la Compagnie à l'Île de France (1742).

15   AOM: DFC IV Mémoire /10: Île de France: pièce 49: Charpentier Cossigny, Journal concernant les travaux des fortifications, 30 September 1753.

16   A version of the Code Noir was enacted on Île de France in 1723. On the Code Noir, see Sala-Molins 1987.

17   E series in AOM: E 337/bis: Pobequin, Jean-Louis: Charpentier a l'Île de France. Throughout, all translations from the French are mine unless otherwise noted.

18   This was the Custom of Paris, which governed marriage and inheritance of free people in the French colonies. A form of partible inheritance was a feature of this.

19   Morcellement refers to the sub-division of land holdings.

20   The Company used different types of vessels for different purposes, the largest those sailing between France and the Indies, generally of 1,200 tons. Daily rations for a sailor consisted mainly of biscuit and salt beef or bacon, supplemented with a pint of wine daily (Boudriot, 1983, 138–139).

21 These figures are unlikely to be accurate, as Philip Baker's exhaustive discussion of the demographic evidence for 1735 shows. Baker estimates that in 1735 there was a total of 901 slaves on the island, including Company-owned slaves and children (Baker 1982, 31). I am very grateful to Philip Baker for this information from his unpublished thesis.

22 A list of enterprises formed with the participation of Labourdonnais is provided by Ly-Tio-Fane Pineo (1993, 268).

23 His personnel record, detailing his service, is in AOM: E 111.

24 See, for example, the accusations made against him concerning his ownership of a large habitation and sawmill in AN: C4/7: Correspondance Générale 1751–1753, n.d. Réponse de M. David au mémoire présenté à la Compagnie au mois d'août 1752.

25 AN: C4/7: Correspondance Générale 1751–1753: Mémoire, August 1752.

26 AN: C4/7: Correspondance Générale 1751–1753, Dupleix to Lozier-Bouvet, 31 August 1753.

27 AN: C4/7: Correspondance Générale 1751–1753: Lozier-Bouvet, 20 March 1753.

28 AN: C4/7: Correspondance Générale 1751–1753: Les Directeurs de la Compagnie des Indes à Conseil Superieur, 6 February 1753.

29 AN: C4/7: Correspondance Générale 1751–1753: Lozier-Bouvet, 31 December 1753.

30 AN: C4/7: Correspondance Générale 1751–1753: M. Abbé de la Tour, Projet concernant les Isles de France et de Bourbon 1753.

31 AN: C4/7: Correspondance Générale 1751–1753: Lozier-Bouvet, 31 December 1753.

32 AOM: DFC IV: Mémoires/10: pièce 49: Cossigny's journal entry dated 1 April 1754.

33 AN: C4/7: Correspondance Générale 1751–1753: Mémoire dated 1753 sur les Isles de France et de Bourbon.

34 AN: C4/7: Correspondance Générale 1751–1753: Mémoire of 1753.

35 AN: C4/9: Correspondance Générale 1755–1757: Mémoire (n.d.): La necessité du commerce particulier aux isles de France et de Bourbon.

36 See, for example, the views of Father Teste in a letter to Paris of 1 March 1764, Congrégation de la Mission (Paris), 1504, ff. 189.

37 AN: C4/7: Correspondance Générale 1751–1753: Abbé de la Tour 1753.

38 "Extraits du Journal de Godeheu," *Revue Retrospective de l'Île Maurice* 9.4: 217.

39 AN: C4/9: Correspondance Générale 1755–1757: Mémoire (n.d.): La necessité du commerce particulier aux isles de France et de Bourbon.

40 See his personnel record in AOM: E 296.

41 This journal is to be found in AN: C4/9, Correspondance Générale 1755–1757, C4/10, Correspondance Générale 1758, and C4/86: Île de France.

42 AN: C4/10: Correspondance Générale 1758, Conseil Supérieur to M. d'Aché, Recensement des gens qui prennent leurs vivres dans les magasins de la Compagnie, 20 October 1758.

43 AN: C4/87: Île de France 1760, letter (author unknown), 28 September 1760.

44 On the conduct of the war in India, see Perrod (1993).

45 For the later War of American Independence, for example, the Mauritius archives contain a file on slaves who had died in combat or of disease on Royal vessels: MNA: OC 72a: Bureau de classes et armament, 1785–1788.

46 The archives for this period reveal frequent accusations and disputes over "ateliers pour le coup du bois." For example, AN: C4/87: Conseil Supérieur, 9 January 1760.

47 AN: C4/15: Île de France 1763–1765, Mémoire, vers 1764.

Chapter 3: Enlightenment Colonialism and Its Limits, 1767–1789

1 Richard Grove has similarly argued that "before the end of the eighteenth century, Mauritius had come to occupy a central and innovative place across a whole field of new thinking in French philosophy, botanical science and literature" (1995, 172).

2 See John Donovan's introduction to his 1982 English translation. On the iconography of the novel, see Toinet 1963. See also Bernardin de St. Pierre's personnel record (and letters) in AOM: E 363. I discuss specific aspects of the novel in later chapters.

3 The role of Mauritius in the history of environmental thinking and the career of Pierre Poivre are discussed in detail by Richard Grove (1995, chapter 5).

4 I owe any understanding I have of French naval history of this period to Robin Briggs, who has kindly shared his knowledge with me. Any mistakes, however, are mine.

5 In 1768 the duc de Praslin authorized an expedition to Fort Dauphin by Maudave, a soldier and adventurer based on Île de France. In 1774 the French government backed a similar plan by the Polish count Benyowsky. Both ended in failure. France did not finally "conquer" Madagascar until the next century.

6 Most of the relevant mémoires are contained in: AN: C4/15: Île de France 1763–1765.

7 See the detailed discussion of his thinking in Grove 1993, chapter 5.

8 AN: C4/15, Île de France, 1763–1765.

9 AOM: G1/505, no. 2, Tableau Général de l'État de Population et de Culture ou étoit L'Isle de France, 1766.

10 AN: C4/15: Île de France 1763–1765: Mémoire sur les blancs, 1763.

11 There are many examples of this practice in following chapters.

12 This problem is also noted by Richard Allen (1999).

13 AN: C4/15: Île de France 1763–1765: Mémoire relatif à l'Île de France (vers 1763).

14 AN: C4/15: Mémoire concernant les établissements de la France au delà du Cap de Bonne Esperance et sur le commerce de la Compagnie des Indes.

15 In his study of medical and scientific institutions in St. Domingue in this period, James McClellan argues " 'science' more than 'Enlightenment' appears to be the appropriate criterion by which to analyse French colonialism in the eighteenth century" (1992, 293). In many ways Île de France was a less likely setting for "Enlightenment colonialism" than was the much more developed and sophisticated island of St. Domingue. However, I am using the term here to characterize the aspirations (largely unfulfilled) of administrators such as Poivre.

16 Poivre's life and work have been described in detail by Madeleine Ly-Tio-Fane

1958. His career as a botanist and administrator are dealt with at length in Richard Grove's 1995 study of colonial environmental thinking. I draw heavily on both authors here, but also on Poivre's own works and on the administrative documentation of his period as intendant. See also the commemorative booklet on Poivre edited by Philippe Lenoir (1993).

17 AN: C4/87: Instructions to Dumas and Poivre.

18 See chapter 9 below.

19 See especially the summarized correspondence between Dumas and Poivre in AN: C4/21: Île de France, Correspondance Générale 1768.

20 See chapter 5 below.

21 AN: C4/21: Île de France, Correspondance Générale 1768, Extrait de la lettre de M. Dumas, 10 September 1767; Lettre de M. Poivre, 21 February 1768.

22 AN: C4/22: Île de France, Correspondance Générale 1768, M. Poivre, 8 January 1768.

23 For an account of a similar attempt to promote "order" and "harmony" on Île Royale, see Johnston (2001).

24 See the entry for Cailleau in the *Dictionary of Mauritian Biography* (hereafter *DMB*), no. 22 (February 1944): 658.

25 On the history of the Port Louis hospital, see L'Hortalle 1980. I have discussed the role of medicine in this period and during the Revolution in Vaughan 2000.

26 "Extraits du Journal de Godeheu," *Revue Retrospective de l'Île Maurice* 4.4: 215.

27 These are in the National Archives of Mauritius (hereafter MNA): OC 53: Bureau de l'hôpital, 1760–1770.

28 See Aublet's personnel record in AOM: E 10.

29 See Vaughan 2000. My information on Dazille comes primarily from his personnel record (AOM: E112), supplemented by his entry in *DMB*, no. 6 (October 1942): 202. Dazille's work in relation to medicine and slavery is also discussed by Quinlan (1996) and by McClellan (1992).

30 Dazille 1776 describes this dispute.

31 On Dazille's career and publications, see Vaughan 2000, McClellan 1992, and Quinlan 1996.

32 As Johnston (2001, 139) points out, census taking was very much an innovation of the colonies in the eighteenth century—no national census was undertaken in France until 1791.

33 For this, see also Campbell 1993. For the role of the French in the East African slave trade, see Alpers 1970, Akinola 1970, and Freeman-Grenville 1965.

34 Indian textiles had always been an important item of exchange for slaves in Africa, and to this extent the Indian Ocean and Atlantic trades had always been linked.

35 According to Raymond d'Unienville (1998, 34), some 550 slaves in French uniform boarded Suffren's ships in 1781.

36 See AOM: E280.

37 See *DMB*, no. 36 (January 1977): 1063–1064.

38 Thomas de Conway's career began with the rank of lieutenant in the Regiment of

Clare. From there he moved to the Regiment of Anjou and then, as colonel, in the Regiment of Pondichéry. In 1783 he was petitioning the king to formally recognize his Irish noble ancestry: AOM: E90: De Conway. Le Comte.

39 On the wider question of the role of the law in colonial cultures, see recent brilliant work by Lauren Benton (2002), which compares different colonial legal regimes and their encounters with "local" cultures from 1400 to 1900. See also work by Stephen Greenblatt (1991) on the role of the law in "taking possession" over American Indians.

40 These must surely exist among the private papers of the island's elite families—but I have had no access to them.

41 These records are also used by Deryck Scarr (1998) in his work on slaving in the Indian Ocean. For a discussion of the interpretation and use of similar records in early modern Europe, see Muir and Ruggiero 1994. For the interpretation of early-twentieth-century court records in the context of French West Africa, see the very interesting work of Richard Roberts (1990).

42 This was in part a reflection of the growing importance of the legal profession in France in this period; see Bell 1994 and Geirson 1984.

43 My brief survey of records for the Antillean island of Martinique in the same period, however, revealed repeated references to the Code Noir in judicial records.

44 On the operation of the courts in the regulation of slavery in North America, see also Lazarus-Black 1994 and Schwartz 1988.

45 In the very different (largely non–slave-owning) situation of Île Royale in Canada, Johnston also notes the importance of the law in regulating colonial society (Johnston 2001, 24; 154–155).

46 For a fascinating account of the use of the law and of the "moral economy of the lash" in South African slavery, see Mason 1990.

47 For very similar issues on Île Royale, see Johnston 2001.

48 Greenburg's argument, however, differs very markedly from my own—but this may reflect the very different slave regimes we are dealing with.

49 Women who owned slaves were in a somewhat ambiguous position in this regard, as I shall discuss below.

50 I also draw here on Langui and Legibre 1979, but most importantly on the contemporaneous legal manual by Daniel Jousse (1771). As far as I have been able to tell, criminal procedure on Île de France followed closely that described by Jousse.

51 On the "problem of confession" in law and literature, see the very stimulating work of Peter Brooks (2000).

52 On legal and cultural intermediaries, see also Benton 2002, 15–18.

53 Johnston (2001) notes a similar problem for the criminal records of Île Royale.

54 "Constant provocation" is Lois McNay's phrase, used in her discussion of Foucault's theories of power. I am indebted to Lois McNay's written work (1994) and discussions with her.

Chapter 4: Roots and Routes: Ethnicity without Origins

1 National Archives of Mauritius (hereafter MNA): JB 27: Procédure Criminelle, 1777, case 11.

2 The judge in this case was Nicolas François Barbé de Marbois, originally from Metz: AOM : E Series (Personnel): E16.

3 Frustratingly, the record seems to be incomplete, but see MNA: OB 58, Jurisdiction Royale, Registre des sentences en matière criminelle, 25 March 1777–8 June 1780: "Tout consideré, avons rejetté et rejettons du proces la deposition du Pierre Nicolas Lambert, cinquième temoin de l'information, et en consequence disons qu'il n'en sera faire lecture, avons declaré et declarons le nommé Adonis convaincu d'avoir reçu et conservé drogues et ingrediens dans le dessein de nuire à son maitre, pour reparation de quoi avons condamné et condamnons le dit Adonis à être attaché à la chaine du roi pour y servir comme forcat pendant trois ans."

4 See Jousse (1771) for the seriousness with which the crime of poisoning was regarded in eighteenth-century France.

5 I draw particularly on Diane Fuss's work (1995, chapter 5); and on Bhabha 1984.

6 On race and performativity (and its limits), see the very interesting discussion by Kalpana Seshadri-Crooks (1998). I am in no way suggesting that "anything went" in the Île de France courtroom, but that the creation of Adonis's and Diamante's positions within that courtroom was not given. The question of performativity in the construction of subjectivity has been most famously and thoroughly addressed in relation to gender and sexuality by Judith Butler (1993) and her critics.

7 This is based on my own reading of the Martinican archives for this period, and also Moitt 1996; Peytraud 1974, 319; and Debien 1974, 399.

8 Palmié 2002a makes this point forcefully in relation to Cuba in the nineteenth century.

9 See Croix 1995, 168–173, on sorcery in Brittany, the origin of many early settlers on Île de France.

10 See Vaughan (1998) in which I discuss these issues in more detail. I am drawing particularly on the work of Antze and Lambek (1996). Of course, this begs the larger question of the definition of trauma and whether different kinds of trauma are comparable.

11 Most of this work (as Ned Alpers has recently pointed out) concentrates on Africans in the Americas and the "Black Atlantic" (Gilroy 1993). See Mintz and Price 1976; Palmié 1995; Palmié 2002a; Lovejoy 2000; Morgan 1997, 1998; Thornton 1992; Olwig 1985; and Craton 1979. For a recent, and particularly relevant, discussion of this literature and the question of memory under slavery, see Larson 2000. Until recently there was little in the way of studies of the culture of slaves and the historical memory of slavery in Mauritius. Pioneering work on Réunion by Gerbeau (1997) was not replicated on Mauritius. However, recent work by Vijayalakshmi Teelock of the University of Mauritius is beginning to fill this large gap. The volume edited by Teelock and Alpers (2001) is representative of this new historiography.

12 The most useful survey and analysis of these regimes is Blackburn 1997.

13 Thanks to Stephen Ellis for patiently explaining aspects of Malagasy history to me. I also rely heavily on recent work by Larson (2000).

14 This, of course, was a practice all over the slave world. For a discussion of the debates on ethnicity under slavery, see the introduction to Lovejoy 2000.

15 The volume and importance of trade from Madagascar to the Mascarenes, particularly in the last third of the eighteenth century, has recently been emphasised by Larson (2000).

16 The French did not finally attain formal colonial control over Madagascar until 1896. In the seventeenth century they attempted to create a base in Fort Dauphin, but this ended in their expulsion (see chapter 1 above). Less formal settlements of foreigners did, however, exist on the east coast of Madagascar throughout the seventeenth and eighteenth centuries—these consisted of communities of pirates and privateers, preying on Indian Ocean trade. On the history of Madagascar, see Brown 1978, Deschamps 1960, and Mack 1986.

17 Benyowsky was eventually killed in Madagascar in 1786. See his personnel file in AOM: E: 26 (Benyowsky, Aladar); and his memoirs, Benyowsky 1790. His colorful life was also the subject of a play (Kotzebue 1798).

18 The Merina peoples have been a particular focus of anthropological attention, with their famous funerary rites documented by the anthropologist Maurice Bloch (1971, 1985). But see also the recent work of Pier Larson (2000), which historicizes these practices and places them in the context of the slave trade. Earlier French scholarship on Madagascar included the monumental work of Grandidier (1908).

19 On the importance of hairstyling in Malagasy culture and politics, see Larson 2000, 240–253.

20 Analyzing the statistics for late-eighteenth-century marroonage, Richard Allen concludes that "Malagasy slaves marooned less frequently during the late eighteenth century than either their reputation or their numbers might otherwise suggest" (1999, 42–43).

21 Larson (2000) also notes the importance of Malagasy women in trade and political negotiation with the French.

22 DMB 1022, no. 35 (January 1975), 70–72.

23 See in particular, the work of K. N. Chaudhuri (1985, 1990). On the long history of slavery and the slave trade in the Indian Ocean, see Harris 1971.

24 On slavery and the slave trade on Madagascar, see Larson 1997, 2000; Barendse 1995; Campbell 1989; Raison-Jourde 1997, Evers and Spindler 1995.

25 On the colonial and ethnographic construction of ethnicities in Madagascar and the notion of ethnic hierarchies, see the discussion by Albert Roca Alvarez (1995). On "Ambolambe," see Larson 1996, Deschamps 1960, and the 1777 Mayeur manuscript in the British Museum, titled "Voyage au pays d'Ancove autrement dit des Hovas ou Amboalambo." I am very grateful to Stephen Ellis for this last source.

26 This is Larson's argument (2000), but a similar argument was also made by Feely-Harnik (1991). The history and historicization of Malagasy burial practices is discussed in an illuminating way in Middleton 1999.

27 The importance of the history of slavery to any understanding of Malagasy identities and cultural practices is acknowledged by many of the contributors to the 1999 volume on Madagascar edited by Karen Middleton. See especially contributions by Evers and Graeber.

28 The most comprehensive study of this process in Africa is Lovejoy 2000.

29 The attitudes of Milbert and Bernardin de St. Pierre quoted earlier were greatly extended and expanded in the nineteenth century, when Madagascar became the focus for much ethnographic attention.

30 See Astuti's (1995) work on the Vezo, for example.

31 But see Larson for the changing meaning of *mainty* (2000, xix, 90–91).

32 Raymond Kent has argued that some of the earliest dynasties in Madagascar had African origins (1970), but his theory is contested.

33 On memory and slavery in Madagascar, see Larson 2000 and Graeber 1999.

34 On the Makua in Île de France, see Alpers 2001.

35 For example, in MNA: z2B/6: Journal de Police, 1790–1791.

36 MNA: z/2/B/6: Journal de Police, 1790–1791, entry for 14 November.

37 On Andrianampoinimerina, see Larson 2000, 41, quoting a thesis by Gilbert Ratsivalaka I have not been able to consult.

38 Roger Bastide (1978) made the same point in his study of the African religious heritage in Brazil.

39 See Lovejoy and Trotman 2002. Lovejoy and Trotman draw on earlier work on Virginia by Michael Sobel (1987).

40 Graeber 1999 discusses the relationship between slaves, loss of ancestors, and adoption of the "Vazimba" spirits.

41 My thanks to Dr. Tim Harper for pointing this out to me at an early stage in this project.

42 Congrégation de la Mission 1504, f. 216, Philippe Caulier to Archevêque de Paris, 20 July 1772.

43 Note that Michael Gomez (1998) takes a rather different view, for though he also cautions that *Bambara* became a generic term in the eighteenth century, he goes on to reconstruct a Bambara worldview and its survival into the new world.

44 On David, see his personnel record: AOM: E111.

45 See Governor Dumas's diary of 1768, AN: C/4/21. On Indian slaves more generally, see Carter 1988–1989; Allen 1999, 2002a; Napal 1965; and Reddi 2001. On Lascars, see also Ewald 2000.

46 This defense was clearly closely connected to French policy toward India. Dumas observed that "these Asians are connected by bonds of blood, of nationality and of religion to the peoples inhabiting the coasts of Coromandel, of Malabar and of Orissa, and asked whether it might not be impolitic to remove from those who come to Isle de France their freedom to practice their religious ceremonies." AN: c4/21.

47 I am very grateful to Professor Alpers for sharing the results of his work with me: Alpers 1997; 2000; 2003. See also recent work by Viyaya Teelock (1999a; 1999b).

48 For the early nineteenth century, however, we have the evidence of the 1823

Mauritius Slave Census, which lists a large number of ethnic groups comprising "Mozambiques." This evidence is reproduced in Alpers 2001, 119.

49 Congrégation de la Mission 1504, f. 171: Voyage des trois missionnaires (Gaudon, Monet et Trogueux) se rendant en Chine, 12 September 1732, Port Louis.

50 MNA: JB 26 Procédure Criminelle, 1777, contre Pèdre et Jouan: Empoisonnement.

51 MNA: JB 80 Procédure Criminelle, 1794, Tribunal d'Appel, 8 pluviôse, contre Cherubin.

52 See Rey (1992, 1557). Gomez (1998, 50) says that *gris-gris* comes from the Mande word *gerregerys* and means a harmful charm.

Chapter 5: A Baby in the Salt Pans: Mothering Slavery

1 MNA: JB30: Procédure Criminelle: 8 September 1778.

2 Barbé de Marbois was son of the duc de la Monnoye of Metz and advocate at the parlement of Metz. His brother was intendant of St. Domingue. He came to Île de France as a judge in 1777. In the interval he had engaged in commerce (to China and elsewhere) but "regretted" not using his talents as a lawyer (AOM: E16). Jean Pierre Aufray was born in Rennes in 1737 and arrived in the island around 1770. He was nominated as a "notaire du Roi" in 1773, *DMB*, no. 17 (October 1945): 536–537.

3 AOM: DPPC* GR 3080, Île de France, Greffes: Arrêts du Conseil Supérieur 1778–1780: 7 July 1778.

4 AOM: E33: Guillaume Blancheteste.

5 Indian slaves on Île de France were usually described as either "Malabar" (indicating southern Indian origins) or "Bengali." On the difficulties in determining the origins of these slaves, see Allen 2002a.

6 This may describe the symptoms of diphtheria.

7 Congrégation de la Mission 1504, Teste: Directoire des Paroisses de l'Isle de Bourbon pour l'Isle de France 1776. Priests complained that just about everyone felt themselves authorized to baptize a newborn baby whose life appeared to be in danger, and that midwives were particularly prone to this.

8 I discuss the position of "free black" women in more detail in chapter 9. See also Allen 2002b.

9 Chinese immigration into Mauritius is generally thought not to have begun until the nineteenth century; however, according to Anthoine Chelin (quoted in the *Gazette des Isles* 10–11 [1986]: 9), in 1760 a boat arrived from Batavia with 300 "Chinois" on board. The next year their wives arrived to join them. Note also that the Chinese are described as a "nation" as opposed to a "caste."

10 This is not quite the same as the Freudian term *family romance*, which has been applied illuminatingly by Lynn Hunt in her analysis of the French Revolution (Hunt 1992), and in a colonial version by Françoise Vergès (2000) in her account of métissage on La Réunion, but there are connections. I am referring here not to Revolutionary or Republican discourse, as Vergès does, but to the family discourses and realities of ancien régime slavery and colonialism. Like Vergès, I see much in this story that is suppressed, if not disavowed.

11   There were very few white women on the island, despite attempts to foster the colonist family. In 1776, there was a total of 6,386 whites, of whom only 651 were women. In the same year there were enumerated 593 white boys and 555 white girls. AOM: DPPC: G/1/473: Dépôt des Papiers publics des Colonies: État Civil: Recensement général de l'Isle de France, 1776.

12   Congrégation de la Mission 1504, Teste: Directoire des Paroisses de l'Isle de Bourbon pour L'Isle de France, 1763.

13   I have not found any complete figures for Christian conversion on the island in the archives of the Lazarist priests. The *Calendrier des Isles de France et de Bourbon*, however, recorded baptisms, marriages, and deaths. In 1774, 670 slaves were recorded as having been baptised in that year, and in 1780 the figure was 919.

14   For discussions of the construction of whiteness, see especially work by Ann Stoler (1991, 1995), Ware 1992, and Hall 1992;. In her discussion of Fanon's work, Diane Fuss refers to the "fantasy" of white, which is the "fantasy of escaping the exclusionary practices of psychical formation" (1995, 146). In other words, white simply *is*, whereas, in Fanon's words, "The Negro is comparison." See also Seshadri-Crooks 1998.

15   Here I am drawing on Bergner 1998, but also on discussions of Fanon's problematic views of masculinity and sexuality under colonialism. See Hall 1996.

16   bell hooks long ago challenged and modified this picture of black emasculation under slavery. The fact that male slaves were deprived of their patriarchal role, she argued, did not mean that they were deprived of their sexuality. Their sexuality, rather, became available for exploitation. See hooks 1981. Recent discussions of this theme have arisen in part out of a reevaluation of Fanon's account of masculinity under colonialism in *Black Skins, White Masks*. See in particular contributions by Stuart Hall, Kobena Mercer, bell hooks, and Lola Young in Read 1996.

17   This "economy of kinship" under slavery is discussed in Bergner 1998. See also Robert Shell's (1994) analysis of the slave family and patriarchy at the Cape.

18   Francoise Vergès discusses this in her account of métissage in La Réunion. "Thinking métissage," she argues (2000, 11), requires accepting genealogies (of slavery, rape, and violence).

19   This draws on recent work on the figure of the mother under slavery and colonialism, whom Fanon appears to "disavow." My formulation is somewhat different. I do not wish to generalize from it, but it does appear to have some plausibility in relation to the specific situation in eighteenth-century Île de France. See Bergner 1995; Abel, Christian, and Moglen 1997; and Young 1996. I discuss the issue of métissage in Île de France in more detail in chapter 9.

20   I have no figures for the incidence of this. Some cases were reported, and I refer to these, but more, presumably, went unreported.

21   MNA: OA 69: Procureur-Général: Régistre pour la consignation de divers plaintes et déclarations, 16 December 1772–17 May 1794, 19 April 1776.

22   MNA: OA 69: Procureur-Général: Régistre pour la consignation de divers plaintes et déclarations, December 1772–17 May 1794, 4 October 1775.

23   MNA: OA 69: 13 July 1777.

24 MNA: Z2B/2: Bureau de Police, Journal pour la consignation des rapports de police, 15 April 1785–31 March 1787.

25 MNA: Z2B/6: 17 November 1790.

26 MNA: JB 50: Procédure Criminelle, 1785, 24 September 1785.

27 MNA: Z2/B/2: 4 August 1776.

28 MNA: Z2/B/2: 28 December 1775.

29 Census data for the eighteenth century have been carefully analyzed by both Richard Allen (1999) and Baker and Corne (1982). They draw on d'Unienville (1885–1886) and the analysis of Kuczynski (1949). I have also consulted the following archival sources: AOM: DPPC: G/1/473: État Civil: recensement général de l'Isle de France 1776; AOM: DPPC: G/1/505: Île de France: Recensements et pièces diverses, 1785; AOM: DPPC: G/1/505: Recensements, Île de France; AOM: DPPC: G/1/475: Île de France, Recensement 1788; AOM: DPPC: Île de France, Recensement, 1780. AN: C/4/15: Corréspondence: Depouillement du Recensement Général de l'Isle de France.

30 This is the argument made by North-Coombes (1978, 92–93).

31 See Moitt's discussion of slave women and reproduction in the French Antilles in the same period (2001, chapter 5).

32 AN: C4/22: Correspondance, 1768.

33 AN:C4/16: Correspondance, 1766, 20 April, letter from M. Le Borgne to M. Anthoine.

34 This was Jean-Barthelemy Dazille, author of *Observations sur les maladies des nègres: Leurs causes, traitemens et les moyens de les prévenir* (1776) and *Observations Générales sur les Maladies des Climats Chauds, leurs causes, leur traitement et les moyens de les prévenir* (Paris, 1785). For a fuller discussion of medical practice on Isle de France, see chapter 3 and Vaughan 2000.

35 AOM: DPPC: G/1/473.

36 AN: C4/15 Correspondance: Mémoire dated 1763.

37 MNA: OA3: Intendant: Documents concernant les Forges de Mon Desir 1768–1789, list of slaves at sale of Forges to the king, 1775.

38 This phenonenom is also described by Eugene Genovese (1975, 482).

39 This name may indicate Malagasy or Indian rather than West African origin.

40 MNA: OA 127: Jardin du Roi: Documents concernant Monplaisir, 1772–1806. Liste des noirs de l'habitation de Monplaisir, 1772.

41 AN: C4/15: Correspondance: Mémoire dated May 1763.

42 MNA: Z2B/6: Journal de Police, 1 juillet–29 janvier 1791.

43 A somewhat later example of this view is that of J. Arago (1817–1820), an apologist for the slave regime of what was by then, British Mauritius: "Abortion is frequent among the negro women, because, concealing their pregnancy for as long as possible, lest they should be separated from the great gang of negroes and be sent under the inspection of overseers to work in the garden, or to make sacks, baskets and mats, they continue to labor in the fields and meet with serious accidents, of which even their owners are not apprized. Their nocturnal excursions, their dances, from which, in spite of pregnancy, they will not abstain, and their un-

bounded licentiousness, all contribute greatly to the frequent miscarriages which occur in most establishments. . . . To all these causes must be ascribed the almost general aversion of the negresses from the performance of the duties of maternity, which induces them to take infusions of savin, and other pernicious plants" (1823, 142). Women slaves in the French Antilles were also frequently accused of deliberately aborting their babies; see Moitt 2001, 93. Induced abortion and infanticide among slaves have sometimes been interpreted as forms of "gynaecological resistance" (Bush 1993). See also the discussion of this issue in Lovejoy and Trotman 2002, 81.

44 Congrégation de la Mission 1504, f. 141, Voyage des trois missionaires se rendant en Chine.

45 There is good reason to believe that many slave women did not voluntarily become maroons but were abducted. However, it was clearly in their interest, once captured, to present themselves as victims.

46 MNA: JB4: Procédure Criminelle, 1741–1746, 9 September 1746.

47 MNA: JB6: Procédure Criminelle, 1750–1751.

48 On Bernardin de St. Pierre's career as a botanist, see Grove 1995. His personnel file (AOM: E363) contains correspondence relating to his brother, who in the 1780s was imprisoned in the Bastille and who went mad. See also the 1996 study by Lieve Spaas of correspondence between him and his sister Catherine.

49 At this time the term *creole* referred to persons of French origin born on the island. In the second half of the nineteenth century the use of the term would shift, and it came to refer to persons of mixed race born on the island.

50 Pierre Marie Le Normand was a military man, *capitaine des milices* on the island from 1750s until his retirement in 1782. He had served in India and was a member of the Colonial Assembly. AOM: E278.

51 Milbert was explicit on this point: "Un grand nombre de mes lecteurs verra sans doute avec curiosité et attendrissment les montagnes de Trois Mamelles, l'eglise des Pamplemousses, et les autres sites que la plume élégante de Bernardin de St. Pierre, non moins fidèle, mais plus seduisante que nos crayons, a gravés dans la mémoire de tous lecteurs sensibles" (1812, 1:xii).

52 On the complex and sometimes contradictory representations of the creole in the Mascarenes, see Racault (1996), whose argument is similar to my own.

53 In 1788 there was a total of 4,457 whites on the island, of whom 1,782 were men, 836 women, 948 boys, and 891 girls. According to the same census, there were 2,456 "gens libres" and 37,915 slaves. AOM: G1/505, no. 13b: Extrait des recensements des Isles de France et de Bourbon.

54 AOM: E124: Desranges de Richeteau, Guillaume.

55 AOM: E224: Horque, Claude.

56 MNA: JB 30: Procédure Criminelle, 1778, case 14, 27 November 1778.

57 AOM: DPPC: G/1/473: Recensement général de l'Isle de France, 1776, Moka district.

58 MNA: OA 85: Jurisdiction Royale, Bureau de Police: Livre pour servir à l'enregistrement de divers ordres, lettres et autres pièces ayant trait aux fonctions de police, 20 November 1779–14 April 1787.

59 MNA: Z2/B/2 Bureau de Police: 12 January 1776.

60 MNA: JB 70: Procédure Criminelle: Case against Sophie et Carton" 30 December 1790.

61 MNA: OA 57: Affranchissements: 25 October 1781, Henriette, négresse creole.

62 On wet nursing in a colonial context, see Stoler 1995, chapter 5, and on wet nursing by slaves at the Cape, see Shell 1994, 304–314.

63 See Butler's (1997) discussion of the Hegelian dialectic and Patterson's (1982) analysis of its relationship to the "real" social relations of slavery.

64 On the various meanings of bodily fluids in African societies, see, for example, Weiss 1998; White 1990, Hunt 1999, and comparative anthropological discussion in Boddy 1998.

65 The phrase is Kaja Silverman's (1992, 47). She argues that the ideological alignment of masculinity with mastery makes it particularly vulnerable.

Chapter 6: Love in the Torrid Zone

1 Jean Lousteau was clerk to the Conseil Supérieur from 1775 to 1791. See AOM: E 292. Some of the records of his legal practice are contained in AOM: NOT MAUR 393.

2 MNA: JB 45: Procédure Criminelle, 1785.

3 The term *Topas* usually referred to a group from southern India of mixed Portuguese and Tamil origin, as discussed in chapter 4.

4 MNA: JB 20: Procédure Criminelle, 1774.

5 This area of Port Louis (which still exists) was originally the home of Wolof West African slaves owned by the king.

6 If this is true, it implies that the initial description of him as a créol was incorrect.

7 AN: SOM NOT, BOB 143, Touraille, 16 January 1789. On property ownership among free women of color, see chapter 9 and Allen 2002b.

8 It is unclear whether any equivalent shift took place in the terminology applied to women. My impression is that it did not: *négresses* remained *négresses.*

9 On homosexuality in France, see Maccubbin 1987; Trumbach 1987; Rey 1980, 1987; and Merrick and Ragan 1996.

10 On sodomy, George Rousseau (1987) makes the important point that in the eighteenth century a "sodomite" was a penetrator of either sex. Of particular relevance to Île de France was the association of sodomy with the navy and with piratic communities.

11 I am very grateful to Dr. Colin Lucas of the University of Oxford for pointing this out to me.

12 Dr. Polly O'Hanlon has generously shared and discussed her work with me.

13 For a thorough examination of Foucault's thesis on bourgeois sexuality and its relationship (or nonrelationship) to colonial realities, see Stoler 1995.

14 Criminal cases and wills of free blacks from this period indicate the importance of clothing to people at all levels of Île de France society.

15 There appear to have been no sumptuary laws enacted on Île de France (as there

were in other parts of the slave world in this period). However, the wearing of shoes by slaves was regarded with deep hostility and suspicion by whites.

16 These local discourses clearly are part of larger eighteenth-century debates—on the "luxury trade," for example, on the nature of the "exotic," and on nature, sexuality, and gender. See Rousseau and Porter 1989, 1990; Laqueur 1990; Brewer and Porter 1993; and Outram 1995.

17 Congrégation de la Mission: 1504, Jean Baptiste Borthon and Gabriel Igou to Paris, 10 November 1728.

18 Congrégation de la Mission: 1504, Father Teste to Paris, 1 March 1764.

19 Congrégation de la Mission: 1504, Father Philippe Caulier to M. Archevêque de Paris, 20 July 1772.

20 Congrégation de la Mission: 1504, Father Borgne to Paris, 24 September 1759.

21 See Journel 1940: for example, Mme. Journel's account of the exploits of André Demol (42–43).

22 Moreau de St. Méry was from St. Domingue; see Dayan 1998. I discuss his views in chapter 9.

23 AN: F3/48: Collection Moreau de St. Méry: Réflexions sur les colonies asiatiques vers 1780, Isle de France.

24 AN: C4/44: M. Maillart Dumesle, intendant to Ministère de la Marine, 30 June 1777.

25 AN: C4/16: 12 April 1766.

26 On anxieties about social inequalities in marriage, see Mousnier 1979, 59.

27 AOM: E 352: Rivaltz de St. Anthoine, conseiller au Conseil Supérieur, 1768–1781.

28 MNA: OA 69: Procureur Général: Régistre pour la consignation de diverses plaintes et déclarations, 16 December 1772–17 May 1794, entry for 25 April 1781.

29 AOM: E 280: Jacques Leroux de Kermoseven, described as a proprietor, merchant, and a shipowner of Île de France and Madagascar. He had at one time more than six hundred slaves. During the colony's regular food shortages, he often came to the rescue of the government by selling them livestock.

30 Congrégation de la Mission: 1504, Father Teste to Paris, 1764.

31 Though in general, as we have seen, there were many more male slaves than women on the island. Congrégation de la Mission: 1504, Father Criais to Paris, 28 January 1742.

32 Congrégation de la Mission: 1504, Caulier, 1772.

33 Congrégation de la Mission: 1504, "Petit Catéchisme de l'Isle Bourbon tourné au style des esclaves nègres," written by Father Caulier, n.d., probably from the 1760s or 1770s. I came across this important document in the archives of the Congréga- tion de la Mission in Paris. It has been transcribed and analyzed by Philip Baker, of the School of Oriental and African Studies, University of London, to whom I am very grateful. This is my own translation.

34 For maroons in the French Antilles in this period, see Debbasch 1961. On ma- roons more generally, see Heuman 1986 and Price 1979. For women maroons in the French Antilles, see Moitt 1996; 2001, chapter 7. Work on the Caribbean by Agorsah (1994) and others aims to recover a maroon "heritage." This would be a

far less plausible exercise in Mauritius, where large-scale maroon communities did not exist. Allen 1999 provides the best analysis of the extent and nature of maronnage on Île de France. See also Nagapen 1999.

35 New Year was a much-celebrated holiday for slaves and, judging from the cases I have read, many took the opportunity to maroon around this time.

36 MNA: JB 45: Procédure Criminelle: Case of Rose, 18 May 1785.

37 MNA: Z2B/6: Journal de Police, 1 July 1790–29 July 1791.

38 MNA: Z2B/2: Journal de Police, 1 January 1776.

39 MNA: JB 4: Procédure Criminelle, 1741–1746, Case against Monique, Marie, and Louison, 9 September 1746.

40 According to Le Clézio and Le Clézio (1990, 82), there is a forest in southwestern Mauritius that takes its name from a maroon, Machabe.

41 De Ternay was governor between August 1772 and December 1776.

42 The cruelty of a slave "commander" is frequently cited as the precipitating factor in a case of maronnage. Only larger slave holders would have had slave commanders.

43 From this and other documentary evidence it would appear that this became the normal greeting among slaves, irrespective of their ethnic origins. See chapter 8 on language.

44 In all the excerpts from original court cases, I have attempted to transcribe these as they were written—this sometimes means without accents. Written French on Île de France at this time was unstable, as we shall see in chapter 8.

Chapter 7: Reputation, Recognition, and Race

1 MNA: Z2B/6: Journal de Police, 1 juillet 1790–29 janvier 1791, entry for 8 January 1791. A M. Commarond is mentioned in chapter 8 as a member of the "house of gossip," a "crazy tavern keeper."

2 On the issue of punishment, honor, and the law, see the work on Cape Colony by John Edwin Mason (1990), Wayne Dooling (1992), Robert Ross (1999) and John Iliffe (2004).

3 See, among others, the work of Philip Morgan (1998, 284–296). Morgan draws on journals and letters of slave owners; we have only one or two equivalent sources for Île de France. Paternalism in North America is in part associated with the rise of evangelicalism—which was not, of course, a factor on Île de France. How far the colonists of Île de France were influenced by the kind of sentimental humanitarianism emanating from writers like Bernardin de St. Pierre is also hard to know.

4 It would be possible to argue that Île de France society fell under Patterson's definition of a slave-owning society in which almost all free persons were slave masters. In this case, he argues, there is a crisis of "recognition" within the slave-owning class, one result of which can be that masters abandon all claims to honor and recognize that slavery is degrading to themselves (Patterson 1982, 98).

5 AOM: E357/bis: Rostaing, Philippe Joseph, Comte de. See also AN 100/AP/2: Philippe Joseph, Comte de Rostaing.

6 Details of the dispute are contained in AOM: E292.

7 This case can be found in JB 24: Procédure Criminelle, 1776.

8 AOM: E 340: Pourcher de la Serré: Mémoire pour être presenté à Monsiegneur Le Marquis de Castres par Madame Lancel, veuve de la Serré. Versailles, 19 January 1785.

9 A blow-by-blow account of this can be found in AN C4/21: Île de France, Correspondance Générale: Journal de M. Dumas, 1768, and AN C4/22: Île de France, Correspondance Générale, M. Poivre, Intendant, 1768.

10 AOM: E352: Rivaltz de St. Anthoine, conseiller au Conseil Supérieur, Île de France, 1768–1781.

11 MNA: JB 23: Procédure Criminelle, 1774.

12 MNA: JB 20: Procédure Criminelle, 1774.

13 MNA: JB 52: Procédure Criminelle, 1787 and MNA: OB 48: Jurisdiction Royale: Régistre des sentences en matière criminelle, 16 June 1783–22 October 1788.

14 For a full discussion of codes of male honor in France at this time, see Nye 1993.

15 On honor in Africa, see Iliffe 2004. On issues of honor within the social and political systems of Madagascar and their relationship to servitude, see Larson 2000.

16 MNA: JB 29: Procédure Criminelle, 1777–1778: 13 September 1777, La Poëze and Joseph.

17 For the question of translation and interpretation of the slave's words, see my discussion in the following chapter. My thanks to Philip Baker for checking and correcting my translations.

18 The correspondence concerning Giraud between the Ministère de la Marine (the duc de Praslin) and the intendant of Île de France, Maillart Dumesle, is found in AN: C4/44: Île de France: Correspondance: M. Maillart Dumesle, Intendant, 1777, and in MNA: OA 10B. The records of Giraud's trial are in MNA: JB 26: Procédure Criminelle, 1777.

19 AOM: E190: Denis-Nicolas Foucault. Foucault was born in Quebec in 1723, the son of François Foucault, President of the Conseil Supérieur of Quebec. He had begun working as an *écrivain* for the Bureau de la Marine in Canada, rising to commissaire de la marine and then ordonnateur in Louisiana and in Pondichéry, before becoming intendant of Île de France. He died in Tours, France, in 1807. He was for a time implicated in a rebellion of habitants in Louisiana and was imprisoned in the Bastille in 1770.

20 I can find no evidence of Foucault having spent any time in Martinique, so presumably he and Giraud first met in Paris.

21 Though in St. Domingue this was a cause of much hostility on the part of white colonists.

22 See my review of David Macey's biography of Frantz Fanon (Vaughan 2001).

23 See Homi Bhabha's foreword to the 1986 edition of *Black Skins, White Masks* (1986); see also the critique of Bhabha's interpretation by Henry Louis Gates (1991), and Stuart Hall's brilliant discussion of all of this in Hall 1996.

24 This argument is discussed in an illuminating way by Diane Fuss (1995, 143).

25 See Judith Butler's recent discussion (2000) of *Antigone*, which has many resonances with the story of Giraud.

26 This echoes Kaja Silverman's (1992) argument on masculinity as "masquerade."

Chapter 8: Speaking Slavery: Language and Loss

1 MNA: Procédure Criminelle: JB 29, 1777, discussed in chapter 7.

2 Chaudenson's *Textes Creoles Anciens* is critiqued in Corne 1983. My own independent transcription of the dialogue in this court case is rather different—lacking some of the accents and cedillas included in Chaudenson's. My thanks again to Philip Baker for translations.

3 On French criminal procedure and the texts which it produced, see Andrews 1994. Roberts 1990 is an interesting discussion of the use of court testimony in colonial French West Africa. Mason 1990 discusses court testimony and slavery in the rather different legal context of the Dutch Cape.

4 For other discussions of Mauritian creole and the linguistic situation in Mauritius, see Baker 1972, Baggioni and de Robillard 1990, Holm 1989, Dinan 1986, and Moorghen 1982.

5 On the Fon language in the context of slavery in Brazil, see Yai 2000.

6 This is the term used for a "target language" by Jacques Derrida in his account of monolingualism (1998, 60).

7 This "Afrogenetic" theory is applied more widely to the study of language in the former slave world. See Philip Morgan's 1998 discussion as it relates to the southern United States.

8 See Corne's critique of Chaudenson and the latter's response in Corne 1983.

9 My interpretation of the contemporary situation in Mauritius, and the role of language within it, is very different to that of Françoise Lionnet, who, in a comparison between Mauritius and La Réunion (1993), argues that linguistic plurality in Mauritius is evidence of genuine "pluriculturalism," mutual respect, and tolerance.

10 Stephan Palmié asks a similar question in his critique of the literature on creolization (2002b).

11 As Morgan (1998, 563) points out, many linguists believe that there are universal human grammars found in all languages.

12 This is my reading of the account written in 1755 by the missionary Father Savary, who stopped on the island on his way to China. He described the appalling conditions in the hospital, which was full of sick and dying soldiers and sailors. What made their condition all the more pitiable, he wrote, was their inability to understand the French language and therefore their inaccessibility to spiritual "aid." Some apparently understood German, since another priest was able to conduct confession in that language. Wellcome Library, London, MS 6065, SAVARY, F. 1755, Journal du Voyage de France en Chine, 39–40.

13 For accounts of linguistic creolization, see Bickerton 1975, Valdman 1977, Chaudenson 1979, and Byrne and Holm 1993. For a more socially based account, see

contributions in Le Page and Tabouret-Keller 1985. Many linguists now eschew evolutionist accounts and argue for a much more flexible view of the evolution of these languages.

14 Baissac (1831–1892) taught at the Collège Royale at Curepipe.

15 The central texts of the *créolité* movement are Bernabé, Chamoiseau, and Confiant, *Éloge de la Créolité* (1993) and Glissant's *Le discours antillais* (1981). There is now a large literature on the *créolité* movement and on cultural and linguistic creolization in the Caribbean. See in particular Britton 1999, Condé and Cottenot-Hage 1995, Balutansky and Sourieau 1998, and Burton 1997. The influence of *créolité* has been felt in the study of the history, culture, and society of La Réunion, particularly in the work of Francoise Vergès (1995; 1996; 1999), but is much less evident in the literature on Mauritius, but see Lionnet (1993).

16 Derrida argues rather differently that though the *I* is important, it can be uttered in different ways, depending on the language (1998, 28).

17 Though we should remember that such "blanking out" is not the only response to trauma—in some cases a trauma results in an excess of memory: Antze and Lambek 1996, Kirmayer 1996.

18 Recent work on the literature of the Middle Passage also traces the route from trauma to imaginative reconstruction (Diedrich, Gates, and Pedersen 1999).

19 This phenomenon is described for the Caribbean in the same period in Burton 1997. See also Britton's 1999 analysis of Glissant's novels.

20 *Sega* derives from a Bantu language root meaning "to play," and varieties of this dance form are to be found around the southwest Indian ocean; see Lee 1990.

21 On riddling, see contributions in Hasan-Rokem and Shulman 1996; Haring 1974, 1985; Blacking 1961; and Finegan 1970. Baker 2003 traces the origins of Mauritian riddles.

22 These are, of course, Freudian terms referring to processes within the unconscious: Laplanche and Pontalis 1973, 82–83, 121–123. Freud developed both concepts largely in relation to dreams.

23 Though relationships between the priests and officials did improve, there is still plenty of evidence of conflict in the latter part of the century. See AOM: F/5a/8: Isles de France et de Bourbon, Missions et Cultes Religieux 1674–1775, in which it is clear that priests were involved in the dispute between Poivre and Dumas in the 1760s; AOM: F/5a/10: Isles de France et de Bourbon et Madagascar: Missions et Cultes Religieux, 1783–1808. On the beginnings of Christianity on Île de France, see also Moutou 1996, Ly-Tio-Fane Pineo 1993, and Mamet 1972.

24 AOM: F/5a/11: Madagascar, Bourbon et Isle de France: Missions, Cultes Religieux, 1775–1782, letter from Souillac and Foucault, Port Louis, 28 February 1780.

25 On religion in the Code Noir, see Noel n.d., Sala-Molins 1987, and Blackburn 1997.

26 More material exists for the Catholic missions to slaves in the Antilles, as outlined in Sue Peabody's recent article (2002). The real impact of popular Catholicism on Mauritius would come in the post-Emancipation period with the work of the legendary Père Laval (Michel 1988).

27 Caulier was born in Liège in 1723 and spent from 1749 to 1771 on the islands. He died in Paris in 1795. In 1785 he published a catechism in the Malagasy language and was at work on a dictionary of the Malagasy language, which was destroyed during the Revolution when the house of St. Lazare in Paris was pillaged.

28 Congrégation de la Mission 1504, Caulier to Archevêque de Paris, 20 juillet 1772.

29 Congrégation de la Mission 1504, Directoire des Paroisses de L'Isle de Bourbon pour L'Isle de France, 1 October 1763.

30 Peabody (2002, 60–61) notes similar practices in the mission of mid-seventeenth-century Jesuits and Dominicans in the Antilles, where missionaries also created a creole version of the Passion according to Saint John.

31 Congrégation de la Mission 1504, Caulier to Archevêque de Paris, 20 juillet 1772.

32 Congrégation de la Mission 1504, Directoire des Paroisses de l'Isle de Bourbon pour l'Isle de France, 1 October 1763.

33 Congrégation de la Mission 1504, Catechisme abregé en la langue de Madagascar pour instruire sommairement ces peuples, les inviter et les diposer au Baptême (written in 1770s, but published in 1785); and Petit catechisme de L'Île de Bourbon tourné au style des Esclaves Nègres, and Profession de Foy, en jargon des esclaves nègres. This is not dated, but appears was probably written in the 1770s. The latter two items are not mentioned by Nagapen in his 1994 history of the catechism on Mauritius. My thanks to Philip Baker for transcribing and translating this last two documents.

34 This was not, of course, true. Slaves came from a variety of religious cultures, but the missionaries did not recognize "paganism" as a form of religious belief. In addition, a minority of slaves were Christians from southern India, and a larger minority were Muslims.

35 John Thornton (1998) has described the implantation of Catholicism in the Kongo people, for example. It is possible that some of the West African slaves who reached Île de France were Christianized, though we have no direct evidence for this, and the Congo was not a known source of slaves in Île de France.

36 The comparative literature on religion in the slave world is now very large. Recent studies include Sandra Greene's 2000 study of Yoruba culture and religion under slavery, George Brandon's 1993 study of Santeria in Cuba, and Maureen Warner-Lewis's 2000 study of religious plurality among slaves in Trinidad. For a classic account of slave religious beliefs in the American plantation system, see Genovese 1975. As Peabody (2002) points out, until now little attention has been paid to slaves' appropriation and transformation of Catholicism in the French colonies of the New World, though Debien (1974) discussed religion in his study of slaves in the Antilles, and earlier works also exist, especially for St. Domingue. For an important critical discussion of the literature of slavery and religion see Palmié 2002a, 2002b.

37 This would become yet more evident in the nineteenth century, during the mission of Père Laval. Caulier complained that though the slaves confessed readily to their sins, such confessions were often "routine" and "without consequence" and had to be regarded as the confessions of "children." He also argued that virtually all slaves, if

able, asked for a confession when they were close to death: Congrégation de la Mission 1504, Caulier to l'Archevêque de Paris, 12 November 1772.

38   Congrégation de la Mission 1504, Teste, Directoire . . . 1 October 1763.

39   Congrégation de la Mission 1504, Caulier 1772.

40   Congrégation de la Mission 1504, Teste, Directoire . . . 1 October 1763.

41   Congrégation de la Mission 1505, 1787, copy of Lettres Patentes du Roi.

42   Congrégation de la Mission 1504, Teste, Directoire . . . 1 October 1763.

43   Olivier Caudron (1996), however, argues that the percentage of books circulating on Île de France in this period was "respectable," and possibly greater than in many towns in France at the time. He has surveyed wills for their library contents. I have only one example (from a will) of the contents of a personal library. André de Fleury, a colonel employed in Île de France, died of "consumption" on his way back to France in 1782, in possession of the following works:

> 6 vols. of history of philosophy
>
> 2 vols. on wars in India
>
> 1 volume on philosophical researches
>
> 1 volume essay on India
>
> 2 vols. of la Politique Naturel
>
> 2 vols. by M. Montcrieff
>
> 2 vols. Caractères a la Bruyère
>
> 1 small Royal Almanac
>
> 3 vols. of Etat Militaire
>
> 1 vol. romance by M. Berquin
>
> 1 vol.—ordonnance des Dragons
>
> 1 vol.—works of Montcrieff
>
> 1 vol.—German grammar
>
> 1 vol.—"homme morale"
>
> 1 vol.—cavalry exercises
>
> 1 vol.—voyage of Ch.Chardin
>
> 1 vol.—History of Persia
>
> 1 vol.—works of an unknown
>
> 2 vols.—leisure of a soldier
>
> 2 vols.—Ordonnance of the King and of the Marine.

AOM: E 185: De Fleury, b. 1750, d. 1782.

44   On the relationship between oral and written forms in colonial India, see the very interesting work of Ajay Skaria (1996). See also de Certeau 1984.

45   The question of the rendering of creole into a written form is discussed by Antillean intellectuals and writers: Metellus 1998; De Souza 1995. It is also a central issue in Patrick Chamoiseau's novels, particularly *Texaco* (1997). Chamoiseau writes in different registers of creole and explores the relationship between writing and memory.

46   MNA: Z2B/3: Jurisdiction Royale, Régistre pour l'enregistrement des declarations de filouteries, éscroqueries, et autres délits semblables et les contraventions découvertes par les inspecteurs et les gardes de police, 31 October 1779–1 April 1784.

47   MNA: Z2B/6: Journal de Police, 1 juillet, 1790–29 January 1791, Observations de Commissaire Brun à la Municipalité, 12 November 1790.

48   MNA: OA 85: Jurisdiction Royale: Livre pour servir à l'enregistrement de divers ordres, lettres et autres pièces ayant trait aux fonctions de police, 20 November 1779–14 April 1787, entry for 24 December 1779.

49   MNA: OA 85: Entry for 16 février 1787.

50   Entry for Laglaine in *DMB*, no. 19 (June 1946): 589.

51   On masquerade and carnival in slavery and postslavery Caribbean societies, see especially Burton 1997.

52   MNA: JB 30: Procédure Criminelle, 1778.

53   MNA: JB 22: Procédure Criminelle, 1775. This genre of satire was also common in France at this time; see Darnton 1997.

54   Maillart Dumesle was the intendant.

55   MNA: E72: Gouvernement Republicain. Directoire: Régistre des Délibérations, 12 February 1792–10 September 1792, *Séance* 142, 8 June 1792.

56   My thanks to Pavi Ramhota of the Mahatma Gandhi Institute for introducing me to this informant and for conducting the interview with me.

Chapter 9: *Métissage and Revolution*

1   On François Letimié (or Letimier), see d'Unienville 1989, 241–242.

2   MNA: E 77: Directoire 1793–1794: Séance 443, 21/12/93.

3   MNA: JB 70: Procédure Criminelle, 1791, case against Jean Toinette.

4   My account of Revolutionary events on Île de France relies heavily on d'Unienville's three-volume work (1975, 1982, 1989), on Pitot 1899, and on consultation of archival documents. See also the volume edited by Bissoondoyal and Sibartie (1989). On the impact of the Revolution on the Indian Ocean region, see the volume edited by Wanquet and Jullien (1996), and for La Réunion, see Wanquet's exhaustive 1984 study. On the Revolution and French colonies in general, see Bénot 1988.

5   Thomas de Conway came from an Irish background, joined the Regiment of Anjou in 1778, and became colonel in the Regiment of Pondichéry in 1781. He was appointed as governor general of all French establishments east of the Cape in 1789 and arrived on Île de France in November of that year. AOM: E90.

6   AN: C4/107: Le Boucher to Ministère de la Marine, 12 August 1792.

7   Rousseau's *Considerations sur le Gouvernement de Pologne*, cited in l'Assemblée Coloniale, 3 May 1796: AN: C4/110.

8   For a rare personalized account of this event, see the journals of Mme. Journel (Journel 1940).

9   The descriptions of these festivals as celebrated in the island come from Pitot 1899. On the Festivals of the Revolution, see Ozouf 1988.

10   The contradictions of revolutionary ideology are explored for the neighboring island of La Réunion in Vergès 1999.

11   On Pondichéry, see Dominique Taffin's 1996 account. On the Antilles, see Butel

2002, Chauleau 1989, and Martin and Yacou 1989. On St. Domingue in particular, see Pluchon 1989.

12 This unstable terminology was also evident in France at this period; see Boulle 1996 and Peabody 1996.

13 See Debbasch 1967.

14 AN: C4/16: 20 August 1766.

15 MNA: JK 10: Insinuations: 10 September 1793. This issue of ethnic designation among free blacks is also discussed by Richard Allen (2002b).

16 MNA: B1A/A31/22: Plan de la Ville de Port Louis dans l'Île de France.

17 Richard Allen is similarly tentative, but also comes to this conclusion in Allen (2002b).

18 AN: C4/15: Mémoire of M. Courcy, 1764.

19 AN: F3/49: Collection M. de St. Méry: M. Houbert, 6 November 1785. The use of gens de couleur in the militia was a contentious issue in the French Antilles.

20 MNA: JS1: Tribunaux de paix, Port Louis: Sentences civiles, 1791–1792.

21 Presumably *bougresse*, slang for "woman."

22 Though Brizard clearly considered this insulting, in the creole language it would have been quite standard, and not an indication of lack of respect.

23 AN: C4/110: 10 fructidor An 4: General Magallon to Directoire Executif re. Isles de France et de Bourbon.

24 AN: F3/48: Moreau de St. Méry: Réflexions (vers 1780). On Moreau de St. Méry, see Benot 1989 and also the discussion of his thought in Dayan's 1998 book on Haiti.

25 AN: C4/106: 1792, Extrait des instructions aux deputés.

26 AN: C4/111: 10 fructidor An 4: General Magallon to Directoire Executif.

27 MNA: JB 74: Procédure Criminelle, 1792.

28 MNA: A39: Affranchissements, Port Louis 1796–1800, 12 August 1793.

29 MNA: A39: Affranchissements, Port Louis 1796–1800, 19 October 1793.

30 MNA: A39: Affranchissements, Port Louis 1796–1800, 29 October 1793.

31 MNA: A39: Affranchissements, Port Louis 1796–1800, 19 Messidor An 2.

32 MNA: JK10: Insinuations 1792–1794, 23 May 1792.

33 AN: C4/110: Motifs de l'arrêté de l'Assemblée Coloniale du 24 ventôse . . .

34 AN: C4/110: Motifs de l'arrêté de l'Assemblée Coloniale du 24 ventôse . . .

Chapter 10: Sugar and Abolition

1 Quoted in Barker 1996, 57–58. I draw heavily here on Anthony Barker's insightful study on slavery and antislavery in Mauritius at the beginning of the nineteenth century.

2 For an account of the flight of one family, see Journel 1940.

3 Butel 1996; see also Eric Saugera's 1996 work on French involvement in the East African slave trade.

4 This was a wider phenomenon, of course, as Pierre Boulle has demonstrated (1988), and, as Sue Peabody has shown (1996), has pre-Revolutionary antecedents.

5   Satyendra Peerthum is completing a master's thesis in history at the University of Cape Town, South Africa.

6   Île Bourbon was returned to the French in 1814.

7   This particularly tragic group is the subject of ongoing study by Marina Carter (see Carter 1998b).

8   An arpent equals 1.043 acres.

9   There is a rich historiography of indentured labor in Mauritius, which has received a great deal more attention than the history of slavery, in part because of the sponsorship afforded by the government of India through the Mahatma Gandhi Institute in Mauritius. In particular, see the many works on this subject by Marina Carter (1992, 1993, 1994, 1995, 1996) that of Huguette Ly-Tio-Fane Pineo (1984), and the earlier work of K. Hazareesingh (1975), in addition to that of Richard Allen (1999).

10   For the comparative history of the creation of a bourgeois family form in the colonial world, see the work of Ann Stoler (1991, 1995).

11   See chapter 4 above. There is, however, scope for a great deal more work on religious practice in Mauritius, particularly for the nineteenth century.

12   On this issue, see also Vijaya Teelock's discussion of the role of slavery in the formation of Creole identity on Mauritius (1999b).

13   De Froberville's work was conducted well after the abolition of slavery and decades after the official ending of the slave trade. It appears, however, that even in the mid–nineteenth century, East Africans were being imported into the Mascarene islands under the guise of being freely recruited—but in practice as forced migrants (see Alpers 2001, 136; Ly-Tio-Fane Pineo 1980).

14   For an exploration of this issue in relation to neighboring Réunion, see Vergès 1999.

15   Allen 1999, 132–133. Allen's own account is rather contradictory on this point.

16   In 1838 there were 37,865 persons of free status, 53,220 apprentices, and 23,909 Indian indentured laborers in the colony (Kuczynski 1949, 774).

17   From Ollier's editorial in *La Sentinelle*, 3 June 1843, quoted in Prosper 1995, 76. Emphases in original.

18   One exception is Vijaya Teelock's article on Creole identity (1999b).

19   Further work on the mission of Père Laval among ex-apprentices would undoubtedly illuminate important aspects of this history. Existing work includes Michel 1972; Michel 1988; and Mamet 1972.

20   See Le Brun quoted in Barker 1999, 140.

21   Hervé Charles Gustave du Hecquet, comte de Rauville (1858–1935): DMB, no. 9 (May 1943): 282–283.

Works Cited

ARCHIVAL SOURCES

Archives Nationales, Paris (AN)

(note: these documents were consulted in Paris but are now housed in the Archives d'Outre-Mer, Aix-en-Provence)

FOND DES COLONIES: C SERIES:
CORRESPONDANCE GÉNÉRALE DE L'ISLE DE FRANCE

C4/1 Correspondance Générale, 1714–1732

C4/86 Correspondance Générale (complementary series), 1731

C4/87 Correspondance Générale (complementary series), 1760

C4/107 Correspondance Générale, 1792

C4/110 Correspondance Générale, 1795–1796

C4/111 Correspondance Générale, 1796–1797

C4/106 Correspondance Générale, 1792

C4/7 Correspondance Générale, 1751–1753

C4/9 Correspondance Générale, 1755–1757

C4/10 Correspondance Générale, 1758

C4/15 Correspondance Générale, 1763–1765

C4/16 Correspondance Générale, 1766

C4/21 Correspondance Générale, 1768

C4/22 Correspondance Générale, 1768

C4/44 Correspondance Générale, 1777

Congrégation de la Mission (Rue du Sèvres, Paris)

Recueil 1504, Bourbon, 1732–1800

Archives d'Outre-Mer, Aix-en-Provence (AOM)

COLLECTION MOREAU DE ST. MÉRY:
F3/48 Reflexions sur les colonies Asiatiques (vers 1780)
F3/49 Recueil des documents concernant l'Île de France, 1654–1806

DÉPÔT DES FORTIFICATIONS COLONIALES (DFC):
DFC 1V, Mémoires/10 Ile de France

DÉPÔT DES PAPIERS PUBLICS DES COLONIES, ÉTAT CIVIL:
DPPC G1/473 Recensement général de l'Isle de France, 1776
DPPC G1/474 Recensement de l'Isle de France, 1780
DPPC G1/474 Recensement de l'Isle de France, 1758
DPPC* GR 3080 Isle de France, Greffes, Arrêts du Conseil Supérieur, 1778–1780
DPPC G1/505 Isle de France, Recensements et pièces diverses

NOTARIAT:
NOT MAUR 393 Lousteau, Jean, 1772–1781
NOT MAUR 394 Lousteau, Jean, 1782–1784
SOM NOT Isle de France, Bobine 143: Touraille, Antoine, 1773–1791

F SERIES:
F5a/8 Isles de France et de Bourbon, Missions et Cultes Religieux, 1674–1775
F5a/10 Isles de France et de Bourbon, Mission et Cultes Religieux, 1783–1808
F5a/11 Madagascar, Bourbon et Isle de France: Missions, Cultes Religieux, 1775–1782

E SERIES (PERSONNEL COLONIAL ANCIEN):
E 337/bis, Pobequin, Jean-Louis, Charpentier à L'Isle de France
E 111, David, Pierre-Felix Barthélemy, Gouverneur des Isles de Franace et de Bourbon
E 296 Magon, René, Ancien Gouverneur des Isles de France et de Bourbon
E 363 Saint Pierre, Bernardin de, Jacques Henri
E10 Aublet, Jean-Baptiste Christophe Fuisée, botaniste du Roi aux colonies, 1773–1774
E112 Dazille, Jean-Barthélemy
E90 De Conway, Le Comte, Gouverneur des établissements français dans l'Inde
E280 Leroux de Kermoseven, proprietaire, negociant et armateur à l'Isle de France et
    à Madagascar
E 16 Barbé de Marbois, Nicolas François, Lieutenant de Juge de la Jurisdiction de l'Isle
    de France
E 33 Blancheteste, Guillaume, Geolier des prisons de l'Isle de France, 1782–1790
E 278 Le Normand, Pierre Marie, Capitaine des milices à l'Isle de France, 1741–1792
E 124 Desranges de Richeteau, Guillaume, Habitant à l'Isle de France, Inspecteur de
    Police à l'Isle de France
E 357/bis, Rostaing, Philippe Joseph, Comte de
E 353, Rivaltz de St. Anthoine, conseiller au Conseil Supérieur, 1768–1781
E 224 Horque, Claude, employé dans La Compagnie des Ouvriers de M. Daumur à
    l'Isle de France, 1770

E 292 and E 293 Lousteau, Jean, greffier au chef de Conseil Supérieur à l'Isle de France

E 340 Pourcher de la Serré, Jacques Philippe, Ancien conseiller au parlement de Bourgogne, Juge Royal à l'Isle de France.

E 185 De Fleury

E 190 Foucault, Denis-Nicolas

National Archives of Mauritius, Coromandel (MNA)

JB 4 Procédure criminelle, 1741–1746

JB 6 Procédure criminelle, 1750–1751

JB 20 Procédure criminelle, 1774

JB 23 Procédure criminelle, 1774

JB 24 Procédure criminelle, 1776

JB 26 Procédure criminelle, 1777

JB 27 Procédure criminelle, 1777

JB 29 Procédure criminelle, 1777

JB 30 Procédure criminelle, 1778

JB 39 Procédure criminelle, 1778

JB 45 Procédure criminelle, 1785

JB 50 Procédure criminelle, 1785

JB 52 Procédure criminelle, 1787

JB 70 Procédure criminelle 1790–1791

JB 74 Procédure criminelle, 1792

JB 80 Procédure criminelle, 1794

OC 72a: Bureau de classes et armament, 1785–1788

OC 53: Bureau de l'hôpital, 1760–1770

OA 57 Affranchissements

A 39 Affranchissements, Port Louis, 1796–1800

OB 58 Jurisdiction Royale, Régistre des sentences en matière criminelle, 25 March 1777–8 June 1780

OA 48 Jurisdiction Royale: Régistre des sentences en matière criminelle, 16 June 1783–22 October 1788

Z2B/6 Journal de Police, 1790–1791

Z2B/2 Bureau de Police, Journal pour la consignation des rapports de police, 15 April 1785–31 March 1787

Z2B/3 Jurisdiction Royale: Régistre pour l'enregistrement des déclarations de filouteries, éscroqueries, et autres délits semblables et les contraventions découvertes par les inspectures et les gardes de police, 31 October 1779–1 April 1784

OA 69 Procureur-Général: Régistre pour la consignation de divers plaints et déclarations, December 1772–May 1794

OA 3 Intendant: Documents concernant les Forges de Mon Desir, 1768–1789

OA 127 Jardin du Roi: Documents concernant Monplaisir, 1772–1806

OA 85 Jurisdiction Royale, Bureau de Police. Livre pour servir à l'enregistrement de divers orders, letters et autres piecès ayant trait aux fonctions de police, 20 November 1779–14 April 1787

E72 Gouvernement Republicain, Directoire: Régistre des Déliberations, 12 February
1792–10 September 1792
E 77 Directoire, 1793–1794
JK 10 Insinuations, 12 April 1792–17 March 1794
B1A/A-31/22 Plan de la Ville de Port Louis
JS1 Tribunaux de paix, Port Louis, Sentences civiles, 1791–1792

Wellcome Library, London
MS 6065 SAVARY, F. 1755. Journal du Voyage de France en Chine

BOOKS AND ARTICLES

Abel, Elizabeth, Barbara Christian, and Helene Moglen, eds. 1997. *Female subjects in black and white.* Berkeley: University of California Press.

Agorsah, Emmanuel Kofi. 1994. *Maroon heritage: Archaeological, ethnographic and historical perspectives.* Barbados: Canoe Press.

Akinola, G.A. 1970. The French on the Lindi Coast, 1785–1789. *Tanzania notes and records* 70: 13–20.

Allen, Richard, B. 1999. *Slaves, freedmen and indentured labourers in colonial Mauritius.* Cambridge: Cambridge University Press.

Allen, Richard. 2001. Licentious and unbridled proceedings: The illegal slave trade to Mauritius and the Seychelles during the early nineteenth century. *Journal of African History* 42: 91–117.

Allen, Richard. 2002a. Carrying away the unfortunate: The exportation of slaves from India during the late eighteenth century. Paper presented at St. Antony's College, Oxford, 22 October 2002.

Allen, Richard 2002b. Femmes de couleur libres and socio-economic marginality in Mauritius, 1767–1830. Paper presented to the International Conference on Women and Slavery in Honour of Suzanne Miers, Avignon, 16–18 October 2002.

Alpers, Edward A. 1970. The French Slave Trade in East Africa (1721–1810). *Cahiers d'Études Africaines* 10.37: 80–124.

Alpers, Edward A. 1975. *Ivory and slaves: Changing patterns of international trade in East Central Africa to the later nineteenth century.* Berkeley: University of California Press.

Alpers, Edward A. 1997. The African diaspora in the northwestern Indian Ocean: Reconsideration of an old problem, new directions for research. *Comparative Studies of South Asia, Africa and the Middle East* 13.2: 62–81.

——. 2000. Recollecting Africa: Diasporic memory in the Indian Ocean world. *African Studies Review* 43.1, 83–99.

——. 2003. The African diaspora in the Indian Ocean: A comparative perspective. In *The African diaspora in the Indian Ocean*, ed. Shihan de Silva Jayusuriya and Richard Pankhurst, 19–50. Trenton: African World Press.

Alpers, Edward A. 2001. Becoming "Mozambique": Diaspora and identity in Mauritius. In *History, memory and identity*, ed. Vijayalakshmi Teelock and Edward A. Alpers, Mauritius: Nelson Mandela Centre for African Culture and University of Mauritius.Alvarez, Albert Rosa. 1995. Ethnicity and Nation in Madagascar. In *Cultures of Madagascar: Ebb and flow of influences*, ed. Sandra Evers and Marc Spindler, 67–83. Leiden: IIAS.

Anderson, Clare. 2000. *Convicts in the Indian Ocean: Transportation from South Asia to Mauritius, 1815–1853*. Basingstoke: Macmillan.

Andrews, Richard Mowery. 1994. *Law, magistracy and crime in old regime Paris*. 2 vols. Cambridge: Cambridge University Press.

Antze, Paul, and Michael Lambek. 1996. Introduction. In *Tense past: Cultural essays in trauma and memory*, ed. Antze and Lambek, xi–xxxviii. New York: Routledge.

Arago, Jacques. 1823. *Narrative of a voyage round the world, 1817–1820*. London: Treuttel and Wurtz.

Arno, Toni, and Orian, Claude. 1986. *Île Maurice: Une société multiraciale*. Paris: L'Harmattan.

Astuti, Rita. 1995. *People of the sea: Identity and descent among the Vezo of Madagascar*. Cambridge: Cambridge University Press.

Azema, Georges. 1859. *Histoire de l'Île Bourbon depuis 1643 jusqu'au 20 décembre. 1848*. Paris: Plon.

Baggioni, Daniel, and Didier de Robillard, eds. 1990. *L'Île Maurice: Une francophonie paradoxale*. Paris: Harmattan.

Baissac, Charles. 1880. *Étude sur le patois créole mauricien*. Nancy: Imprimerie Berger-Levrault.

Baker, Philip. 1972. *Kreol: A description of Mauritian creole*. London: Hurst.

——. 1982. The contribution of non-francophone immigrants to the lexicon of Mauritian Creole. PhD diss., University of London.

——. 2002. Creole linguistics. Paper presented at the Conference on Creolization, University College, London.

Baker, Philip. 2003. Sur les origines africaines et européenes des devinettes mauriciennes de Baissac (1880, 1888). In *Variation et Francophonies*, ed. Aidan Coveney and Carol Sanders. Paris: Harmattan.

Baker, Philip, and Chris Corne. 1982. *Isle de France creole: Affinities and origins*. Ann Arbor, Mich.: Karoma Publishers.

Balutansky, Kathleen, and Marie-Agnes Sourieau, eds. 1998. *Caribbean creolization: Reflections on the cultural dynamics of language, literature and identity*. Gainesville: University of Florida Press.

Barendse, R. J. 1995. Slaving on the Malagasy Coast, 1640–1700. In *Cultures of Madagascar: Ebb and flow of influences*, ed. Sandra Evers and Marc Spindler, 137–155. Leiden: IIAS.

Barker, Anthony J. 1996. *Slavery and antislavery in Mauritius, 1810–1833*. Basingstoke: Macmillan.

Barnwell, P. J. 1948. *Visits and despatches, Mauritius, 1598–1948*. Port Louis: Standard Printing Establishment.

Barry, Boubacar. 1998. *Senegambia and the Atlantic slave trade*. Cambridge: Cambridge University Press.

Bastide, Roger. 1978. *The African religions of Brazil*. Baltimore: Johns Hopkins University Press.

Bayly, Susan. 1989. *Saints, goddesses and kings: Muslims and Christians in South Indian society, 1700–1900*. Cambridge: Cambridge University Press.

Beaton, Patrick. 1859. *Creoles and coolies, or Five years in Mauritius*. London: James Nisbet.

Bell, David. 1994. *Lawyers and citizens: The making of a political elite in Old Regime France*. New York: Oxford University Press.

Benedict, Burton. 1965. *Mauritius: The problems of a plural society*. London: Pall Mall Press.

Benitez-Rojo, Antonio. 1996. *The repeating island: The Caribbean in postmodern perspective*. Durham, N.C.: Duke University Press.

Benjamin, Jessica. 1998. *Shadow of the other: Intersubjectivity and gender in psychoanalysis*. New York: Routledge.

Bénot, Yves. 1988. *La Révolution française et la fin des colonies*. Paris: Éditions La Decouverte.

Benton, Lauren. 2002. *Law and colonial cultures: Legal regimes in world history: 1400–1900*. Cambridge: Cambridge University Press.

Benyowsky, Maurice Auguste Aladar. 1790. *Memoirs and travels of Mauritius Auguste, Count de Benyowsky*. Trans William Nicholson. London: G. G. J. and J. Robinson.

Bernabé, Jean, and Chamoiseau, Confiant, and Raphaël Confiant. 1993. *Éloge de la créolité*, ed. bilingue. Paris: Gallimard.

Bergner, Gwen. 1998. Myths of Masculinity: The Oedipus Complex and Douglass's 1845 Narrative. In *The Psychoanalysis of Race*, ed. Christopher Lane, 241–261, New York: Columbia University Press.

Berlin, Ira. 1996. From Creole to African: Atlantic Creoles and the Origins of African-American Society in Mainland North America. *William and Mary Quarterly*, 3rd ser., 53: 251–289.

Berlin, Ira, and Philip D. Morgan. 1993. Introduction: Labor and the shaping of slave life in the Americas. In *Cultivation and Culture*, ed. Ira Berlin and Philip D. Morgan, 10–45. Charlottesville: University of Virginia Press.

Berlin, Ira, and Philip D. Morgan, eds. 1991. *The slaves' economy: Independent production by slaves in the Americas*. London: Frank Cass.

Bernabé, Jean, Patrick Chamoiseau, and Raphael Confiant. 1993. *Éloge de la créolité*. Paris: Gallimard.

Bernardin de St. Pierre, Jacques-Henri. [1773] 2002. *Journey to Mauritius*. Trans. Jason Wilson. Oxford: Signal Books.

Bhabha, Homi. 1984. Of mimicry and man: The ambivalence of colonial discourse. *October* 28: 125–133.

Bhabha, Homi. 1986. Remembering Fanon. Foreword to *Black Skins, White Masks*, by Frantz Fanon, vii–xxvi. London: Pluto Press.

Bickerton, Derek. 1975. *Dynamics of a creole system*. Cambridge: Cambridge University Press.

Biondi, Jean-Pierre. 1987. *Saint-Louis du Senegal: Mémoires d'un métissage*. Paris: Denoel.

Bissoondoyal, Uttama, and Asha L. Sibartie, eds. 1990. *L'Île Maurice et la Révolution française*. Moka, Mauritius: Mahatma Gandhi Institute.

Blackburn, Robin. 1997. *The making of new world slavery: From the baroque to the modern, 1492–1800*. London: Verso.

Blacking, John. 1961. The social value of Venda riddles. *African Studies* 20: 1–32.

Bloch, Maurice. 1971. *Placing the dead: Tombs, Ancestral villages and kinship organisation in Madagascar*. London: Seminar Press.

———. 1985. *From blessing to violence: History and ideology in the circumcision ritual of the Merina of Madagascar*. Cambridge: Cambridge University Press.

Blussé, J. L. 1986. *Strange company: Chinese settlers, women and the Dutch in VOC Batavia*. Dordrecht: Foris.

Boddy, Janice. 1998. Afterword: Embodying ethnography. In *Bodies and persons: Comparative perspectives from Africa and Melanesia*, ed. Michael Lambek and Andrew Strathern, 252–274. Cambridge: Cambridge University Press.

Bolster, W. Jeffrey. 1997. *Blackjacks: African American seamen in the age of sail*. Cambridge: Harvard University Press.

Bongie, Chris. 1998. *Islands and exiles: The creole identities of post/colonial literature*. Stanford, Calif.: Stanford University Press.

Boudriot, Jean. 1983. *Compagnie des Indes (1720–1770)*. 2 vols. Paris: A.N.C.R.E.

Boulle, Pierre. 1988. In defense of slavery: Eighteenth-century opposition to abolition and the origins of racist ideology in France. In *History from below*, ed. Frederick Krantz, 219–246. Oxford: Oxford University Press.

———. 1996. Les "non-blancs" de L'Ocean Indien en France à la fin de l'ancien régime. In Wanquet and Jullien 1996, 11–21.

Bourde de la Rogerie, Henri. 1934. *Les Bretons aux Îles de France et de Bourbon au XVII et XVIII siècles*. Rennes: Imprimerie Oberthur.

Bowser, Frederick P. 1974. *The African Slave in Colonial Peru, 1524–1650*. Stanford, Calif.: Stanford University Press.

Boxer, C. R. 1977. *The Dutch seaborne empire, 1600–1800*. London: Hutchinson.

Brandon, George. 1993. *Santeria from Africa to the New World*. Bloomington: Indiana University Press.

Brewer, John, and Roy Porter, eds. 1993. *Consumption and the world of goods*. London: Routledge.

Brockliss, Laurence, and Colin Jones. 1997. *The medical world of early modern France*. Oxford: Clarendon.

Brodeur, Raymond, and Brigitte Caulier, eds. 1997. *Enseigner le catéchisme: Autorités et institutions, XVIe–XXe siècles*. Saint Nicolas, Quebec: L'Université de Laval.

Brooks, Peter. 2000. *Troubling confessions: Speaking guilt in law and literature*. Chicago: University of Chicago Press.

Britton, Celia M. 1999. *Edouard Glissant and postcolonial theory: Strategies of language and resistance*. Charlottesville: University Press of Virginia.

Brown, M. 1978. *Madagascar rediscovered*. London: Damien Tunnacliffe.

Burroughs, Peter. 1976. The Mauritius Rebellion of 1832 and the Abolition of British Colonial Slavery. *Journal of Imperial and Commonwealth History* 4: 243–265.

Burton, Richard D. E. 1997. *Afro-Creole: Power, opposition and play in the Caribbean.* Ithaca, N.Y.: Cornell University Press.

Bush, Barbara. 1993. Hard labour: Women, childbirth and resistance in Caribbean slave societies. *History Workshop* 36: 83–99.

Butel, Paul. 1996. Les ports atlantiques français et l'ocean indien sous la Révolution et l'empire, l'exemple de Bordeaux. In Wanquet and Jullien 1996, 85–95.

———. 2002. *Histoire des antilles françaises, xviie–xxe siècle.* Paris: Perrin.

Butler, Judith. 1992. Contingent foundations: Feminism and the question of "postmodernism." In *Feminists theorize the political*, ed. J. Butler and J. Scott. New York: Routledge.

———. 1993. *Bodies that matter: On the discursive limits of "sex."* New York: Routledge.

———. 1997. *The psychic life of power: Theories in subjection.* Stanford, Calif.: Stanford University Press.

———. 2000. *Antigone's claim: Kinship between life and death.* New York: Columbia University Press.

Byrne, F., and J. Holm, eds. 1993. *Atlantic meets Pacific: A global view of pidginisation and creolisation.* Amsterdam: John Benjamins.

Campbell, Gwyn. 1980. Labour and transport problems in imperial Madagascar. *Journal of African History* 21: 341–356.

———. 1989. Madagascar and Mozambique in the slave trade of the west Indian Ocean. In *The economics of the Indian Ocean slave trade in the nineteenth century*, ed. G. Clarence-Smith, 166–194. London: Cass.

———. 1993. The structure of Trade in Madagascar, 1750–1810, *International Journal of African Historical Studies* 2 6.1: 111–148.

Caron, Peter. 1997. Of a nation which others do not understand: Bambara slaves and African ethnicity in colonial Louisiana, 1718–1760. *Slavery and Abolition* 18: 98–122.

Carter, Marina. 1988–1989. Indian slaves in Mauritius (1729–1834). *Indian Historical Review* 15: 233–247.

———. 1992. The family under indenture: A Mauritian case study. *Journal of Mauritian Studies* 4: 1–21.

———. 1993. The Transition from slave to indentured labour in Mauritius. *Slavery and Abolition* 14: 114–30.

———. 1994. *Lakshmi's legacy: The testimonies of Indian women in the nineteenth century.* Rose Hill, Mauritius: Éditions de l'Océan Indien.

———. 1995. *Servants, sirdars and settlers: Indians in Mauritius, 1834–1874.* Delhi: Oxford University Press.

———. 1996. *Voices from indenture: Experiences of Indian migrants in the British Empire.* London: Cass.

———. 1998a. Founding an island society: Inter-ethnic relationships in Isle de France. In *Colouring the rainbow: Mauritian society in the making*, ed. Marina Carter, et al., 1–30. Port Louis: Centre for Research on Indian Ocean Societies.

——. 1998b. Recapturing the African past: Nineteenth-century Afro-Creole genealogies. In *Colouring the rainbow: Mauritian society in the making*, ed. Marina Carter, et al., 119–134. Port Louis: Centre for Research on Indian Ocean Societies.

——, et al., ed. 1998c. *Colouring the rainbow: Mauritian society in the making*. Port Louis: Centre for Research on Indian Ocean Societies.

Carter, Marina, and Hubert Gerbeau. 1989. Covert slaves and coveted coolies in the early-nineteenth-century Mascareignes. In *The Economics of the Indian Ocean Slave Trade in the Nineteenth Century*, ed. William Gervase Clarence-Smith, 194–208. London: Cass.

Carter, Marina, and James Ng Foong Kwong. 1998. Creoles and immigrants in the nineteenth century: Competition and cooperation in Mauritius. In Carter 1998c, 41–60.

Caudron, Olivier. 1990. Le livre dans la société de l'Île de France du dernier quart du XVIIIe siècle. In Bissoondoyal and Sibartie 1989, 175–191.

——. 1996. Livre, lecture et révolution aux Mascareignes: Quelques pistes de recherches. In Wanquet and Jullien 1996, 149–154.

Chamoiseau, Patrick. 1997. *Texaco*. London: Granta.

Chaudenson, Robert. 1974. *Le lexique de parler créole de la Réunion*. Paris: Champion.

——. 1979. *Les créoles français*. Paris: Nathan.

——. 1981. *Textes créoles anciens*. Hamburg: Helmut Buske.

Chaudhuri, K. N. 1985. *Trade and civilisation in the Indian Ocean: An economic history from the rise of Islam to 1750*. Cambridge: Cambridge University Press.

——. 1990. *Asia before Europe: Economy and civilisation of the Indian Ocean from the rise of Islam to 1750*. Cambridge: Cambridge University Press.

Chan Low, Jocelyn. 1999. Aux origines du "Malaise Créole?" Les ex-apprentis dans la société Mauricienne (1839–1861). Paper presented at the Conference Commemorating the 160th Anniversary of the End of Apprenticeship, June 1999. Mahatma Gandhi Institute, Moka, Mauritius.

——. 2000. L'importance de l'occupation néerlandaise dans l'histoire de l'Île Maurice. In Evers and Hookoomsingh 2000, 57–67.

Chauleau, Liliane, ed. 1989. *Antilles, 1789: La Révolution aux Caraïbes*. Paris: Nathan.

Chelin, Anthoine. 1954. *Le théâtre à L'Île Maurice*. Port Louis: Port Louis Printing Ltd.

——. [1949] 1987. Les premiers habitants de l'Isle de France. *La Gazette des Isles*, no. 17, December, 722–724.

Cobham-Sander, Rhonda. 1995. Colin Ferguson, "Me" and "I": Anatomy of a creole psychosis. *Transition*, no. 67: 16–21.

Cohen, Sulomith. 1996. Connecting through riddles, or the riddle of connecting. In *Untying the Knot*, ed. Galit Hans-Rokem and David Dean Shulman, *Untying the knot: On riddles and other enigmatic modes*, 294–315. New York: Oxford University Press.

Colloque international sur l'esclavage à Madagascar. 1997. *L'Esclavage à Madagascar: aspects historiques et résurgences contemporaines: actes due colloque international sur l'esclavage, Antananarivo 24–28 septembre 1996*. Antananarivo: Institut de civilizations, musée d'art et d'archéologie.

Condé, Maryse, and Madeleine Cottenot-Hage, eds. 1995. *Penser la créolité*. Paris: Karthala.

Corne, Chris. 1983. À propos de l'ouvrage de Robert Chaudenson: Textes Créoles Anciens (La Réunion et Île Maurice) comparaison et essai d'analyse. *Études Créoles* 5: 94–108.

Cornevin, Robert, and Marianne Cornevin. 1990. *La France et les français outre-mer*, Paris.

Craton, Michael. 1992. The transition from slavery to free wage labour in the Caribbean, 1780–1890: A survey with particular reference to recent scholarship. *Slavery and Abolition* 13: 37–67.

———, ed. 1979. *Roots and branches: Current directions in slave studies*. Toronto: Pergamon.

Crepin, P. 1922. *Mahé de La Bourdonnais, gouverneur général des Îles de France et de Bourbon, 1699–1753*. Paris: Éditions Ernest Leroux.

Croix, Alain. 1995. *Cultures et religion en Bretagne aux 16e et 17e siècles*. Rennes: Éditions Apogée.

———. 1997. Catéchiser les sauvages de Bretagne au XVIIe siècle: De la conversion à l'instruction. In Brodeur and Caulier 1997, 73–86.

Curtin, Philip. 1975. *Economic change in Precolonial Africa: Senegambia in the era of the slave trade*. Madison: University of Wisconsin Press.

Darnton, Robert. 1995. *The corpus of clandestine literature in France, 1769–1789*. New York: Norton.

———. 1997. *The forbidden best-sellers of pre-Revolutionary France*. London: Fontana.

Davis, David Brion. 1970. *The problem of slavery in Western culture*. Harmondsworth.

Dayan, Joan. 1998. *Haiti, history and the gods*. Berkeley: University of California Press.

Debbasch, Yvan. 1961. Le marronnage: Essai sur la désertion de l'esclave antillais. *L'Année Sociologique*, 3rd ser.: 1–112.

Debbasch, Yvan. 1967. *Couleur et liberté: Le jeu de critère ethnique dans un ordre juridique esclavagiste*. Vol. 1: L'affranchi dans les possessions françaises de la Caraïbe (1635–1833). Paris: Librairie Dalloz.

Debien, Gabriel. 1974. *Les esclaves aux Antilles françaises, XVIIe–XVIIIe siècles*. Basse Terre: Société de l'histoire de la Guadeloupe.

———. n.d. Le journal de traite de la *Licorne* au Mozambique, 1787–1788. *Notes d'Histoire Coloniale*, no. 220: 91–116.

De Certeau, Michel. 1984. *The practice of everyday life*. Berkeley: University of California Press.

De Froberville, Eugène. 1847. Notes sur les moeurs, coutumes, et traditions des Amakoua, sur le commerce et la traité des esclaves dans l'Afrique orientale. *Bulletin de la Société de Géographie*, 3rd ser., 7: 311–329.

De la Caille, M. l'Abbé. 1763. *Journal historique du voyage fait au Cap de Bonne Esperance*. Paris: Guillyn.

Delesalle, Simone, and Lucette Valensi. 1972. Le mot "nègre" dans les dictionnaires français d'ancien régime: Histoire et lexicographie. *Langue française* 15: 79–104.

De Souza, Pascale. 1995. Inscription du créole dans les textes francophones: De la cita-
tion a la créolisation. In Condé and Cottenot-Hage 1995, 173–191.

Derrida, Jacques. 1998. *Monolingualism of the other, or The prothesis of origins*. Stanford, Calif.: Stanford University Press.

Deschamps, Hubert. 1960. *Histoire de Madagascar*. Paris: Éditions Berger-Levrault.

De Rauville, Hervé. 1889. *L'Île de France legendaire*. Paris: Challamel et Cié.

——. 1908. *L'Ile de France contemporaire*. Paris: Nouvelle libraire nationale.

Diedrich, Maria, Henry Louis Gates, and Carl Pedersen, eds. 1999. *Black imagination
and the Middle Passage*. New York: Oxford University Press.

Dina, Jeanne. 1997. Les Makoa dans le Sud-Ouest de Madagascar. In Colloque international sur l'esclavage à Madagascar 1997.

Dinan, Monique. 1986. *The Mauritian kaleidoscope: Languages and religions*. Rose
Hill, Mauritius: Éditions de l'Ocean Indien.

Dommen, Edward, and Dommen, Bridget. 1999. *Mauritius: An island of success: A
retrospective study, 1960–1993*. Wellington: Pacific.

Donzelot, Jacques. 1979. *The policing of families*. Trans. Robert Hurley. New York:
Vintage.

Donovan, John. 1982. Introduction. In *Paul and Virginie*, by Jacques-Henri Bernardin
de St. Pierre, trans. John Donovan. London: Penguin.

Dooling, Wayne. 1992. *Law and community in a slave society: Stellenbosch District,
South Africa, c. 1760–1820*. Communications (University of Cape Town, Centre
for African Studies), 23. Rondebosch, South Africa: Centre for African Studies.

D'Unienville, Baron. 1885–86. *Statistiques de l'Île Maurice et ses dependences suivie
d'une notice historique sur cette colonie et d'un essai sur l'Île de Madagascar*. 2nd
ed., 3 vols. Maurice: Imprimerie de The Merchants and Planters Gazette.

D'Unienville, Raymond. 1975. *Histoire politique de l'Isle de France (1789–1791)*.
Mauritius Archives Publications, no. 13. Port Louis: Government Printer.

——. 1982. *Histoire politique de l'Isle de France (1791–1794)*. Mauritius Archives Publications, no. 14. Port Louis: Government Printer.

——. 1989. *Histoire politique de l'Isle de France (1795–1803)*. Mauritius Archives Publications, no. 15, Port Louis: N.I.M.

——. 1998. Whites, creoles, and indians: Vignettes from a history of mutual dependence. In *Colouring the rainbow: Mauritian society in the making*, ed. Marina Carter, et al., 31–40. Port Louis: Centre for Research on Indian Ocean Societies.

Durand, Jean-Pierre, and Joyce Durand. 1975. *L'Île Maurice: Quelle indépendance? La
reproduction des rapports de production capitaliste dans une formation sociale domi-
née*. Paris: Éditions Anthropos.

Elizabeth, Léo. 1989. La société Martiniquaise aux xvième et xviiiième siècles, 1664–
1989. Doctorat d'État, Paris 1.

Engerman, Stanley. 1992. The economic response to emancipation and some economic aspects of the meaning of freedom. In *The meaning of freedom: Economics,
politics and culture after slavery*, ed. Frank McGlynn and Seymour Drescher, 49–
68. Pittsburgh: University of Pittsburgh Press.

Eriksen, Thomas Hylland. 1998. *Common denominators: Ethnicity, nation-building and compromise in Mauritius*. Oxford: Berg.

——. 1999. Tu dimmun pu vini kreol: The Mauritian creole and the concept of creolization. Working paper, University of Oxford/ESRC project on Transnational Communities.

Evers, Sandra. 1995. Stigmatization as a self-perpetuating process. In Evers and Spindler 1995, 157–185.

Evers, Sandra, and V. Y. Hookoomsingh, eds. 2000. *Globalisation and the south-west Indian Ocean*. Réduit: University of Mauritius and International Insititute for Asian Studies.

Evers, Sandra, and Marc Spindler, eds. 1995. *Cultures of Madagascar: Ebb and flow of influences*. Leiden: IIAS.

Ewald, Janet J. 2000. Crossers of the sea: Slaves, Freedmen and other migrants in the northwestern Indian Ocean, c. 1750–1914. *American Historical Review* 105: 69–92.

Fairchilds, Cissie. 1984. *Domestic enemies: Servants and their masters in old regime France*. Baltimore: Johns Hopkins University Press.

Falola, Toyin, and Paul Lovejoy, eds., 1994. *Debt bondage in historical perspective*. Boulder, Colo.: Westview Press.

Feely-Harnik, Gillian. 1991. *A green estate: Restoring independence in Madagascar*. Washington, D.C.: Smithsonian Institution Press.

Filliot, Jean-Michel. 1974. *La traite des esclaves vers les Mascareignes au xviiie siècle*. Paris: ORSTOM.

Finegan, Ruth. 1970. *Oral literature in Africa*. Oxford: Oxford University Press.

Freeman-Grenville, G. S. P. 1965. *The French at Kilwa Island*. London: Oxford University Press.

Frémont, Georges. 1993. Un comptoir en plein essor. In Rose 1993, 67–88.

Freud, Sigmund. 1993. *On psychopathology: Inhibitions, symptoms and anxiety and other works*. Penguin Freud Library, vol. 10. London: Penguin.

Fuss, Diana. 1995. *Identification papers*. London: Routledge.

Gates, Henry Louis. 1991. Critical Fanonism. *Critical Inquiry* 17.3: 457–470.

Geirson, Gerald L., ed. 1984. *Professions and the French state*. Philadelphia: University of Pennsylvania Press.

Genovese, Eugene. 1975. *Roll, Jordan, roll: The world the slaves made*. London: André Deutsch.

Gerbeau, Hubert. 1997. Histoire oubliée, histoire occultée? La diaspora malgache a La Réunion: entre esclavage et liberté. In Colloque international sur l'esclavage à Madagascar 1997, 3–29.

Gilroy, Paul. 1993. *The black Atlantic: Modernity and double consciousness*. Cambridge: Cambridge University Press.

Glassman, Jonathan. 1995. *Feasts and riot: Revelry, rebellion and popular consciousness on the Swahili coast, 1856–1888*. Portsmouth, N. H.: Heinemann.

Glissant, Edouard. 1981. *Le discours antillais*. Paris: Éditions du Seuil.

Gomez, Michael A. 1998. *Exchanging our country marks: The transformation of African identities in the colonial and antebellum South*. Chapel Hill: University of North Carolina Press.

Graeber, David. 1999. Painful memories. In Middleton 1999, 319–349.

Grandidier, A. 1908–1928. *Ethnographie de Madagascar*. 4 vols. Paris: Imprimerie nationale.

Grant, Charles. 1801. *The history of Mauritius or the Isle of France and the neighbouring islands*. London: W. Bulmer and Co.

Greenblatt, Stephen. 1991. *Marvelous possessions: The wonder of the New World*. Chicago: University of Chicago Press.

Greenburg, Kenneth, S. 1996. *Honour and slavery*. Princeton, N.J.: Princeton University Press.

Greene, Sandra. 2000. Cultural zones in the era of the slave trade: Exploring the Yoruba connection with the Anlo-Ewe. In Lovejoy 2000, 86–102.

Grove, Richard. 1995. *Green imperialism*. Cambridge: Cambridge University Press.

Hall, D. 1978. The Flight from the estates reconsidered: The British West Indies, 1838–1842. *Journal of Caribbean History* 10–11: 7–24.

Hall, Gwendolyn Midlo. 1992. *Africans in colonial Louisiana: The development of an Afro-Creole culture in the eighteenth century*. Baton Rouge: Louisiana University Press.

Hall, Stuart. 1996. The After-Life of Frantz Fanon: Why Fanon? Why Now? Why *Black Skins, White Masks?* In Read 1996, 12–38.

Handelman, Don. 1996. Traps of transformation: Theoretical convergences between riddle and ritual. In Hasan-Rokem and Shulman 1996, 37–61.

Haring, Lee. 1974. On knowing the answer. *Journal of American Folklore* 87: 197–207.

——. 1985. Malagasy riddling. *Journal of American Folklore* 98: 163–90.

Harris, Joseph E. 1971. *The African presence in Asia: Consequences of the East African slave trade*. Evanston, Ill.: Northwestern University Press.

Hasan-Rokem, Galit, and David Shulman, eds. 1996. *Untying the knot: On riddles and other enigmatic modes*. London: Oxford University Press.

Haudrère, Philippe. 1989. *La Compagnie des Indes au XVIIIe siècle (1719–1795)*. Paris: Librarie de l'Inde.

——. 1993. La Compagnie des Indes. In Vincent 1993, 44–67.

——. 1996. Quelques aspects du commerce entre la France et l'Asie à la fin du XVIIIe siècle. In Wanquet and Jullien 1996, 31–39.

Hayot, Émile. 1971. *Les gens de couleur libres du Fort-Royal, 1679–1823*. Paris: Société Française d'Histoire d'Outre-Mer.

Hazareesingh, K. 1975. *History of Indians in Mauritius*. 2nd ed. London: Macmillan Education.

Herskovits, Melville. 1941. *The myth of the Negro past*. New York: Harper and Row.

Heuman, Gad, ed. 1986. *Out of the house of bondage: Runaways, resistance and marronage in Africa and the New World*. London: Cass.

Ho, Hai Quang. 1997. L'Esclavage à l'Île Bourbon de 1664 à 1714. In Colloque international sur l'esclavage à Madagascar 1997, 29–53.

Holm, F. S. 1989. *Pidgins and creoles*. Cambridge: Cambridge University Press.

hooks, bell. 1981. *Ain't I a woman: Black women and feminism*. London: Pluto Press.

———. 1996. Feminism as a persistent critique of history: What's love got to do with it? In Read 1996, 76–86.

Hufton, Olwen. 1982. *The poor of eighteenth-century France, 1750–1789*. Oxford: Oxford University Press.

Hunt, Lynn. 1992. *The family romance of the French Revolution*. London: Routledge.

Hunt, Nancy Rose. 1999. *A colonial lexicon: On birth ritual, medicalization and mobility in the Congo*. Durham, N.C.: Duke University Press.

Iliffe, John. 2004. *Honour in African history*. Cambridge: Cambridge University Press.

Jacobus, Mary. 1995. *First things: The maternal imaginary in literature, art and psychoanalysis*. New York: Routledge.

Johnston, A. J. B. 2001. *Control and order in French colonial Louisburg, 1713–1758*. East Lansing: Michigan State University Press.

Jones, P. M. 1995. *Reform and revolution in France: The politics of transition, 1774–1791*. Cambridge: Cambridge University Press.

Journel, Henry Morel, ed. 1940. *Le fond de mon tiroir: Cahiers confidentels de Madame Journel . . . 1774 à 1833*. Montbrison: Imprimerie Eleuthère Brassart.

Jousse, Daniel. 1771. *Traité de la justice criminelle*. 4 vols. Paris.

Jumeer, Musleem. 1984. Les affranchis et les indiens libres à l'Île de France au xviiie siècle. Thèse de 3eme cycle, Université de Poitiers, Faculté des Sciences Humaines.

Kent, Raymond K. 1970. *Early kingdoms in Madagascar, 1500–1700*. New York: Holt, Rinehart and Winston.

Kirmayer, Laurence. 1996. Landscapes of memory: Trauma, narrative and dissociation. In *The past imperfect: Cultural essays in trauma and memory*, ed. Paul Antze and Michael Lambek, 173–198. New York: Routledge.

Knight, Franklin. 1970. *A slave society in Cuba during the nineteenth century*. Madison: University of Wisconsin Press.

Kopytoff, Igor, and Suzanne Miers. 1977. African "slavery" as an institution of marginality. In *Slavery in Africa: Historical and Anthropological Perspectives*, ed. Miers and Kopytoff, 3–81. Madison: University of Wisconsin Press.

Kotzebue, August von. 1798. *Count Benyowsky, or The conspiracy of Kamtschatka: A tragic-comedy*. London: W. J. and J. Richardson.

Kuczynski, R. R. 1949. *Demographic survey of the British colonial empire*. Vol. 11. London: Oxford University Press.

Lacan, Jacques. 1982. *Écrits: A selection*. London: Tavistock Publications.

Lagesse, Marcelle. 1972. *L'Île de France avant La Boudonnais (1721–1735)*. Port Louis: Imprimerie Commerciale.

———. 1987a, 17 décembre. 1761. Séparation des époux Bulle et Masson: L'éloquence des actes notaries. *La Gazette des Îles*, no. 16, September, 8–9.

———. 1987b, Les enfants naturels de La Bourdonnais. *La Gazette des Îles*, no. 14, April, 4–5.

Lagesse, Marcelle. 1988. Une escale: A six heures nous avons desaffourché . . . . *La Gazette des Îles*, no. 20, July, 999–1000.

Laingui and Lebigre 1979. *Histoire du droit pénal*. Paris: CUJAS.

Lambek, Michael. 1998. Body and mind in mind, body and mind in body: Some anthropological interventions in a long conversation. In *Bodies and persons: Comparative perspectives from Africa and Melanesia*, ed. Michael Lambek and Andrew Strathern, 103–127. Cambridge: Cambridge University Press.

Lambek, Michael, and Andrew Strathern, eds. 1998. *Bodies and persons: Comparative perspectives from Africa and Melanesia*. Cambridge: Cambridge University Press.

Laplanche, J., and J-B. Pontalis. 1973. *The language of psychoanalysis*. London: Karnac.

Laqueur, Thomas. 1990. *Making sex: Body and gender from the Greeks to Freud*. Cambridge: Harvard University Press.

Larson, Pier. 1996. Desperately seeking "The Merina": Reading ethnonyms and their semantic fields in African identity histories. *Journal of Southern African Studies* 12: 541–560.

——. 2000. *History and memory in the age of enslavement: Becoming Merina in highland Madagascar, 1770–1822*. Portsmouth, N.H.: Heinemann.

Lazarus-Black, Mindie. 1994. Slaves, masters and magistrates: Law and the politics of resistance in the British Caribbean, 1736–1834. In *Contested States: Law, Hegemony and Resistance*, ed. Mindie Lazarus-Black and Susan F. Hirsch, 252–280. New York: Routledge.

Lebrun, François. 1998. *La vie conjugale sous l'ancien régime*. Paris: Armand Colin.

Le Clézio, J. M. G., and J. Le Clézio. 1990. *Sirandanes*. Paris: Éditions Seghers.

Lee, Jacques, K. 1990. *Sega: The Mauritian folk dance*. London: Ludo.

Lenoir, Philippe, ed. 1993. *Pierre Poivre, 1719–1786*. Les Pailles, Maurice: Précigraph.

L'Hortalle, A. S. 1980. *Hôpital Civil [de Port Louis], 1740–1980*. Port Louis: Regent Press.

Le Page, R. B., and A. Tabouret-Keller. 1985. *Acts of identity: Creole-based approaches to language and ethnicity*. Cambridge: Cambridge University Press.

Linebaugh, Peter, and Marcus Rediker. 2000. *The many-headed hydra: The hidden history of the revolutionary Atlantic*. London: Verso.

Liebbrandt, H. C. V. 1896. *Précis of the archives of the Cape of Good Hope: Letters received, 1695–1708*. Cape Town: W. A. Richards.

Lionnet, Françoise. 1993. *Créolité* in the Indian Ocean: Two models of cultural diversity. *Yale French Studies* 82: 101–111.

Lokke, Carl Ludwig. 1932. *France and the colonial question: A study of contemporary French opinion, 1763–1801*. New York.

Lougnon, Albert, ed. 1933. *Correspondance du Conseil Supérieur et de la Compagnie des Indes, 10 mars 1732–23 janvier 1736*. St. Denis: Ernest Laroux.

——, ed. 1937. *Mémoire des Îles de France et de Bourbon*. Port Louis.

Lovejoy, Paul. 1983. *Transformations in slavery: A history of slavery in Africa*. Cambridge: Cambridge University Press.

——, ed. 2000. *Identity in the shadow of slavery*. London: Continuum.

Lovejoy, Paul E., and David. V. Trotman. 2002. Enslaved Africans and their expectations of slave life in the Americas: Towards a Reconsideration of models of "creolisation." In *Questioning Creole: Creolisation Discourses in Caribbean Culture*, ed.

Verene A. Shepherd and Glen L. Richards, 67–91. Kingston, Jamaica: Ian Randle Publishers and James Currey.

Ly-Tio-Fane Pineo, Huguette. 1980. Aperçu d'une immigration forcée: L'importation d'africaines liberés aux Mascareignes et aux Seychelles, 1840–1880. In *Minorités et gens de mer en Ocean Indien, xixe–xxe siècles*. Institut d'Histoire de Pays d'Outre-Mer, Université de Provence, Études et Documents 12, Aix-en-Provence, 73–85.

——. 1993. *Île de France, 1715–1746*. Vol. 1. Moka, Mauritius: Mahatma Gandhi Institute.

——. 1984. *Lured away: The life history of Indian cane workers in Mauritius*. Moka, Mauritius: Mahatma Gandhi Institute.

Ly-Tio-Fane Pineo, Madeleine. 1958. *Mauritius and the spice trade: The odyssey of Pierre Poivre*. Port Louis: Esclapon.

Maccubbin, R. P., ed. 1987. *'Tis nature's fault: Unauthorized sexuality during the Enlightenment*. Cambridge: Cambridge University Press.

Mack, John. 1986. *Madagascar: Island of the ancestors*. London: British Museum.

Mamet, J. 1972. *Les Lazaristes: Fondateurs de la Chrétienté de l'Île de France*. Port Louis: Diocese of Port Louis.

Martin, Michell, and Alain Yacou, eds. 1989. *De la Révolution française aux revolutions créoles et nègres*. Paris: Éditions caribéennes.

Mason, John Edwin. 1990. Hendrik Albertus and his ex-slave Mey: A Drama in Three Acts. *Journal of African History* 31: 423–445.

Mayer, Jean, Jean Tarrade, Annie Rey-Goldzeiger, and Jacques Thobie. 1991. *Histoire de la France coloniale des origines à 1914*. Paris: Armand Colin.

McClellan, J. E. 1992. *Colonialism and science: Saint Domingue in the old regime*. Baltimore: Johns Hopkins University Press.

McNay, Lois. 1994. *Foucault: A Critical Introduction*. Cambridge: Polity.

Merrick, Jeffrey, and Bryant T. Ragan, eds. 1996. *Homosexuality in modern France*. Oxford: Oxford University Press.

Metellus, Jean. 1998. The process of creolization in Haiti and the pitfalls of the graphic form. In Balutansky and Sourieau 1998, 118–129.

Michel, Joseph. 1972. *Le Père Jacques Laval: Le saint de L'Île Maurice*. Paris: Beauchesne.

——. 1988. *De l'esclavage à l'apostolat: Les auxiliaires laïcs du Bienheureux Jacques Laval, apôtre de l'Île Maurice*. Paris: Beauchesne.

Middleton, Karen, ed. 1999. *Ancestors, Power and History in Madagascar*. Leiden: Brill.

Milbert, Jacques Gérard. 1812. *Voyage pittoresque à l'Île de France, au Cap de Bonne Esperance et àl'Île de Teneriffe*. Paris.

Miles, William F. S. 1999. The creole malaise in Mauritius. *African Affairs* 98: 211–228.

Mintz, Sidney. 1974. *Caribbean transformations*. Baltimore: Johns Hopkins University Press.

——. 1985. *Sweetness and power*. New York: Penguin.

Mintz, Sidney, and Richard Price. 1992. *The birth of African-American Culture: An anthropological perspective*. Boston: Beacon Press.

Moglen, Helene. 1997. Redeeming history: Toni Morrison's *Beloved*. In Abel, Christian, and Moglen 1997, 201–223.

Moitt, Bernard. 1996. Slave women and resistance in the French Caribbean. In *More than chattel: Black women and slavery in the Americas*, ed. David Barry Gaspar and Darlene Clark Hine, 239–258. Bloomington: Indiana University Press.

——. 2001. *Women and slavery in the French Antilles, 1635–1848*. Bloomington: Indiana University Press.

Moorghen, Pierre Marie. 1982. Multilingualism in Mauritius. *International Journal of Sociology of Language* 34: 51–66.

Moree, P. J. 1998. *A concise history of Dutch Mauritius, 1598–1710*. London: Kegan Paul International.

Morgan, Philip D. 1997. The cultural implications of the Atlantic slave trade: African regional origins, American destinations and New World developments. *Slavery and Abolition* 18: 122–145.

Morgan, Philip D. 1998. *Slave counterpoint: Black culture in the eighteenth century Chesapeake and Low Country*. Chapel Hill: University of North Carolina Press.

Mousnier, Roland E. 1979. *The institutions of France under the absolute monarchy, 1598–1789: Society and the state*. Trans. Brian Pearce. Chicago: University of Chicago Press.

Moutou, Benjamin. 1996. *Les Chrétiens de l'Île Maurice*. Port Louis: Best Graphics.

Muir, Edward, and Guido Ruggiero, eds. 1994. *History from crime*. Baltimore: Johns Hopkins University Press.

Nagapen, Amédée. 1990. Il y a 300 ans naissait J.-B. Garnier du Fougeray. *La Gazette des Îles*, no. 26, January, 1576–1582.

——. 1994. *Le catéchisme à L'Île Maurice avant la Concile Vatican II*. Port Louis: Diocese of Port Louis.

——. 1999. *Le marronnage à l'Isle de France-Île Maurice: Rêve ou riposte de l'esclave?* Port Louis: Centre Culturel Africain.

Napal, D. 1965. *Les Indiens à l'Île de France*. Port Louis: Éditions Nationales.

"New Light Shed on the Mysteries of the Dodo." 1999. *Oxford University Gazette*, 21 January, 631.

Noel, Karl. 1991. *L'Esclavage à L'Isle de France (Ile Maurice) de 1715 à 1810*. Paris: Éditions Two Cities ETC.

North-Coombes, M. D., 1978. Labour problems in the sugar industry of Île de France or Mauritius, 1790–1842. M.A. thesis, University of Cape Town.

——. 2000. *Studies in the political economy of Mauritius*. Compiled and ed. W. M. Freund. Moka, Mauritius: Mahatma Gandhi Institute.

Nye, Robert. 1993. *Masculinity and male codes of honor in modern France*. Oxford: Oxford University Press.

O'Hanlon, Rosalind. 1997. Issues of masculinity in north Indian History: The Bangash Nawabs of Farrukhabad. *Indian Journal of Gender Studies* 4: 2–19.

——. 1999. Manliness and imperial service in Mughal North India. *JESHO* 42: 47–92.

Olwig, Karen Fog. 1985. *Cultural adaptation and resistance on St. John: Three centuries of Afro-Caribbean life*. Gainesville: University of Florida Press.

Ong, Walter. 1982. *Orality and literacy: The technologizing of the word*. London: Methuen.

Outram, Dorinda. 1995. *The Enlightenment*. Cambridge: Cambridge University Press.

Ozouf, Mona. 1988. *Festivals and the French Revolution*. Trans. Alan Sheridan. Cambridge: Harvard University Press.

Palmié, Stephan, ed. 1995. *Slave cultures and the cultures of slavery*. Knoxville: University of Tennessee Press.

——. 2002a. *Wizards and scientists: Explorations in Afro-Cuban modernity and tradition*. Durham, N.C.: Duke University Press.

——. 2002b, Creolization and its discontents, or Is there a model in the muddle? Paper presented at the Conference on Creolization, University College, London.

Patterson, Orlando. 1982. *Slavery and social death: A comparative study*. Cambridge: Harvard University Press.

Payet, J. V. 1990. *L'histoire de l'esclavage à l'Île Bourbon*. Paris: L'Harmattan.

Peabody, Sue. 1996. *"There are no slaves in France."* New York and Oxford: Oxford University Press.

——. 2002. "A dangerous zeal": Catholic missions to slaves in the French Antilles, 1635–1800. *French Historical Studies* 25: 53–90.

Peerthum, Satyendra. 2000. The frenzy for freedom: A study of manumission in British Mauritius during the last years of slavery and the apprenticeship period, 1827–1839. Unpublished paper.

Pérotin-Dumon, Anne. 2000. *La ville aux Îles, la ville dans l'île: Basse-Terre et Pointe-à-Pitre, Guadeloupe, 1650–1820*. Paris: Karthala.

Perrod, Pierre-Anthoine. 1993. La fin du rêve d'empire. In Vincent 1993, 221–233.

Peytraud, Lucien. 1897. *L'esclavage avant 1789*. Paris: Hachette et Cie.

Phillips, Adam. 1995. *Terrors and experts*. London: Faber and Faber.

Picon, Anthoine. 1992. *French architects and engineers in the age of the Enlightenment*. Cambridge: Cambridge University Press.

Pitot, Albert. 1899. *L'Île de France: Esquisses historiques, 1715–1810*. Port Louis: Coignet Frères et Cie.

——. 1905. *T'Eylandt Mauritius: Esquisses historiques, 1598–1710*. Port Louis: Coignet Frères et Cie.

Pluchon, Pierre. 1989. *Toussaint-Louverture, un révolutionnaire d'ancien régime*. Paris: Fayard.

Poivre, Pierre. 1768. *Voyages d'un philosophe et observations sur les moeurs et les arts des peuples de l'Afrique, de l'Asie et du l'Amérique*. Yverdon.

——. 1797. *Oeuvres complettes de P. Poivre*, précédés de sa vie, et accompagnées de notes. Paris.

Price, Richard. 1979. *Maroon societies: Rebel slave communities in the Americas*. Baltimore: Johns Hopkins University Press.

Priestley, Herbert Ingram. 1939. *France overseas through the old regime: A study of European expansion*. New York: D. Appleton Century Co.

Prosper, Jean-Georges, ed. 1995. *Memorial Rémy Ollier: 150e anniversaire de la mort de Rémy Ollierr*. Moka, Mauritius: Mahatma Gandhi Institute.

Quinlan, S. 1996. Colonial bodies, hygiene and abolitionist politics in eighteenth century French history. *History Workshop Journal* 42: 107–25.

Racault, Jean-Michel. 1996. Pastorale ou "dégéneration": L'image des populations des Mascareignes à travers les récits des voyages dans la seconde moitié du XVIIIe siècle. In Wanquet and Jullien 1996, 71–83.

——, ed. 1986. *Études sur Paul et Virginie et l'oeuvre de Bernardin de St. Pierre*. Paris: Diffusion.

Raison-Jourde, Françoise. 1997. Familiarisation de l'esclavage, asservissement des libres. Le paradoxe Merina d'une mutuelle privation du desir de liberté. In Colloque international sur l'esclavage à Madagascar 1997, 117–131.

Rajabally, Houssain. 1997. *La couleur du communalisme*. Vacoas, Île Maurice: Éditions Le Printemps.

Ramanantsoa Ramarcel, Benjamin. 1997. Mainty=Andevo, un amalgame statutaire de l'Imerina. In Colloque international sur l'esclavage à Madagascar, 141–161.

Randriamaro, Jean Roland. 1997. L'emergence politique des Mainty et Andevo au xxe siecle. In Colloque international sur l'esclavage à Madagascar, 357–383.

Read, Alan, ed. 1996. *The fact of blackness: Frantz Fanon and visual representation*. London: ICA.

Reddi, Sadasivam. 2001. Aspects of Indian Culture in Île de France between 1803 and 1810. In Teelock and Alpers 2001, 33–41.

Reid, Roddey. 1993. *Families in jeopardy: Regulating the social body in France, 1750–1910*. Stanford, Calif.: Stanford University Press.

Rey, Alain, et al., eds. 1992. *Dictionnaire historique de la langue française*. Paris: Le Robert.

Rey, Michel. 1980. Attitudes to homosexuality in eighteenth-century France. *Journal of European Studies* 10: 231–255.

——. 1987. Parisian homosexuals create a lifestyle, 1700–1750, the police archives. In Maccubbin 1987, 179–191.

Roberts, Richard. 1990. Text and testimony in the *Tribunal de Première Instance*, Dakar, during the early twentieth century. *Journal of African History* 31: 447–463.

Roche, Daniel. 1998. *France in the Enlightenment*. Cambridge: Harvard University Press.

Ross, Robert. 1999. *Status and respectability in the Cape Colony, 1750–1790: A tragedy of manners*. Cambridge: Cambridge University Press.

——. 2000. The Dutch as globalizers in the western basin of the Indian Ocean. In Evers and Hookoomsingh 2000, 7–15.

Rosset, Alfred. 1967. *Les premiers colons de L'Île Bourbon*. Paris: Éditions du cerf-volant.

Rousseau, G. 1987. The pursuit of homosexuality in the eighteenth century. In Maccubbin 1987, 132–161.

Rousseau, G., and R. Porter, eds. 1987. *Sexual underworlds of the Enlightenment*. Manchester: Manchester University Press.

——, eds. 1990. *Exoticism and the Enlightenment*. Manchester: : Manchester University Press.

Saintoyant, Jules François. 1929. *La colonisation française sous l'ancien régime (du xve siècle à 1789)*. Paris: La Renaissance du Livre.

Sala-Molins, Louis. 1987. *Le Code Noir, ou le calvaire de Canaan*. Paris: Presses Universitaires de France.

Saugera, Eric. 1996. Les armements négriers français vers l'Ocean Indien sous le Consulat. In Wanquet and Julien 1996, 103–113.

Scarr, Deryck. 1998. *Slaving and slavery in the Indian Ocean*. Basingstoke: Macmillan.

Schama, Simon. 1987. *The embarrassment of riches: An interpretation of Dutch culture in the Golden Age*. London: Fontana.

Schwartz, Philip J. 1988. *Twice condemned: Slaves and the criminal laws of Virginia, 1705–1865*. Baton Rouge: Louisiana University Press.

Searing, James. 1993. *West African slavery and Atlantic commerce: The Senegal river valley, 1700–1860*. Cambridge: Cambridge University Press.

Seshadri-Crooks, Kalpana. 1998. The comedy of domination: Psychoanalysis and the conceit of whiteness. In *The Psychoanalysis of Race*, ed. Christopher Lane, 353–380. New York: Columbia University Press.

Shell, Robert. 1994. *Children of bondage: A social history of the slave society at the Cape of Good Hope, 1652–1838*. Hanover, N.H.: University Press of New England.

Sheridan, Richard. 1993. From chattel to wage slavery in Jamaica, 1740–1860. *Slavery and Abolition* 14: 13–40.

Silverman, Kaja. 1992. *Male subjectivity at the margins*. New York: Routledge.

Simmons, Adele Smith. 1982. *Modern Mauritius: The politics of decolonization*. Bloomington: Indiana University Press.

Singaravelou. 1993. La côte de Coromandel. In Vincent 1993, 30–44.

Skaria, Ajay. 1996. Writing, orality and power in the Dangs, western India, 1800s–1920s. In *Subaltern studies ix: Writings on South Asian history and society*, ed. Shahid Amin and Dipesh Chakrabarty, 13–59. New Delhi: Oxford University Press.

Sleigh, Daniel. 2000. The economy of Mauritius during the second Dutch occupation (1664–1710). In Evers and Hookoomsingh 2000, 51–57.

Sobel, Michael. 1987. *The world they made together: Black and white values in eighteenth century Virginia*. Princeton, N.J.: Princeton University Press.

Spaas, Lieve. 1996. *Lettres de Catherine de St. Pierre à son frère Bernardin*. Paris: L'Harmattan.

Spillers, Hortense J. 1997. "All the things you could be by now if Sigmund Freud's wife was your mother": Psychoanalysis and race. In Abel, Christian, and Moglen 1997, 135–159.

Stein, Robert Louis. 1979. *The French slave trade in the eighteenth century: An old regime business*. Madison: University of Wisconsin Press.

Stepan, Nancy. 1982. *The idea of race in science*. London: Macmillan.

Stoler, Ann Laura. 1991. Carnal knowledge and imperial power: Gender, race and morality in colonial Asia. In *Gender at the crossroads of knowledge: Feminist anthropology in a postmodern era*, ed. Micaela di Leonardo, 55–101. Berkeley: University of California Press.

———. 1995. *Race and the education of desire: Foucault's history of sexuality and the colonial order of things*. Durham, N.C.: Duke University Press.

Sussman, George D. 1982. *Selling mother's milk: The wet-nursing business in France, 1715–1914*. Urbana: University of Illinois Press.

Sussman, Linda K. 1980. Herbal medicine in Mauritius. *Journal of Ethnopharmacology* 2: 259–78.

Taffin, Dominique. 1996. Citoyens et Malabars à Pondichéry pendant la Révolution française, 1790–1793. In Wanquet and Jullien 1996, 235–257.

Taub, France. 2000. New Hypothesis on the dodo's true morphology from an ecological consideration of its available diet. In Evers and Hookoomsingh 2000, 67–77.

Taylor, Jean Gelman. 1983. *The social world of Batavia: European and Eurasian in Dutch Asia*. Madison: University of Wisconsin Press.

Teelock, Vijaya. 1998. *Bitter sugar: Sugar and slavery in nineteenth-century Mauritius*. Moka, Mauritius: Mahatma Gandhi Institute.

———. 1999a. Historical relations between Mauritius and Mozambique: An overview. Paper presented to the Conference in Commemoration of the 160th Anniversary of the Abolition of Apprenticeship, University of Mauritius, 22 June 1999.

———. 1999b. The influence of slavery in the formation of creole identity. *Comparative Studies of South Asia, Africa and the Middle East* 29.2: 3–8.

Teelock, Vijayalakshmi, and Edward A. Alpers, eds. 2001. *History, memory and identity*. Mauritius: Nelson Mandela Centre for African Culture and University of Mauritius.

Thornton, John. 1992. *Africa and Africans in the making of the Atlantic world, 1400–1680*. Cambridge: Cambridge University Press.

Thornton, John. 1998. *The Kongolese Saint Anthony: Dona Beatriz Kimpa Vita and the Antonian movement, 1684–1706*. Cambridge: Cambridge University Press.

Toinet, Paul. 1963. *Paul et Virginie: Répertoire bibliographique et iconographique*. Paris: Maisonneuve et Larose.

Toorawa, Shawkat. 2000. Imagined territories: The pre-Dutch history of the southwest Indian Ocean. In Evers and Hookoomsingh 2000, 31–41.

Toussaint, Auguste. 1936. *Port Louis: Deux siècles d'histoire, 1735–1935*. Port Louis: Typographie moderne.

———. 1967. *La route des Îles*. Paris: S.E.V.P.E.N.

———. 1969. *Early printing in Mauritius, Réunion, Madagascar and the Seychelles*. Amsterdam: Vangendt & Co.

Thomas, Nicolas. 1997. *In Oceania: Visions, artifacts, histories*. Durham, N.C.: Duke University Press.

Titmuss, Richard M. 1968. *Social policies and population growth: A report to the governor of Mauritius.* Port Louis, Île Maurice: Government Printer.

Trumbach, Randolph. 1987. Sodomitical sub-cultures, sodomitical roles and the gender revolution of the eighteenth century: The recent historiography. In Maccubbin 1987, 109–119.

Valdman, Albert. 1992. On the socio-historical context in the development of Louisiana and Saint-Domingue Creoles. *Journal of French Language Studies.* 2: 75–95.

——, ed. 1977. *Pidgin and creole linguistics.* Bloomington: Indiana University Press.

Van den Heuvel, Laetitia. 2000. Dodo's virtual reality. In Evers and Hookoomsingh 2000, 77–89.

Vanmeerbeck, E. 1865. *Rémy Ollier et son époque.* Maurice: Dupuy et Dubois.

Vaughan, Megan. 1996. The character of the market: Social identities in colonial economies. *Oxford Development Studies* 24:61–77.

——. 1998. Slavery and colonial identity in eighteenth-century Mauritius. *Transactions of the Royal Historical Society,* 6th series, vol. 8: 189–214.

——. 2000. Smallpox, slavery and revolution: 1792 on Île de France (Mauritius). *Social History of Medicine* 13: 411–428.

——. 2001. I am my own foundation. *London Review of Books* 23.20, 18 October 2001: 15–18.

Vaxelaire, Daniel. 1997. *Le grand livre de l'histoire de la Réunion.* 2 vols. La Réunion: Orphie.

Vergès, Françoise. 1995. Métissage, discours masculin et deni de la mère. In Condé and Cottenot-Hage 1995, 69–85.

——. 1996. Chains of madness, chains of colonialism: Fanon and freedom. In Read 1996, 46–76.

——. 1999. *Monsters and revolutionaries: Colonial family romance and métissage.* Durham, N.C.: Duke University Press.

Vincent, Rose, ed. 1993. *Pondichéry, 1674–1761: L'échec d'un rêve d'empire.* Paris: Éditions Autrement.

Walton, Jean. 1997. Re-placing race in (white) psychoanalytic discourse: Founding narratives of feminism. In Abel, Christian, and Moglen 1997, 223–252.

Wanquet, Claude. 1984. *Histoire d'une revolution: La Réunion, 1789–1803.* 4 vols. Marseilles: Jean Lafitte.

Wanquet, Claude, and Benoit Jullien, eds. 1996. *Révolution française et Ocean Indien: Premices, paroxysmes, heritages et deviances.* Paris: Éditions L'Harmattan.

Ware, Vron. 1992. *Beyond the Pale: White women, racism and history.* London: Verso.

Warner-Lewis, Maureen. 2000. Ethnic and religious plurality among Yoruba immigrants in Trinidad in the nineteenth century. In Lovejoy 2000, 113–129.

Weber, Jacques. 1993. La mosaïque pondichérienne. In Vincent 1993, 144–164.

Weiss, Brad. 1998. Electric vampires: Haya rumours of the commodified body. In *Bodies and persons: Comparative perspectives from Africa and Melanesia,* ed. Michael Lambek and Andrew Strathern, 172–197. Cambridge: Cambridge University Press.

White, Luise. 1990. Bodily fluids and usufruct: Controlling property in Nairobi, 1917–1939. *Canadian Journal of African Historical Studies* 24: 418–438.

Worden, Nigel. 1985. *Slavery in Dutch South Africa*. Cambridge: Cambridge University Press.

Yai, Olabiyi. 2000. Texts of enslavement: Fon and Yoruba vocabularies from eighteenth and nineteenth-century Brazil. In Lovejoy 2000.

Index

Note: Slave names are followed by parentheses indicating ethnicity and/ or owners' name where possible.

Houbert, M., 242

Hova, 108

Hugo, Hubert, 11–12

Humanitarianism, and slavery, 85

"I" in Creole, absence of, 211

Idealist, Poivre as, 65–66, 71–72

Identity, gender, and sexuality, 159

Identity, slave, 101–102, 104–105, 128–129

Île Bourbon (La Réunion), 1; agriculture on, 62; British capture of, 259; Creole from, 205; early inhabitants of, 22–24; French occupation of, 20–21; and Île de France, 45; inhabitants of, 31–32; *métissage* on, 244–245; and private trade, 75; after Seven Years' War, 61; slave population on, 77

Île de France: aristocracy on, 105–107 (*see also* Elites); and Batavia, 60; British capture of, 259 (*see also* British colonization); conditions of, 102–103; costs and benefits of, 67–68; engineering of, 33–55; flourishing of, 75; French reasons for keeping, 37; and French Revolution, 255–256; historical occupation of, 1–33; hospitals on, 72–74; inhabitants leaving, 31–32; maintenance of, 48–49; naming of, 21; population of, 76–77, 234–235, 245–246; poverty of, 135; and slave traders, 77–78; sugar industry in, 261; and war, 34–35, 51–54, 59, 61. *See also* Mauritius

Île Royale, 45

Illicit affairs, children of, 168–169

Indentured labor, Indian, 267, 269–272

India: cultural roots from, 117; indentured labor from, 267, 269–272; slaves from, 113, 116–118. *See also* Lascars (Indian sailors); Pondichéry

Insults, and performance, 223–224

Intimacy, male, 154

Investigations, criminal, 85–88, 95–96, 174–175; of maroons, 16–18, 185–187.

See also Confession; Punishment, of slaves

Island motif, in thought, 57

Jacobins, 232

Janetton (Le Normand), 146

Jansz, Pieter, 15

Jasmin (Dureau), 186

Jean-Louis (maroon), 252

Jeremie, John, 263–264

Johnston, A. J. B., 45

Joseph (Malagasy), speech of, 202–204, 227

Joseph (Mozambique), 190–192

Jouan (Lousteau), 152–158, 160–161, 166, 230, 266

Journel, Mme., 144, 164

Jousse, Daniel, 89

Jumeer, Musleem, 234–235, 238

Kel, Katherina, 16

Kermoseven, Leroux de, 79, 168

Kinship, 110–113, 247. *See also* Families

Kwong, James Nyu Foong, 271

Labor: indentured, 267, 269–272; in the colonies, 42–43; in Port North-West, 39–40; sale of slave, 138; slave, 69–70; and the sugar industry, 261–262

Labourdonnais, Mahé de, 59, 71, 116, 126, 135, 174, 181; background of, 35–36; children of, 131; on Company policies, 45–46; design of colony, 33; and labor, 39–41; plans for Port North-West, 38–39; on private trade, 47; on slave supply, 46–47

La Basserie, Elizabeth, 29

Lacan, Jacques, 211, 214

La Chaumière (Sans-Culottes), 232–233

Lacroix (Indian), 136

Ladouceur (Malagasy), 136

Lagesse, Marcelle, 131

Laglaine, Joseph, 224

"La Grande Barbe," 140, 173

Megan Vaughan is Smuts Professor of Commonwealth History
at the University of Cambridge and a Fellow of King's College.

Library of Congress Cataloging-in-Publication Data
Vaughan, Megan.
Creating the Creole Island : slavery in eighteenth-
century Mauritius / Megan Vaughan.
p. cm.   Includes bibliographical references and index.
ISBN 0-8223-3402-X (cloth : alk. paper)
ISBN 0-8223-3399-6 (pbk. : alk. paper)
1. Mauritius—History—To 1810. 2. Slavery—Mauritius—
History—18th century. 3. Racially mixed people—
Mauritius—History—18th century. 4. Creole dialects—
Mauritius—History—18th century. I. Title.
DT469.M465V378 2005   969.8'201—dc22   2004015807